EAST ASIAN
VISIONS

EAST ASIAN VISIONS
PERSPECTIVES ON ECONOMIC DEVELOPMENT

EDITORS
INDERMIT GILL • YUKON HUANG • HOMI KHARAS

AUTHORS
AUN PORN MONIROTH • ROBERTO F. DE OCAMPO
TOYOO GYOHTEN • YUJIRO HAYAMI • JOMO K. S.
CAO SY KIEM • TOMMY KOH • HARUHIKO KURODA
LONG YONGTU • KISHORE MAHBUBANI
FELIPE MEDALLA • MARI PANGESTU • MINXIN PEI
ANDREW SHENG • WU JINGLIAN • JOSEPH YAM
ZHENG BIJIAN

A copublication of the World Bank and the
Institute of Policy Studies (Singapore)

©2007 The International Bank for Reconstruction and Development / The World Bank and The Institute of Policy Studies

The International Bank for Reconstruction
and Development / The World Bank
1818 H Street NW
Washington DC 20433
Telephone: 202-473-1000
Internet: www.worldbank.org
E-mail: feedback@worldbank.org

The Institute of Policy Studies
29 Heng Mui Keng Terrace #06-06
Singapore 119620
Tel: +65-6215-1010
Fax: 6215-1014
Internet: www.ips.org.sg
E-mail: ips@ips.org.sg

All rights reserved

1 2 3 4 5 10 09 08 07

This volume is a product of the staff of the International Bank for Reconstruction and Development / The World Bank. The findings, interpretations, and conclusions expressed in this volume do not necessarily reflect the views of the Executive Directors of The World Bank or the governments they represent.

The World Bank does not guarantee the accuracy of the data included in this work. The boundaries, colors, denominations, and other information shown on any map in this work do not imply any judgement on the part of The World Bank concerning the legal status of any territory or the endorsement or acceptance of such boundaries.

Rights and Permissions
The material in this publication is copyrighted. Copying and/or transmitting portions or all of this work without permission may be a violation of applicable law. The International Bank for Reconstruction and Development / The World Bank encourages dissemination of its work and will normally grant permission to reproduce portions of the work promptly.

For permission to photocopy or reprint any part of this work, please send a request with complete information to the Copyright Clearance Center Inc., 222 Rosewood Drive, Danvers, MA 01923, USA; telephone: 978-750-8400; fax: 978-750-4470; Internet: www.copyright.com.

All other queries on rights and licenses, including subsidiary rights, should be addressed to the Office of the Publisher, The World Bank, 1818 H Street NW, Washington, DC 20433, USA; fax: 202-522-2422; e-mail: pubrights@worldbank.org.

ISBN-10: 0-8213-6745-5
ISBN-13: 978-0-8213-6745-2
eISBN: 0-8213-6746-3
DOI: 10.1596/978-0-8213-6745-2

Library of Congress Cataloging-in-Publication data

East Asian visions : perspectives on economic development / Indermit Gill, Yukon Huang, and Homi Kharas editors.
    p. cm.
    Includes bibliographical references and index.
    ISBN-13: 978-0-8213-6745-2
    ISBN-10: 0-8213-6745-5
    ISBN-10: 0-8213-6746-3 (electronic)
    1. East Asia—Economic integration. 2. East Asia—Economic policy. 3. East Asia—Foreign economic relations. 4. China—Economic policy. I. Gill, Indermit Singh, 1961- II. Huang, Yukon. III. Kharas, Homi J., 1954-
    HC460.5.E277 2006
    338.95—dc22

2006037028

The *Institute of Policy Studies* (IPS) is a think-tank dedicated to fostering good governance in Singapore through strategic policy research and discussion. It focuses on Singapore's domestic developments and its external relations. It takes a multidisciplinary approach in its analysis, with an emphasis on long-term strategic thinking. IPS began operations in 1988. Key activities include research projects, conferences, and publications.

The institute's mission is threefold:
- Analysis: To analyze policy issues of critical concern to Singapore and contribute to policy development
- Bridge-building: To build bridges among diverse stakeholders, including government, business, academia, and civil society
- Communication: To communicate research findings to a wider community and generate a greater awareness of policy issues

---

Cover design by Drew Fasick.

Contents

ACKNOWLEDGMENTS ix
ACRONYMS AND ABBREVIATIONS x

1. Perspectives on East Asian Development: An Introduction 1
Indermit S. Gill, Yukon Huang, and Homi Kharas

2. Economic Integration in East Asia: Cambodia's Experience 24
Aun Porn Moniroth

3. The Case for East Asian Financial Cooperation 53
Roberto F. de Ocampo

4. The Future of Asia 69
Toyoo Gyohten

5. Rural-Based Development in East Asia
    under Globalization 82
Yujiro Hayami

6. Economic Development and Regional Cooperation
    in East Asia 107
Jomo K. S.

7. East Asian Economic Integration: Problems for
    Late-Entry Countries 128
Cao Sy Kiem

12.2 Export Growth Rates in Selected Asian Countries ... 211
12.3 Growth in Philippine Exports ... 212
12.4 Share of Worker Remittances and Two Key Exports in Per Capita GNP in the Philippines ... 218
12.5 Worker Remittances, by Source in the Philippines ... 219
12.6 Share of Traditional Manufacturing in GDP in the Philippines ... 220
12.7 Philippine Exports, by Recipient ... 225
12.8 Government Capital Expenditures as a Share of GDP ... 227
14.1 The Leadership Response to Crisis in Selected Asian Countries ... 249
16.1 Impact on Efficiency and Energy Consumption of Unsubsidized Energy Prices in China ... 290
16.2 Per Capita Ownership of Resources in China Relative to the World Average ... 291
16.3 China's Resource Consumption as a Percentage of the World Total ... 295
16.4 GDP Share of the Output Value of the Tertiary Sector, 1980–2004 ... 300

Acknowledgments

This collection of essays was produced by the Office of the Chief Economist, East Asia and Pacific Region of the World Bank. It is the result of a collective effort by a World Bank team led by Homi Kharas (chief economist), Indermit S. Gill (economic adviser), and Yukon Huang (senior adviser). Tommy Koh (chairman) and Arun Mahizhnan (deputy director) of the Institute for Policy Studies (Singapore) provided guidance and wise counsel at all stages of the project.

The editors are grateful for valuable comments and logistical support from a number of people. Foremost, we would like to thank Radu Tatucu for his valuable contributions during all stages of the preparation, which involved not only logistical support, but also an essential coordinating role that ensured the timely completion of this publication. Without his assistance, this volume would not have been possible.

At the World Bank, among the many colleagues who contributed their ideas and inputs are Nisha Agrawal, Adelma Bowrin, Huot Chea, Jianqing Chen, Tianshu Chen, Doris Chung, Kazi Matin, Vera Songwe, Thang-Long Ton, William Wallace, and Chunlin Zhang. We are also grateful to Arun Mahizhnan, Kee Wee Tan, Chang Li Lin, and Andrea Wong of the Institute of Policy Studies, Singapore, and to Made Marthini in Indonesia, Junko Mogi in Japan, and Sunny Yung in Hong Kong (China).

Robert Zimmermann has done a fantastic job as language editor, and Patricia Katayama, Susan Graham, Stuart Tucker, and Santiago Pombo, of the Office of the Publisher, have steered the publication and dissemination efforts for the book.

No region is as diverse as East Asia. Not only does per capita income (excluding Japan) vary from about US$500 to over US$25,000, but major differences in less quantifiable factors such as language, culture, resource endowments, and political systems also persist. Despite this or perhaps because of this diversity, East Asia is integrated as never before. Goods, money, and, increasingly, knowledge are being traded across the region. The new terminology emphasizes regional production networks rather than country policies or leaders as keys to success. In many ways, East Asia is now undergoing a renaissance: redefining itself from a collection of disparate nations that once looked mainly to export markets in the West to a more self-reliant, innovative, and networked region. In the process, countries in the region are seeking to build stronger economic and political relationships among themselves, as well as more strategic partnerships with the rest of the world.

In this complex landscape, East Asians are debating options for the region. Much is at stake, including ensuring that any new East Asian economic architecture complements the evolving global architecture. This volume provides an opportunity to understand, firsthand, how some of the most influential thinkers in East Asia view the challenges for the region.

East Asian Visions: Perspectives on Economic Development is a collection of essays by 17 eminent East Asians who represent a broad spectrum of backgrounds and experiences.[1] All are senior policy makers, statesmen, or scholars who have either had to deal with or think through some of the most critical financial and developmental issues confronting their countries and the region. Collectively, 10 of them have, at some point in their careers, been at the head of key ministries and central banks; nearly a dozen have been academics and scholars of distinction; several have served as ambassadors to the West and bring a more global strategic perspective; and many have been influential policy advisers and decision makers in governments and international financial agencies.

Table 1.1 lists the authors, where they come from, and key positions they have held. Their essays reflect individual experiences at critical economic junctures and are occasionally quite personal, not surprising since each author selected a topic of his or her own choosing. Given their backgrounds, they have chosen to write about the highly diverse country experiences of East Asia, covering rich, middle-income, and poor countries, and they speculate on how their countries fit into a rapidly changing region and globalizing world.

TABLE 1.1 **Contributing Authors**

Author	Country	Key position(s)
Aun Porn Moniroth	Cambodia	Secretary of State, Ministry of Economy and Finance; Chairman of the Supreme National Economic Council
Roberto F. de Ocampo	Philippines	President, Asian Institute of Management; former Secretary of Finance
Toyoo Gyohten	Japan	President, Institute for International Monetary Affairs; former Chairman, Bank of Tokyo; former Vice Minister of Finance
Yujiro Hayami	Japan	Chairman, Foundation of Advanced Studies of International Development, Japan; former Professor, Tokyo University and Cornell University
Jomo Kwame Sundaram	Malaysia	United Nations Assistant Secretary-General for Economic Development; former Professor, University of Malaya
Cao Sy Kiem	Vietnam	Academy of Social Sciences; former Governor, Central Bank
Tommy Koh	Singapore	Ambassador at Large, Singapore; Chairman, Institute of Policy Studies; former Ambassador of Singapore to the United Nations and to the United States
Haruhiko Kuroda	Japan	President, Asian Development Bank; former Vice Minister of Finance; Professor, Hitotsubashi University
Long Yongtu	China	Secretary-General, Boao Forum for Asia, China; former Vice Minister; former Chief Negotiator for China, World Trade Organization
Kishore Mahbubani	Singapore	Dean, Lee Kuan Yew School of Public Policy; former Ambassador of Singapore to the United Nations
Felipe Medalla	Philippines	Professor, University of the Philippines; former Secretary for Planning; former Director General, National Economic and Development Authority
Mari Pangestu	Indonesia	Minister of Trade; Board Member, Center for International and Strategic Studies, Indonesia
Minxin Pei	China	Senior Associate and Director, China Program, Carnegie Endowment for International Peace, Washington, DC
Andrew Sheng	Malaysia	Visiting Professor, University of Malaya, Malaysia, and Tsinghua University, Beijing; former Chair, Securities Commission; Deputy Chief Executive, Hong Kong Monetary Authority, Hong Kong (China)

continued

TABLE 1.1 **Contributing Authors** *(continued)*

Author	Country	Key position(s)
Wu Jinglian	China	Professor, Chinese Academy of Social Sciences; Senior Fellow, Development Research Center, State Council; Member, Standing Committee, Chinese People's Political Consultative Conference, China
Joseph *Yam*	Hong Kong, China	Chief Executive, Hong Kong Monetary Authority
Zheng Bijian	China	Chairman, China Reform Forum; Executive Vice-President, Communist Party School

Source: Compiled by the editors.
Note: The names in italics are the last names. "Country" refers to place of birth or residence during the bulk of the individual's career.

Four themes permeate these essays (see table 1.2):

- What explains East Asia's growth and developmental success? Will it continue? Can all countries in the region benefit from China's success or will some be crowded out and left behind?
- Will the powerful forces of regional integration build efficiency or become a source of vulnerability? What if there is a disruption in China?
- Can East Asia avoid domestic disintegration given growing public intolerance of increasing inequities, pollution, and corruption?
- From where will East Asia find its next generation of leaders? Are meritocratic elites and bureaucracies in decline? Can national sovereignty be partially set aside in favor of more effective regional associations?

None of these questions draws a ready answer. But by writing reflective essays, rather than technical pieces, the authors have the freedom to move between politics, economics, culture, physics, and ethics. What is lost in formality of approach is more than made up for by breadth of reasoning. Not surprisingly, the authors have a keen sense of the need to get the politics right: within countries, within the region among countries competing for leadership, and between the region and the West. And, because politics is rooted in history and culture and because East Asia has a long tradition in these areas, many authors start by looking backward. De Ocampo goes the furthest in this historical approach by

TABLE 1.2 A Road Map to the Essays

Themes	Approach	Key questions
Growth and development strategies	Historical perspectives	What are the lessons of history?
	Postwar performance	Was the crisis indicative of some deep-rooted weaknesses or simply a pause in the miracle saga?
	Future prospects and country differences	Is China an opportunity or a threat?
		Can laggards thrive in the new Asia?
Networks and regional integration	Trade-production sharing network	Will the production-sharing network still drive regional growth and trade?
	Financial network	Can East Asia create a viable regional financial network?
	Old regionalism versus new regionalism	Will East Asia move beyond market-based (old) regionalism to more politically driven (new) regionalism?
		What is the region: the Association of Southeast Asian Nations (ASEAN), ASEAN+3 (plus China, Japan, and Rep. of Korea), the East Asian Community, Asia-Pacific Economic Cooperation?
		Is regionalization or globalization driving East Asia?
Globalization and avoiding domestic disintegration	Social justice	Does increasing domestic or regional inequality matter?
	Sustainable development	Do East Asians still believe in growth at any cost?
	Ethics and corruption	Is corruption an ethical or a developmental concern?
Leadership and change agents	National: senior leadership, bureaucrats	Does leadership matter?
		Is there still a role for meritocratic elites and dedicated bureaucracies?
	Regional: ASEAN, China, Japan, Rep. of Korea, others	Is ASEAN up to the task?
		Will China or Japan play a more active leadership role?
		Can Japan and China work out their differences?
	Global: United States and the West	Is the West still relevant for East Asia?

Source: Compiled by the editors.

In the same manner, Gyohten, one of Japan's most influential international monetary policy figures in a career spanning over three decades, expresses astonishment at the lack of concern about Asia, because of its small economic size, when he first attended meetings at the Bank for International Settlements, in Basel, in 1967. He recalls, "I thought uneasily that, for those bankers, the world seemed still to end somewhere near the Dardanelles." He pinpoints a catch-up mentality in Asia as the common ground upon which the successive development of Japan, the four tigers, the Association of Southeast Asian Nations (ASEAN), and now China has been established. He also notes that successful countries benefited from enlightened leadership, or, to put it more bluntly, "developmental dictatorship," but cautions that collective dynamism, which a benevolent dictator may mobilize, may conflict with individual initiative in business activity. The trick is to find the right moment to shift between these two forces.

Not all the contributors feel the same sense of historical inevitability. While the miracle experience spawned a search for unique success factors in East Asia, the financial crisis of 1997–98 vindicated those who were skeptical about the origins and sustainability of the miracle, including some who characterized the achievements as simply the result of massive increases in investment and Asians working harder, but not necessarily smarter (Stiglitz and Yusuf 2001). The scars left on policy makers by the crisis can be seen in several essays that call for vigilance and an acceleration of reforms now when times are good.

So does the crisis indicate some deep-rooted weaknesses in East Asia or merely a pause in the unfolding of a miracle? As observed by de Ocampo, who was the chair of the Asia-Pacific Economic Cooperation Finance Ministers at the time, the crisis exposed glaring faults in the regulatory regimes and governance structures for financial institutions and corporations. It called into question the viability of family- and relationship-based conglomerates and their links with governments. And it tested the mettle of meritocratic bureaucracies in coping with complex and rapidly changing market conditions. The institutional weaknesses revealed by the crisis will surely take time to be fully addressed. Yet, East Asia has recovered speedily, surprising even the most ardent proponents of strong East Asian fundamentals. Fears of a long stagnation have now totally subsided. The growth of the emerging economies in East Asia since 1998 has been remarkable; gross domestic product (GDP) almost doubled by 2005. Concerns have shifted from broad regional weaknesses to questions such as whether China is growing too rapidly or how East Asia's economies can find the right balance between the quality and the speed of growth.

Competition with China Is a Concern

China's rise has undoubtedly changed the dynamics of regional economic relations. With its economies of scale and other advantages, it has leapfrogged up the technological ladder. No other country in East Asia has the capacity to produce at all points between the lower and the upper ends of the technology spectrum. China now represents one-half of emerging East Asia's GDP and one-third of its exports. Its import-to-GDP share is now 34 percent, roughly triple the corresponding share of Japan and the United States. Although, in absolute terms, Japan's GDP is still much larger than China's at current market prices, China imports more from the world and significantly more from East Asia and so has shaped changes in regional trade volumes and commodity prices. Over the past decade, China (including Hong Kong) has accounted for as much as 40–60 percent of the growth of exports from neighboring countries.

Pangestu, a distinguished intellectual and minister of trade in the current Indonesian government, writes that the rise of China implies that "the rest of the world, including developed countries, will have to make adjustments. In the interim, there may yet be greater tensions because of more protectionism as countries seek to cope with the fresh competition." For many countries, there is a real preoccupation with whether China is an opportunity or a threat in the medium term, notwithstanding the short-term benefits to the region from China's huge imports. Gyohten refers to Napoleon, who it is claimed, warned, "China is a sleeping giant. Let her sleep, for, when she awakes, the world will tremble."

These concerns are frankly expressed by Kiem, a former governor of the Central Bank of Vietnam, and Medalla, from his perspective as a former secretary for planning in the Philippines. They elaborate on the past pattern of country growth during the Asian miracle and nostalgically recall the model of the flying geese formation, with Japan at the tip of the formation, and the four tigers next, followed by middle-income countries and then low-income countries producing at lower technology levels. This model provided a structure within which all economies could operate. There was a clear path for laggards to move up the production chain. China's emergence has changed this orderly progression.

But, if truth be told, there is more to it than simply China's emergence. Jomo, one of Malaysia's most noted and frank commentators on political economy matters, never bought into the flying geese model and contrasts the less-than-stellar growth experiences of Southeast Asia relative to Northeast Asia. He attributes the latter's strengths to domestic entrepreneurship and financing, as well as attention to social equity, rather than to Japanese technology and finance.

Bearing in mind the prevalence of such concerns, Zheng, a prominent strategist in the Communist Party of China and the originator of the concept of "China's peaceful rise," acknowledges the widespread apprehension over the so-called China threat. He offers reassurances that China seeks to manage its development in ways that would foster regional benefits and reduce frictions. Yet, at the same time, he is steadfast in affirming that the time has come for China to take its place as a global economic power. The coming years will be China's "golden age of development" leading to a "great renaissance of the Chinese nation," confirming Mao Zedong's prediction in the 1950s that "China would become a big, powerful, yet amicable country."

Most countries have, in fact, found a niche in which they may retain competitiveness relative to China. In the last few years, all countries in the region have been growing rapidly, and the gap between the richest and the poorest has been shrinking, the reverse of the global trend of relatively poor performance among middle-income countries (Garrett 2004). Kiem notes that countries have the choice of (1) investing in China and selling to China or world markets; (2) exporting components to China and making it the assembly plant for exports to others; or (3) exporting raw materials to China. The United States and the European Union are focusing on the first channel. The four tigers and the more industrialized countries within ASEAN are focusing on the second. The less-developed countries that possess natural resources are focusing on the third.

Kiem's concern is whether the third path is a viable long-term option for low-income countries. Aun, the leader of Cambodia's young reformists, acknowledges that future growth in Cambodia will depend on exports, but worries about the social inequalities this may bring. Medalla argues that the Philippines did not gain as much as its more dynamic neighbors and "has the worst of both worlds: slow economic growth that is overly concentrated in and around Metro-Manila." He points out that many Philippine stakeholders are not convinced about the benefits of globalization or their ability to tap Chinese markets, especially because their nation's contributions appear largely to take the form of exporting labor rather than goods.

Pangestu also cautions that, without major internal reforms, the prospects for countries such as Indonesia may be grim. Given the current production-sharing system driven by economies of scale, relatively small changes in cost can cause significant changes in the volume of trade flows. Thus, competitive pressures may be brutal. Low-income countries with natural resources may come out well if improvements in global terms of trade hold up, but, unlike the newly industrialized countries, they have not been fully integrated into the production chain and fear being left out of the transition to the second path. Pangestu therefore argues that the prospects for many countries might be enhanced by collective action within ASEAN so as to supplement domestic reforms in individual countries.

Production-Sharing Networks and Financial Networks

Many authors comment on the significance of the transformation of East Asian production and finance into a complex of intraregional networks. East Asia's share of world trade has increased from 10 percent in the 1970s to more than 25 percent today. Intraregional trade, which is increasingly based on components, has increased from 35 percent to 55 percent of the total and provided the biggest stimulus to the shifts taking place in the composition of trade. With such a wide range of factors at play, no single country within East Asia can dominate the production chain, but much of the activity is centered on China as the "assembly plant of the world."

A New Mode of Production: Regional Networks

By 1990, foreign affiliates already accounted for 30 to 90 percent of the total manufactured exports from China and other middle-income countries in East Asia. Japanese multinational companies now send more than 80 percent of their exports from Asian affiliates to other Asian countries and obtain 95 percent of their imports from Asian plants. Firm-level surveys suggest that outsourcing is almost 40 percent more prevalent in this region than in the rest of the world. The technological basis of product lines, however, is shifting rapidly. Low-skill, labor-intensive products such as garments and toys are becoming less important even for China and now account for only 15 percent of total exports. Improved logistics, supply-chain management, and specialization among countries have inspired a dynamic, but still largely uncharted process regarding the future location of production.

There is a strong link between much of this production-sharing-related trade and foreign direct investment. Since 1980, inflows of foreign direct investment into East Asia have more than quadrupled, reaching 31 percent of the world inflows in 2004. Two-thirds of the regional inflows are going to China, which is now the premier destination for foreign investment globally.

The numbers suggest that, thus far, the production-sharing network has been a boon for the region. It has fostered efficiencies and lifted the competitive position of East Asia relative to the rest of the world. But much of this depends on what happens in China. Initially, China's role was constrained by its lack of secure market access and inability to join the World Trade Organization (WTO), while the state still dominated production. Long, who played a key role as China's chief WTO negotiator, traces the country's 15-year struggle to join WTO and reveals the extent to which integrating with the global economy has been part of a longer-term strategy of transition from plan to market. He now feels that the WTO-membership process has been as important as the outcome in helping to convince millions of domestic stakeholders about the virtues of globalization. Despite fears that WTO membership might initially impact negatively on the domestic economy, it clearly reinforced the already existing incentives for investment and exports and put aside any doubts about the merits of liberalizing trade in goods and services.

The worry today is no longer that China might be isolated, but that it will consolidate production networks inside its own borders. Kiem frets that production processes in China are likely to be interlinked more with its own hinterland than with low-income countries in Southeast Asia, and, if so, these countries may continue to lag behind. But such fears are minimized by Wu, the dean of China's first generation of reform-minded economists. Wu elaborates on the long-standing debate among Chinese policy makers on industrial strategies and the country's past dependence on heavy industries. He appears confident that China will rely more on services, resource sustainability, and technology-based activities in the future, moving up the value added ladder and leaving more room for industrialization in low-income countries.

Kuroda, as president of the Asian Development Bank, is well placed to survey how market-based trade and financial activities have transformed the region. He emphasizes the ability of crossborder infrastructure cooperation to reduce transaction and logistics costs, as well as stepped-up regional cooperation and integration in trade, investment, finance, and the prevention of regional public bads. He points to the need to design this cooperation in a way that gives preferential treatment to the least developed countries and helps to close development gaps.

Regional Financial Networks: Topology and Vulnerability

If Asia's production-sharing network has been a source of strength thus far, then, as many authors note, the region's financial network was its Achilles' heel in the past. As discussed in Sheng's essay, the rise of Asia's production network revolutionized industrial processes, but the concept was not new and evolved naturally from historically similar networks in Japan and Korea. Patterns of foreign direct investment and related financing helped shape the nature of supply chains, but depended on the strength of the Japanese financial system, which extended dollar-denominated credit for goods ultimately being sold in the United States.

Sheng describes how the political decision to allow the yen to depreciate against the U.S. dollar after 1995 boosted the yen value of these outstanding dollar assets of Japanese banks. At the same time, the falling Nikkei stock market index and a need to provision against bad domestic loans decreased the equity base of Japanese banks. This combination proved to be a recipe for a major credit retrenchment from East Asia. Both Sheng and de Ocampo highlight the contagion effects of the regional credit crunch. In the year and a half preceding the financial crisis, nearly US$90 billion flowed into Indonesia, Korea, the Philippines, and Thailand, but in the subsequent year and a half, nearly US$80 billion flowed out, mostly back to Japanese banks.

Sheng frames his discussion in topological terms, calling the centralized financial network efficient, but describing it as lacking in robustness when the node came under pressure. He goes on to advocate the development of a distributed network for production and finance,[2] a combination which he believes would deliver both efficiency and robustness and which has become familiar in the region as the Toyota way of doing business. His assessment camouflages a warning: if the failure of the centralized node in Japan caused the financial crisis, does this imply that regional production networks, with centralized nodes in China, are similarly brittle?

For many of the authors, the trauma of the financial crisis has clearly not disappeared from the Asian psyche, causing them to ask whether the region is prepared to join together and reap the benefits of more integrated financial systems. Yam, who, as head of the Hong Kong Monetary Authority, sits at the crossroads of East Asian financial flows, is pushing for regional financial integration to increase market size and thereby reduce vulnerability to financial instability. But he cautions about any rush toward deeper monetary cooperation, noting the "intensely political" nature of any decision to yield power to a single common central bank in the region. He also notes the very different approaches taken in the region toward monetary policy independence, free capital mobility, and fixed exchange rates, approaches that would need to be harmonized if regional monetary cooperation is to progress.

The discussion of the crisis inevitably centers around the controversial role played by global institutions. For Sheng, it was only fitting that Japan initiated a number of proposals to provide more financing for the region, as he believes that Japanese banks were indirectly the culprit that triggered the collapse. But Japan also had to balance its interests with the West, and, as Jomo notes, the first proposal for an independent regional financing mechanism was thwarted by Western opposition, especially in the United States. At that time, the prevalent view throughout the region was that "vulnerability had been greatly increased by ill-considered economic liberalization policies, especially financial liberalization . . . By early 1998, . . . it was clear that [International Monetary Fund] solutions were part of the problem." But this view was not unanimous. Other financial observers consider that the conditions imposed by the International Monetary Fund on Korea, for example were instrumental in helping the country tackle deep-rooted institutional and financial problems.

Understandably, what permeates many essays is the sense that East Asia needs to be more self-reliant, mirroring the subtle shift toward regionalization rather than globalization as the focus of attention among policy makers. But Yam recognizes that the other side of the regionalization coin is the greater role that must be played by Asian governments in the international financial architecture. Because much of East Asia's huge savings are invested in debt instruments in industrialized countries, while its investments are being financed by capital from those very same countries, the region is becoming more globally integrated at the same time that it becomes more regionally integrated. The policy implication is to strengthen regional capital markets so that East Asia's surpluses can be intermediated within East Asia to meet the needs for major infrastructure and other capital investments. If successful, such reforms might transform a past vulnerability into a future advantage.

Regionalism and Regionalization

The center of economic gravity in East Asia has shifted toward China and Northeast Asia. Regionalism, which is based on formal economic and trade agreements, and regionalization, which is steered by market processes, are shaping the production and financial networks that are driving growth and innovation. Are these trends compatible with globalization?

The most obvious indicator of growing regionalism is the proliferation of free trade agreements, usually between two countries, but increasingly also between ASEAN and other countries, including some outside the region. In the last 10 years, 24 such agreements involving at least one East Asian country have come into effect, and another 34 are being negotiated. Most authors feel that trade issues are being appropriately addressed in these discussions and do not see them as conflicting with global approaches such as the WTO Doha Development Round (for example, Kuroda, Long, and Pangestu). Moreover, in light of the recent breakdown in the Doha round, many will likely continue to push for bilateral or regionally oriented processes despite warnings that this so-called noodle bowl approach will eventually turn out to be too complex or fraught with contradictions. Bilateralism seems to have gained the upper hand as a pragmatic alternative, but it is hope rather than experience that says this will work out as intended.

Free trade agreements are being negotiated almost as a matter of course, and most authors see making progress on regional financial integration as the near-term challenge. Following through on the Chiang Mai Initiative and the Asian Bond Markets Initiative, creating regional surveillance mechanisms, harmonizing standards, facilitating crossborder transactions, and establishing the framework for an eventual common currency are addressed in depth in many essays measures and higher taxes, which could reduce investment and eventually lead to slower growth. This has been the unhappy experience in some Latin American countries. East Asian policy makers have to respond proactively to address inequality, but, because this is a recent phenomenon, there is not much practical experience to build on.

An alternative to government redistribution is offered by Hayami, Japan's most distinguished rural development economist. In his view, the case that scale economies and agglomeration are unique to industrialization and urbanization is overdone. Drawing on experiences in rural development dating back to Meiji Japan, he notes that rural sectors, too, may benefit from economies of scale. He describes several cases where there is potential to form rural, community-based production and trade networks that rely on informal relationships and self-monitoring to reduce costs and that can link the domestic hinterland with international markets. If these could be developed with better internal infrastructure so as to reduce farm-to-market costs and increase the speed of delivery of perishables, it would help narrow rural-urban income differences and reduce pressures on Asia's sprawling megacities, which are increasingly less able to deal with their social and environmental problems.

Asia's environmental concerns flow largely from the rapid urbanization already under way, which, by global standards, is unprecedented. Air and water pollution, loss of biodiversity, and deforestation: all have crossborder consequences (Hayami, Koh, and Kuroda), but such outcomes also reflect the resource-intensive and historically excessive focus on growth and industrialization in countries such as China (Wu and Zheng). Given East Asia's substantial achievements in recent years, will the growth-at-any-cost strategy continue? China's senior leadership has clearly signaled its concerns over the prospects for more sustainability and more balanced development, and, everywhere across the region, leaders are talking about the need for more balanced growth, more well-rounded societies, and sustainable development. Yet, how many of them really mean it when faced with stiff competitive pressures and a preoccupation with employment generation? So far, environmental sustainability in most of the region is still sadly lagging.

Aun believes that globalization inevitably draws attention to issues of weak governance and corruption. He voices concern over the developmental aspects. Koh and Pei go further, stressing the ethical issues as well. Some authors argue that there is an Asian paradox, that corruption coexists with rapid growth. The nature of corruption in East

Asia does not seem to be as damaging to efficiency as is the case elsewhere in the world. Yet, others argue, corruption, if unchecked, can bring down governments and reverse decades of economic progress, as evidenced by regime changes in Indonesia and the Philippines. There is no evidence that East Asians are more tolerant of corruption than citizens of Western democracies. They demand that their political systems address the corrosive effects of corruption. Thus, East Asians appear to have the foresight to realize that governance is likely to be increasingly important in the future, especially as globalization exerts pressures for more transparency and the rule of law (Pangestu, Long). But the challenge of building sound institutions has been complicated by the political choice to decentralize most public spending to the local level. The speed of decentralization has run ahead of the speed of building accountability and transparency into local public systems.

Leadership: Finding Change Agents Nationally, Regionally, and Globally

The citizens of some East Asian countries, frustrated over inadequate social services, inequality, urban decay, and weak governance structures, are increasingly holding their leaders accountable and demanding that bureaucracies shape up. In moving forward, are Asian institutions now sufficiently robust that the emergence of a heroic leader no longer matters? Some feel strongly that East Asia's future will depend on the quality of its top leadership (de Ocampo, Gyohten, Mahbubani, Pangestu, Pei, and Sheng). In the absence of inspired leadership, weak reform coalitions are the rule. Medalla wryly notes that the need is greatest where leadership is in shortest supply: "protectionist development strategies require much better governments than those the lagging countries have (and may, in fact, be the reason why they are lagging in the first place)."

Others argue that the challenge is to reestablish accountable, technocratic bureaucracies. They emphasize the need for a high-quality administrative system to manage a globalized and more complex environment. Over time, talent has tended to gravitate away from the public sector to the private sector (except perhaps in Singapore), but only at considerable cost. Sheng stresses that Asian bureaucracies "must make the important transition from a paternalistic top-down governance structure to a pluralistic market economy structure" since "a small elite can no longer manage large complex market economies open to wide public choice."

Pei notes that two of the institutional pillars for maintaining growth and mobilizing public support—the rule of law and the creation of political mechanisms for government accountability and integrity—were often not established during past periods of reform. "Crises also provide new elites with a fresh political mandate," but, in many cases, such as the financial crisis, the duration of crisis may be too short to inspire durable changes in governance structures. Mahbubani sees superior performance among the elites as one of Singapore's distinctive achievements. Pangestu notes that effective governance is now the paramount issue everywhere. Most authors, however, do not equate good governance with the concept of democracy as defined in the West. Rather, they would argue that Asia needs to find its own way in determining what is effective and acceptable in light of history and social and cultural distinctions.

National leadership is only one part of the puzzle in the age of regionalism and globalization. Many authors also see the need for stronger regional associations. Perhaps more out of expediency than proven effectiveness, ASEAN is now at the center of an energized search to link regional interests in institutional ways that can deflect concerns about the primacy of particular countries or coalitions. Through overlapping and more inclusive geopolitical groupings such as ASEAN+3, the East Asian Community, and Asia-Pacific Economic Cooperation and reinforced by the proliferation of bilateral and multilateral free trade agreements and financial arrangements, regional cooperation is now a must-have topic for discussion whenever Asian policy makers come together.

Yet, many bemoan the lack of substantive progress because ASEAN has chosen to operate by consensus and to adhere to the principle of noninterference in the affairs of member states. No single country or grouping has stepped forward to help bridge differences and drive the process of forging purposeful direction, unlike the case during the formation of the European Union. Not surprisingly, these essays often wonder whether ASEAN is up to the task (Kiem).

The focus on regional leadership extends well beyond ASEAN to more geopolitical questions. What role will China and Japan play in the broader East Asian context? Is the West still a factor? Inevitably, such questions cannot be answered without considering the influence of Europe and the United States. Countries in the region are trying to balance all these relationships and hedge their bets. Gyohten elaborates on three trilateral relationships that will likely shape Asia's future:

China-Japan, China–United States, and Japan–United States. Each has its own complexities, and all are potentially intractable. All authors would probably therefore agree that, whether the goal is to promote accountability within democratic-type frameworks or move toward real integration within East Asia and in its relationships with the rest of the world, progress will require fresh thinking and more visionary leadership.

In conclusion, perhaps it is worth reflecting on what was lost during the centuries that Asia was in decline. The current Asian renaissance is about more than simply revived prosperity. It is also about creativity, cohesion, and civilization. In reflecting on Asia's future and the challenges ahead, Koh raises the bar by suggesting that "we have to solve these and other shortcomings if we want the West to treat us as equals and if we want the rest of the non-Western world to look to Asia for inspiration."

A Summary Table on the Coverage by the Authors of the Four Main Themes

TABLE 1.3 **Major Themes, by Author**

Author	Country	Growth	Networks	Disintegration	Leadership	An illustrative insight
Aun	Cambodia		☐		☐	Low-income countries will need stronger regional leadership
de Ocampo	Philippines		☐		☐	A lesson of the financial crisis is that more regional integration is needed
Gyohten	Japan	☐	☐		☐	Resolving bilateral relations is key for China, Japan, United States, and ASEAN
Hayami	Japan		☐	☐		Rural supply links can be brought into the regional production chain
Jomo	Malaysia	☐	☐			Asia must be more self-reliant and learn from the past

continued

TABLE 1.3 **Major Themes, by Author** (continued)

Author	Country	Growth	Networks	Disintegration	Leadership	An illustrative insight
Kiem	Vietnam		☐	☐	☐	Low-income countries are in danger of being left behind
Koh	Singapore			☐	☐	Nonincome development challenges must not be forgotten
Kuroda	Japan		☐	☐		Regionalization is central to Asia's future
Long	China		☐			Globalization can be used to build a domestic reform constituency
Mahbubani	Singapore	☐			☐	Leadership and the role of elites are key to development
Medalla	Philippines	☐	☐	☐		Citizens in lagging countries must demand better government
Pangestu	Indonesia		☐	☐	☐	Good governance is even more important than good policies
Pei	China			☐	☐	Economic success can be derailed by social and political vulnerabilities
Sheng	Malaysia	☐	☐		☐	Economic networks have particular strengths and vulnerabilities
Wu	China	☐		☐		China's industries must become more resource efficient
Yam	Hong Kong, China		☐			Regional financial integration is the most pressing challenge
Zheng	China	☐		☐	☐	China's peaceful rise is not a threat, but it is inevitable

Source: Compiled by the editors.

Notes

1. This volume is a companion piece to Gill and Kharas (2006). That volume analyzes the drivers of growth in the new East Asian environment. It looks at how recent economic thought can be used to provide a rich analytical framework for many of the critical policy issues discussed in these essays.

2. A distributed network is like a net in which each node is connected to several other nodes. There are therefore many pathways to connect nodes in the net. The further the nodes from each other, the more the number of potential connecting pathways. This differs from a centralized network that describes a hub-and-spoke arrangement wherein the nodes connect to each other only through a central hub.

References

Garrett, Geoffrey. 2004. "Globalization's Missing Middle." *Foreign Affairs*, November–December: 84–96.

Gill, Indermit S., and Homi Kharas, eds. 2006. *An East Asian Renaissance: Ideas for Economic Growth*. Washington, DC: World Bank.

Maddison, Angus. 2003. *The World Economy: Historical Statistics*. Paris: Organisation for Economic Co-operation and Development.

Stiglitz, Joseph E., and Shahid Yusuf, eds. 2001. *Rethinking the East Asian Miracle*. Washington, DC: World Bank; New York: Oxford University Press.

World Bank. 1993. *The East Asian Miracle: Economic Growth and Public Policy*. World Bank Policy Research Reports. New York: Oxford University Press.

CHAPTER 2

Economic Integration in East Asia
Cambodia's Experience

AUN PORN MONIROTH

Cambodia may be used as a case study in evaluating the benefits and the risks implicit in global and regional economic integration from a country perspective.

In the last five decades, the world has witnessed dramatic changes. The Cold War has ended, and geopolitical relations among the major powers have been generally stable and tranquil. Moreover, the end of colonialism has allowed newly independent countries to play a greater role in the international arena, and countries that used to be foes have now joined hands to develop their economies and raise the living standards of their peoples. At the same time, economic integration, both regional and global, has taken a strong hold. There is a growing realization that, for the survival of the modern world, with increasing cross-country links and externalities, global cooperation is a necessity. The economic and business climate has changed remarkably. Countries not necessarily sharing political ideologies have come together to benefit from mutual interdependencies, and small nations are resorting to regionalism to enhance their bargaining leverage and to gain some degree of international political influence. Countries integrate because they do not want to lose out in the global competition for export markets and foreign direct investment (FDI). Moreover, they also realize that their lives and economic options are being determined not only by themselves, but by an international environment over which they have little control, and that the inherent risks are best minimized through group and not individual country action.

The pace of international economic integration accelerated in the 1980s and 1990s. The sweep of economic reform and spectacular economic growth in China and the commitment to market-based reforms by India have added fuel to this process. Moreover, the establishment of the World Trade Organization (WTO) in 1995 has created a favorable environment for settling multilateral international trade issues in an amicable manner. As a consequence of these developments, hundreds of global, regional, and bilateral integration processes have emerged, and many of them have taken root. The number of regional trade agreements notified to the WTO from 1995 to May 2003 was 265 (though not all are in force). The Association of Southeast Asian Nations (ASEAN), a regional trade agreement established in 1967, has slowly gained momentum and has made considerable progress in forging a regional free trade area. ASEAN aims to achieve a fully integrated ASEAN Economic Community by 2020.

The rapid progress of economic integration has sparked an intense debate over the advantages and disadvantages. While it is more or less clear that integration would bring about stronger economic growth, it is less clear whether the economic benefits of this growth would be equitably distributed to reduce poverty. The opponents of integration argue that integration is a guise for exploiting the people in developing countries, which will cause massive disruptions of lives and few benefits to the poor. Others consider it with hostility and believe that it increases inequality within and between nations, threatens employment and living standards, and thwarts social progress in the weaker economies. The proponents point to the significant reduction in poverty in countries that have adopted economic integration, such as China, India, and Vietnam. Others consider this integration as a key process for future world economic development. They believe it is inevitable and irreversible.

Since the mid-1980s, Cambodia has gradually moved away from a planned economy to a market-based economy supported by a wide range of economic reforms and increasing involvement in regional and global integration activities. Cambodia is a small economy, and, to benefit from economies of scale, we have to be competitive in export markets. After many years of effort, Cambodia has succeeded in becoming a member of ASEAN and the WTO. In spite of its narrow economic base, it is carrying out the major structural adjustment of the economy required by these affiliations. We realize that Cambodia has no choice but to be integrated with the world community to survive in the evolving global environment. The pain we are suffering today is in the interest of the long-term development of Cambodia.

This essay outlines the perspectives on economic integration, particularly in the context of East Asia, and uses Cambodia as a case study in evaluating the merits and demerits of integration. The essay begins by discussing the strengths and weaknesses of economic integration from global and regional perspectives and then analyzes the impacts of economic integration on Cambodia. Finally, the essay provides some thoughts on how best to manage the risks implicit in the rapid changes in the economic structure resulting from integration.

Key Perspectives on Economic Integration

Economic integration may be interpreted in several ways. In a broad sense, it may be considered identical to globalization, which might be defined as increasing economic interdependence among countries. In this essay, "economic integration" and "globalization" will be used interchangeably. At a more technical level, economic integration may be defined as the rise of international trade through cross-country links in the markets for goods, services, and some factors of production. The increasing role of FDI, multinational corporations, and international capital markets in supporting higher growth, higher employment, and the exports of several countries reflects some of the tangible outcomes of economic integration across the globe.

In general, economic integration is expected to provide a slew of benefits to consumers. It would result in lower consumer prices because of increasing allocative efficiency through production structures based on comparative advantage, the exploitation of economies of scale in the bigger domestic and international markets, and the adoption of new technologies. As a consequence of expanded consumer choices because of greater quantities and ranges of imports and exports, more competition, the dismantling of vested monopolies in domestic markets, higher productivity growth, and lower price markups, the average consumer in a country will be more well off with more trade rather than with less.

The poor might also conceivably benefit from the growth of international trade. At least, they would benefit as consumers from lower prices. Additionally, there is evidence that greater economic integration has played an important role in accelerating growth and reducing poverty in an increasing number of developing countries and, hence, in reducing overall global inequality in income distribution. Three channels have been identified as contributing to reducing poverty. First, economic integration promotes growth, which will have significant trickle-down effects. Second, the higher demand for relatively abundant factors of production, such as unskilled labor in most of the Asian countries, will improve the incomes of the poor. Third, the use of better technology will raise productivity and, consequently, factor incomes.

Another major benefit from economic integration is good governance. The failure of governance can lead to an overall political breakdown. Weak governance has contributed to the poor economic performance of several countries. Globalization has put a high premium on good governance. An increasingly competitive global marketplace leaves little room for corruption, which adds to transaction costs. As a result, governments are rendered more accountable to their citizens for the higher costs of economic mismanagement. Globalization has also raised new challenges for public policy that go beyond halting corruption. Technological gains, shifting geopolitics, expanding trade and financial flows, and cheaper communications have created tremendous opportunities and lifted barriers to global knowledge and problem solving. They have likewise raised new risks and challenges, for example, financial instability, disease transmission, and crossborder criminality. Nations will have to adapt their political and governance institutions to the new technological, financial, and economic realities. This is also a challenge.

Alongside the benefits, economic integration is thought to create many problems. Oxfam (2000) critiques globalization as antigrowth and antipoor because globalization ignores the crucial role of income distribution in poverty reduction. The poor have virtually no access to productive resources. Since economic integration benefits only those with resources, people who lack resources, typically the poor, are left behind. Therefore, globalization has contributed to a growing divide between the haves and the have-nots.

The distribution of per capita income between countries has become more unequal in recent decades. For example, in 1960, the average per capita gross domestic product (GDP) in the richest 20 countries in the world was 15 times that in the poorest 20 countries. Today, this gap has widened to 30 times since rich countries have, on average, also grown more rapidly than poor ones. Indeed, per capita incomes in the poorest 20 countries have hardly changed since 1960 and have even fallen in several countries. Moreover, the hopes of some of the poorest countries that the demand for low-skilled labor will increase once a country has opened up may not be realized because low-skilled labor may no longer be needed following the introduction of new technologies.

Job insecurity may also result from globalization. In the developed countries, integration will provide job security to those with the skills and mobility to exploit opportunities in global markets, while low-skilled workers will be left out because their jobs and earnings will be displaced by labor-intensive imports from low-wage countries or shifted overseas by multinational corporations to reduce costs. On the surface, it appears that unskilled and semiskilled workers in developing countries have benefited from integration through improved employment prospects and higher earnings, as there is more FDI. However, this apparent benefit is also at risk since globalization exposes these economies to business cycles that originate in the developed world. Moreover, the investments of multinational corporations are often fickle. They have no permanent stake in any country and tend to relocate production facilities to emerging centers of competitive advantage. Overall, labor in the developing world experiences no less job insecurity than their counterparts in the developed world. Moreover, recent evidence shows that trade liberalization leads to growing wage gaps between the educated and uneducated not only in the countries of the Organisation for Economic Co-operation and Development, but in the developing world as well. Between 1991 and 1995, wage gaps increased for six of seven Latin American countries for which reliable wage data are available. It was inevitable that this led to massive social protests in these countries.

Another major problem of economic integration is the stress it places on the scarce administrative resources of governments in the less developed countries. The world has become increasingly borderless, and governments have lost control over many areas of public policy management. With financial integration, nation states have lost part of their sovereignty and control to capital markets and speculators driven by the profit motive and not by considerations of public good. Technological advances and the lowering of border barriers have increased the problems involved in monitoring and controlling crossborder crimes such as commercial fraud, drug and human trafficking, money laundering, environmental pollution, and terrorism. And, while integration raises the demands for governments to provide social safety nets, it reduces the ability of governments to provide these nets because governments are discouraged from raising taxes on the capital and earnings of skilled labor, the main beneficiaries of globalization.

The most serious charge against economic integration is that it was the primary cause of the 1997–98 Asian financial crisis, which brought to an abrupt halt the smooth economic progress regional economies had been making for more than a decade. The crisis showed that regionally integrated economies might be quickly affected by a contagion arising from the economic weakness of one country in the group. Thus, economic integration may cause volatility and vulnerability in some countries due to no fault of their own.

The crisis also showed that excessive reliance on foreign capital to support higher economic growth is a high-risk strategy. Short-term capital inflows to Southeast Asia were massive in the early 1990s mostly by way of private sector commercial bank borrowings and portfolio investments. The inward surge of capital occurred in response to the strong economic growth, capital account liberalization, and domestic financial market liberalization witnessed in these countries. In the six quarters preceding the onset of the crisis in July 1997, capital inflows into Indonesia, the Republic of Korea, the Philippines, and Thailand totaled US$86.8 billion. However, in the subsequent six quarters, there was a huge outflow of US$77.9 billion. These funds were largely utilized for domestic purposes and were, by and large, not hedged against exchange rate risks. The pegged exchange rate provided an implicit government guarantee against exchange rate risk, spurring domestic borrowers to access the cheaper international funds. The huge capital inflows contributed to overvalued exchange rates, asset bubbles in real estate and stock markets, overinvestment in productive capacity, and falling quality in investment projects. Short-term debt was used to finance longer-term investments, resulting in risky maturity mismatches. When the crisis struck, foreign capital fled, and regional currencies depreciated sharply. Since the size of the foreign funds was huge and exceeded official reserves, central banks were unable to defend their currencies in most cases. Even though the affected economies have, by and large, adjusted since the shock, some effects of the crisis are being felt even today.

The last argument against economic integration is the threat of social disintegration. Economic integration is perceived to undermine traditional values and cultural identities because of the increasing intrusion of global, primarily Western, norms, practices, and values into societies and local communities. The Internet has increased the rapidity and ubiquity of this process. The change has been so rapid in several countries that centuries-old domestic institutions, norms, and practices have fallen by the wayside in the name of economic progress.

East Asian Economic Integration

Even though it seems to be a mixed blessing at best, countries in the region are keen to go forward with economic integration. Economies such as Hong Kong (China), Korea, Taiwan (China), and the original five ASEAN member countries (Indonesia, Malaysia, the Philippines, Singapore, and Thailand) opened up a long time ago to trade and investment. They have become well integrated with the world economic community. Indeed, a major goal of ASEAN is to foster this integration. The new ASEAN members are also eager to join the world community. In fact, Cambodia, the Lao People's Democratic Republic, and Vietnam opened up their economies even before they gained ASEAN membership. Overall, Asia has become a dominant supplier to consumers in developed economies. The East Asian countries were able to expand their share of global trade from 5.4 percent in 1975 to 18.7 percent in 2001, while their share in manufactured exports increased from 52 percent in 1981 to 88 percent in 2001.[1]

However, East Asian countries wish to strengthen economic integration since they realize there is no viable alternative growth strategy to sustain growth momentum in the future. The ASEAN countries have started to put in place the structure for the ASEAN Economic Community, while the East Asia Vision Group has proposed the formation of an East Asian Economic Community that will include the 10 ASEAN member countries, plus China, Japan, and Korea. The proposal to create this economic community has been boosted by the creation of the East Asia Summit. The rationale for the community is that some of the economies in the group are too small to be able to participate effectively in the global market, and they need to integrate with the large economies in the region to enhance the benefits from economic cooperation and integration.

Recent economic research reveals that integration has been naturally motivated by market forces, economic complementarity, and the economic dynamism of the region. However, this process has been impaired because of the Asian financial crisis and the failure of the WTO world trade talks at Cancun in September 2003. Therefore, it has been recognized that strong government support through formal regional institutional agreements will be needed to supplement market forces in accelerating integration. These developments are elaborated below.

Market-Driven Initiatives

Alongside rapid economic growth, there has been a notable expansion of intraregional trade in East Asia. In fact, intraregional trade has been expanding much more rapidly than the trade of the region with areas outside the region. A study by Ng and Yeats (2003) shows that, while the share of the trade of the East Asian countries increased threefold between 1975 and 2001, the intraindustry trade increased by sixfold. The share of intraregional trade in East Asia in the region's total trade rose from 23 percent in 1980 to 41 percent in 2001 (excluding Japan).[2] The increased intraregional trade and investments were a natural process of economic development because economies in close proximity tend to grow together by taking advantage of economies of scope and scale.

Moreover, within the region, the export profiles of some countries increasingly match the import profiles of others. This complementarity is strong for the group comprising Hong Kong (China), Indonesia, Malaysia, the Philippines, Taiwan (China), and Thailand, which reflects the importance of intraindustry trade and the strengthening of two-way trade among these countries. Between 1985 and 2001, the share of intraregional exports in total exports increased substantially, from 9.9 percent to 27.2 percent for Indonesia, from 10.1 percent to 34.1 percent for Korea, and from 14.8 percent to 41.1 percent for Taiwan (China). In the same period, the share of intraregional imports in total imports also rose significantly, from 13.8 percent to 37.3 percent for Indonesia, from 13.4 percent to 25.8 percent for Korea, and from 12.7 percent to 31.4 percent for Taiwan (China) (see table 2.1).

The increase in intraregional trade was initially accompanied by an increase in foreign investment, which was led by Japan, in the newly industrialized economies and in Southeast Asian countries in the 1980s. Subsequently, investment from the newly industrialized economies flowed to Southeast Asia and China. In fact, the share of these countries in investment among ASEAN members continues to rise. Japan

TABLE 2.1 **Share of Intraregional Trade in Total Trade, 1985–2001**

Country	Exports 1985	Exports 2001	Imports 1985	Imports 2001
China	35.1	30.8	23.0	49.8
Hong Kong (China)	27.5	35.2	46.8	60.0
Indonesia	9.9	27.2	13.8	37.3
Korea, Rep. of	10.1	34.1	13.4	25.8
Malaysia	38.1	42.0	44.4	51.6
Philippines	17.5	34.4	34.1	37.1
Singapore	35.1	44.9	39.2	43.5
Taiwan (China)	14.8	41.1	12.7	31.4
Thailand	25.5	33.5	33.5	36.2

Source: Ng and Yeats 2003.

appears to be the largest investor in ASEAN countries, especially Indonesia and Thailand. Multinational corporations began to fragment their production processes into subprocesses and locate the fragmented production facilities in countries in the region according to available national factor proportions and technological capabilities. This strategy has generated a web of intraregional trade networks in parts, components, semifinished products, and finished products within East Asia, contributing to a more efficient division of labor and deeper integration in the region. The FDI-trade nexus is a distinctive feature in the region. FDI is a complement to trade rather than a substitute for trade.

Public Sector Initiatives

Integration in the East Asia countries has not been driven by market forces alone. Since the early 1990s, governments in the region, prompted by many motives, have played a proactive role in cementing regional economic integration.

First, the governments have had to respond to escalating pressure from a private sector clamoring for policies and strategies to facilitate trade and investment. The macroeconomic interdependence within the region has recently become stronger, as evidenced by the simultaneous contraction of economic activity throughout East Asia in 1998 and the expansion in 1999–2000. Though regional economies may be affected by some common factors, such as economic cycles in the United

States and stock-price movements in the information technology sector, many of the recent, synchronized economic activities in the region can be attributed to growing macroeconomic interdependence and the recent efforts to develop a network of free trade areas in the region by ASEAN+3 (plus China, Japan, and Korea), ASEAN and the Australia and New Zealand Closer Economic Relations Trade Agreement, and ASEAN and India. The increasing interdependence in trade and investment will not be sustained if there is no formal policy support from the governments. Problems such as harmonization in rules, regulations, laws, standards, procedures, dispute settlement, and so on will need to be addressed before integration may be taken to a higher level.

Second, even though there has been strong economic growth in many countries in East Asia in the last two decades, the threat of rising poverty and unemployment remains. Regional governments cannot turn a blind eye to this issue. They must become actively involved in regional integration initiatives so that they are able to manage effectively the social and political fallout from economic integration. This is crucial for the sustainability of economic growth and integration. It is not a coincidence that most of the poor and the people who have been left behind in these countries are located along the borders, where infrastructure is weak and social services are virtually nonexistent. Realizing this threat to the sustainability of economic integration, the governments have initiated infrastructure development and generated employment opportunities in border regions.

A notable example of shared infrastructure that forges closer trading relationships among countries with common borders is cooperation in the Greater Mekong Subregion, which includes Cambodia, Lao PDR, Myanmar, Thailand, Vietnam, and Yunnan Province and the Guanxi Zhuang Autonomous Region in China. In 1992, with assistance from the Asian Development Bank (ADB), these countries embarked on a program of regional economic cooperation to raise the standards of living of their peoples. Through the program, three major economic corridors are being developed that, when completed, will significantly boost trade and investment across the region. The Greater Mekong Subregion has emerged as a strong regional entity and one of the most rapidly growing subregions in the world.

The need for strong financial governance was highlighted by the Asian financial crisis. It is now realized that poor financial and corporate governance in the affected countries contributed significantly to the deepening of the crisis and was a direct result of government failure. There is a clear need for governments to engage in the prevention, management, and resolution of financial crises and contagion. Governments are responsible for ensuring that strong corporate and financial management structures are put in place so that there is no repeat of the 1997–98 catastrophe. The global initiative for a new international financial architecture was moving slowly when the crisis struck. The crisis-affected economies were also dissatisfied with the level of assistance from the European Union (EU) and the United States and the inappropriate conditionalities of multilateral financial assistance that treated the crisis as though it had originated from current account imbalances, while the problem was centered on capital account management. It was clear that the region had to devise self-help mechanisms to prevent and manage possible crises in the future. The creation of the ASEAN+3 process of regional financial cooperation is a direct result of the crisis. Since the crisis, economic integration has become an attractive option for sustainable economic recovery because it provides better security of market access, attracts investment resources, and creates internal pressure for domestic economic reforms and restructuring.

The failure at Cancun and the slow progress of Asia-Pacific Economic Cooperation has had serious repercussions for the economic welfare of many developing countries. While the developments in the international forums have been slow, economic integration in the Americas and Europe has strengthened appreciably. The EU is expanding rapidly by bringing erstwhile countries of the Council for Mutual Economic Assistance into the fold. The Free Trade Area of the Americas is also forging ahead. By 2003, 184 regional trade agreements in force throughout the world had been reported to the WTO. Regional governments fear that, unless they form their own free trade areas, they will be disadvantaged in global competition. Firms are being forced to adopt and adapt to regional and global strategies of doing business in order to survive and stay competitive. East Asia has been obliged to respond somehow to show the world that, even in the face of complex diversity within the region, there is an avenue for closer regional cooperation, coordination, and integration. The East Asian governments have realized that their countries will not be able to maintain the status quo in the global production network in the rapidly changing global competitive equation if there is no integration. The East Asian economies also believe they need to secure a bigger market within their own region so that economies of scale and efficiency gains may be exploited more effectively. The region needs to establish an extensive network of regional production and trading arrangements with key economic players. This will open up and expand opportunities for economic links in the region and beyond and strengthen regional competitiveness and attractiveness globally. At the same time, closer economic integration will enhance competitiveness and bargaining leverage and offer safeguards for continued market access for exports. Obtaining all these advantages would require active government participation in regional integration processes.

Lastly, regional governments have had to respond to the severe adjustment problems emerging because of the rapid economic rise of China. However, this challenge may be converted into an opportunity. The emergence of China as a world economic power has led to a growing realization that the region might form a large and dynamic economic bloc by integrating with China, harnessing regional resources and efforts to resolve regional problems, and meeting the common challenges of regionalism from America and Europe. With China included, the East Asian region will hold one-third of the world's population, one-quarter of the world's GDP, and two-fifth of the world's foreign reserves.

Financial Integration

There was a realization following the 1997–98 crisis that self-help mechanisms are needed in the region for the effective prevention, management, and resolution of financial crises and contagion. This has sparked several initiatives that should be quick in response, wide in scope, and effective in impact. Intensive policy dialogue and mutual surveillance, the establishment of regional liquidity support arrangements, and the development of bond markets denominated in local currencies are among several regional initiatives that have been launched to strengthen regional financial integration.

The East Asian economies have liberalized their financial systems to integrate them with the global financial system so that they may have better access to capital markets, especially those in the developed economies. But more efforts are needed for a better deployment of regional financial resources. Currently, a sizable portion of gross savings in Asia finds its way into debt instruments of governmental and quasi-governmental issuers in industrialized economies, while investment in Asia is financed, to a significant degree, by capital from those same countries. This reflects the relative lack of integration in financial markets in the Asian economies. Moreover, financial liberalization and innovation initiatives in East Asia do not appear to have strengthened the financial links among the financial markets of individual East Asian countries. Instead, financial liberalization has led to the diversification and strengthening of East Asian financial ties with global financial markets rather than closer financial cooperation within the region.

While individual East Asian countries have made considerable progress in deregulating and opening their financial markets, they have not been able to coordinate their liberalization efforts collectively. As a result, they have achieved little harmonization in legal systems at the regional level for the protection of minority stockholders, for regulatory systems, and for the tax treatment of crossborder financial transactions. They have achieved little harmonization in standards governing banking, accounting, auditing, disclosure, and corporate governance. Lagging cooperation in the regional harmonization of legal and regulatory systems and standard-setting has been by far the most important cause of the slow progress in financial integration in the region.

Potential Benefits of Financial Integration

If a deep and well-functioning corporate bond market were to become established in the region, the considerable pool of savings, much of which now flows to industrial countries, might instead be utilized within the region. As financial intermediation becomes rationalized, the cost of capital for enterprises in Asia would become lower. The dependence of regional investment on funds from nonregional sources is not only incongruous; it also exposes the region to the risk that the flows of capital might dry up abruptly because of developments in international financial markets, thus wreaking havoc on regional economic activity.

Financial market deregulation and liberalization generally facilitate the migration of capital in the long run and the crossborder financing of current account imbalances in the short run, thereby reducing the costs of adjustment to shocks. Financial liberalization also allows the extensive sharing of the investment risks associated with macroeconomic shocks across countries because it broadens the range for diversification by including foreign bonds and equities in individual portfolios. By lowering transaction costs and eliminating exchange rate risks, the formation of a common currency area can help area members reap these benefits of financial liberalization. Therefore, countries with close international financial links would have the incentive to join a common currency arrangement.

Expanding the effective size of regional financial markets through greater integration across national jurisdictions may increase the ability of our economies to absorb the volatility of international capital movements as effectively as the European and U.S. markets. Several official initiatives toward closer financial links in the region are bearing fruit, notably the Chiang Mai Initiative and the Asian Bond Fund.

Moreover, with financial market liberalization, domestic residents can diversify their asset portfolios internationally by holding securities issued by firms and financial institutions of other countries in addition to domestic ones. The possibility of portfolio diversification across a large array of assets means that a country suffering an adverse terms-of-trade shock could share some of the loss with its trading partners to the extent that it holds claims on their output.

An adverse supply shock such as an oil price increase may result in a deficit on the current account in addition to both an increase in unemployment and a decrease in real wages. As they adjust to the shock, countries with an open financial regime have better access to regional and global capital markets so that it would be easier and less costly for them to borrow to finance their current account deficits. External borrowing sourced from international capital markets at reasonable terms might make the real adjustment smaller and less arduous for these countries than recourse to higher-cost, arranged borrowings.

Current Development of Financial Integration

While East Asian countries have been unable to coordinate their institutional reforms at the regional level, they have been pressured to adopt the codes and standards for financial sector regulation, accounting, and corporate governance developed by advanced countries. Whatever its rationale, the effort of the advanced countries to graft the Western systems and standards on East Asia has not been successful (Park 2002). East Asia has recently recognized the need to get a regional consensus on this issue, and the ASEAN+3 Finance Ministers' Meeting process has taken it up as a high priority.

In other areas, East Asia has made significant progress in monetary and financial cooperation. This process has been led by the ASEAN+3 group in response to the 1997–98 financial crisis and has been assisted in various ways by the ADB. In its efforts to integrate their financial markets, ASEAN+3 countries have created two important initiatives, the Chiang Mai Initiative and the Asian Bond Markets Initiative. These two initiatives have been progressing well and provide major benefits to member countries.

A salient feature of the *Chiang Mai Initiative* is the provision of liquidity support to participating countries through a network of bilateral swap agreements. In May 2006, ASEAN+3 took a major step by strengthening the initiative and doubling the size of the swaps.

ASEAN+3 has also instituted a number of mechanisms to support policy dialogue and promote open discussion on financial and economic issues. It has implemented the *Asian Bond Markets Initiative* to mobilize the region's vast pool of savings for direct, efficient use in the region's long-term investments. During this period, the following have been achieved.

- Various international and foreign institutions have issued bonds denominated in local currencies. The World Bank issued ringgit-denominated Islamic Bonds in Malaysia in May 2005. In Thailand, the ADB and the Japan Bank for International Cooperation issued baht-denominated bonds in May and September 2005, respectively. These were the first baht-denominated issuances by an international institution and by a foreign government institution. In October 2005, the International Finance Corporation and the ADB issued renminbi-denominated so-called Panda Bonds, in China. The ADB also issued peso-denominated bonds in the Philippines. The proceeds of the issue will be used to buy up nonperforming loans from the National Home Mortgage Finance Corporation. The issuance of the Japanese Samurai Bonds recovered in 2005.
- Bonds denominated in local currencies have also been issued through securitization. The China Development Bank and the China Construction Bank issued assets-backed securities with trust investment companies as special purpose vehicles in late 2005. In Japan, the issuance amount of mortgage-backed securities by the Government Housing Loan Corporation recorded a noticeable growth. Korea started issuing Student Loan-Backed Securities based on the loans originating through the new student loan system. In Singapore, the Commercial Mortgage-Backed Securities market is thriving in line with the real estate investment trust. In April 2006, the government supported the launch of the Small- and Medium-Sized Enterprise Access Loan Scheme.

Cambodia's Experiences in Globalization

Since liberation day on January 7, 1979, the government of Cambodia has been strenuously involved in rehabilitation efforts. In the early 1980s, Cambodia experimented with a centrally planned economy. Realizing the vast potential provided by the world community and FDI, Cambodia embraced a market-based economic system in the mid-1980s. Cambodia has never been hesitant to join regional and global communities. As a result, it has become a member of many regional and global organizations, such as ASEAN, the Greater Mekong Subregion, and, at the global level, the WTO. All these initiatives have meant considerable structural adjustment and reform on Cambodia's part.

Cambodia's trade with the world has also increased substantially in the last decade. Trade has been the main source of economic growth in Cambodia. The normalization of relationships with EU countries and the United States that culminated in trade agreements has been widely hailed as a success. Cambodia has gained jobs and investments, along with better working conditions for labor. After Cambodia gained access to the European and U.S. markets, its garment exports increased in value from only around US$20 million in 1995 to almost US$2 billion in 2005. Growing employment in the garment and textile sectors has been a major factor in stabilizing the economy. These sectors currently employ 280,000 skilled and unskilled workers.

Economic growth averaged 8 percent in the last decade. This spectacular growth was made possible by sharp increases in trade and investment. Economic growth rose to 9.5 percent in 2004 and accelerated to 13.4 percent in 2005 despite negative external developments such as higher oil prices, terrorism, and the spread of epidemic diseases. Political stability, accompanied by greater investor confidence, has provided the basis for this robust growth performance, which has been driven mainly by the superb growth in the agricultural sector, the expanding tourism sector, continued robust garment exports, and increased construction activities. The growth rates in the agricultural sector, industrial sector, and services sector have generally been quite robust, from 11.7 percent, 12.1 percent, and 2 percent, respectively, in 2003 to 1.1 percent, 16.7 percent, and 10.1 percent in 2004 and 17.3 percent, 13.3 percent, and 9.4 percent in 2005, respectively.

The value of total trade has also risen significantly. The value of exports reached almost US$3 billion in 2005, while the value of imports reached almost US$4 billion. Cambodia has established trading relationships with a wide range of partners, including the EU, Japan, many other Asian countries, and the United States. At the same time, Cambodia has also received considerable foreign investment from several sources. The value of FDI rose substantially, from US$74 million in 2003 to US$381 million in 2005. The increase in trade and investment reflects the growing integration of Cambodia in the world trading system.

With around 75 percent of the population still living in the countryside and an economy heavily dependent on tourism and garment exports, the integration of Cambodia into regional and global communities, especially the entry into the WTO, is fraught with opportunities and challenges. Some skeptics have questioned the merits of Cambodia, with its vulnerable economic structure, joining the WTO. They have noted the situation of several members of the WTO that are least developed countries and that, despite their membership, have been unable to secure trading opportunities commensurate with their development needs. However, from its past experience, Cambodia remains hopeful of gaining substantial benefits from its accession to the WTO. Nevertheless, it realizes that the risks inherent in this initiative will need to be carefully managed.

Perceived Benefits of Integration

The perceived benefits of integration range from building a new national image within the world community to improving exports, investment, and governance. In the case of a poor country such as Cambodia, integration is seen as a necessary means to achieve economic growth. To survive in the harsh and fierce environment of global competition, Cambodia must grasp all available opportunities. Integration represents one way to guarantee we seize these opportunities.

Cambodia's recent history has been traumatic; it is still going through the aftermath of a genocidal regime, prolonged internal conflict, and neglect. The image of violence, poverty, and hardship has stuck with the country. The integration of Cambodia into the world community is therefore viewed as a deliberate step toward breaking away from the image as a poor, war-stricken country isolated from the international community. Moreover, integration may be considered a means to fulfill broader strategic goals, one of which is to facilitate the peaceful reemergence of Cambodia as a trading nation.

Economic integration will afford Cambodia access to markets in other countries. Integration will also intensify competition between foreign and local producers. The resulting market environment will be more efficient and in a better position to cope with global competition. This, in turn, will attract more investment, creating a virtuous circle of higher productivity, higher incomes, and higher growth. Cambodia's industrial environment will eventually converge toward international norms through a reduction in the impediments to export competitiveness.

Cambodia's membership in the WTO implies that investors wishing to locate production facilities in Cambodia will not be subject to price discrimination in export markets. Moreover, Cambodian exporters will be able to know in advance the maximum legal duties that may be assessed on exported goods because WTO members have "bound" (that is, set legal ceilings on) most of their tariff lines. Furthermore, a Cambodian exporter may be assured that the exports will not be subject to quotas or quantitative restrictions on export markets. For all of these reasons, WTO membership reduces the uncertainty facing an investor who wants to produce in Cambodia for export to other markets.

Integration will also provide exporters with access to raw materials and intermediate inputs at world market prices. Cambodia has always recognized this, and, under the Law on Investment, has provided export industries with duty-free access to imported capital and intermediate goods and raw materials. For example, membership in ASEAN allows Cambodia to import fabrics from ASEAN countries to produce garments for the EU market. When Cambodia was not a member of ASEAN, it had to ask for derogation from the EU every year in order to import fabrics to produce garments for the EU market so that it might satisfy the requirements of the Rules of Origin under the EU generalized system of preferences scheme.

The ability to export with free access to raw materials and to benefit from fair and nondiscriminatory treatment in foreign markets is very important for Cambodia because it needs more exports to generate jobs. Cambodia is a small country with a relatively small population, a large proportion of which is impoverished. However, Cambodia's population has been growing rapidly. The number of young people entering the job market has been rising and will continue to rise at a rapid pace in the years ahead. Expanding employment opportunities commensurately is therefore a major challenge. Given the lack of purchasing power in the domestic economy, the rapid creation of new jobs in the short term will only result from production for external markets. Exports will play a key role in creating employment and reducing poverty in Cambodia until domestic markets are able to generate sufficient employment opportunities to absorb the growth in the labor force. Moreover, exports will allow Cambodian producers to access the world's resources, technology, and ideas; enable greater efficiency and productivity through the exploitation of comparative advantage, economies of scale, competition, and innovation; and provide for wider consumer choice.

To be able to export and generate employment, Cambodia needs foreign investment because adequate savings, skills, and technology are not available within the country. Cambodian firms must therefore cooperate with foreign firms to get the benefits of what they are missing at home. Foreign investment has an important role in upgrading technology levels and transferring commercial and industrial knowledge. Cambodia has much to learn from the foreign firms that know foreign markets the best and possess the technology, managerial experience, and marketing channels needed to export successfully.

Cambodia's textile and garment industry well illustrates the role of exports and investment in generating employment and helping to reduce poverty. More than half the current 280,000 skilled and unskilled jobs in the industry have been created during the past five years, making the industry by far the largest source of job growth during this period. The workers are generally from low-income families in the countryside, and their earnings usually flow back to these families in the countryside, where they support rural development. Garment exports have also helped manage the balance of payments; they rose sharply from around US$20 million in 1995 to almost US$2 billion in 2005.

Cambodia understood from the beginning that the country's attractiveness to investors depends on the availability and quality of the physical and financial infrastructure required by business. The investment environment is also enhanced by the availability of an educated and trained labor force. Economic integration may be seen as an opportunity to encourage foreign investment in key services infrastructure and therefore as an opportunity to enhance the country's overall environment for business. Likewise, foreign participation in adult education and training would help develop the skilled workforce that is necessary to attract skills-based industries and allow for increased wages because of higher productivity.

The agricultural sector also stands to benefit greatly from integration. The productivity of the agricultural sector in Cambodia is considered low. Relative to neighboring countries, agricultural yields are much smaller. However, through economic integration, the small yields might also be turned into a good opportunity to enhance productivity in the sector. Because of the vast area of cultivation and the huge untapped potential in all agricultural crops, economic integration would open up foreign markets to Cambodian agricultural products, while also obliging Cambodian farmers to become more competitive so as to succeed in local and foreign markets.

Even though integration may be considered a source of inequality, the benefits from integration offset the negative impacts. Integration can act as a motivating force among people who have been left behind; they will work harder, learn more, and equip themselves with more professional skills because they will see the benefits obtained by others from integration in terms of better living standards and greater prosperity. In Cambodia, we have realized the benefits of higher education and greater skills, and we are experiencing a huge increase in the demand in education for places both in private and public universities. Many people with lower-level degrees or diplomas have gone back to tertiary education.

Finally, integration will force Cambodia to carry out the necessary reforms in legal and institutional structures and improve governance standards. This is a major challenge. For example, WTO membership requires an intensified effort by Cambodia to put in place the legal framework required by business. For some time, the government has been actively engaged in drafting and submitting to the National Assembly the laws necessary to establish a modern, liberal, business-friendly legal environment. A member of the WTO must likewise enact laws that embody WTO rules on international trade and activities related to trade.

In terms of legal obligations, the first and most obvious challenge is to fulfill the commitments to legislative and administrative change that Cambodia has accepted through the protocol of WTO accession. In a decision taken on February 27, 2004, the Council of Ministers identified 98 separate tasks that flow from the protocol and that needed to be accomplished before the end of 2005, and it apportioned the responsibility for completing these tasks among 20 ministries and agencies. Its agreements to abide by international treaty rules and the rule of law in the conduct of trade and in domestic policy will push

Cambodia to accelerate the implementation of legal and domestic policy reform, ensuring the uniform and impartial implementation of trade accords with much greater transparency and strengthening prudential regulation and supervision. However, a modern, liberal, business-friendly, and WTO-compliant legal regime will only be as good as the level of implementation and enforcement. The magnitude of the multiple challenges that Cambodia faces in this respect is widely recognized. Cambodia is at the very earliest stages in developing a properly functioning judicial system. It must push ahead with reform as a matter of urgency and, in the meantime, ensure that nonjudicial measures such as arbitration and administrative enforcement are used to the fullest to ensure that laws are put into practice and obeyed.

Negative Impacts of Integration

Similar to other countries undergoing integration, Cambodia is also facing several problems. Rapid economic change is altering social relationships, with some positive and some negative effects. Even though the opportunities provided by integration are substantial, Cambodia does not possess a sufficiently robust social framework to seize on those opportunities fully. It continues to experience the many social ills, such as drug use and crime, that are often attributed to globalization.

Integration will likewise mean that, in future, Cambodia will not be spared from the shocks emanating from the international financial and commercial systems. For example, the Asian financial crisis resulted in a sharp drop in FDI in Cambodia. The ratification of trade agreements between other countries will also have an impact on Cambodia, for example, the United States–Vietnam Trade Agreement. The end of safeguard measures by the EU and the United States on textile products from China in the future will also pose a threat to the Cambodian garment sector.

One of the biggest challenges relates to the rising inequality resulting from the differential impact of integration on segments within society. Those people who are not able to seize the opportunities provided by integration are being left out of the process. With its sustained high growth over the last decade, Cambodia has reduced poverty incidence from 47 percent in 1993–94 to 35 percent in 2004. The peace dividend in the aftermath of the end of civil strife and the low initial conditions prevailing in the economy have enabled Cambodia to sustain high growth during the early stages of development without severely straining capacity. This growth has generally been unbalanced, centered in Phnom Penh and other urban areas, and narrowly based, driven as it is by such activities as garment making, construction, and tourism.

Cambodia is experiencing considerable inequality in income distribution: the Gini coefficient was 0.42 in 2004. If the situation worsens because of integration, the social consequences will be heavy. This is the most pressing issue in Cambodia today. We have enjoyed economic success because of a high growth rate, but we have not been able to reduce inequality, and this may threaten stability and future growth. Cambodia is considered to suffer from the greatest inequality in income distribution in the region. Much of this has been due to growing differences within the rural population, with considerable variation in the rate and distribution of growth in different localities, in the security of land tenure, in remoteness from markets and services, and in the lack of productive assets.

Inequality in Cambodia can be classified into two kinds. First is the inequality represented by those people with good education and financial background who are able to seize the new opportunities and the inequality represented by those people with less education who are unable to capitalize on these opportunities. In Cambodia, those who possess advanced degrees, the ability to speak foreign languages, and the skills demanded by the market are living comfortably because they are able to work for reasonable salaries in the private sector or with nongovernmental organizations and other international organizations. Meanwhile, the other people, those without skills and education, are stuck in low-paying jobs without proper medical care or a social safety net. For example, many women employed in garment factories must live at a subsistence level as they struggle to remit large shares of their wages to their families. This is not unique in Cambodia. It is a problem common to all countries. The government understands that an appropriate redistribution policy would play a key role in mitigating this problem by improving and strengthening the education sector, the health sector, and access to public services. Various strategies are being implemented in the education sector, including "education for all and all for education," to ensure free and quality access to education, and the Priority Action Plan to channel funds directly to the proper budget entities. In the health sector, the government has created the Health Sector Strategic Plan to achieve priorities in regard to health services delivery, behavioral change, quality improvements, human resource development, health financing, and institutional development.

The second kind of inequality has resulted from asymmetric information. Those who understand the potential of the new opportunities may advance quickly, while those who are unable to access the relevant information remain more vulnerable. Integration definitely involves a lot of business opportunities. People who have access to information—for example, about promising areas for new investment or potential areas for investment—or people who are able to determine the positive impacts of integration on areas of investment will be able to make huge profits in land speculation, business deals, and so on. Thus, in Siem Reap Province, those people who have understood the potential of this area to become a new tourist destination in Asia may make a lot of money through land speculation. Meanwhile, those who have not been able to understand this potential have lost significantly by selling their land to speculators at bargain prices and moving to more remote areas or becoming landless.

Cambodia is experiencing rising landlessness, and this problem has contributed to inequality significantly. Economic integration is one of the major causes of landlessness in Cambodia. As the price of land has risen because of the increase in foreign investments and the growing demand for land for hotel and factory construction, farmers have sold their lands cheaply. Moreover, because they lack knowledge about how to manage this sudden financial gain, the money has vanished quickly, and many farmers have become landless and poor. The proportion of landless rural households increased from 13 percent in 1997 to 16 percent in 1999 and 20 percent in 2004. The rise in landlessness has been relatively rapid given that land distribution was more or less equal when land was formally allocated to households in 1989. The problem has been exacerbated by the related problem of unclear property rights (as many as 80 percent of rural households that owned land were without titles to the land in 2004) and the ambiguous legal status of land ownership. The rising value of land in many parts of the country has complicated the issue. The result is an emerging phenomenon of increasing landlessness juxtaposed with the existence of uncultivated land. Realizing that this is not an easy problem to solve, the government has set up the Ministry of Land Management, Urbanization, and Construction for the sole purpose of managing land, clarifying land titling, and reviewing land concessions.

Finally, it is widely known that economic integration is accompanied by corruption. No country has been spared this unfortunate activity. Integration exposes countries to corruption, which contributes to a deterioration in the business environment. Since Cambodia began integrating with the world economy, we have experienced this phenomenon. Corruption definitely slows the integration process because investors are afraid to pour money into a corrupt environment, which, in turn, leads to slower growth in trade and other forms of integration. In the Cambodian case, corruption has not had a strong impact on integration into regional and global communities. One of the reasons for this is the fact that the government has been quite aware of the problem. The integration of Cambodia into regional and world communities means that the country must make commitments to reform so as to improve governance, the rule of law, and the establishment of an appropriate regulatory environment. To achieve this, the government has set up numerous mechanisms to tackle corruption, such as the Rectangular Strategy, which aims at good governance, and various reforms, including public financial management reform, judicial reform, and civil administration reform, along with the relevant joint working groups. Moreover, the government has also set up the Government–Private Sector Forum, in which the private sector may meet with the government to express complaints and grievances that the government then seeks to address.

Conclusion: The Management of Economic Integration

Economic integration has been increasing, and the process is irreversible. It is difficult to conclude a priori that integration is either good or bad for Cambodia. Much will depend on how adroitly the process is managed. In any case, economic integration will definitely have both positive and negative impacts. The positive impacts will have to be maximized, and the negative impacts will have to be well managed if Cambodia is to benefit unequivocally from integration.

The government needs to maintain macroeconomic stability so as to create the proper conditions for investment and savings, to push for outward-oriented policies to promote efficiency through increased trade and investment, to promote structural reform to encourage domestic competition, and to create strong institutions to foster good governance.

Even though structural adjustment in many countries in East Asia has meant a decreasing share of agriculture in GDP, agriculture is still an important sector, providing employment and livelihoods for millions of people in rural areas. In many countries, even as the share of the agricultural sector in GDP has declined to around 30 percent, its share in total employment is still actually around 75–80 percent. Without agricultural development, it will be difficult to reduce rural poverty and release the resources needed for industrial development. In many areas, growth in the supply of basic staples is critical to ensure household food security and to sustain adequate real wages in agriculture. Moreover, the gains in agricultural productivity will reduce poverty by lowering food prices, raising farmer incomes, and creating employment opportunities.

The agricultural sector is often characterized as a classic case of market failure. More attention to the investments by the government in this sector is needed. At the same time, to promote the growth of agricultural productivity, the government must focus on the development of adequate rural infrastructure and communication networks and take steps to minimize transaction costs. Monetary policy must be geared to improving the access of farmers to formal institutional credit, particularly short-term seasonal credit. Land reform must ensure tenure and property rights. Simultaneously, efforts must be made to diversify to high-value cash crops and the provision of broader employment opportunities for the rural poor. Access to skills, information, and technology, such as access to current price information on agricultural products, to machinery, and to fertilizers should also be improved, particularly in lagging regions where market failures are likely to become more pronounced.

Though there has been some progress, much more remains to be done to improve transparency and accountability in the formulation of public policy, in public-private relationships, and in the rules and procedures governing the allocation of public resources. To a significant extent, the issues all revolve around the requirement for a better understanding of the governance needs of the poor. These needs appear to lie in the following areas: (1) better service delivery, particularly in health care and education; (2) a reduction of leakage in targeted antipoverty programs; (3) access to justice for all; (4) regulatory support for the informal and unorganized sectors of the economy, where a majority of the poor pursue their livelihoods; and (5) a reduction in the threats of erosion in the incomes of the poor because of various forms of income insecurity and the improper application of administrative authority. In this sense, improving governance also means improving service delivery to poor and marginalized groups. The quantity and quality of the services delivered by governments in the areas of health care, education, clean water, sanitation, and so on are still lagging in many countries. One in three people in Asia's urban centers lack access to basic services, water, sanitation, and secure housing. The plight of those left behind has to be accorded top priority in the reform of governance.

More transparency and accountability in government expenditures and more well-targeted spending on the poor will definitely contribute to better service delivery. The government needs to ensure that the money it spends reaches the poor. A key requirement is the tight monitoring of the outputs and outcomes of public expenditure programs.

Decentralization is also important for improving the effectiveness of service delivery. There has been notable progress in decentralization and in achieving innovations through public-private partnerships in service delivery in several countries. The decentralization of public administration and the empowerment of local institutions have recently been promoted in many Asian countries, including Cambodia, China, India, Indonesia, and Pakistan. Decentralization has widened the scope for citizens at the grassroots to influence decision making in resource allocation and to become responsible for the outcomes of their decisions.

Moreover, there is a need to provide social protection to the poor because most of the poor are vulnerable to adverse weather, economic recession, natural disasters, and ill health. Without social protection, some marginal families may easily fall into the poverty trap. Therefore, to protect these people, governments need to create sound risk-pooling mechanisms, social insurance schemes, social security systems, and pension systems. This is easier said than done and has posed challenges even in advanced economies. Although the task is daunting for the developing world, it may be ignored only at the risk of perpetuating poverty. We have to start rethinking the priorities in the allocation of public expenditures.

Overall, economic integration has done more good than harm. However, many of the concerns of those who oppose economic integration are also legitimate, and these should not be ignored. Greater efforts need to be made by national governments and by international institutions to address these concerns and assist the losers in the integration process without undermining the process itself. The winners must also contribute adequately to compensating the losers. However, there is no need to reverse direction or return to autarky. Since most of the costs of globalization are costs of adjustment, analogous costs would arise if we moved in the opposite direction.

Indeed, given how far the world has already come in the establishment of efficient global markets, continued economic integration may well be less painful for all stakeholders than a return to the inward-looking policies of the past. The best way to deal with the challenges being raised by the international integration of markets is to be open and honest in recognizing the risks involved and address these risks in a transparent and humane way.

Notes

1. For additional details, see Chaturvedi et al. (2006).
2. Including Japan, the rise was from 34 to 51 percent.

References

ASEAN (Association of Southeast Asian Nations). 2004. "AFTA and Beyond: What Drives Economic Integration in ASEAN?" *ASEANOne* 1 (November 11): 5–6. http://www.aseansec.org/Lens%20-%20Myrna.pdf.

Aun Porn Moniroth. 1995. "Democracy in Cambodia: Theories and Realities," trans. Khieu Mealy. Paper, January, Cambodian Institute for Cooperation and Peace, Phnom Penh, Cambodia.

———. 1996a. "Economic Development in Cambodia: Challenges and Opportunities." Paper, January, Cambodian Institute for Cooperation and Peace, Phnom Penh, Cambodia.

———. 1996b. "Strategy for Cambodia's Participation in the ASEAN Free Trade Area (AFTA)." Discussion Paper, November, Cambodian Institute for Cooperation and Peace, Phnom Penh, Cambodia.

Aun Porn Moniroth and Keat Chhon. 1998. *Economic Development in Cambodia in the ASEAN Context: Policies and Strategies.* Cambodian Institute for Cooperation and Peace, Phnom Penh, Cambodia.

Aun Porn Moniroth, Keat Chhon, and Vongsey Vissoth. 1998. "Managing the Challenges of Globalization." Paper, January, Economics and Finance Institute, Phnom Penh, Cambodia.

Chaturvedi, Sachin, John Humphrey, Nagesh Kumar, and Hubert Schmitz. 2006. "Asian Economic Integration: Dynamics and Impacts." Paper prepared for the "Workshop on Asian and Other Drivers of Global Change," Seventh Annual Global Development Conference, "Institutions and Development: At the Nexus of Global Change," St. Petersburg, Russia, January 18–19.

Dixon, Joly. 2000. "Further Economic Integration in Asia?: Some Lessons from the European Experience." Paper presented at the Institute for International Monetary Affairs, Tokyo, December 18. http://jpn.cec.eu.int/home/speech_en_Speech%2027/00.php.

IMF (International Monetary Fund). 2000. "Globalization: Threat or Opportunity?" IMF Issue Brief 00/01 (April 12), Washington, DC: International Monetary Fund. http://www.imf.org/external/np/exr/ib/2000/041200.htm.

Kawai, Masahiro. 2004a. "Regional Economic Integration, Peace and Security in East Asia." Paper presented to the Economists for Peace and Security session on "Real

Homeland Security" held during the Allied Social Science Association Annual Meetings, San Diego, CA, January 3-5.

———. 2004b. "Regional Economic Integration and Cooperation in East Asia." Paper presented to the Experts' Seminar on the "Impact and Coherence of OECD Country Policies on Asian Developing Economies," organized by the Policy Research Institute, Japanese Ministry of Finance and the Secretariat of the Organisation for Economic Co-operation and Development, Paris, June 10-11.

Keat Chhon and Aun Porn Moniroth. 1997. "Strategy for Cambodia's Participation in the ASEAN Free Trade Area (AFTA) and Its Implementation of the Agreement on the Common Effective Preferential Tariff (CEPT)." Paper, Cambodian Institute for Cooperation and Peace, Phnom Penh, Cambodia.

Lamberte, Mario B. 2005. "An Overview of Economic Cooperation and Integration in Asia." In *Asian Economic Cooperation and Integration,* ed. Asian Development Bank, 3-41. Manila: Asian Development Bank. http://www.adb.org/Documents/Books/Asian-Economic-Cooperation-Integration/chap1.pdf.

Lerman, Robert I. 2002. "Globalization and the Fight against Poverty." Paper presented at the 8th European Forum Berlin, "Europe in World Politics," Berlin, November 15-16. http://www.urban.org/url.cfm?ID=410612.

Ng, Francis, and Alexander Yeats. 2003. "Major Trade Trends in East Asia: What Are Their Implications for Regional Cooperation and Growth." Policy Research Working Paper 3084, World Bank, Washington, DC. http://econ.worldbank.org/view.php?type=5&id=27878.

Oxfam. 2000. "The White Paper on Globalisation." Parliamentary Briefing 12 (December), Oxfam, Oxford.

Park, Sung-Hoon. 2002. "East Asian Economic Integration: Finding a Balance between Regionalism and Multilateralism." Draft EIAS Briefing Paper, February, European Institute for Asian Studies, Brussels.

Park, Yung Chul, and Kee-Hong Bae. 2002. "Financial Liberalization and Economic Integration in East Asia." Paper presented at the PECC Finance Forum Conference, "Issues and Prospects for Regional Cooperation for Financial Stability and Development," Honolulu, August 11-13.

Pich, R. 2001. "Impacts of Economic and Trade Liberalization on Cambodia." Paper presented at the "Globalization Conference: Business and Law Perspectives," Phnom Penh, Cambodia, July 27-28.

Schuh, G. Edward. 2001. "Globalization, Governance, and Policy Reform." Paper presented at the "Workshop on International Economic Policy," Orville and Jane Freeman Center for International Economic Policy, Humphrey Institute of Public Affairs, University of Minnesota, Minneapolis, November 27.

Sok, Siphana. 2003. *Mainstreaming Trade for Poverty Alleviation: A Cambodian Experience.* World Bank Development Outreach, July, 7-12, World Bank Institute, Washington, DC. http://www1.worldbank.org/devoutreach/july03/article.asp?id=205.

———. *Lessons from Cambodia's Negotiations and Entry into the World Trade Organization.* Tokyo: Asian Development Bank Institute.

Teune, Henry. 2001. "The Developmental Consequences of Globalization." Paper presented at the International Convention of the International Studies Associations, "Globalization and Its Challenges in the 21st Century," Hong Kong (China), July 26-28.

Yam, Joseph. 2006, "A Case for Financial Integration in Asia." Paper presented at the conference organized by the Directorate General for Economic and Financial Affairs, European Commission on "The Euro: Lessons for European and Asian Financial Markets," Hong Kong (China), February 24. http://www.news.gov.hk/en/category/ontherecord/060224/html/060224en11001.htm.

Yip, Wei Kiat. 2001. "Prospects for Closer Economic Integration in East Asia." *Stanford Journal of East Asian Affairs* 1 (1): 106–11. http://www.stanford.edu/group/sjeaa/journal1/geasia1.pdf.

Yue, Chia Siow. 2003. "Globalization and Inequality in Asia." Paper prepared for presentation at the Global Development Network Forum, Cairo, January 19–20.

Yue, Chia Siow, and Mari Pangestu. 2003. *The Rise of East Asian Regionalism*. Paper prepared for the 29th Pacific Trade and Development Forum meeting, Jakarta, December 15–17.

Yusuf, Shahid. 2001. "Globalization and the Challenge for Developing Countries." Policy Research Working Paper 2618, World Bank, Washington, DC.

World Bank. 2000. "Poverty in an Age of Globalization." Briefing paper, World Bank, Washington, DC.

———. 2006. *Cambodia: Halving Poverty by 2015?, Poverty Assessment 2006*. Report 35213-KH prepared for the Consultative Group Meeting, Phnom Penh, Cambodia, February, East Asia and the Pacific Region, World Bank, Washington, DC.

CHAPTER 3

The Case for East Asian Financial Cooperation

ROBERTO F. DE OCAMPO

The Asian financial crisis made clear that better financial supervision and domestic capital markets were urgently needed to sustain growth.

In the past few years, East Asian regional economic cooperation has again become fashionable. I write "again" because, in a sense, it's nothing new in the millennia of Asia's history. Southeast Asian economies were trading with each other as early as the seventh century, when the Sumatra-centered Srivijaya Empire controlled both the spice route traffic between India and China and local trade along the coasts of Southeast Asia with Chinese, Indian, and Malay merchants. Flash forward to the so-called Asian miracle spanning the 1970s to the mid-1990s. During these three decades, the region sustained an average growth rate in gross domestic product (GDP) of 7 percent on the back of postwar Japan, which grew at an average of 10.4 percent from 1961 to 1969, and, later, on the backs of Hong Kong (China), the Republic of Korea, and Singapore (see table 3.1). Growth in Southeast Asian economies such as Indonesia, Malaysia, and Thailand gained momentum in the early 1990s. As a result, intraregional trade as a share of total trade rose from about 20 percent in 1980 to about 30 percent in 1990 (Burton, Tseng, and Kang 2006).

During the same period, the region became a top destination of foreign direct investment (FDI). In 1970, East Asia received only 16.4 percent of

TABLE 3.1 Average Annual GDP Growth Rate
percent

Country	1970–96	1970–79	1980–89	1990–96
China	9.1	7.4	9.7	10.5
Hong Kong, China	7.4	9.3	7.3	4.9
Indonesia	7.3	7.8	6.4	8.0
Japan	3.9	5.3	3.7	2.3
Korea, Rep. of	8.0	8.3	7.7	7.9
Malaysia	7.5	7.7	5.9	9.5
Philippines	3.6	5.8	2.0	2.8
Singapore	8.5	9.3	7.5	8.9
Thailand	7.7	7.5	7.3	8.6
Average	7.0	7.6	6.4	7.0

Source: World Bank 2005.

all FDI inflows to developing countries. Ten years later, the corresponding FDI inflows to the region stood at 44.7 percent, sharply rising to 64.3 percent by 1990 (see figure 3.1).

However, even as these economies became more closely linked with each other through regional trade, the financial sectors of the various East Asian countries remained in the national domain and

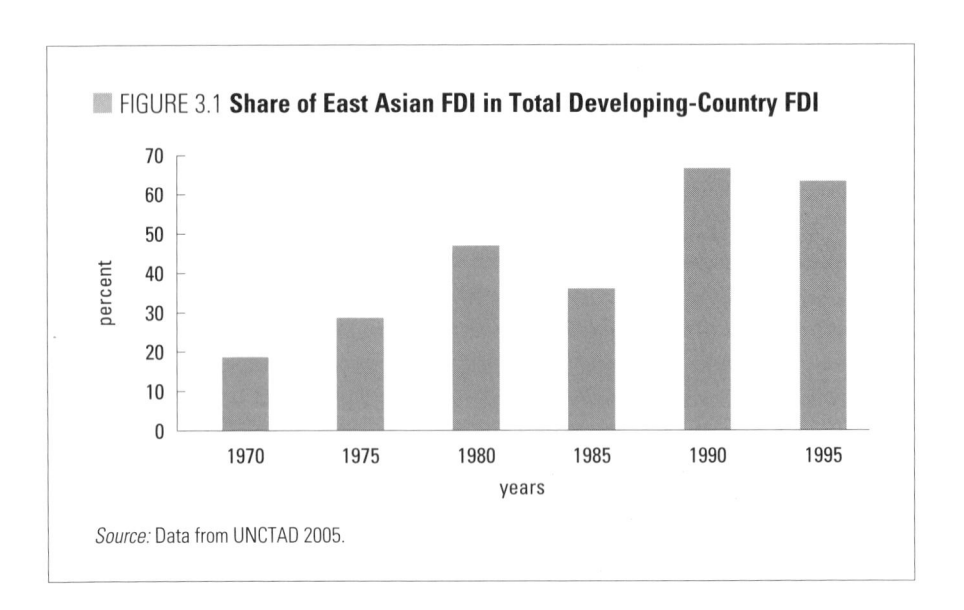

FIGURE 3.1 Share of East Asian FDI in Total Developing-Country FDI

Source: Data from UNCTAD 2005.

were mostly left out of regional discussions. The creation in 1967 of the region's first formal attempt at cooperation, the Association of Southeast Asian Nations (ASEAN), successfully put together the industrial cooperation scheme and the agreement on industrial complementation, which promoted trade, investment, and tourism among member countries. The common effective preferential tariff scheme for the ASEAN Free Trade Area, signed in 1992, paved the way for free trade in the region. These early economic arrangements in the ASEAN notwithstanding, little attention was paid to the financial sector.

That changed seemingly overnight with the onset, in 1997, of the Asian financial crisis, which brought the region's high-growth years to a screeching halt. Average growth that year slowed to 5 percent, from 7 percent in the previous years (see table 3.2). By 1998, the region's economies had suffered output contractions. Indonesia and Thailand posted the largest declines in output, at 13 and 10 percent, respectively. On average, the region's growth plummeted by 4 percent.

At the onset of the Asian financial crisis, I was finance minister of the Philippines and had the fortune (or misfortune) of being the chair of the Asia-Pacific Economic Cooperation Finance Ministers. Asia and the rest of the world were in shock at what had just happened. Many openly wondered if it meant an end to decades of economic progress; others questioned if the main paradigms associated with the Asian

TABLE 3.2 **Pre- and Postcrisis GDP Growth**
percent

Country	1990–96	1997	1998
China	10.5	8.8	7.8
Hong Kong, China	4.9	5.1	−5.0
Indonesia	8.0	4.7	−13.1
Japan	2.3	1.9	−1.1
Korea, Rep. of	7.9	4.7	−6.9
Malaysia	9.5	7.3	−7.4
Philippines	2.8	5.2	−0.6
Singapore	8.9	8.5	−0.9
Thailand	8.6	−1.4	−10.5
Average	7.0	5.0	−4.2

Source: World Bank 2005.

model, such as the export orientation riding on the back of low-priced labor, were inappropriate or faulty to begin with. Some asked if the region had embarked on its economic journey too fast too soon. I keenly remember the informal, but raging debate that took place during the 1997 World Bank–International Monetary Fund meeting held in Hong Kong (China) between Malaysian Prime Minister Mahathir Mohamad and George Soros on who was to blame for the economic disaster: Asian economies steeped in "cronyism" or "heartless" fund managers engaged in global currency speculation.

Clearly, both were factors, but, more importantly, what the Asian crisis did was highlight the region's weaknesses, as well as the changing global economic scene. First, the inevitability of globalization brought with it both opportunities and risks. In the case of East Asia, openness indeed boosted growth, but also increased the region's susceptibility to external shocks. Second, the Asian crisis was unique in the sense that it stemmed from private sector weaknesses, which, in turn, highlighted poor government regulation and supervision. By eventually addressing these weaknesses, the private sector became stronger and eventually played an important role in both national and regional economic growth and stability. Third, technology permanently altered the size, nature, and speed of capital flows. Observers are in agreement that the huge reversals in capital flows in the months following the collapse of the Thai baht greatly hurt the region's economic stability. Fourth, the paradigm of export-led growth, combined with trade liberalization, was no longer, by itself, enough to sustain progress. It had to be coupled with the development of domestic capital markets, which also involved improving governance and regulation, especially in the financial sector. Fifth, regional cooperation was an increasingly important feature of the region's economic stability.

Let us take a closer look at how each feature manifested itself.

In the 1970s and the 1980s, the Asian economies tried to be major players in the global economy. Export-oriented growth was the main strategy of the eight so-called tiger economies of Hong Kong (China), Indonesia, Korea, Japan, Malaysia, Singapore, Taiwan (China), and Thailand. For example, Korea's exports as a share of GDP increased from 13.3 percent to 31.8 percent (see table 3.3). By 1985, the exports of the emerging markets in Southeast Asia exceeded 20 percent of GDP. The establishment of the ASEAN Free Trade Area was a major initiative that ensured the free flow of goods and services in Southeast Asia. Exports and imports flourished as the region embarked on trade liberalization.

TABLE 3.3 **Exports as a Share of GDP**
percent

Country	1970	1975	1980	1985
China	1.8	4.2	7.6	10.0
Hong Kong, China	93.5	83.8	89.1	108.1
Indonesia	13.5	24.0	34.2	22.2
Japan	10.7	12.7	13.6	14.3
Korea, Rep. of	13.3	26.3	31.7	31.8
Malaysia	41.4	43.0	56.7	54.1
Philippines	21.6	21.0	23.6	24.0
Singapore	—	146.0	215.4	168.0
Thailand	15.0	18.4	24.1	23.2

Source: World Bank 2005.
Note: — = no data are available.

East Asia also became a top destination of FDI. Efficiency-seeking multinationals located their operations in these countries, where trade barriers were low and goods could be easily shipped out to other parts of the world. Undoubtedly, economic openness helped advance growth, but, at the same time, it heightened the exposure of individual economies to the risks posed by external factors.

As the growth process unfolded, the East Asian countries became more closely linked with each other, but this development heightened the tendency of fund managers to view the region as a single market. This became strongly evident when, at the collapse of the Thai baht in July 1997, contagion swept through the rest of the economies as fund managers and other foreign investors pulled out funds regionwide despite the individual merits and economic fundamentals of individual countries. The trouble in Thailand spread quickly to Indonesia, Korea, Malaysia, and the Philippines.

This contrasted with experiences prior to the crisis, whereby countries in the region had, at various times, undergone periods of economic difficulty, but with hardly any effect on the regional economy. My country, for example, experienced a severe recession in 1983, which eventually led to a fiscal crisis in 1985. Weak macroeconomic fundamentals and political instability strained the economic and financial systems, but the ramifications did not go beyond the domestic economy.

The Asian financial crisis was particularly surprising to most observers since not only did East Asia exhibit superior economic performance prior to 1997, but the crisis, unlike other financial crises prior to this one (such as the Mexican financial crisis), had its origins in the private rather than the public sector and found its roots in the private banking sector in particular because of a lack of an arm's-length relationship between the banks and their borrowers.

Thus, banks funded risky projects in the absence of more prudent credit processes, and, when some of these projects became unviable, corporations experienced difficulties, and banks were literally left holding the proverbial empty bag that wreaked havoc on their balance sheets. Investors lost confidence, which soon led to reversals in capital flows that strained the financial sector and caused problems in the real economy because of the unprecedented increase in the speed and volume of private capital flows.

Looking back, I observe that there may have been a tendency among many financial analysts to pay less attention to private capital flows, and, thus, they ended up somewhat caught by surprise by the phenomenon, since, historically (up to that point, at least), capital flows had been dominated by bilateral and multilateral fund movements. These movements were gradual because of the lengthy approval processes involved. I myself worked in the World Bank for several years and recall that the period of time between project identification and loan approval was almost invariably nine months, followed by an almost equally lengthy time period for the fulfillment of the conditions before actual loan release. It was a bit of an inside joke among World Bank country officers as I then was that a World Bank loan was rather like pregnancy: no matter how much effort or how many people were involved in the job, it would inevitably take nine months. Not so with the private sector, which included massive treasure chests of pension funds, aided as it was by the rapid and continued development of new technology that allowed the instantaneous transfer of enormous amounts of private capital across countries worldwide without the need for the processing protocols guiding bilateral and multilateral capital flows. Between 1990 and 1996, private flows increased at least threefold in four Southeast Asian economies (see table 3.4), and arbitrage thrived as private firms searched for the best place to park their funds or the place where returns would be the highest.

The Asian financial crisis made it increasingly evident that the paradigms of export-oriented growth and trade liberalization were no longer sufficient to sustain growth; the need for improved financial supervision

TABLE 3.4 **Net Total Private Capital Flows**
current US$ millions

Country	1990	1991	1992	1993	1994	1995	1996
Indonesia	2,923.30	3,451.30	4,431.70	411.50	5,973.10	8,141.60	14,882.50
Malaysia	476.30	3,480.43	8,380.17	17,157.60	12,609.07	10,062.99	11,116.82
Philippines	639.20	398.10	(1,102.30)	1,822.40	2,460.80	2,372.30	5,784.30
Thailand	4,370.45	4,990.69	4,736.52	7,110.18	4,606.34	10,016.28	13,320.38

Source: World Bank 2005.
Note: Data are drawn from the World Bank's Debtor Reporting System.

and the development of domestic capital markets was gaining urgency. The heavy dependence of countries in the region on bank financing was largely due to the lack of alternative financial instruments that more well-developed domestic capital markets might have provided. Banks used foreign funds borrowed on a short-term basis to finance long-term projects that did not generate foreign currency. A number of economists cited the double mismatch problem—mismatches in currency and maturity—as another major cause of the crisis.

By nature, banks are short-term lenders. Large-scale projects that require long-term financing are best funded by bonds and other instruments, which were not developed in the domestic markets at that time. As a finance minister raising funds in the international market, I had to ask myself many times if this situation jibed with the region's high savings. The availability of more regional financial instruments might have better mobilized East Asia's enormous amount of savings in the region; instead, they were being placed in financial markets in the West, which made them susceptible to the herd mentality that manifests itself now and then among global fund managers. This welcome view about financial instruments is now being strongly propounded by, among others, Donald Tsang (more recently in his speech before the Boao Forum for Asia in April 2006).

The features of the crisis shared a common theme: the region's economies had become closely intertwined, and, interestingly enough, as things turned out, the solution to the crisis was in more and not less regional cooperation. In fact, the crisis did not last as long as some people expected, partly because of the region's closer economic ties. Prior to the crisis, the region's export orientation targeted the consumers of the American, European, and Japanese markets based on a then prevailing view and experience that a slack in the U.S.

economy and, thus, a slack in export demand would usually be taken up by Japan and vice versa. But then when the financial crisis struck, the economies of both Japan and the United States were in the doldrums, and it was growing intraregional trade that served as a buffer for East Asia and saved the day. By 2005, intraregional trade had grown to more than 40 percent of total trade, comparable to that of the North American Free Trade Area (Burton, Tseng, and Kang 2006). Increased intraregional trade helped provide an alternative market for the region's exports, which, in turn, truly helped the East Asian economies get back on track in a shorter period of time than many had anticipated. Clearly, therefore, immediate and long-term solutions to the crisis necessitated a more vigorous pursuit of greater regional cooperation.

During my chairmanship of the Asia-Pacific Economic Cooperation Finance Ministers at the height of the crisis in 1997–98, a number of meetings were held that resulted in the drafting of the Manila Action Plan (or the Manila Framework). Its provisions[1] included the following: (1) the development of regional surveillance to complement global surveillance, (2) the implementation of technical assistance and support to strengthen the financial sectors of related countries, (3) the call for expanding the resources of the International Monetary Fund to manage future crises, and (4) the establishment of a regional financing arrangement to complement assistance programs of the International Monetary Fund and other international financial institutions. This framework reiterated the importance of a free and open economic environment that was grounded on policy coordination at both the national and regional levels. The Manila Framework paved the way for initiatives in and the strengthening of regional dialogue and the expansion of regional financing facilities.

A significant development in the area of policy dialogue was the coming together of the ASEAN+3 economies (the 10 ASEAN countries, plus China, Japan, and Korea). Previously, formal dialogues in ASEAN were limited to the member countries. The crisis brought together the leaders of the ASEAN 10, plus China, Japan, and Korea, to discuss issues such as regional growth and stability. Since 1999, the ASEAN+3 have been meeting to discuss issues such as economic surveillance, financing facilities, and bond market development through the ASEAN+3 framework. These dialogues have formalized the cooperation among ASEAN members and the East Asian countries, giving rise to genuine East Asian cooperation.

The Chiang Mai Initiative, an effort born out of the ASEAN+3 Finance Ministers' Meeting in Chiang Mai, Thailand, in May 2000, was the first regional financing arrangement aimed at assisting countries in managing swings in capital flows and maintaining exchange rate stability. Its aim was to expand the existing ASEAN Swap Arrangement by (1) providing coverage to all ASEAN members, (2) raising the size of the swap arrangements, and (3) creating a network of bilateral swap agreements among the ASEAN+3 economies (Wang and Andersen 2003).

Long-term postcrisis initiatives focus rightly, I believe, on the development of capital markets, including the improvement of regulation and supervision in the financial sector. Efforts to realize the development of local-currency bond markets are now in full swing, led by the Asian Bond Markets Initiative. I think these efforts must be relentlessly pursued to successful completion since, among other effects, bond markets will decrease the region's heavy dependence on banks for financing. Furthermore, East Asia has huge savings; the gross national savings of most countries exceeded 30 percent of GDP from 1993 to 2003. These funds can be better utilized to fund the region's investment needs (for instance, in supporting private sector–led infrastructure development). It is also ironic that most of these savings leave the region essentially only to loop back because Asian firms have had to borrow from Western banks. The development of bond markets can potentially correct this situation (see table 3.5).

There has been considerable progress in developing domestic capital markets. The Asia Cooperation Dialogue has been tasked to draft guidelines for developing sound bond markets in the region. At the Asia Cooperation Dialogue Informal Meeting on Promoting Supply of Asian Bonds, held in Bangkok in May 2004, the representatives of the member countries recognized the need to create a sufficient supply of bonds through the regular issuance of investment-grade local-currency-denominated

TABLE 3.5 **East Asian Savings as a Share of GDP, 1993–2003**
percent

Country	Gross national savings
China	41.6
Hong Kong, China	32.6[a]
Indonesia	23.7[b]
Japan	29.4
Korea, Rep. of	34.4
Malaysia	35.6
Philippines	22.2
Singapore	48.9
Thailand	32.2
Vietnam	27.2[c]

Source: World Bank 2005.
a. No data for 1993–97.
b. No data for 2001.
c. No data for 1993–95 and 2003.

bonds at different maturities to create benchmark yield curves. In addition, member countries agreed to find ways and means to trade these bonds actively across countries with ample liquidity in the region and the world.[2]

The discussion on developing domestic capital markets has now progressed toward the harmonization of rules and regulations in the bond market. The Asian bond market has enormous potential, given the strong recovery of the region and its huge accumulation of foreign reserves, amounting to more than US$1 trillion. Since bond markets in emerging economies in East Asia are in different stages of development, seven areas must be harmonized to promote the development of regional bond markets. These are the legal and regulatory framework, rating agencies, trading platforms, clearing settlement, accounting and auditing standards, taxation, and foreign exchange regulation.

At the heart of regional financial reforms is the development of a strong institutional and regulatory policy framework. The financial sector must be able to manage the risks that come with the capital flows and to provide an early warning of impending crisis. It is important that financial institutions across the region are properly supervised. Efforts to strengthen the regulatory and supervisory framework in the region must be complemented by global prudential regulation standards such as Basel II and the international accounting standards. Developing strong regulatory and supervisory frameworks in the individual countries is important for the region's financial stability. There has to be a convergence in the quality of financial institutions if regional cooperation is to work effectively. For one thing, as we saw during the crisis, trouble in one country may cause massive investor panic and quickly spill over to neighboring economies. Thus, it is important that all countries in the region implement reforms aimed at improving their respective financial sectors.

The reforms and initiatives, of course, necessitate greater engagement among the region's individual-country central banks. In fact, the Chiang Mai Initiative is a collaborative effort of the individual central banks. The Executives' Meeting of East Asia–Pacific Central Banks (EMEAP) is a strong anchor of central bank cooperation in the region. It is a caucus of the 11 central banks and monetary authorities of Australia, China, Hong Kong (China), Indonesia, Japan, Korea, Malaysia, New Zealand, the Philippines, Singapore, and Thailand. A prominent effort of the EMEAP is the Asian Bond Fund. This fund invests in sovereign and quasi-sovereign bonds issued by EMEAP members (except Australia,

Japan, and New Zealand). On the one hand, Asian Bond Fund 1, which was launched in 2003, invests in dollar-denominated bonds, and access is limited to EMEAP central banks. On the other hand, Asian Bond Fund 2, which was introduced in 2005, invests in local-currency-denominated bonds and is accessible to private investors.

While the Asian crisis has, in a way, sealed the case for greater regional financial cooperation, developments in trade and investment in recent years provide a further impetus for such cooperation. As intraregional trade has gained momentum, so has intraindustry trade. Research shows that the automotive, electronics, and health care products industries in ASEAN are now highly integrated. Production processes for goods are broken down into several stages and are located throughout the region depending on the comparative advantage of the host countries. These regional production networks are the strong drivers of FDI, which has become an important source of capital for East Asian economies.

The potential of intraregional trade and investment to be drivers of growth must be harnessed. Achieving this entails stronger financial cooperation in the region since the financing of trade and development requires a developed financial market. For example, regional production networks, which are trade driven, require huge financing. This means that capital markets must be well developed. A regional bond market can help address this need. Intraregional trade, on the other hand, requires exchange rate stability among the participating economies. To some extent, this also necessitates continuing improvements in regional exchange rate coordination.

Given these issues, we have to ask ourselves a number of questions. How far and how rapidly are we going to implement regional financial cooperation? How do we advance from policy dialogue and surveillance to more concrete initiatives? What form of regional financial arrangement best suits us? Are we headed toward the direction of a monetary union? At this point, it is useful to review some of the proposals that have been put forward.[3]

Some posit using the U.S. dollar standard to achieve regional exchange rate stability. The advantage of using a dominant international currency—the U.S. dollar standard is simple and involves no extra cost in ensuring exchange rate stability—is that it is beneficial to the emerging markets in the region. The danger, however, lies in the fluctuations in the effective exchange rates in the face of erratic movements in yen-dollar exchange rates.

Another proposal is to use a currency-basket system whereby a currency's central rate is linked to a basket of major currencies (such as the euro, the Japanese yen, and the U.S. dollar) rather than to one dominant currency (such as the U.S. dollar). This system prevents excessive fluctuations in effective exchange rates in the face of volatile yen-dollar or euro-dollar rate movements, while leaving room for East Asian currencies to move within a certain range. However, monetary authorities must determine the weights for each currency in the basket, and this has to be coordinated throughout the region.

Of course, the possibility of moving toward a common currency area is also on the horizon. A number of studies argue that East Asia is an optimal currency area. However, a sine qua non for monetary integration is to begin the process of economic convergence among the region's economies. This is not an easy task given the diverse levels of income and development in the region. Assuming this is successfully accomplished, then the next step, the introduction of a regional currency unit, can be contemplated. Some have advanced the notion that this can be done by first constructing a basket of regional currencies that includes the 13 currencies of the ASEAN+3 countries. The weights of the regional currencies would reflect the relative importance of the countries in the region. A regional currency unit, thus derived, could be used to denominate economic transactions (trade and capital flows) and asset stocks (foreign exchange reserves and crossborder bonds), as well as to measure the degree of each currency's exchange rate deviation from the regional average. From this point, movement toward a monetary union could be eventually made.

Unfortunately, I believe, it may not be as straightforward as that. Perhaps, as East Asia embarks on greater financial cooperation, it should look at some of the lessons imparted by the experience in the European Union (EU) in this regard. First, the process of arriving at a common currency took the EU states decades, not merely years of adjustment. (It took 50 years for the euro to became a reality. The process of convergence among the EU economies was a long process, given the members' diverse levels of development. Clearly, the levels of development and the differences in culture of East Asian countries are even more diverse.) Second, monetary integration requires strong institutions at both the national and regional levels. A monetary union can only be sustained if countries are sufficiently credible to commit to regional policies. Third, monetary integration requires stronger leadership and policy coordination at the regional level. There has to be strong political will to see the integration through, and, more importantly, one or two countries should clearly take the lead.

East Asia need not and, in fact, should not take the EU model wholesale and use it as a blueprint for the region. However, given these lessons, East Asian economies must address some issues that might affect regional financial cooperation. At the onset, three factors might make the process longer and more difficult than usual. These are (1) income disparities and poverty, (2) inconsistencies in institutional quality and governance across the region, and (3) the lack of solid leadership at the regional level.

Despite decades of stellar economic performance, income disparities remain. Per capita incomes in Hong Kong (China), Singapore, and Taiwan (China) are among the highest worldwide. The region is also home to about 280 million people each living on US$1 a day. The idea that financial cooperation leads to greater economic openness remains unpopular in some sectors. These sentiments ultimately delay the process, as governments find it hard to convince their citizens of the benefits of a regional economy. Conditions look optimistic though. The World Bank reports impressive poverty reduction in the region in 2005. The share of the population living on less than a dollar fell to 8 percent in 2005 from 9 percent in 2004 (World Bank 2006). To make integration more acceptable, the region must strengthen its poverty reduction efforts. Improvements in living standards will make it easier for people to see the benefits of a regional economy.

Another potential impediment to financial cooperation is the poor quality of institutions and governance in some East Asian countries. The role of institutions in the development process has become very important in recent years. Although Hong Kong (China), Japan, and Singapore are home to high-quality institutions, the rest of the economies in the region are plagued with governance problems. Looking at the corruption perceptions index score in 2005, only four countries garnered a score halfway to a perfect score of 10 (least or virtually no corruption). Singapore scored 9.4, one of the highest scores in the world. In contrast, China, Indonesia, the Philippines, and Vietnam are some of the worst performers in the world (see table 3.6). If East Asia is serious about

TABLE 3.6 **Corruption Perceptions Index, 2005**

Country	Score
China	3.2
Hong Kong, China	8.3
Indonesia	2.2
Japan	7.3
Korea, Rep. of	5.0
Malaysia	5.1
Philippines	2.5
Singapore	9.4
Thailand	3.8
Vietnam	2.6

Source: Transparency International 2005.

stronger integration, it must resolve the perceived poor quality of institutions in these countries. High-quality institutions will make the region's efforts more credible and help to fast track financial cooperation.

Lastly, there is a need for clearer leadership at the regional level. At present, policy making in East Asia is consensus based, which has its benefits. However, as the process of integration deepens, such consensus should address the need to reduce tensions between countries with less than friendly relations. Hostile relations hinder effective cooperation and might prolong the integration process. Individual countries must set aside their differences for the common good.

Admittedly, there are other issues equally crucial in realizing closer financial cooperation. The foregoing are, I think, among the more pressing issues that should be addressed.

East Asia's successful recovery from the crisis has made it once again a destination for capital and investment. Of course, it is common knowledge as well that the rapid growth of China has become an irresistible magnet for large investments in the region. China's emergence, seen as a threat in the past, has presented abundant opportunities in the region. China's import spending was estimated at US$413 billion in 2003 and was expected to grow by 30 percent in 2004 (Wattanapruttipaisan 2005). Given this, China is a major buyer of Southeast Asian goods and services. In fact, every Southeast Asian country has a positive and growing trade surplus with China. Another positive observation is that China's exports from ASEAN are composed of high-value goods such as machinery, transportation equipment, and chemical products (Wattanapruttipaisan 2005).

The region's recovery, coupled with the emergence of China, brings a positive economic outlook. China will continue to be an important source of needed stimulus for regional growth as the United States orchestrates a managed soft landing to more healthy fiscal and current account balances. The opportunities and, more importantly, the risks that come with China's progress must be properly managed if the region is to benefit from this phenomenon.

In closing, let me summarize the key points I have raised in this discussion. First, the Asian crisis highlighted five lessons that brought the concept of greater financial cooperation in East Asia to the fore of regional discussion. The crisis emphasized the close link among the region's economies, the growing importance of the economic role of the private sector, the impact of technology in altering the size and speed of capital flows, the need for a new growth paradigm that involves the appropriately sequenced development of domestic capital markets, and the need for greater regional financial cooperation. Second, in the aftermath of the crisis, reforms and initiatives were launched toward the realization of closer financial ties in the region. These included greater engagement among the region's financial and monetary leaders, the expansion of regional financing facilities, and the development of a regional bond market. Third, as East Asia traverses the path of recovery, observers are beginning to ask if we are headed toward the direction of the EU. Is an Asian currency on the horizon? Certainly, this is a question that cannot be answered definitively at the moment because several issues still need to be addressed before the region can embark on the process of a common currency. There has to be greater convergence among the region's economies and institutions; at the same time, there has to be strong leadership at the regional level. I dare say, however, that, at this point, achieving monetary union is not the most pressing issue of the day. What East Asia must instead realize is that establishing the building blocks for a monetary union is as good a goal for the region for now as actual monetary union itself, since these building blocks will lead to greater financial cooperation, which, in turn, promotes regional economic stability.

It took a massive financial crisis for the region to realize more fully the need for stronger financial cooperation and to take more definitive steps in that direction. East Asia has learned its lesson well. Whether we move toward the direction of a monetary union or a different form of financial integration, it is clear that the financial sector can no longer be left out of or play second fiddle in the regional agenda. As the region accelerates its economic growth once more, it needs to ensure the stability of its progress, and stronger regional financial cooperation can definitely serve as East Asia's economic anchor for that process.

Notes

1. The Web site of Japan's Ministry of Finance (http://www.mof.go.jp) provides detailed information on the provisions of the Manila Framework.

2. The information provided in this paragraph has been culled from the Asian Bond Market Initiatives Web site, at http://aric.adb.org/asianbond/index.htm.

3. Some of the proposals on monetary integration presented here are discussed in Kuroda and Kawai (2003).

References

Burton, David, Wanda Tseng, and Kenneth Kang. 2006. "Asia's Winds of Change." *Finance and Development* 43 (2). http://www.imf.org/external/pubs/ft/fandd/2006/06/burton.htm.

Kuroda, Haruhiko, and Masahiro Kawai. 2003. "Strengthening Regional Financial Cooperation in East Asia." PRI Discussion Paper 03A-10 (May), Policy Research Institute, Japanese Ministry of Finance, Tokyo.

Transparency International. 2005. "Table 1: TI 2005 Corruption Perceptions Index." Transparency International, Berlin. http://www.transparency.org/cpi/2005/cpi2005.sources.en.html#cpi.

UNCTAD (United Nations Conference on Trade and Development). 2005. *World Investment Report 2005: Transnational Corporations and the Internationalization of R&D.* Geneva: UNCTAD.

Wang, Seok-Dong, and Lene Andersen. 2003. "Regional Financial Cooperation in East Asia: The Chiang Mai Initiative and Beyond." *Bulletin on Asia-Pacific Perspectives 2002/03,* United Nations Economic and Social Commission for Asia and the Pacific, Bangkok.

Wattanapruttipaisan, Thitapha. 2005. "Background Note on China and ASEAN Part Two: Risks and Opportunities for ASEAN." BEI Studies Unit Paper 06/2005, Bureau for Economic Integration, ASEAN Secretariat, Jakarta.

World Bank. 2005. *World Development Indicators 2005.* Washington, DC: World Bank.

———. 2006. "East Asia Update: Solid Growth, New Challenges," March. East Asia and Pacific Region, World Bank, Washington, DC.

CHAPTER 4

The Future of Asia

TOYOO GYOHTEN

An almost feverish enthusiasm for development has spread throughout East Asia. The dynamo of economic development has been ignited in the region.

Regional Dynamism

Asia's ascent in the global landscape has been a long one. In 1964, Japan was accepted as a member of the Organisation for Economic Co-operation and Development. If you had gone to the Organisation for Economic Co-operation and Development at that time, you would have seen that the delegates met in a large, elegant conference room in Paris and that there were 24 countries around the table. And, when the members of the Japanese delegation found themselves in that room for the first time, they would have seen that they were the only delegation whose members were so different, so non-Caucasian. I still remember vividly the day when I went to a meeting at the Bank for International Settlements in Basel as an observer. It was the year the Cultural Revolution was sweeping China. Red Guards were rampaging there, and it was of high concern to neighboring Asian countries. But at the meeting at the Bank for International Settlements, central bankers from all the European countries were gathered, had cocktails, luncheons, and dinners, and talked endlessly about gold, the dollar, and the pound sterling, switching among English, French, and German. There was absolutely no interest in the upheavals in China. The Vietnam War was at a critical stage, but, apparently, the bankers had little interest in such events. I thought uneasily that, for those bankers, the world seemed still to end somewhere near the Dardanelles.

For Asians who have memories of those days, the interest in Asian issues shown today by political and business leaders in the West, the frequency of reports about Asian affairs now appearing in the Western media, and the volume of articles and books published in the West on things Asian are dazzling. This reminds me of an ancient Asian saying, "The history of man never stops flowing."

The Asian ascent started in the 1960s. Japan, defeated in World War II, had lost 70 percent of its industrial output. It made a rapid recovery from the destruction. The factors that enabled this performance were certainly not singular. Skillful economic policy management (such as the income doubling plan in the 1960s), the free access to the U.S. market, the undervalued exchange rate of ¥360 per dollar, the favorable demographic situation, and the highly motivated business leaders and workers all made important contributions. In less than three decades, after near-total destruction, the Japanese economy recovered and was the second largest economy in the world. The recovery of Japan was remarkable. But more remarkable was the fact that the success of Japan has turned out to be the harbinger of the development of the entire East Asian economy over the last four decades. An almost feverish enthusiasm for development has spread throughout the region. The East Asian dynamo of economic development has been ignited.

One unique feature of Asian economic development is that it has always been led by a forerunner. After Japan, it was the four tigers in the 1970s, that is, Hong Kong (China), the Republic of Korea, Singapore, and Taiwan (China). Each with a competent and stable government supported by a high-quality labor force, the four tigers started stalking successful development in the wake of Japan. They focused their resources on the promotion of exports.

During the 1980s, the member countries of the Association of Southeast Asian Nations joined the race. Most of these countries had been relatively underdeveloped. Various diversities within society, the relatively low level of public education, and the inadequacy of social and economic infrastructure meant that these countries lagged behind the four tigers. But they were stimulated and inspired by the achievement of the four tigers, and they quickly recognized their economic and strategic importance within the region. They accelerated their efforts at economic development in parallel with their cooperative endeavor to strengthen their ties as a group.

In the 1990s, the world was mesmerized by the stunning economic growth rates in China. The historic ascent of the Chinese economy started in 1979 when Deng Xiaoping launched the Opening and Reform campaign. Deng's reform policy was unquestionable evidence that he was a true political genius. He succeeded in unleashing the dynamism needed to awake the sleeping lion. He proved that Napoleon's ominous prophecy 200 years earlier had been correct. ("China is a sleeping giant. Let her sleep, for, when she awakes, the world will tremble.") Deng departed from communist orthodoxy by discarding some of the fundamental principles. Yet, he managed to uphold the political legitimacy of the communist dictatorship after skillfully overcoming serious difficulties, including the protests at Tiananmen Square in 1989. The Chinese economy entered a period of tremendous growth. In a matter of only two decades, China has become a world-leading producer of many consumer goods.

At the beginning of the 21st century, it seems increasingly clear that the Asian ascent will continue. India, another sleeping giant for many centuries, is looming on the horizon. With its vast human resources of high quality and its resilient democracy, India has clear potential of becoming the next Asian economic powerhouse.

Numerous books have already been written exploring the secret of the ascent of Asia. The most intriguing feature of the phenomenon is the fact that, while Asia is admittedly a region of great diversity, there has clearly been a regional dynamism common in all the economies. One factor that exists universally in the region is the sense of strong national aspiration to development. In Asia, there is a shared target; all societies try to catch the forerunner. The catch-up mentality seems to have provided a common ground upon which the development of each economy could be established. Also important was the enlightened and motivated leadership in most economies, though not in all. Leaders succeeded in stimulating a sort of collective dynamism in their nations and in directing this dynamism toward the national goal of economic development. Equally important, many of them knew that the promise of freedom could unleash individual initiative in business activities.

Developmental Dictatorship

This political style is often dubbed developmental dictatorship. It cannot be denied that developmental dictatorship is not always compatible with the principles of democracy. It was, in most cases, accompanied by a certain amount of planning and control by the government. It was not a system based on the free action of market forces. Yet, it cannot be denied that developmental dictatorship did serve the purpose when social and market infrastructure was not mature enough to generate an autonomous thrust toward development. This situation represents a dilemma for many developing economies. It is almost natural for a developing economy, particularly one driven by the urge to catch up with forerunners, to consider powerful government leadership necessary in mobilizing and organizing otherwise listless forces.

However, the value of developmental dictatorship has a clear limit. If the dictatorship tries to outlive its historical usefulness, it will quickly become a detriment. The dictator must turn over the reins to private market forces. Thus, the success of a developing economy depends on the quality of leadership. The leaders must be sufficiently wise to discern when the dictatorship is no longer needed. They must be courageous enough to relinquish power that has outlived its usefulness. Inertia, complacency, and vested interests are the worst enemies of any leader in a developing economy.

The first serious challenge for the galloping Asian economy came with the tide of globalization. The first victim of the challenge was Japan. Until the 1980s, Japan was the role model for East Asian economies in their quest for an ideal development strategy. In a sense, Japan played an exemplary role in demonstrating the value of developmental dictatorship. The enlightened and motivated government guided the economy skillfully, while the dynamic, yet well-disciplined, well-organized private business sector ran the economy. The dexterous combination of control and protection worked well in mobilizing the potent dynamism that had been stored in an economy effectively secluded from outside influence. However, the wave of globalization undermined the very foundation of the system.

The basis of globalization was to be found in a new sort of environment for economic activities. This environment was, first of all, symbolized by the free flow of information and financial resources on a global scale. As the result of the information technology revolution, the traditional monopoly on information by the government and business managers had been effectively broken. Now, every voter, taxpayer, shareholder, consumer, and employee might share the same information universally and instantaneously. This new situation made the competition for efficiency global, and it made values such as transparency and accountability the most important in governance and business management.

Unfortunately, the traditional Japanese model, which had been so successful, lacked these ingredients. Beginning in the mid-1980s, the economic bubble ballooned and then burst. The economy suffered more than a decade of stagnation. In hindsight, the whole disaster seems to have been caused by a series of mistakes in economic policy decision making that had their root in Japan's inability to adapt to the new environment of globalization. The system of control and protection by the government, the lack of awareness about global competition, and the disregard for transparency and accountability all contributed to Japan's inability to made bold changes. The sense of complacency and inertia that was the child of the experience of past successes aggravated the situation. Only after the traumatic shock of the near collapse of the financial system in 1997 did Japan finally awaken and undertake, in earnest, the structural reforms that are bearing fruit in the current impressive recovery.

Asian economies also learned painful lessons. The 1997–98 Asian financial crisis was caused by a combination of factors. Yet, the most immediate cause was a combination of the massive, volatile flow of short-term capital and a weak banking system under inadequate supervision. The fragile banking system in East Asia simply could not withstand the onslaught of speculative international capital. The tragedy occurred because, although these economies were not big or strong, they opened up their capital markets after incessant prodding by U.S. advocates of globalization. In hindsight, they should have opened their capital markets according to a properly sequenced schedule. They miscalculated the monstrous force of globalization.

Regional Cooperation

In any event, East Asians realized, with a sense of remorse, that their economies were not fully prepared to join the globalizing world in spite of the remarkable physical development they had achieved. In dealing with the aftermath of the crisis, they became convinced that the region needed to become equipped to prevent and manage crises more effectively. Their particular concerns were that there was no mechanism to facilitate emergency financing, no market for mobilizing domestic savings for the development of the region, and no arrangement to reduce exchange rate volatility. Indeed, this fresh awareness marked the start of efforts to foster Asian economic cooperation that, in the following years, gained great momentum.

Certainly, Asian economic cooperation was not a new concept. The Association of Southeast Asian Nations was created in 1967, and a variety of efforts have been undertaken to encourage intraregional trade and investment and to coordinate industrial policy. Only following the 1997 crisis, however, were concerted and conscious steps launched to promote Asian regional economic cooperation in an organized, institutionalized fashion.

Many different vectors are operating in the region; all are moving toward some sort of regional economic cooperation. There are several tracks. However, I think we can group the efforts into two broad categories. One is government led, and the other is market driven. The first category of cooperation includes a network of free trade agreements. Indeed, during the last decade, bilateral and intraregional free trade agreements have mushroomed. These agreements will probably contribute to increasing the aggregate volume of trade within the region. There is some concern over these flourishing arrangements, however. First, at present, with few exceptions, the arrangements are designed only to reduce tariffs bilaterally. They are not intended to liberalize and stimulate broader economic activities in the region. Second, because tariff reduction is carried out by discriminating against outsiders, the proliferation of such arrangements may not support the overall balanced development of intraregional trade.

Other types of cooperation are practiced mostly in the area of finance. Cooperative projects have been initiated directly following on the lessons of the Asian financial crisis of 1997–98. After the crisis, many Asian economies suffered severe shortages of foreign currency. Many Asians felt that the International Monetary Fund was not forthcoming in providing adequate financing. They felt they had been discriminated against relative to other regions such as Latin America. Many Asians became convinced they needed their own regional financing facility.

As a first step toward financial and monetary cooperation, central banks in the region have established a network of currency swap agreements. Already, 18 such agreements have been concluded, at a total of US$40 billion equivalent. Central banks are expected to try to develop the network into a centralized pool of reserves that may function as a regional monetary fund. For success, such a facility must have an appropriate degree of conditionality and sufficient authority over policy surveillance.

A second step is the development of capital markets to receive investments of the region's internal savings through instruments of obligation issued by public and private borrowers in the region. The idea of a regional bond market has been prompted by the fact that, so far, most of the region's excess savings have been invested in nonregional instruments, particularly U.S. Treasury obligations, and then have detoured back into the region through nonregional investors. Asia was not the master of its own savings.

A regional bond market will succeed only if a standard, dependable market infrastructure is in place, including settlement, accounting, auditing, rating, and so on. An adequate degree of liquidity and appropriate arrangements for credit enhancement will also be required.

The third step in financial and monetary cooperation is the creation of some sort of common Asian currency. This idea arose because, although East Asian countries have around US$3 trillion in official reserves, international economic activities in the region are conducted predominantly in nonregional currencies, particularly the U.S. dollar, and the Asian economy is still susceptible to fluctuations in the dollar exchange rate. All these irregularities might be solved, in theory at least, through the creation of a common reserve currency in Asia. The creation of a common currency is a project for the long haul. Even in Europe, where conditions are much more favorable, it took 50 years to issue the first euro. Still, if Asia wants to establish itself as an integral economic power in the world, Asia needs its own currency. Theoretical studies on the desirable shape of the common currency and the proper sequence of preparatory stages have been flourishing. On a more practical level, the Asian Development Bank is reported to be working on the idea of a notional composite currency unit that would be a representative indicator of Asian currencies.

Thus, there are several schemes for Asian financial and monetary cooperation proceeding at different speeds. The enthusiasm for and momentum of financial and monetary cooperation will continue to mount in coming years. As the integration of the real economy progresses, it will provide increasing support for the need to integrate the superstructure. In the process, the most serious challenge will be securing a consensus among all governments in the region that they should surrender national sovereignty as soon as possible and as much as possible. Without a surrender of national sovereignty, no surveillance mechanism will work effectively, and no common currency will be feasible.

In addition to government-led cooperation, there has been a strong movement toward market-driven economic cooperation in Asia. The rapid development of the Asian economy was supported in the 1960s primarily by exports. All Asian countries, taking advantage of their cheap labor and imported foreign technology and techniques, were racing against each other to produce competitive products and export them outside the region, notably, to the United States. There was not so much intraregional trade and investment. Then, in the middle of the 1980s, there emerged a fundamental change in the picture. The change was triggered by the surge in Japanese direct investment in the region. Motivated by the sharp appreciation of the yen following the Plaza Accord in October 1985, Japanese manufacturing industries moved their factories into neighboring Asian countries. This set off new flows of goods and capital within the region. Japanese industries exported parts and components to their overseas factories and shipped finished products back to Japan and to other Asian countries. This pattern of operation was replicated by other relatively developed economies such as Hong Kong (China), Korea, Singapore, and Taiwan (China). In this respect, the overseas Chinese capitalists who are scattered all around Southeast Asia have played an important role. Apparently, the new pattern in the movement of production factors stimulated indigenous economic development in all countries in the region, and a beneficial regional chain reaction had started.

Now, the level of intraregional trade and investment in East Asia is comparable to that in the European Union and the North American Free Trade Agreement. The complementarity of exports and imports is also high. The interprocess division of labor among regional countries has likewise risen markedly. East Asia has grown into a huge integrated manufacturing plant. Energy resources and raw materials are imported from outside the region. Within the plant, Hong Kong (China), Japan, Korea, Taiwan (China), Singapore, and others produce high-grade industrial materials, parts, and components and ship them to China, Indonesia, Thailand, and Vietnam, where they are processed into final products and exported outside the region. It is intriguing that such a large-scale transformation of industrial structure has occurred with virtually no government support. The entire process has been accomplished through market-driven private initiative.

What implications might this have for the global economy? The world economy today depends on the robust growth of the U.S. economy, which, in turn, is supported by strong growth in household consumption. The problem is that the import component of U.S. consumption is high. This reflects the eroding manufacturing base for many consumer goods. The bulk of the soaring U.S. trade deficit since the beginning of the 21st century is attributable to the increase in imports of various consumer goods. The large trade deficit is financed by capital inflows from surplus countries, aggravating the debtor position of the United States. The debt servicing cost is increasing. In 2005, the U.S. current account deficit reached US$800 billion, about 7 percent of the gross domestic product of the United States. Roughly half the deficit is with East Asia. East Asia is now an integrated manufacturing plant. It is true that many U.S. multinational companies have set up operations in the plant. They are an important part of the production process. However, as a national economy, the United States is not integrated in the plant. It is an end buyer of products made in the plant. The situation implies that the imbalance between the United States and East Asia has become almost structural; it has become less elastic to changes in prices and incomes. Indeed, the success of Asian economic cooperation seems to have added a new problem to the issue of global imbalances.

There is also the other important aspect of the large imbalance between the United States and East Asia. East Asian governments have amassed US$3 trillion in official reserves, most of which is invested in U.S. Treasury obligations. The huge national assets of East Asia are exposed to exchange rate risk and interest rate risk. At the same time, any major shift in portfolio will trigger a fluctuation in the U.S. dollar rate and the U.S. long-term rate. In a sense, East Asian governments are overloaded with double-edged swords. The relationship between the United States and East Asia is at the core of the issue of global imbalances.

In many respects, the achievements in Asian cooperation and integration have been impressive. However, one has to admit that, so far, most of the progress has been made at the functional level, but not at the institutional level. Many people argue that this is inevitable considering the vast diversity in the region. They believe that Asia should continue to expand the scope for functional cooperation in whatever areas regional consensus may be secured. Environmental protection, human security, cultural and personal exchanges, energy conservation, research and education, and so on are cited as possible areas for functional integration. I am ready to recognize that these areas are indeed of great importance for the region as a whole, and progress in these areas will contribute greatly to the welfare of all people in the region.

A Trilateral Relationship and Three Bilateral Relationships

If Asians dream of truly accomplishing any substantive integration in the region following the example of the European Union, no matter how long it may take, then they must consider seriously whether their dream has any chance of realization. What are the obstacles they face? In my view, the fundamental problem facing Asian integration is the lack of a stable leadership structure. More concretely, it is the instability in the trilateral relationship between China, Japan, and the United States. In this respect, Asia is totally different from the European Union and the North American Free Trade Agreement.

For Asia, the trilateral relationship can be decomposed into three bilateral relationships, that is, China-Japan, China–United States, and Japan–United States. Naturally, all three bilateral relationships are affected by developments in the other two. It is not possible to discuss any one of the bilateral relationships to the exclusion of the other two.

I would not consider the Japan–United States relationship the easiest; yet, it is at least more predictable than the others. The Japan–United States relationship since the end of World War II has had phases. On the whole, it has become more natural and more mature. The countries know each other better, their respective strengths and weaknesses, the opportunities, and the risks. Their economies are reasonably intertwined. Although there is still a large trade imbalance, this does not create serious trade disputes. Above all, Japan is committed to being a solid member of the democracies on the Pacific Rim. The ties between Japan and the United States reflect a relationship between two countries with well-established democracies and open, mature markets.

The challenge for Japan and the United States in coming years will be to identify common objectives and other areas of cooperation. One objective should certainly be to establish and maintain markets of the highest quality, markets that ensure dynamism, openness, fairness, self-discipline, and efficiency. If this is done, the influence of this success, as an exemplar, will penetrate throughout Asia and well into Eurasia. A second objective should be to cooperate so as to awaken the world to the need for a multilateral effort in addressing the problem of global imbalances. The problem of global imbalances cannot be solved unilaterally or even bilaterally. It needs to be addressed through economic policy coordination at a multilateral level. Japan and the United States should cooperate to take the lead so as to move the world. The core of the problem of global imbalances is the disequilibriums in savings ratios and exchange rates. All countries must recognize the need to join in the process of adjustment in their respective ways.

The China-Japan relationship has many unique features. It currently seems to be characterized by a dichotomy, that is, a close economic relationship and a strained political relationship. We should take a long-term historic view, and we should not forget that there will always be some competition and rivalry. China and Japan have a bilateral relationship spanning over 2,000 years. There have been wars, but we have also enjoyed the richest interaction in culture, religion, human exchanges, trade, and so on.

The balance of power between the two countries has shown major shifts since the middle of the 19th century. Then, China suffered a major setback and humiliation. The incompetence and corruption of the Qing Dynasty hurt the country badly. This invited colonization by Western powers, defeat in a war with Japan in 1895, ongoing internal conflicts, and the Japanese invasion from 1931 to 1945. Since 1949, however, under communist rule, China has made a spectacular resurgence. At the beginning of the 21st century, China is ascending toward the apex of a historical cycle of power. Its national pride has fully recovered.

Meanwhile, Japan was emerging as the first Asian country to fend off the wave of Western colonization and become an important world power. However, overblown ambition resulted in a traumatic defeat in 1945 that forced Japan to give up its illusion of becoming the hegemon of Asia. Still, in the 60 years since the end of the war, Japan has also rebuilt itself as a democratic country and a world economic power.

Against this backdrop, shouldn't it even seem natural that these two countries feel they are in competition with each other in the quest for leadership in the region?

On the economic front, China and Japan are now functioning as two important partners supporting the Asian manufacturing plant. At present, 35,000 Japanese companies are operating in China, paying ¥800 billion in taxes to the Chinese government, and 100,000 Japanese are working in China. Almost 10 million Chinese are employed by Japanese firms.

How may we establish a stable, nonhostile relationship? Given the complexity of the geopolitical issues and all the other issues, one should not expect a quick, permanent solution. The element of competition is deeply embedded. It is quite possible for both of us to become convinced that the maintenance of a stable, nonhostile relationship will serve the best interests of others as well. We should deepen and broaden our cooperation in all noncontroversial areas, and these exist in abundance. We should also establish a constant, frank dialogue between leaders so that they can gradually build a relationship of mutual trust and free of unnecessary suspicion. We should continue to take these doable steps. Beyond that, we must be content to ask history.

The China–United States relationship has, no doubt, global implications. Both sides have many issues to take into strategic consideration. For the time being, the relationship is being conducted as if it were a bargaining game. What pattern of development will China follow? Will it develop into a country that embraces the same value standards as Western democracies, thus vindicating the hopeful American dictum that "democracy is inevitable"? Or, will China develop into an economic and military superpower that is ruled by a communist dictatorship? Or, will there be some sort of hybrid? If we look back over the 4,000 years of Chinese history, with 15 or so dynasties that rose and fell, we discover that China prospered best when the country was ruled by an enlightened, benevolent, but ruthless emperor, the Child of Heaven. It should not seem too far from the truth to affirm that the Communist Party of China is playing the same role as the Child of Heaven. This means the basic framework of China as a country has not departed far from its historical legacy. Will China change? That is the question. If China does not change, we may see, in the long run, a competition between two sets of ideologies: if I may paraphrase, the competition between individual democracy and collective democracy. The United States has triumphed over fascism and communism and is now engaged in a deadly battle against Islamic fundamentalism. It may turn out that the United States will fight another ideological war sometime during the 21st century.

If the surrender of national sovereignty is a prerequisite for Asian integration, then Asian integration in the style of Europe will not happen in the foreseeable future. Three major powers that have big stakes in the region have too much national interest involved. As long as the trilateral relationship lacks enduring stability, they have no compelling reason to sacrifice national sovereignty. Other Asian countries, particularly those in the Association of Southeast Asian Nations, have a strong sense of ambivalence toward each of the three powers. They are eager to act as a balancing counterweight lest they become submerged in the trilateral power game. There will be ample opportunity for them to play that role.

Regional cooperation will surely continue to progress. Everybody is firmly convinced that regional economic cooperation, be it market driven or government led, brings benefits to the majority. Here is a big hope. If regional economic cooperation, in alliance with significant public and private effort, succeeds in promoting economic development and enhancing the living standards in every country in the region, this will accelerate structural change in society, which, in turn, will prompt political reform. A political structure based on the divisions between the ruler and the ruled may remain viable only as long as the majority of people have time to think of nothing else but how to improve their daily lives. When people become sufficiently affluent, they will carefully consider issues about political systems. Some may prefer collective democracy to individual democracy, but the important point is that the choice will be a choice by the people themselves.

CHAPTER 5

Rural-Based Development in East Asia under Globalization

YUJIRO HAYAMI

This essay illustrates the critical role of domestic trade networks in supporting agricultural and industrial production in East Asia's hinterlands in response to rising global demand.

In common with other developing regions, the current wave of globalization in East Asia has been associated with a concentration of economic activities in megalopolises. The price paid for the benefit of the agglomeration economies resulting from this urban concentration has been formidable congestion and pollution. Income inequality has also increased. Migrants, who typically find initial employment in the urban informal sector, generally receive wages that are much lower than those of workers employed in the formal sector, where labor is protected by labor codes and unions. The widening income disparities have been a major source of social and political instability, as epitomized by higher crime rates and the greater frequency of riots.

A popular perception prevails that identifies these trends as an inevitable consequence of the integration of developing economies with the world economy as globalization progresses. However, globalization, which is characterized by the freer movement of goods and services across national borders, does not necessarily cause urban concentration and rural marginalization. Many industrial activities, especially labor-intensive manufactures such as cloth, garments, and standard electronic parts, which are characterized by weak economies of scale and modest transportation costs, need not be located in megalopolises.

Still, if these activities are to be located in the hinterland, there must be domestic trade networks linking foreign demand and rural producers. In the absence of such networks, the emerging demand for labor-intensive manufactures in developing economies tends to be met exclusively by factories located in metropolises, to which labor has migrated from the hinterland. However, cottage industries might be stimulated in rural areas, where the manufacturing costs are lower. This perspective is clearly supported by the experience of rural-based industrialization in Meiji Japan (1868–1912) and the striking success of balanced rural-urban growth in Taiwan (China) after World War II.

This essay aims to illustrate the critical role of the domestic trade network in supporting agricultural and industrial production in East Asia's hinterlands in response to rising global demand. The essay also discusses the ways and means to foster such networks.

The following section describes the unique nature of urbanization and industrialization in developing economies under the current wave of industrialization through a review of history and theory. The importance of the development of community-based trade networks to link rural producers with global markets is illustrated in the subsequent section with respect to industrial commodities and, in the section thereafter, with respect to agricultural commodities. Finally, policies that support these trade networks are discussed in the last section.

The Megalopolis-Centered System: Theory and History

In this essay, the term megalopolis-centered system is used to characterize the economic system in developing economies in the modern era. In this system, economic, political, and cultural activities and resources are disproportionately concentrated in the primate cities and surrounding areas that constitute megalopolises. The megalopolis complex, typically only one in each economy (such as Bangkok in Thailand or Manila in the Philippines) or in each major region of larger economies (such as Shanghai in the lower Yangtze area of China), dominates the economy by occupying on the order of 10 percent of the total population and 20 to 40 percent of the total gross domestic product.

How has this system been created?

The Colonial Legacy

The belief that globalization is a major force underlying the megalopolis-centered system through urban concentration and rural marginalization is widespread. It appears to have evolved out of a neo-Marxian perspective whereby global capitalism seeks to marginalize developing economies at the expense of advanced capitalist economies (Furtado 1963; Frank 1967; Baran 1957). In this perspective, free trade and foreign direct investment destroy indigenous industries, forcing rural people to specialize in primary commodity production at a mere subsistence level, while primate cities prosper as commercial and financial centers to support the business of shipping out primary commodities to advanced economies and distributing the industrial commodities imported from advanced economies. In this way, the global integration of developing economies gives rise to the dominance of primate cities in these economic systems.

This explanation of the role of globalization in creating the megalopolis fits well with the situation in developing economies under colonialism in the late 19th and early 20th centuries. When colonial powers imposed the free trade system on tropical economies, these economies were forced to specialize in the production of primary commodities (Bairoch 1975). Competition from industrial commodities imported from the West, which had already completed the industrial revolution, typically destroyed indigenous manufacturing among farm households and among cottage industries for the local consumption of home-produced goods (Hymer and Resnick 1969; Resnick 1970). Rural labor sought alternative employment on plantations and in mines geared to creating exports to industrialized economies. Colonial governments took various measures to enhance this process. They allocated available virgin land for the exclusive use of colonial planters, often even permitting the enclosure of the commons recognized among native communities so that they could be turned into plantations. Publicly funded agricultural research concentrated on cash crops grown on plantations to the neglect of subsistence food crops. Investments in infrastructure such as ports, roads, and railways were directed at facilitating the transport of cash crops and minerals for export. Native peasants shouldered a significant share of the cost of building infrastructure through various taxes and levies such as land and poll taxes. This taxation forced cashless peasants to seek wage employment, thereby expanding the supply of labor to colonial enclaves. All these policies increased the comparative advantage of cash crops and minerals over subsistence crops and domestically manufactured commodities (Myint 1965; Lewis 1970).

This process produced large port cities, typically one in each colony, linking domestic economies with international markets not only for trade, but also for financial and other services. These cities were usually sites of colonial administration and strong agglomeration economies. All private and public services were networked, and there were close connections between private firms and government offices. Because of the influx of colonial government officials, traders, shippers, and financiers, plus a large number of native employees and a swarm of coolies, the colonial primate city grew to a size incomparably larger than precolonial towns. Such a primate city gained a dominating role in each of the colonial economies. The megalopolis-centered system is thus a legacy of colonialism.

The Impact of Import Substitution

After World War II, newly independent nations almost unanimously made industrialization a top priority. To counter the de-industrialization effect of free trade under colonialism, these nations commonly adopted the so-called import-substitution industrialization strategy. The strategy advocated the use of tariffs and quotas to reduce the competition from imports, thereby protecting large-scale modern industries at home. However, the tariffs and quotas raised the domestic prices of goods produced by such industries. Meanwhile, the same industries were given import quotas for the capital and intermediate goods they needed, which could be bought at low prices because of the overvaluation of the government-controlled foreign exchange rate. The victims of this strategy were consumers, but also unprotected industries, which were obliged to sell their products at lower prices and buy their inputs at elevated cost. Agriculture and small- and medium-scale industries suffered especially (Little, Scitovsky, and Scott 1970). For example, when large-scale synthetic fiber industries were protected, the high yarn prices that resulted damaged downstream textile-processing industries, which were usually run by small and medium enterprises using labor-intensive technologies. Note that weaving and garment making are among the industries most suitable for rural households and cottage industries. The protection of chemical fertilizers had the same negative effect on farmers. Thus, the scope for rural-based development was narrowed under import-substitution industrialization, which fostered the growth of industries supplied by large urban-based factories. Ironically, though intended to break the colonial economic system, the strategy strengthened it instead.

The Nature of the Second Wave of Globalization

The first wave of globalization in the 19th century under colonialism set the stage for the megalopolis-centered system to emerge through the de-industrialization of developing economies. Yet, this system was not counteracted, but strengthened through industrialization under the autarky-oriented import-substitution regime. In terms of chronological history, globalization may therefore appear to have promoted megalopolis-centered urbanization. Nonetheless, curbing globalization alone is unlikely to be effective in stopping urban concentration. If policies are to promote more balanced and equitable growth in the rural and urban sectors, they must be grounded on an understanding of the difference between the current wave of globalization and the earlier wave.

The first wave of globalization in the 19th century was generated by the rise of industrial power in Western nations, which resulted in the de-industrialization of developing economies under the dictate of comparative advantage (Baldwin and Martin 1999). In contrast, the second wave, currently in progress, has been characterized by the shift of comparative advantage in advanced economies from the industrial production of standardized commodities to the production of services, especially new knowledge and information. Under the present structure of comparative advantage, the integration of domestic with international markets is stimulating the growth of manufacturing activities in developing economies, unlike the first wave of globalization. In fact, East Asia is the region that has best exploited the industrialization opportunity created by the second wave.

In applying strategic trade theory to economic geography, Krugman (1991) assumed that the concentration of industrial activities in urban centers would generate strong, increasing returns to industrial production at significant costs in transportation. Rural areas were expected to specialize in agricultural production, which would be characterized by constant returns. This assumption is flawed to the extent that Krugman's dichotomy between agriculture and industry with respect to economies of scale lacks empirical validity.

Indeed, strong evidence exists for the absence of economies of scale in agriculture in developing economies, though agriculture in developed economies is generally characterized by increasing returns (Hayami 1996; Hayami and Ruttan 1985). However, many industrial commodities, especially among labor-intensive manufactures such as cloth, garments, and standard electronic parts, are characterized by narrow ranges of increasing returns and modest transportation costs. Moreover, the share of commodities with weak economies of scale has been rising because global demand has been shifting from standardized products to differentiated products with shorter product cycles (Piore and Sabel 1984; Feenstra 1998). Indeed, the enormous expansion in the production of industrial commodities of this nature, that is, industrial commodities that represent a major link in the global value chain or commodity chain, is considered by some to underlie the East Asian economic miracle (Gereffi 1999; Tewari 2005). There is no reason to doubt the possibility that the hinterlands are able to produce such industrial commodities at lower cost than megalopolises to the extent that there are rural-urban differentials in the cost of labor and land.

Even for commodities characterized by strong increasing returns and high transportation costs, such as automobiles, the greater integration with external markets may induce industrial entrepreneurs to shift their production base to rural areas closer to export markets, such as to the border with the United States in the case of Mexico, as Krugman himself recognizes (Krugman and Elizondo 1996). Evidence for the existence of a tendency for trade liberalization to reduce urban concentration has been found in a cross-country study by Ades and Glaeser (1995).

Even if the integration of a domestic market with the international market stimulates the growth of industrial activities, there must be a domestic trade network linking foreign demand and rural producers if a significant share of these activities are to be located in the hinterland far from the trade entrepôt. A domestic trade network is vitally important in mobilizing a large number of peasant farmers for the production of labor-intensive, high-value agricultural commodities such as fresh fruits, vegetables, and flowers, for which international demand has been rising sharply.

The Community-Based Trade Network for Rural Industrialization

Trade liberalization, coupled with domestic deregulation, has greatly facilitated the effective use of the abundant labor in developing economies in response to the rising demand in high-income countries for labor-intensive products. However, these manufactures have been located disproportionately in major cities and their outskirts, such as Bangkok, Jakarta, and Manila.

This is different from the experience in Japan during the Meiji era (1868–1912) and in Taiwan (China) after World War II, when rural towns and villages were being developed as production sites for labor-intensive industrial and agricultural commodities (Ho 1982; Ranis and Stewart 1993). It was the domestic trade network of large numbers of small traders and processors tied together by community relationships that enabled the mobilization of labor in the hinterland for rural-based production geared for international markets.[1]

In Meiji Japan, if an urban trader received a large order of cotton or silk cloth for export, for example, he usually entered into contracts with local collectors in rural areas to assemble the needed amounts from many small weavers living in their native villages. To meet the demand, the trader had to put together a large bulk of commodities by a specified delivery date. The commodities had to meet a quality standard specified by the foreign buyer. If his collectors violated the contracts by mistake or opportunism, the export trader might have been obliged to pay a large cash penalty, and he would lose face among foreign customers. Thus, he normally endeavored to establish a relationship of mutual trust with collectors through repeated dealings over time, while interlinking commodity trades with credit and other transactions.

The same applied to local collectors in relation to cottage weavers operating in rural villages and towns. Typically, a local collector developed contracts with weavers by providing yarn in advance and collecting cloth at a prescribed piece rate. Relatives, friends, and neighbors were preferred in the selection of contracting partners. Long-term, repeated contracts were offered so as to discourage opportunistic behavior, such as the embezzlement of yarn by weaving cloth at lower density than contracted. Opportunism was suppressed because of the expectation that contract violations would be punished socially through damage to reputations and ostracism within the small rural community. Once community sanction reduced opportunism, small-scale, family-based rural enterprises became more efficient than large factories under hierarchical management. This was so because of the advantage of the family firm in monitoring low-cost labor in the case of labor-intensive industries characterized by weak economies of scale. It was on the basis of such community-based trade networks that industrial activities spread widely throughout rural areas in Meiji Japan (Smith 1988; Itoh and Tanimoto 1998; Tanimoto 1998).

Contrary to the assumption of Krugman (1991), it is not the physical cost of transportation that makes the location of industries near the urban center advantageous, but the high transaction costs involved in enforcing contracts at the various stages of domestic trading from rural producers to urban exporters. It is not practical to rely on legal procedures for contract enforcement, since the costs of formal court procedures often exceed the expected gains from dispute settlement over the small transactions typical of rural entrepreneurs. Thus, rural-based industrialization in Japan critically depended on the successful use of the community mechanism to correct the agency problem stemming from information asymmetry.

Meanwhile, the wide dispersion of industrial activities to rural areas through community-based trade networks has already progressed in developing Asia, but, so far, it has not extended much beyond the outskirts of metropolises, unlike in the case of Japan (Hayami 1998). It may be argued that decentralized production systems such as the system of putting contracts out among small rural producers is only effective at a primitive stage of industrial production, but is not adequate at a more advanced stage. Indeed, a popular assumption based on the historical experience in Europe is that a system for outsourcing contracts is a premodern form of industrial organization. Though it was effective in promoting protoindustrialization before the industrial revolution, it was bound to fail in the modern era because it could be replaced by the modern factory system based on teams of hired wage laborers working together under the supervision of managers and foremen (Landes 1969; Pollard 1965). The factory system has the advantage of being able to mass-produce standardized goods with large-scale machinery so as to meet the demand of large national and international markets.

In Japan, however, there is evidence to indicate that the outsourcing system became more common after the beginning of modern economic growth with the nation's opening to international trade in the late 19th century. A case study in Saitama Prefecture shows that, before the Meiji Restoration (1868), farmers would weave cloth from yarn spun from their own harvested cotton and sell their products in cash to guild merchants in towns. The opening of international trade and subsequent national unification brought large increases in demand for striped cotton cloth and major declines in the price of cotton yarn imported from abroad. This opportunity was exploited by rural traders outside the guild system who organized outsourcing contracts to lease looms and provide stocks of yarn to women weavers in farm households (Kandachi 1975; Tanimoto 1998). The enforcement of the contracts of the rural traders, not only with these cottage weavers, but also with large wholesalers who shipped the cloth to distant markets, critically depended on the strong community ties characteristic of rural Japan (Itoh and Tanimoto 1998). This example seems to indicate that the outsourcing system may be an efficient mechanism for meeting dynamic demand expansion by mobilizing labor at a low opportunity cost and a low supervisory cost since community relationships can be relied upon as the basis of contract enforcement. Indeed, this system served as a major instrument in organizing industrial production in the early stages of Japan's modern economic growth. Without a similar mechanism, the wide diffusion of industrial activities in rural areas through subcontract arrangements would not have been possible in Taiwan (China) either (Amsden 1991; Gereffi and Pan 1994).

An important point is that the traditional outsourcing system organized by local traders was eventually transformed into the modern subcontracting system that is a mainstay of industrial strength in Japan. Although the scale of the establishments became larger among the contract agents and although household production gave way to factory production, the outsourcing system in its original form is still commonly practiced in the textile industry in Japan, similar to the case in Taiwan (China) (Ho 1982). Today, the system is used by large chemical-fiber manufacturers and large trading houses based in metropolises as an instrument for the organization of small- and medium-scale enterprises in local industrial clusters so as to meet national and international demand. Large chemical companies still prefer to contract out weaving, dying, and garment-making activities rather than vertically integrating these downstream activities with fiber production. This is so partly because of the cheaper labor, but more because of the low cost of supervision, the strong work incentives available to management, and the flexibility created in employment and staffing (Itoh and Urata 1994).

In Japan today, the outsourcing system for processing chemical textiles is only one of many variations of the subcontracting system practiced in high-technology industries. The relationship between automobile producers and parts suppliers is well known. Their transactions are not only long term, but also multistranded. including technical guidance and credit guarantees. The subcontractors try to observe product-quality and delivery requirements. The assembler also tries to guarantee the appropriate treatment of subcontractors to maintain supply. Because the mutual trust thus created eliminates the danger of delays in the production chain, the subcontractors do not hesitate to invest heavily in the formation of specific skills and equipment consistent with the demands of the final producers. This establishment of an artificial community relationship is said to underlie the competitive strength of the Japanese automobile industry (Asanuma 1985; Abegglen and Stalk 1985; Fujimoto 1999).

It is interesting to note that Kiichiro Toyota, the founder of the Toyota Motor Company, intended to build a "pastoral factory" in Koromo City (today's Toyota City), a typical rural town with few industrial activities when he began automobile production in the 1930s. Toyota's idea was not only to locate the factory in a pastoral environment with cheap land and labor, but also to surround it with trustworthy parts suppliers connected by a community spirit. Toyota initially tried to contract with manufacturers who were receptive to Toyota's guidance even if they had no previous experience in precise, sophisticated metal processing (Wada 1998). It appears that Toyota's idea originated from his experience as a supplier of automatic looms for rural-based weavers. His idea has borne fruit today as Toyota's highly efficient, modern subcontracting system known as *kanban*, the just-in-time system.

It is important to remember that the community-based contract enforcement mechanism in the subcontracting system in Japan today, as well as in the outsourcing system in the Meiji era, is not a mere remnant of a premodern agrarian society. Instead, it is an institutional innovation created by modern entrepreneurs in response to modern needs. They have installed community relationships in their business organizations to make these organizations consistent with social norms ingrained in the minds of people, thereby lowering the cost of contract enforcement. From this experience, entrepreneurs in the high-performing East Asia of today may learn a lesson on the opportunity for improving production and trade organizations through the exploitation of their own cultural endowments.

Mobilizing Farm Producers for Global Markets

Another issue of importance in promoting balanced rural-urban growth in a context of globalization is the forging of adequate links between farmers in the hinterland and the emerging international demand for agricultural products.

The traditional marketing system for peasant crops such as rice and corn is characterized by a relatively loose network of traders at various levels. Typically, the system consists of a hierarchy composed of a large number of self-employed agents and small traders specializing in the collection of minute marketable surpluses from peasants in villages (perhaps one might call these small traders village collectors) and larger traders in towns who engage in local retailing and in transshipment (one might call them town traders). The town traders gradually accumulate surpluses in the commodities supplied by the village collectors. These surpluses are left over after the needs of local retailing have been met. When these surpluses are sufficiently large, they are shipped to urban markets. Received as cargos by urban wholesalers, the rural surpluses are distributed to retailers or shipped on to other domestic markets or abroad. This system is characterized by relatively loose connections among traders. Community ties do exist at the local level and commonly involve repeated transactions; short-term credit frequently flows as advances or arrears, and buying and selling are essentially spot transactions (Dewey 1962; Davis 1973; Hayami 1999; Hayami and Kawagoe 1993).

Such a system works relatively efficiently for traditional peasant crops such as cereals and pulses, which are storable and for which product quality can easily be verified so that information asymmetry is insignificant. However, it does not appear that the system may serve as an appropriate channel to connect small family farms with wide national and international markets with respect to new, high-value commodities. The new agricultural commodities of rising global demand, such as vegetables, fruits, and flowers, are mostly perishable, and rapid delivery by producers to processing plants or directly to consumers is critical. Yet, it is not easy to assemble a large bulk of commodities adequate for marketing and processing so as to meet wide urban or foreign demand. Due to severe information asymmetry, the quality standardization of these commodities is also difficult, especially in the case of products that may be certified organic because the cultivation has involved little or no use of chemicals. For this purpose, farm-level production from planting to harvesting must be much more closely coordinated with the needs of marketing and processing than is the case in the prototype peasant marketing system. In that prototype system, decentralized decisions and production plans, including the choice of crop varieties and cultivation methods, are left to the individual farm producers.

The Plantation System

A traditional approach to achieving sufficient coordination between farm production and processing and marketing for the delivery of tropical agricultural products to international markets is vertical integration into plantations (Hayami 1996, 2002). A typical example is the case of black tea. The manufacturing of black tea at a standardized quality for export requires a modern fermentation plant into which fresh leaves must be fed within a few hours of plucking. The need for close coordination between farm production and large-scale processing underlies the traditional use of the plantation system for black tea manufacture. Unfermented green tea, in contrast, is still predominantly produced on family farms in China and Japan. Another example is the production of bananas for export. In this case, the harvested fruit must be packed, sent to the wharf, and loaded on a refrigerated boat within a day. A boatful of bananas that can meet the quality standards of foreign buyers must be collected within a few days. The whole production process, from planting to harvesting, must therefore be precisely controlled so as to meet the shipment schedule. Thus, the plantation system has a decisive advantage in the production of bananas for export. However, this is not so for the production of bananas for domestic consumption. These bananas are usually produced on family farms.

The large plantation based on hired wage labor working under centralized management was an efficient organization in the effort to open new lands for export crop production. This was so because of the system's ability to erect the necessary infrastructure such as roads and harbors. However, after the land had been opened and the infrastructure had been built, the plantation system became increasingly more inefficient relative to the peasant system because of the high cost of supervising hired wage labor. Peasants who rely on family labor require no supervision. Because of the high cost of supervision in spatially dispersed and ecologically diverse farm operations, plantations usually practice monoculture. Intercropping and crop rotation are complicated and difficult to manage through a command system, implying that both labor input and income per hectare are lower on plantations. The strong bent of plantations toward mechanization further reduces the labor-holding capacity of the hinterland.

Contract Farming

The approach that has recently been advocated as a substitute for the plantation system is the contract-farming or core-satellite system in which an agribusiness enterprise or a cooperative manages processing and marketing and contracts with small growers to guarantee supplies of farm-produced raw materials (Goldsmith 1985). The contract may include stipulations on the quantities of the material to be supplied and on delivery deadlines, but also on prices, credit, and technical extension services. In this way, the advantage of the agribusiness in large-scale processing and marketing and the advantage of the peasant system in farm-level production may be combined. As a system for coordinating activities among economic agents, contract farming is a variation on the subcontracting system. In fact, if the contract used in contract farming includes a stipulation that a principal organizer should provide inputs such as fertilizer to farmer-agents in advance as credit in kind, the system has exactly the same structure as the outsourcing system.

Contract farming has recorded significant successes, notably, in pineapple processing by multinational agribusinesses in Thailand. Because of the system, Thailand has become the top exporter of pineapple products in the world, surpassing the Philippines, where production is based on the plantation system. However, many failures have also been reported (Siamwalla 1992; Jaffee and Morton 1995). The failures have usually stemmed from the difficulty faced by agribusinesses or cooperative management in enforcing contracts with a large number of smallholders in terms of the quantity and quality of their output and the amount of delivery time to processing plants and marketing centers. The moral hazard on the side of farmer-agents often involves opportunistic behavior by agribusiness principals. For example, an agribusiness principal might initially offer a high price to induce agents to specialize in the production of a certain crop under contract and then later breach the price agreement once the agents have specialized (Glover 1987; Singh 2002). Thus, similar to the case of subcontracting systems in manufacturing, the success of contract farming critically depends on the establishment of mutual trust between agents and principals, possibly by exploiting the community relationships prevailing in Asian villages.

The Case of Vegetable Marketing in Java

The case of the informal contract-farming system may be illustrated by my own field study of commercial vegetable marketing in an upland village in Java, Indonesia (Hayami and Kawagoe 1993, chap. 4). The village is located on a hilly plateau near the border between West Java and Central Java, about 300 kilometers east of Jakarta. Typical of upland villages, this village used to possess only meager endowments in land and, hence, low incomes relative to lowland villages endowed with irrigated rice lands. The average farm size was only 0.4 hectares, half of which was under tenancy. Farmers traditionally staked out bare subsistence by using the mixed cropping of upland crops, such as corn, soybeans, and upland rice.

Within about five years beginning in the mid-1980s, the village economy underwent a major change because of the successful introduction of commercial vegetable production mainly geared for metropolitan markets. With this innovation, the average farm income per hectare increased by as much as eight times, surpassing the income level of irrigated rice farming in lowland areas. The relatively cool elevated environment in the study village and its surroundings is suitable for vegetable production. In the 1980s, the rapidly rising urban demand for fresh vegetables in the wake of the success of labor-intensive industrialization in Indonesia based on liberalization in trade and foreign direct investment began to spill over to this hinterland. However, the opportunity this represented for marginal farmers could not have opened up in the absence of a new marketing system for the delivery of large bulks of perishable products to the Jakarta metropolis 300 kilometers away.

The vital consideration in marketing vegetables to distant urban areas is the need to minimize the time required for delivery from producers to consumers. If an entrepreneur is to organize the long-distance shipments efficiently, he must assemble full truckloads of vegetables. For example, if a truck is carrying only a half load, the unit transportation cost will double with respect to a full load. But, in the case of fresh vegetables, unlike the case of storable commodities, the shipper cannot wait until the full truckload is assembled unless the assembly process is speedy. For this reason, marketing must be tightly coordinated with the production and harvesting process.

The organizers of the long-distant shipment of vegetables in the case of the village under study are called intervillage collectors. They assemble vegetables through smaller collectors called village collectors. A typical intervillage collector in the study village was a landowner with about 5 hectares of farmland (which is quite large as a holding in Java). He would contract with some 20 village collectors to assemble vegetables from the village and its surroundings for shipment, mainly to markets in Jakarta.

His daily operations are illustrated in figure 5.1. In the early morning, farmers harvest vegetables and deliver them to the homes of village collectors, which are commonly called depots. Then, the intervillage collector sends chartered trucks, each with one of his agents, to go around the depots to load up the assembled vegetables. As soon as a truck becomes fully loaded, it immediately proceeds to Jakarta. In about five hours, the truck reaches one of the two major wholesale markets in Jakarta. The cargo is delivered to a consignee, who sells vegetables by the sack to resellers. Although formal auctions are not practiced, each operation is a de facto auction because many resellers gather together to buy in competition. The resellers bring their purchases to their stalls within the market and sort out vegetables by grade for sale to retailers, such as grocery shopkeepers and peddlers. As soon as the intervillage collector's agent receives sales proceeds from the consignee, the truck returns to the village. After receiving the money from the agent, the intervillage collector goes around among his village collectors to pay them for the vegetables they collected in the morning. Each receives the rightful share of the sales proceeds taken in Jakarta, less the commission of the intervillage collector. On this occasion, the intervillage collector also seeks to obtain estimates from the village collectors on the amounts of vegetables they can assemble the next morning. He then charters the appropriate trucks from various sources for the next day's operation.

This is a tightly scheduled operation designed for the quick delivery of perishable commodities to metropolitan consumers with a minimum loss in value. For this marketing system to be viable, the intervillage collector must be able to secure (1) a reliable supply from vegetable growers via village collectors and (2) the conscientious services of consignees in metropolitan wholesale markets. Let me explain the second point first. The consignee in the Jakarta markets is not a formal agent officially licensed to preside over auctions based on formal rules, unlike the case of wholesale market agents in developed economies. No official record is kept on the transactions between the consignees and their resellers. Thus, the intervillage collectors cannot check if the sales reports handed to their agents by the consignees are accurate. It is also difficult for the agents to monitor each consignee's dealings with resellers, which occur in an apparently unorganized, chaotic manner. In fact, agents and drivers usually go to lunch when the de facto auction is taking place.

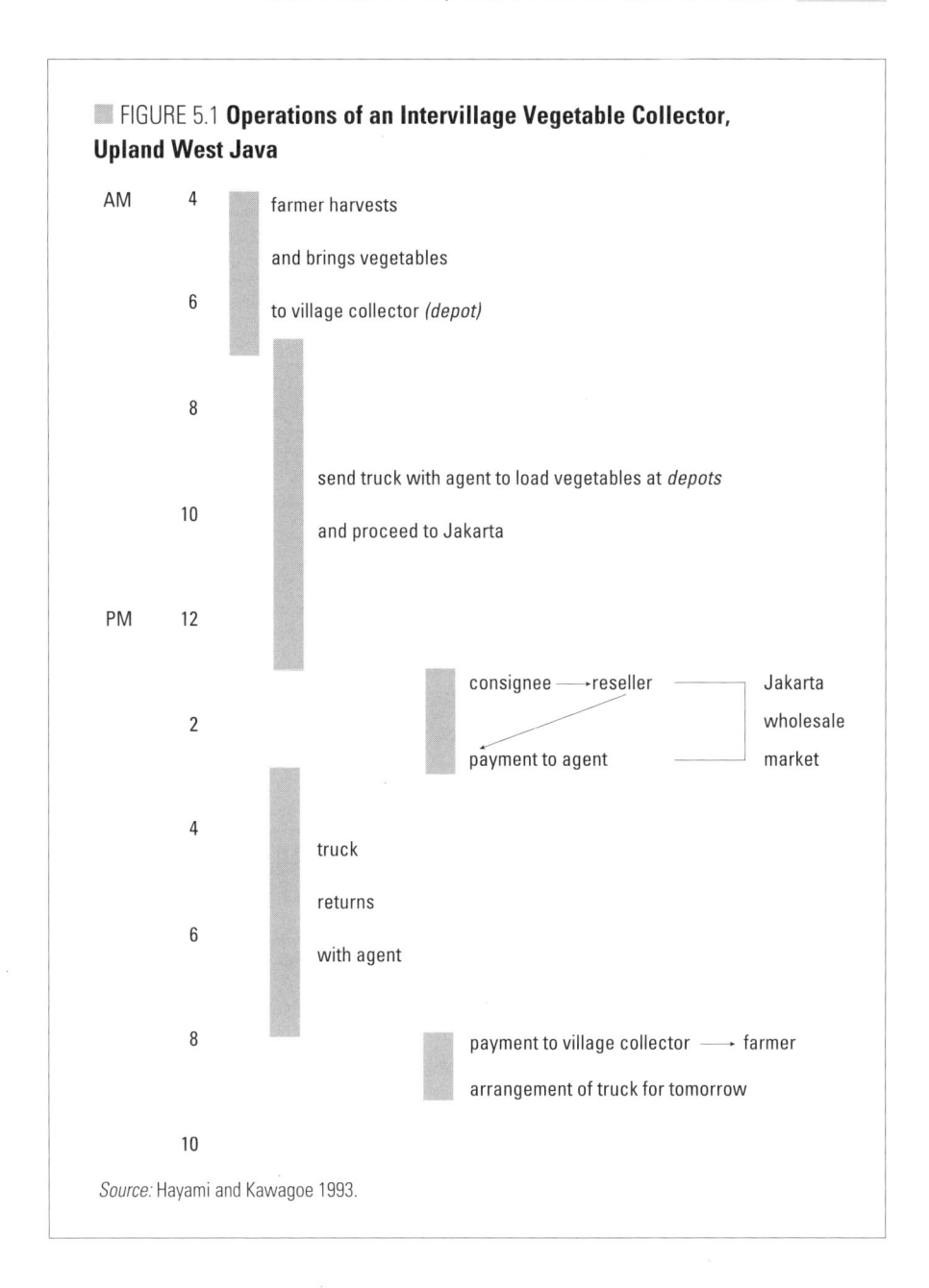

FIGURE 5.1 **Operations of an Intervillage Vegetable Collector, Upland West Java**

Time		Activity
AM	4	farmer harvests and brings vegetables
	6	to village collector *(depot)*
	8	
	10	send truck with agent to load vegetables at *depots* and proceed to Jakarta
PM	12	
	2	consignee ⟶ reseller ⟶ Jakarta wholesale market payment to agent
	4	truck returns
	6	with agent
	8	payment to village collector ⟶ farmer arrangement of truck for tomorrow
	10	

Source: Hayami and Kawagoe 1993.

Under such conditions, a consignee's conscientious services can only be secured on the basis of mutual trust established through regular, long-term transactions. It is easy for a consignee to cheat an intervillage collector on the sale of a single cargo. However, if a consignee underreports prices by too much and too often, the chance becomes high that his opportunism will be detected when the intervillage collector compares trade outcomes with other intervillage collectors in the same community. The consignee might thus lose the business provided not only by this particular intervillage collector, but also by others in the same circle. This would be a serious loss since the consignees live on the commissions they make from the de facto auction sales. In this way, the community mechanism of social opprobrium and ostracism restrains the moral hazard associated with reliance on marketing agents outside a village community, such as consignees in the markets of Jakarta. This mechanism works essentially the same as the threat of group embargo organized by Maghribi traders in North Africa during the Middle Ages to counteract the threat of the confiscation of their property by the rulers of trading posts on the Mediterranean Sea (Greif 1989, 1993).

To sustain this mechanism, an intervillage collector must send a truckload regularly to each consignee, one per wholesale market. Furthermore, more than one truckload is necessary if the intervillage collector is to reduce his risk. As is common with perishable commodities, the price of vegetables fluctuates widely in each wholesale market, depending on variations in the amounts in the cargoes the market receives. In order to reduce the risk involved in these variations in market prices, the intervillage collector has to diversify the destinations of his cargoes. In the case of the intervillage collector under illustration, he usually sent his cargoes to four separate wholesale markets.

Similarly, the task of the intervillage collector's effort to meet the first condition, namely, to secure a reliable supply of vegetables from farmers, is difficult because the needed supply not only is large in volume, but also must be regular and predictable for the sake of accurately scheduling transportation. A device used by intervillage collectors to secure reliable supplies is to tie both village collectors and farmers to themselves through credit. The intervillage collector advances credit to farmers through village collectors to guarantee delivery of the collected vegetables. This practice of supplying credit to cement a business relationship is also occasionally used by large wholesalers in towns in their dealings with small collectors in villages with respect to storable commodities such as corn and soybeans. However, the credits involved in the trade in these crops are short term, ranging from a few days to a few weeks, and seldom flow to the farmers. A unique aspect of vegetable marketing is that this credit practice is universal and involves long-term production credits that are supplied to farmers for two or three months. Typically, a village collector assigns vegetable growers in-kind credits in the form of fertilizer and chemicals in exchange for which the growers agree to deliver their entire harvests to him. The credit repayments of the farmers are deducted from the sales proceeds generated by the vegetables over the course of a harvest season. Village collectors receive the fertilizer and chemicals they need for these credit operations from the intervillage collector, in exchange for which they, in turn, agree to supply the intervillage collector with all the vegetables they assemble. The contracts are seasonal, but they are normally renewed regularly in subsequent seasons.

Interest is not explicitly charged on credits to farmers. Nor do collectors pay credit-receiving farmers lower prices relative to noncredit farmers. Nevertheless, the collectors are able to recover the costs of the credit by taking advantage of differential prices between collectors and farmers. For example, intervillage collectors can buy urea in large lots at Rp 185 per kilogram from fertilizer dealers in towns and allow village collectors to charge Rp 200 to farmers on credit payments because this is the price farmers would have to pay if they were buying fertilizer in small lots at village grocery stores. As illustrated in table 5.1, the average cost of current inputs provided as credit in kind would have totaled Rp 70,500 per farm according to my 1990 survey if farmers themselves were to buy locally in cash, whereas the same inputs could have been purchased by collectors at the cost of Rp 65,550. In a credit operation, collectors would charge farmers Rp 70,750 for these inputs. If the credit is paid back in two months, collectors earn, in effect, an interest rate of 3.9 percent per month. The cost of the credit to intervillage collectors, who generally own sizable land assets, would have been close to 1.5 percent per month, which was the official interest rate on collateral loans from the government bank, Bank Rakyat Indonesia. Thus, collectors may capture a large margin if they are acting as financial intermediaries, which is considered a return to their higher credit monitoring capability with respect to farmer-debtors relative to the bank's monitoring capability.

While this is a lucrative credit operation for collectors, it is also advantageous for farmers. The input cost if a farmer makes a purchase using his own cash (Rp 70,500) relative to the payment the farmer would eventually make to collectors for credit in kind (Rp 70,750) means that the

TABLE 5.1 Cost of Credit to Vegetable Producers under Alternative Schemes, Majalengka District, West Java, 1990

Scheme	Input cost per farm[a] (Rp)	Effective interest rate[b] (% per month) Farmer	Effective interest rate[b] (% per month) Collector
Cash purchase			
Farmer (in small lots)	70,500	n.a.	n.a.
Collector (in large lots)	65,550	n.a.	n.a.
Credit purchase			
Collector's trade credit	70,750	0.2 (2.2)	3.9 (58.1)
Fertilizer dealer's sale on credit	73,250	1.9 (25.8)	n.a.
Bank loan	75,950	3.8[c] (56.3)	1.5[d] (19.6)

Source: Hayami and Kawagoe 1993, 129.
Note: n.a. = not applicable.
a. Cost for 150 kg of urea, 50 kg of triple superphosphate, 100 kg of ammonium sulphate, and 1 l of Azodrin per 125 *bata* (0.18 ha).
b. Interest rates per year are shown in parentheses.
c. The official interest rate, plus transaction costs.
d. The official interest rate for a collateral loan.

effective interest rate is 0.2 percent per month. This is much lower than the interest rate the farmers would have paid if they had purchased the inputs, on credit, from fertilizer dealers (1.9 percent) or if their purchases were based on noncollateral loans from the government bank (3.8 percent), including the high transaction costs in dealing with the bank relative to the small size of the typical farmer credit. Thus, the credit contracts involved in the informal contract-farming system represent a Pareto improvement because they benefit both collectors and farmers.

The credit contract stipulates that, during one season, the farmer will sell his produce exclusively to a particular village collector at the prices offered by the latter (usually defined as the proceeds of sales at metropolitan markets, minus the cost of commissions of a certain percentage going to village and intervillage collectors). The contract does not assign the market power of a monopsonist to the collector. If the prices offered by the collector are judged too low relative to regular market prices, the farmer can shift to another collector in the next season. The same relation holds between an intervillage collector and village collectors. Indeed, one intervillage collector who had been operating in the study site was cut off by discontented farmers and village collectors because he had developed a reputation for paying unfair prices.

Because they have a reliable supply of vegetables assured by a mutually beneficial contract, intervillage collectors are able to organize an efficient system to carry out the long-distance marketing of perishable commodities.

Enforcement of the contract depends solely on relationships among farmers and collectors living in the same village community. It is difficult to enforce such contracts with traders who live outside the community, especially ethnic Chinese traders who are based in towns, despite their dominance in the trade in storable commodities. This vegetable marketing system is also said to be difficult and risky for cooperative managers; because they are not the owners of any residual profit, their incentive to take risks is low.

The intervillage collectors in Java, as sketched out above, resemble closely, in image, the rural entrepreneurs who led industrialization in Meiji Japan (Smith 1956; Itoh and Tanimoto 1998). More remarkable is the fact that the informal contract-farming system they have organized has the same structure as the just-in-time system of Toyota. In both systems, the principal secures reliable supply through agents by relying on community relationships to enforce contracts. Both are successful in securing the just-in-time supply of materials for processing and shipment.

This resemblance may not be mere coincidence. The Toyota Automobile Company began as a rural industry, and managers possessed a community relationship with parts suppliers from the start. Toyota's intricate marketing system was designed and operated by indigenous entrepreneurs rooted in rural villages.

Despite the hypothesis of Geertz (1963), the peasant population of Java is likewise motivated by a modern spirit of entrepreneurship. If there is a way to tap its potential, rural entrepreneurship may become an important basis for balanced rural-urban growth. This growth would involve the development of labor-intensive agricultural and industrial production in the hinterlands of developing economies. The potential appears to be especially strong in East Asia, where tight relationships of community have been forged among stable villages practicing sedentary agriculture, especially irrigated rice culture (Platteau and Hayami 1998).

Some Policy Implications

Investments in transportation and communication infrastructure such as roads, railroads, electricity grids, and information technology networks are indispensable for the development of internal trade. The establishment of industrial clusters within agglomeration economies outside metropolises may be facilitated by the creation of industrial parks and export processing zones (Sonobe and Otsuka 2006). Holding industrial fairs is effective in giving rural entrepreneurs access to urban and foreign markets. Above all, research and development on industrial and agricultural technology geared to rural production, as well as education, training, and extension among rural producers, are vital for rural-based development. Without efforts to upgrade the capacity of rural producers, outsourcing to rural areas by urban manufacturers and traders because of the low wages is unlikely to be sustainable, or it might work, but only as a mechanism to lock workers in developing economies into simple low-wage tasks at the bottom of the global value chain (Gereffi 1999; Humphrey and Schmitz 2002; Tewari 2005).

While national and municipal governments must undertake the maximum effort to provide such public goods, they should refrain from distorting the incentives of market agents. If markets are competitive, profit-seeking private entrepreneurs in rural areas will try to make the best use of community relationships to reduce transaction costs so as to beat the competition. The resulting efficiency improvements in marketing will benefit both consumers and producers, including poor peasants and cottage manufacturers.

On the other hand, if government and the agencies of international development assistance give special favors to cooperatives and self-help associations by granting monopoly rights or exclusive access to subsidized credits and inputs, the benefits will tend to be captured by the political elites in the communities controlling these organizations. This would motivate these elites to allocate their efforts to rent seeking rather than to reducing costs and improving services so as to beat out the market competition.

In organizing contract farming, it is not appropriate to grant exclusive franchises over territories to agribusiness enterprises or cooperatives. This would force farmers operating in these territories to deliver their products to processing or marketing centers controlled by a single principal. Farmers should be given an exit option; they should be allowed to trade with other principals after they have completed their current contracts. Otherwise, the contract-farming system will be oppressive and monopsonistic in exploiting smallholders.

It is important to recognize that, in the absence of competitive markets, community relationships will become mechanisms so the rich and powerful may exploit the poor. The relatively closed corporate groups in the Japanese automobile industry are able to escape this evil because there is strong competition among corporate groups (such as Honda versus Toyota), and this reduces the scope for monopoly price setting. Likewise, assemblers refrain from monopsonistic exploitation of parts suppliers because of the fear that good parts suppliers will migrate to the other corporate group. The same applies in the case of vegetable marketing in Indonesia with respect to the availability of exit options for farmers in counteracting possible monopsony by collectors. However, if the government were to collude with political elites in suppressing competitive markets, the failure of communities would loom large, and the scope for rural-based development would be narrowed.

Certainly, forging an efficient link between rural producers and global demand is only one of the preconditions for rural development. Another important step would be to promote links between industry and commerce within the rural sector and agriculture, where any increase in agricultural productivity in export cash crops and subsistence food crops would be a significant advance (Ho 1982; Ranis and Stewart 1993; Hayami 1998). Strengthening the connection between the hinterlands and international markets will necessarily also promote the links existing within the rural sector of the domestic economy.

Note

1. The analysis in this section is largely based on the experience of Japan. However, the experience of Taiwan (China) does not seem to lead to a different conclusion despite the widely differing political economy environments; see Caldwell (1976); Amsden (1991); Gereffi and Pan (1994); Lane (1998).

References

Abegglen, James C., and George Stalk, Jr. 1985. *Kaisha: The Japanese Corporations*. New York: Basic Books.

Ades, Alberto F., and Edward L. Glaeser. 1995. "Trade and Circuses: Explaining Urban Giants." *Quarterly Journal of Economics* 110 (1): 195–227.

Amsden, Alice. 1991. "Big Business and Urban Congestion in Taiwan: The Origins of Small Enterprise and Regionally Decentralized Industry." *World Development* 19 (9): 1112–35.

Asanuma, Banri. 1985. "Organization of Parts Purchases in the Japanese Automobile Industry." *Japanese Economic Studies* 13 (summer): 32–53.

Bairoch, Paul. 1975. *The Economic Development of the Third World since 1900*. London: Methuen.

Baldwin, Richard E., and Philippe Martin. 1999. "Two Waves of Globalization: Superficial Similarities and Fundamental Differences." In *Globalization and Labor*, ed. Horst Siebert, 3–59. Tübingen, Germany: Mohr Siebeck.

Baran, Paul A. 1957. *The Political Economy of Growth.* New York: Monthly Review Press.
Caldwell, J. Alexander. 1976. "The Financial System in Taiwan: Structure, Functions, and Lessons for the Future." *Asian Survey* 16 (8): 729-51.
Davis, William G. 1973. *Social Relations in a Philippine Market: Self-Interest and Subjectivity.* Berkeley, CA: University of California Press.
Dewey, Alice G. 1962. *Peasant Marketing in Java.* New York: Free Press.
Feenstra, R. C. 1998. "Integration of Trade and Disintegration of Production in the Global Economy." *Journal of Economic Perspective* 12 (4): 31-50.
Frank, Andre G. 1967. *Capitalism and Underdevelopment in Latin America: Historical Studies of Chile and Brazil.* New York: Monthly Review Press.
Fujimoto, Takahiro. 1999. *The Evolution of a Manufacturing System at Toyota.* New York: Oxford University Press.
Furtado, Celso. 1963. *The Economic Growth of Brazil.* Berkeley, CA: University of California Press.
Geertz, Clifford. 1963. *Peddlers and Princes.* Chicago: University of Chicago Press.
Gereffi, Gary. 1999. "International Trade and Industrial Upgrading in the Apparel Commodity Chain." *Journal of International Economics* 48 (1): 37-70.
Gereffi, Gary, and Mei-Lin Pan. 1994. "The Globalization of Taiwan's Garment Industry." In *Global Production: The Apparel Industry in the Pacific Rim,* ed. Edna Bonacich, Lucie Cheng, Norma Chinchilla, Nora Hamilton, and Paul Ong, 126-47. Philadelphia: Temple University Press.
Glover, David J. 1987. "Increasing the Benefits to Smallholders from Contract Farming: Problems for Farmers' Organizations and Policy Makers." *World Development* 15 (4): 441-48.
Goldsmith, Arthur. 1985. "The Private Sector and Rural Development: Can Agribusiness Help the Small Farmer?" *World Development* 13 (10/11): 1125-38.
Greif, Avner. 1989. "Reputation and Coalitions in Medieval Trade: Evidence on the Maghribi Traders." *Journal of Economic History* 49 (December): 857-82.
———. 1993. "Contract Enforceability and Economic Institutions in Early Trade: The Maghribi Traders' Coalition." *American Economic Review* 83 (June): 525-48.
Hayami, Yujiro. 1996. "The Peasant in Economic Modernization." *American Journal of Agricultural Economics* 78 (December): 1157-67.
———, ed. 1998. *Toward the Rural-Based Development of Commerce and Industry: Selected Experiences from East Asia.* EDI Learning Resources Series. Washington, DC: Economic Development Institute, World Bank.
———. 1999. "Middlemen and Peasants in Rice Marketing in the Philippines." *Agricultural Economics* 20 (March): 79-93.
———. 2000. "Toward a New Model of Rural-Urban Linkages under Globalization." In *Local Dynamics in an Era of Globalization,* ed. S. Yusuf, W. Wu, and S. Evnett, 74-83. Oxford: Oxford University Press.
———. 2002. "Family Farms and Plantations in Tropical Development." *Asian Development Review* 19 (2): 67-89.
———. 2004. "Communities and Markets for Rural Development under Globalization: A Perspective from Villages in Asia." Keynote address delivered at the Florence Conference of the European Association of Agricultural Economics, Florence, September 8-11.
Hayami, Yujiro, and Yoshihisa Godo. 2005. *Development Economics: From the Poverty to the Wealth of Nations,* 3rd ed. Oxford: Oxford University Press.
Hayami, Yujiro, and Toshihiko Kawagoe. 1993. *The Agrarian Origins of Commerce and Industry: A Study of Peasant Marketing in Indonesia.* New York: St. Martin's Press.
Hayami, Yujiro, and Vernon W. Ruttan. 1985. *Agricultural Development: An International Perspective,* 2nd ed. Baltimore: Johns Hopkins University Press.

Ho, Samuel P. S. 1982. "Economic Development and Rural Industry in South Korea and Taiwan." *World Development* 10 (11): 973–90.

Humphrey, John, and Hubert Schmitz. 2002. "How Does Insertion in Global Value Chains Affect Upgrading in Industrial Clusters?" *Regional Studies* 36 (9): 1017–27.

Hymer, Stephen, and Stephen Resnick. 1969. "A Model of an Agrarian Economy with Nonagricultural Activities." *American Economic Review* 59 (4): 493–506.

Itoh, Motoshige, and Masayuki Tanimoto. 1998. "Rural Entrepreneurs in the Cotton-Weaving Industry in Japan." In *Toward the Rural-Based Development of Commerce and Industry: Selected Experiences from East Asia*, 47–68. Washington, DC: Economic Development Institute, World Bank.

Itoh, Motoshige, and Shujiro Urata. 1994. "Small- and Medium-Size Enterprise Support Policies in Japan." Policy Research Working Paper 1404, World Bank, Washington, DC.

Jaffee, Steven, and John Morton, eds. 1995. *Marketing Africa's High-Value Foods: Comparative Experiences of an Emergent Private Sector*. Dubuque, IA: Kendall-Hunt Publishing Co.

Kandachi, Haruki. 1975. *Meiji-ki Noson Orimonogyo no Tenkai* [Development of the Rural Textile Industry in the Meiji Period], 2nd ed. Tokyo: Ochanomizu Shobo.

Krugman, Paul. 1991. "Increasing Returns and Economic Geography." *Journal of Political Economy* 99 (3): 483–99.

Krugman, Paul, and Raul Livas Elizondo. 1996. "Trade Policy and the Third World Metropolis." *Journal of Development Economics* 49 (1): 135–50.

Landes, David S. 1969. *The Unbound Prometheus: Technological Change and Industrial Development in Western Europe from 1750 to the Present*. Cambridge: Cambridge University Press.

Lane, David L. 1998. "Political Basis of Rural Entrepreneurship: Korea and Taiwan, China." In *Toward the Rural-Based Development of Commerce and Industry: Selected Experiences from East Asia*, ed. Yujiro Hayami, 187–210. EDI Learning Resources Series. Washington, DC: Economic Development Institute, World Bank.

Lewis, W. Arthur, ed. 1970. *Tropical Development, 1880–1913*. London: Allen and Unwin.

Little, Ian M. D., Tibor de Scitovsky, and Maurice Scott. 1970. *Industry and Trade in Some Developing Countries: A Comparative Study*. London: Oxford University Press.

Myint, Hla. 1965. *The Economics of Developing Countries*. New York: Oxford University Press.

Piore, Michael, and Charles Sabel. 1984. *The Second Industrial Divide*. New York: Basic Books.

Platteau, Jean-Philippe, and Yujiro Hayami. 1998. "Resource Endowments and Agricultural Development: Africa Versus Asia." In *The Institutional Foundation of East Asian Economic Development*, ed. Yujiro Hayami and Masao Aoki, 357–410. London: Macmillan.

Pollard, Sydney. 1965. *The Genesis of Modern Management: A Study of Industrial Revolution in Great Britain*. London: Arnold.

Ranis, Gustav, and Frances Stewart. 1993. "Rural Nonagricultural Activities in Development: Theories and Application." *Journal of Development Economics* 40 (1): 75–101.

Resnick, Stephen. 1970. "The Decline in Rural Industry under Export Expansion: A Comparison among Burma, Philippines, and Thailand, 1870–1938." *Journal of Economic History* 30 (1): 51–73.

Siamwalla, Ammar. 1992. "Myths, Demons and the Future of Thai Agriculture." Paper presented at the Thailand Development Research Institute 1992 Year-End Conference, "Thailand's Economic Structure: Toward Balanced Development," Bangkok, December 12–13.

Singh, Sukhpal. 2002. "Contracting Out Solutions: Political Economy of Contract Farming in Indian Punjab." *World Development* 30 (9): 1621–38.
Smith, Thomas C. 1956. "Landlords and Rural Capitalists in the Modernization of Japan." *Journal of Economic History* 9 (October): 93–107.
———. 1988. *Native Sources of Japanese Industrialization, 1750–1920.* Berkeley, CA: University of California Press.
Sonobe, Tetsushi, and Keijiro Otsuka. 2006. *Cluster-Based Industrial Development: An East Asian Model.* London: Palgrave Macmillan.
Tanimoto, Masayuki. 1998. *Nihon ni okeru Zairai Keizaihatten to Orimonogyo* [Indigenous Economic Development and the Textile Industry in Japan]. Nagoya: University of Nagoya Press.
Tewari, Meenu. 2005. "The Role of Price and Cost Competitiveness in Apparel Exports, Post-MFA: A Review." Working Paper 173, Indian Council for Research on International Relations, New Delhi.
Wada, Kazuo. 1998. "The Formation of Toyota's Relationship with Suppliers: A Modern Application of the Community Mechanism." In *Toward the Rural-Based Development of Commerce and Industry: Selected Experiences from East Asia*, ed. Yujiro Hayami, 69–86. EDI Learning Resources Series. Washington, DC: Economic Development Institute, World Bank.

CHAPTER 6

Economic Development and Regional Cooperation in East Asia

JOMO K. S.

There is more to East Asia's development than the flying geese model or China's emergence. There are also serious risks inherent in the development paths adopted since the 1997–98 crisis.

The East Asian region has suffered from a certain lack of confidence since the regional financial crisis of 1997–98. The earlier hubris, even conceit, following the East Asian miracle disappeared with the East Asian debacle. This came several years after the Japanese big bang, another disaster due to ill-considered financial liberalization. East Asian developments since then, especially greater regional cooperation, offer interesting lessons about the potential and limitations of the responses.

The East Asian Miracle and Differences Within the Region

A dominant explanation for the East Asian miracle—sustained and rapid economic growth in the 1970s and 1980s—saw the phenomenon as essentially due to unfettered market forces (Little, Scitovsky, and Scott 1970). The obvious policy implication was to liberalize, open up, and globalize.

There were other, far less prominent efforts to explain the East Asian miracle, including heterodox viewpoints invoking institutionalist, evolutionary, post-Keynesian perspectives and so on.

During the 1980s, several influential Western authors recast the Northeast Asian experience separately in terms of the so-called developmental state, a conception that was nearly opposite to the emphasis on unfettered market forces (for example, see Johnson 1982; White 1988; Amsden 1989; Wade 1990). Others insisted on Northeast Asian exceptionalism, which was attributed to unique cultural or historical circumstances such as Confucianism and the Cold War. Hence, for them, Northeast Asia was deemed unsuitable for emulation.

Instead, Southeast Asia was promoted as the model for emulation, particularly by other developing countries and especially after the economic liberalization of the economies of Indonesia, Malaysia, and Thailand beginning in the mid-1980s.

Some heterodox economists from the region dissented, arguing that the *East Asian Miracle* volume (World Bank 1993), for example, failed to acknowledge Southeast Asia's inferior achievements. Our dissenting book (Jomo et al. 1997) was published the day before the East Asian financial crisis broke in Bangkok on July 2, 1997, and was wrongly credited with having predicted the debacle. Rather, we had argued that the Southeast Asian success was much more modest than that of Northeast Asia and that the lessons being drawn from the region's experience were misleading, especially because they understated the role of government interventions in the region's economies. Furthermore, the average annual growth of the economies of Indonesia, Malaysia, and Thailand was about 6 percent, compared to about 8 percent for the East Asian newly industrializing economies before the 1990s. With far higher population growth in Southeast Asia, the actual difference in per capita terms was closer to 3 percent.

In Northeast Asia, domestic entrepreneurship and financial resources were more important, and foreign direct investment (FDI) accounted for less than 2 percent of gross domestic capital formation, whereas FDI was far more important in some countries of Southeast Asia than it was in most other developing countries.

Not surprisingly, no significant industrial entrepreneurial class has emerged in Southeast Asia, and this, in turn, accounts for the dominance of rentier elements particularly associated with finance capital. Southeast Asia has also been far more unequal than Northeast Asia. Many reforms in Northeast Asia were anticommunist in inspiration, such as Japanese stakeholder capitalism and the land reforms in Japan, the Republic of Korea, and Taiwan (China). Such initial conditions helped create more egalitarian, rapidly growing economies in which more people felt they had a stake.

There have also been other important policy differences within the East Asian region. For instance, there have been very few trade policy interventions in Singapore and Hong Kong (China). Not surprisingly, then, Hong Kong (China) has been de-industrializing for well over two decades. While Singapore's industrialization has been led by proactive, selective interventions to attract foreign manufacturers such as through so-called free trade areas, the region's free trade areas are actually preferential trade areas. Recent free trade agreements have had little to do with traditional trade issues per se; they have had much more to do with strengthening intellectual property rights, investment incentives, and other privileges that have only mixed consequences on economic development.

Southeast Asia has inadvertently encouraged industrial dualism, while earlier attempts to promote import-substituting industries were followed by the promotion of export processing zones and licensed manufacturing warehouses. There is generally little integration of these manufacturing enclaves with the rest of the national economy, quite unlike the situation in Northeast Asia, where effective protection has often been conditional on export promotion. In other words, industries and firms have been provided with protection and other subsidies, but have also been required to export, so that production for the domestic market leads to production for export, unlike in Southeast Asia, where there is little connection between the two.

Market Failure, Government Intervention, and Other Policy Issues

A different view about the East Asian miracle came about because of a rather fortuitous change in circumstances. Most importantly, beginning in the mid-1980s, the appreciation of the Japanese yen with respect to the U.S. dollar and an increase in Japan's efforts in official development assistance made Japan the second largest contributor to this sort of assistance after the United States. With its new clout, Japan insisted that the World Bank should reflect on why countries that had been following the structural adjustment prescriptions of the 1980s were experiencing only slow per capita growth, if not economic contraction, as well as greater inequality, as in, for example, much of Africa and Latin America. In contrast, much of East Asia, which had adopted more heterodox policies, was experiencing sustained high growth, often with only a little worsening in inequality, until the greater financial liberalization starting in the late 1980s.

The World Bank, meanwhile, argued that there should be a distinction between functional and strategic state interventions. Functional interventions were justified by the concept of market failure. In the face of market failures, governments needed to intervene by providing sound macroeconomic management, physical infrastructure, social services (particularly in health care and education), and other basic state functions such as ensuring the rule of law and so on. For the Bank, since the other sort of interventions—the strategic ones—were not justifiable in terms of market failure, they were likely to fail and should therefore not be pursued. Using moot methodologies, it proceeded to argue that trade policies, as well as industrial policies, had basically failed, though the contribution of directed credit was conceded.[1]

The concept of market failure in economics assumes an inexorable systemic tendency to achieve equilibrium. But even if this is the case, achieving equilibrium has little to do with economic development. The concept of efficient market allocation is based on comparative statics, not on structural transformation to achieve new comparative advantage in a dynamic sense. In the real world, achieving economies of scale is important, especially for economic development, rather than the constant or declining returns assumed in economic models. The challenge is to identify and promote economic activities offering increasing returns to scale, as opposed to activities only offering decreasing returns such as agriculture. This has been the premise for favoring industrialization and for promoting infant industries.

Over the 20th century, there was a secular long-term tendency for the terms of trade of primary commodities to decline against manufactured goods, as suggested by Singer (1950) and Prebisch (1950). The decline in the terms of trade of tropical primary commodities against their temperate counterparts—observed by Arthur Lewis, in, for example, cotton versus wool—has also persisted over recent decades. More recently, in the last three or four decades, there has also been a significant decline in the terms of trade of generic manufactures, that is, those manufactures produced by industries with few entry barriers, compared to products strongly protected by monopolistic intellectual property rights.

The success of well-considered government intervention and its crucial role in late industrialization and economic development all over the world are important reasons for insisting on industrial or investment policy. Besides trade, there are other areas in which such policies have been important in East Asia. Examples are promoting new technology, improving human resources, and offering appropriate investment incentives conditional on meeting performance criteria such as effective protection that is conditional on export targets or export promotion. Preferential credit for desired economic activities and the converse for undesired activities have been justified by the idea of financial restraint, instead of the notion of financial repression, justifying financial liberalization.[2]

In a world of imperfect competition, then, profit maximization inevitably involves rent seeking. The key policy challenge becomes one of managing rents and of minimizing waste in the creation and distribution of rents.

Financial Liberalization: The Onset of Crisis and Beyond

Financial liberalization has been the corollary of the rise of finance capital in the last three decades, especially after the demise of the Bretton Woods system, closely associated with the postwar Keynesian Golden Age when there was relatively rapid growth and some decline in inequality, not only internationally but also within most economies, partly because of social policies in Europe and Japan.

Financial liberalization has had adverse consequences for the developing world, undermining financial arrangements, institutions, and relations conducive to overcoming economic backwardness and market failure problems (Gerschenkron 1962). To make matters worse, most advocates of financial liberalization have ignored the warnings of the gurus of financial liberalization. For example, McKinnon (1989) emphasized that correct sequencing is necessary in pursuing financial liberalization, and capital account liberalization should come last, rather than first as in some East Asian economies before the 1997–98 crisis.

Financial liberalization seemed to be associated with the regional boom beginning in the late 1980s. In much of Southeast Asia, a series of devaluations in Indonesia, Malaysia, and Thailand and some financial liberalization in the mid-1980s were followed by a decade-long boom from the late 1980s until the 1997–98 crisis. There were three devaluations in Indonesia, one in Malaysia, and another in Thailand. This series of devaluations made production costs much cheaper, attracting investments for the boom. But the U.S. dollar pegs of the currencies of Indonesia, Malaysia, and Thailand became more problematic after mid-1995, when Eisuke Sakakibara, then Japanese vice minister for international affairs in the Ministry of Finance, and Larry Summers, then U.S. deputy treasury secretary, agreed to reverse the *endaka* (high yen) by letting the U.S. dollar appreciate against the yen after a decade of yen appreciation.

Other policy changes accompanying devaluation were also important. The Japanese Ministry of International Trade and Industry adopted a new Asia industrial development regional policy, encouraging Japanese firms to relocate not only in the East Asian newly industrialized economies of Korea, Hong Kong (China), Singapore, and Taiwan (China), but especially in the Southeast Asian newly industrializing countries, as well as China. Toward the end of the Chiang Ching-kuo era and with Lee Teng-hui's presidency in Taiwan Province, the government encouraged Taiwanese companies to move south to Southeast Asia, instead of to the mainland, fearing problems from closer integration with the mainland.

Korean efforts to relocate in Southeast Asia were much more modest and largely limited to Indonesia and Vietnam. Singapore's Sijori (Singapore-Johor-Riau) growth triangle initiative with neighboring Johor in Malaysia and Riau in Indonesia beginning in 1986 was followed by other efforts to integrate with China (for example, Suzhou) and India (for example, Bangalore), with rather mixed consequences. Meanwhile, Hong Kong (China) was de-industrializing, and manufacturing was being relocated to the Pearl River delta and beyond.

The impact of financial liberalization in East Asia proved disastrous, starting with the fallout from the big bang in Japan in the late 1980s and its near moribund economy in the decade and a half thereafter. Korea accelerated capital account liberalization to join the Organisation for Economic Co-operation and Development in the early 1990s, distorting the financial incentives for Korean conglomerate (*chaebol*) behavior, again with disastrous consequences. In Indonesia, bank proliferation starting in 1988 undermined monitoring and supervision, with cataclysmic consequences. In Thailand, the postcoup 1993 Bangkok International Banking Facility and the 1994 provincial counterpart had problematic consequences, culminating in the 1997–98 regional crisis.

After a serious banking crisis in the late 1980s, when the share of nonperforming loans reached 30 percent of the total commercial bank loan portfolio, the Malaysian authorities became more cautious with bank regulation. While careful about foreign bank borrowing, the Malaysian authorities aggressively promoted the stock market, especially after the break with the Singapore stock exchange in 1990. These successful efforts to promote the stock exchange in Malaysia attracted tremendous inflows of portfolio investment funds, particularly in 1992–93, which were subsequently reversed, with adverse consequences at the end of 1993. In early 1994, the Malaysian government temporarily introduced capital controls on inflows; these were subsequently removed after intense lobbying, leading to a new stock market bubble in 1995–96 that attracted fresh inflows.

Has international financial liberalization delivered on its own promises, even if not according to developmental criteria? Advocates of international financial liberalization have made three major claims. First, there should have been flows of funds from capital-rich to capital-poor economies. But, for most of Africa, Asia, Latin America, and the so-called transitional economies, the net flows of funds have actually been in the opposite direction, from the poor to the rich economies. East Asia was an exception in the early and mid-1990s, as finance followed investment and growth. Second, financial liberalization promised to lower the cost of funds. However, the cost of funds has not gone down, but has actually gone up until recently, increasing financial rents in the economies of the Organisation for Economic Co-operation and Development. Third, financial liberalization also promised lower volatility and greater stability with financial deepening, especially with the development and availability of new financial derivatives. However, although new financial derivatives have reduced some old sources of volatility and instability, they have also introduced new sources of the same, notably hedge funds (de Brouwer 2001).

Two other adverse implications of international financial liberalization should also be mentioned here. With financial liberalization, financial interests have become far more influential. They have influenced public policy, with typically deflationary consequences. The trend in the last two decades toward more independent central banks has actually reduced the monetary policy discretion available to governments, besides reducing financial policy instruments for economic development. The recent emphasis on inflation targeting, rather than growth or employment targeting, has also resulted in slower employment expansion and growth because of the prioritization of deflationary macroeconomic policies. Financial liberalization has likewise undermined crucial financial industrial policy instruments for accelerating industrialization and other desired structural transformations.[3]

Massive capital inflows are presumed to have desirable consequences for economic growth somehow, though there is little empirical basis for this assumption. By their very nature, short-term inflows rarely contribute to real capital formation and, hence, to growth. Many East Asian countries have adopted monetary policies (for example, sterilization) to limit the adverse consequences of massive capital inflows into their economies, but these also reduce possible gains from such inflows. The claim that massive capital flows would be desirable for economic development is thus misleading.

Instead, massive capital flows have often had adverse consequences. First, there have been asset market bubbles—mainly in the stock and real property markets—and, consequently, the associated construction booms, which have often worsened trade deficits. Second, consumption binges tend to be fueled by cheap credit; thus, the number of luxury cars sold in Thailand during the mid-1990s rose sharply. Not surprisingly, much of the elite and middle class like and support these financial policies, which do not contribute to and may even undermine the long-term development of these economies. Third, the availability of more and cheaper funds may encourage the misallocation of investment funds. While this may be true, the actual significance may be exaggerated by casual empiricism citing misleading anecdotal examples,[4] as in East Asia.

Various circumstances led to the 1997–98 crisis, including domestic and international financial liberalization and the mid-1995 Sakakibara-Summers reversal of the previous decade's dollar depreciation and rising yen. With this reversal, currency speculators began to look for new opportunities. With cheaply available foreign credit mainly denominated in U.S. dollars (even by European and Japanese banks), powerful vested interests in Southeast Asia wanted their currencies to continue to be pegged to the U.S. dollar, although such pegs would now render Southeast Asian economies less competitive.

The foreign debt buildup was mainly short term, rather than long term, even when the debt was deployed for long-term investments, primarily because of the Bank for International Settlements' capital adequacy requirements encouraging short-term lending. Stock markets in so-called emerging markets have been especially fickle and vulnerable to herd behavior by portfolio investors. A significant buildup of foreign assets in regional markets increased the likelihood of contagion from abroad. In Southeast Asia, such external shocks were exacerbated by the official policy responses of authorities in the region, often seriously compromised by influential vested interests, though such cronyism alone could not have caused the debacle.

Thus, economic vulnerability had been greatly increased by ill-considered economic liberalization policies, especially financial liberalization. Also, the initial policy responses in the region to the unfolding crisis were generally procyclical, as recommended or required by international financial institutions, especially the International Monetary Fund (IMF), and desired by market pundits in the business media. Such procyclical policy responses exacerbated the situation in Southeast Asia. Western-trained economists had imbibed currency crisis theories that did not take into account the different circumstances in the region relative to Latin America, for example. Also, many policies recommended to or even forced upon governments in the region were politically biased. For instance, in late 1997 and early 1998, the IMF favored the expanded "Berkeley mafia" in Indonesia and largely acted in concert with them, rather than on the basis of an informed, independent assessment of actual conditions in Indonesia and the causes of these conditions.

By early 1998, however, it was clear that IMF solutions were part of the problem, and there was a substantial shift away from the original diagnosis of the Asian crisis as a currency crisis. Instead, Asian values and business practices were blamed, especially poor corporate governance. Thus, social capital and corporatism were portrayed as cronyism, and profit maximization became rent seeking, as the earlier alleged foundations for the East Asian miracle were turned on their head in the wake of the debacle.

In the first year of the crisis, the tendency among pundits, particularly in the international business press, was to blame the victims and condemn the East Asian economies for alleged malpractices and so on. In mid-1998, U.S. President Clinton and others started talking about the desirability of a new international financial architecture, implicitly recognizing that the international monetary and financial system had developed in an ad hoc fashion after the Bretton Woods system had been undermined by U.S. President Nixon in 1971.

This change of heart was encouraged by the apparent spread of the crisis to Russia in August 1998. The crisis in Brazil and Russia precipitated the collapse of Long-Term Capital Management, a hedge processing fund. Fears that this collapse would have major repercussions on Wall Street encouraged the Federal Reserve Bank of New York to coordinate a private bailout of Long-Term Capital Management. The

U.S. Federal Reserve then lowered interest rates—reversing the outflow of funds from East Asia—in the last quarter of 1998, thereby facilitating economic recovery in the region.

Economic recovery in the following period, especially in 1999 and 2000, was strongest in Korea. In Southeast Asia, the recovery started later, but was stronger in Malaysia compared to Indonesia and Thailand. When the Malaysian government introduced capital controls in September 1998, orthodox economists insisted that the measures would be disastrous. Although it is not possible to attribute Malaysia's strong recovery definitively to the capital controls, there is also no proof that the capital controls caused any significant harm to the Malaysian economy (Jomo 2003).

In the 1990s, more than 80 percent of foreign direct investment consisted of mergers and acquisitions—mainly acquisitions, rather than mergers—in emerging markets. World FDI also declined beginning in the mid-1990s. Much more of the FDI going to East Asia now goes to China, with the proportion rising in less than a decade from under two-fifths to over two-thirds.

China's labor surplus economy has meant that its productivity gains have translated into consumer price deflation there. Consequently, China has become even more competitive, especially with its improving industrial policy initiatives. Thus, contrary to conventional wisdom, a state-owned enterprise, Shanghai Baosteel Group Corporation, has become the most efficient steel producer in the world, overtaking Pohang Steel Corporation (Posco), the Korean state-owned enterprise, once denounced by the World Bank as not worthy of industrial financing. China has thus become an increasingly diverse, formidable, and versatile economic force not only in the region, but in the world.

Lessons from the Crisis

Based on the experiences of the 1997–98 East Asian crisis, one might draw six key lessons for international financial reform. First, existing mechanisms and institutions for financial crisis prevention are grossly inadequate. The continuing trend toward financial liberalization is likely to increase, rather than decrease the likelihood, frequency, and severity of currency and financial crises. Outside Malaysia, too little has been done to discourage short-term capital flows, and too much faith has been invested in the protection expected from international adherence to codes and standards (Rodrik 1999).[5] Korea has joined China,

Hong Kong (China), Japan, Singapore, and Taiwan (China) in building up huge foreign currency assets (mainly U.S. dollars), at great cost, for self-insurance. This regional trend has also reduced the role and influence of the IMF in the region following its bitter experiences during the 1997–98 crisis. Financial liberalization has reduced the macroeconomic instruments available to governments for crisis aversion and has often left governments with little choice, except to react procyclically, tending to exacerbate economic downturns. National macroeconomic policy autonomy should be assured so as to enable governments to intervene countercyclically to avoid crises, which have generally had much more devastating consequences in developing countries than elsewhere.

Second, existing mechanisms and institutions for financial crisis management are also grossly inadequate. The greater likelihood, frequency, and severity of currency and financial crises in middle-income developing countries in recent times—with devastating results for the real economy and also for innocent bystanders in the neighborhood, as in the East Asian crisis—make speedy and effective crisis management imperative. There is an urgent need to increase the availability of emergency financing during crisis and to establish new, adequate procedures for timely and orderly debt standstills and workouts.[6] International financial institutions, including regional institutions, should be able to provide adequate countercyclical financing during a crisis (Ocampo 2000).[7] Instead of the current arrangements that tend to privilege foreign creditors, new procedures and mechanisms are required to ensure that foreign creditors also share responsibility for the outcomes of their lending practices.

Third, the agenda for international financial reform should go beyond the recent preoccupation with crisis prevention and resolution to address the declining availability and provision of development finance, especially to small, poor countries (Ocampo 2000) that have very limited and costly access to capital markets. There is growing pressure on the IMF, in particular, to return to its supposed core function of providing emergency credit and supposed core competencies of crisis prevention and crisis mitigation.[8] Furthermore, the World Bank and other multilateral development banks have abandoned or sharply reduced industrial financing, for example, thereby limiting even further the likelihood that developing countries may secure funding to develop new economic capacities and capabilities. The United Nations Conference on "Financing for Development" in Monterrey, Mexico, in March 2002 did not adequately address this challenge.

Fourth, inertia and vested interests stand in the way of urgently needed international institutional reforms. The governance of existing international financial institutions should be reformed to ensure greater and more equitable developing-country participation in and, hence, ownership of operations, research, and decision making at all levels in various tasks that the international financial system must begin to address more adequately. There is also a related need to consider reducing the concentration of power among peak institutions such as the IMF by, for example, delegating authority to other agencies (for instance, a world financial organization or a world financial authority), as well as by encouraging decentralization, devolution, complementarity, and competition with other international financial institutions, including regional ones.[9]

The exaggerated effects of currency movements for developing countries can only be addressed by greater surveillance and cooperation among the three major international currency issuers, but, unfortunately, there is little evidence that the G-7 or other similar arrangements have had much success in international macroeconomic coordination or even mere monetary coordination in the last two decades. A greater role for the IMF in this regard, especially with a greater voice for developing-country interests, might go a long way, with greater legitimacy, than an arrangement that only involves the major industrial economies. Through the IMF, which they control anyway, the G-7 can more effectively consult developing countries in matters of international macroeconomic governance to minimize oversights, as well as additional loss of legitimacy (Rodrik 1999).

Fifth, the reforms should restore and ensure national economic sovereignty and autonomy, which have been significantly undermined by international liberalization, deregulation, and new regulation and which are essential for more effective macroeconomic management and development efforts. The policy conditionalities[10] accompanying IMF financing must be minimized if not eliminated. It is now clear that one size does not fit all and that externally imposed policies have not contributed much to either economic recovery or growth (Weisbrot, Naiman, and Kim 2000; Weisbrot, Baker, and Rosnick 2005), let alone sustainable development. Such national ownership will ensure greater legitimacy for public policies and must include regulation of the capital account, as well as the choice of the exchange rate regime.[11] Since it is unlikely that international financial reforms will soon adequately provide the global public goods and other affordable international financial services required by most developing countries, it is imperative that, while reforming the international system to serve the needs of these countries more effectively, national policy independence is also assured to serve regulatory and interventionist roles beyond global and regional purview.

Finally, regional monetary cooperation can help in the face of growing capital mobility and the increasing frequency of currency and financial crisis, often with devastating consequences for the real economy. Greater European monetary integration in recent decades arose out of the recognition by governments of their declining sovereignty in the face of expanding capital mobility, especially after their capital accounts were liberalized (Baines 2002). Instead of trying to assert greater national control, with limited efficacy, governments are concluding that regional cooperation is more likely to be effective in the face of the larger magnitude and velocity of capital flows. However, there is no single formula or trajectory for fostering such cooperation, and such cooperation can probably not be successfully promoted independently of cooperation on other fronts.

Regional arrangements also offer an intermediate alternative between national and global levels of action and intervention and reduce the otherwise monopolistic powers of global institutions or arrangements. To be successful and effective, such regional arrangements must be flexible, but credible and capable of effective countercyclical capacity for crisis prevention, as well as crisis management. In East Asia, the Japanese proposal for an Asian monetary facility soon after the outbreak of the East Asian currency crisis might have made a big difference in checking and managing the crisis, but was thwarted by Western opposition. With the growing reluctance in the West, especially in the United States, to allow the IMF to serve as a lender of last resort (as in the more recent Argentine crisis), there should be more tolerance of regional cooperation in monetary and financial affairs.

Regional Financial Cooperation

Following the yen appreciation in the mid-1980s, the East Asian region was poised for greater regional cooperation despite lingering resentment of Japanese hegemony because of its unwillingness to atone fully for its wartime record. In response to the failure to conclude the Uruguay Round of the General Agreement on Tariffs and Trade negotiations in December 1989, then Malaysian Prime Minister Mahathir famously called for an East Asian economic grouping. Earlier, Japanese Prime Minister Nakasone's proposal for East Asian economic cooperation had been referred by the Australian government to the United States for approval. The U.S. response was to insist on Pacific Rim cooperation in the form of Asia-Pacific Economic Cooperation, which has little to show after a seemingly promising start in the mid-1990s.

The 1997–98 East Asian financial crisis and the international responses to it have profoundly reshaped the region. This is apparent not only in the greater official interest in East Asian—as opposed to Asia-Pacific or Pacific Rim—regional cooperation in recent years. The Association of Southeast Asian Nations (ASEAN) seems to have lost some of its earlier relevance and dynamism following its expansion to include Cambodia, Laos, Myanmar, and Vietnam, and the ASEAN Free Trade Area has failed to deliver on expectations.

Yet, the seemingly awkward ASEAN+3 East Asian regional arrangement, including the 10 ASEAN members, plus China, Japan, and Korea, has quickly attained an unanticipated relevance in both political and economic spheres. Admittedly, the European attempt at engaging East Asia through the Asia-Europe meetings has not yielded much, but the fate of the effort may well be a reflection of the difficulties of engaging two rather different and varied regions.

Meanwhile, the decline of Asia-Pacific Economic Cooperation has been apparent since the second half of the 1990s. In 1995, the Osaka Summit checked or altered some of the commitments to trade liberalization made only a year earlier. The Western, especially American, response to the regional financial crisis beginning in July 1997 only served to deepen the Pacific gulf. East Asians perceived some Western glee at the end of the Asian miracle, following the Japanese slowdown after its financial big bang less than a decade earlier, when both the IMF and the market quickly blamed the East Asians themselves for the debacle.

Initially, the problems in East Asia were portrayed as similar to those of Latin American macroeconomic populism because they involved fiscal profligacy. The crisis economies were advised or even forced to adopt contractionary fiscal and monetary measures, which only served to exacerbate the crisis, instead of providing the sorely needed countercyclical impetus. After it became abundantly clear that the East Asian macroeconomic authorities had been fiscally prudent, the IMF reversed itself on fiscal policy, but continued to press for tight monetary measures as the only option consistent with capital account openness.

By early 1998, however, the refrain in Washington had changed. In a succession of speeches at the beginning of the year, U.S. Federal Reserve Board Chairman Alan Greenspan, U.S. Deputy Treasury Secretary Lawrence Summers, and IMF Managing Director Michel Camdessus pronounced the new mantra, blaming the crisis on poor corporate governance in East Asia. Soon, media and academic pundits were waxing eloquent in denouncing the East Asian miracle's ostensible basis in Confucian cultural or social capital because, they said, it was cronyism and stood at the root of the crisis.

Regional responses may actually have reflected growing nationalism when the absence of helpful responses by the West aggravated consternation and resentment. The latter were especially pronounced in long-time U.S. allies such as Korea and Thailand, where the ruling regimes were replaced by the main political opponents. The political discourse turned decidedly nationalist on all sides in Thailand because the crisis provided a rallying point previously absent in a kingdom that had never been formally subjugated by any colonial power. In Korea, the already strong nationalist discourse broadened from its previous anti-Japanese focus, but was also mixed with strong democratic and anti-*chaebol* (anti-conglomerate) impulses.

In Malaysia, Prime Minister Mahathir's unorthodox policy responses played to a nationalist gallery as he disguised his use of state resources to save business cronies and the preemptive elimination of his designated successor, generally perceived as the only available political alternative in the long-standing one-party state. In Indonesia, where the crisis was most protracted and economically damaging, opposition to foreign involvement was less significant than the opportunity to get rid of a 32-year-old military despot and his privileged business cronies.

In September 1997, soon after the regional crisis had begun in Thailand on July 2, the Japanese Ministry of Finance proposed a US$100 billion Asian monetary fund or facility to help authorities in the region cope with the crisis. The initial Chinese response is reported to have been negative because Beijing had not been consulted prior to the announcement and may have been wary of Japanese intentions of strengthening regional hegemony through the new fund, but the Chinese authorities have since been keen to promote this sort of regional cooperation. Japanese Finance Vice Minister for International Affairs Eisuke Sakakibara had assumed there would be U.S. approval for the scheme when he briefed his counterpart, Lawrence Summers, but, instead, faced rebuffs from the United States, as well as the IMF, after the announcement. The United States then convened the Manila Framework Group in November 1997, but offered few real resources, and the group had little perceptible effect. The crisis conditions continued to deteriorate.

Only in mid-1998, a year after the crisis began, did the Clinton administration begin to raise the need for a new international financial architecture. The architecture would avert and manage more effectively the increasing frequency of currency and financial crises following international financial liberalization after the demise of the Bretton Woods system in the early 1970s and the international (sovereign) debt crises of the 1980s. The Russian crisis of August 1998 moved the United States to action. Besides the need to prop up the Yeltsin government after more than a half decade of economic collapse, there was a palpable fear that the East Asian crisis was spreading to the West and threatened other economies closer to home. After the criticism of Asian bailouts as evidence of cronyism, it was proving awkward to need to explain the coordination by the U.S. Federal Reserve of the initiative to contain the collapse of the hedge fund, Long-Term Capital Management, following the Russian crisis. Soon thereafter, the Federal Reserve lowered interest rates, thereby encouraging funds to flow back to East Asia, which helped to stabilize the region's currencies and enabled a sharp, V-shaped recovery everywhere in the region, except in Indonesia, where new political dynamics compromised the economic recovery effort.

Japanese Finance Minister Miyazawa's new initiative for Asia at the annual IMF–World Bank meetings in October 1998 was warmly welcomed by the United States as the prospect of Latin American crisis loomed large. The quid pro quo involved Japan funding a new short-term IMF facility to bail out Latin American countries, while the U.S. Congress appropriated US$18 billion for an IMF capital increase (Tadokoro 2003, 232). The Miyazawa initiative offered bilateral assistance of up to US$30 billion in the form of loans and credit guarantees to help revive the East Asian region's crisis economies. Most importantly, it complemented IMF assistance and was not linked to any alternative multilateral institutional framework for regional cooperation on monetary and financial matters. In the following year, the Japanese established currency-swap backup facilities for the Korean and Malaysian central banks.

Beginning in 1999, the ASEAN+3 finance ministers began meeting annually in conjunction with the Asian Development Bank board of governors meetings (Amyx 2002). At their second meeting in Chiang Mai, Thailand, in May 2000, they announced new arrangements to increase liquidity in the event of a future currency crisis by expanding the existing ASEAN Swap Agreement and setting up a bilateral currency-swap network involving China, Japan, and Korea. Efforts have also been made to enhance related monitoring, surveillance, and training. However, countries need to have an IMF-supported program in place before they may access more than 10 percent of the available funds. Thus, the funds actually available are even less and can barely be expected to withstand concerted speculative attacks. Most important, the arrangements have remained formally bilateral, rather than multilateral, and many of the bilateral currency-swap agreements have not yet actually been signed. Finally, in May 2005, the ASEAN+3 finance ministers agreed to multilateralize the arrangement to enable the relevant bilateral agreements to be collectively activated more promptly in case of emergency.

The memory of the Asian crisis lingers and has encouraged several East Asian economies to develop self-insurance arrangements against the threat of currency crisis. To accomplish this, they have accumulated large foreign exchange reserves, mostly in U.S. Treasury bonds. Such self-insurance is undoubtedly very expensive not only because of the low interest rates accruing to the bonds and the decline of the dollar in recent years, but also because it diminishes funds that might be more productively deployed in an economy or in a region. Recognition of the continuing problems of global and regional hegemony has animated recent debates about alternative arrangements.

The Asian bond market was launched in mid-2003 by the Executives' Meeting of East Asia–Pacific Central Banks. This organization launched the US$1 billion Asian Bond Fund to invest in U.S. dollar sovereign and quasi-sovereign bonds issued in countries of the organization, except Australia, Japan, and New Zealand. Later that year, ASEAN+3 launched the Asian Bond Markets Initiative to provide the necessary infrastructure for a well-functioning regional bond market. Subsequent developments suggest slow but steady progress in local-currency bond market development (Chin 2005). Development of the Asian bond market will broaden financial intermediation within the region, encouraging regional recycling of funds without strengthening the banking sector, while reducing vulnerability to currency mismatch problems.

The two main regional initiatives thus far—the elaborate bilateral currency-swap arrangements for liquidity support and the regional bond market—hardly threaten global hegemonic interests. In fact, development of the regional bond market has secured support from those "outside the region who are eager to benefit from its expected byproducts, including financial liberalization and reform in ASEAN+3 economies" (Amyx 2004, 3). After all, the U.S. dollar remains the anchor currency for most Asian monetary authorities maintaining currency pegs.

However, the region, especially China, is also very mindful of the likelihood that Japan will use regional initiatives to its own advantage. During 2001–02, Japanese Ministry of Finance officials seemed to be trying to use the ASEAN+3 cooperative framework to promote a yen-centered regional exchange rate regime. The promotion of the yen as the region's common currency was seen as an attempt to revive Japanese financial markets, that is, to promote "regional integration through the prism of Japan's national interests rather than through the prism of greater regional collective interests" (Amyx 2004, 9).

In early 2005, the executive secretary of the United Nations Economic and Social Commission for Asia and the Pacific proposed the creation of an Asian Investment Bank, to be patterned after the European Investment Bank, for mobilizing private funds more effectively in order to finance the region's infrastructure finance needs, estimated by the Japan Bank for International Cooperation at around US$200 billion annually. The Asian Development Bank, which was also initially proposed by the United Nations Economic and Social Commission for Asia and the Pacific and is now widely seen as controlled by the Japanese Ministry of Finance, currently provides about a quarter of that amount on concessionary terms. Such a regional infrastructural investment financing facility—drawing on private sector funds, but accessible to sovereign borrowers on better terms than otherwise available in commercial financial markets—may also increase financial intermediation within the region, besides helping to recycle funds for more productive uses.

Notes

1. An exceptional paper authored by Joseph E. Stiglitz, who received the Nobel Prize in Economics in 2001, acknowledged that directed credit had succeeded. (See Stiglitz 1994, 1996.)

2. In 1973, Shaw (1973) and McKinnon (1973) developed their critique of financial repression based on the case of Korea in the 1960s. Ironically, contrary to what

their works suggest, savings and investment rates actually rose in the peninsula despite the ostensibly repressed financial system that had emerged under the military dictator General Park Chung Hee.

3. In Singapore, which has not implemented much trade policy, financial policy has facilitated the emergence and growth of institutions such as the Development Bank of Singapore in its early role, while other financial policies have also been important in the effort to "catch up."

4. It made sense to invest in the production of dynamic random access memory devices in the late 1980s when the unit price was well over US$80. Not surprisingly, a great number of Korean and Taiwanese firms went into this production, driving down the unit cost to under $2 by the mid-1990s. With the benefit of hindsight, it is easy to criticize overinvestment or misallocation of resources, but that was certainly not foreseeable at the time of investment. In any case, procyclical market tendencies (for example, capital following growth or finance following investment) tend to exacerbate such problems.

5. Pistor (2000) has demonstrated that international legal standards are unlikely to have the desired outcomes owing to the significance of historical original conditions and variances in "path dependence."

6. There is a growing consensus on the need to set up standstill and other procedures for international debt workouts akin to U.S. bankruptcy provisions for corporations and municipal authorities, though the Krueger (2001, 2002) proposals have not been well received by those governments most likely to be affected. These governments are wary of the adverse selection consequences on them.

7. Social safety nets should not be seen as a substitute for social policy, which should be adequate to ensure a decent standard of living within a government's means and to develop human resources.

8. Then U.S. Treasury Secretary and former World Bank Vice President and Chief Economist Lawrence Summers is a prominent proponent of this view; for example, see his speech at the London Business School on December 14, 1999, and reported in the *Financial Times* the next day (Summers 1999).

9. As Ocampo (2000) put it, "The required financial architecture should in some cases have the nature of a network of institutions that provide the services required in a complementary fashion (in the areas of emergency financing, surveillance of macroeconomic policies, prudential regulation and supervision of domestic financial systems, etc.), and in others (particularly in development finance) should exhibit the characteristics of a system of competitive organizations."

10. These have been shown to be ill informed, erroneous, and irrelevant to the problems at hand, besides exacerbating the crises in East Asia.

11. Interestingly, then IMF Senior Deputy Managing Director Stanley Fischer (2001) admitted that "*willingly or otherwise*, a growing number of countries have come to accept [the belief that intermediate regimes between hard pegs and free floating are unsustainable] . . . Proponents of the bipolar view—myself included—have perhaps exaggerated their argument for dramatic effect."

References

Amsden, Alice. 1989. *Asia's Next Giant*. New York: Oxford University Press.
Amyx, J. A. 2002. "Moving beyond Bilateralism?: Japan and the Asian Monetary Fund." Pacific Economic Paper 331, East Asian Bureau of Economic Research, Canberra.
———. 2004. "A Regional Bond Market for East Asia?: The Evolving Political Dynamics of Regional Financial Cooperation." Pacific Economic Paper 342, East Asian Bureau of Economic Research, Canberra.

Baines, Adam. 2002. "Capital Mobility and European Financial and Monetary Integration: A Structural Analysis." *Review of International Studies* 28: 337–57.

Chin, Kok-Fay. 2005. "East Asian Monetary and Financial Cooperation: The Long Road Ahead." In *Monetary and Exchange Rate Systems: A Global View of Financial Crises*, ed. Louis-Philippe Rochon and Sergio Rossi, Chapter 4. Cheltenham, United Kingdom: Edward Elgar.

de Brouwer, Gordon. 2001. *Hedge Funds in Emerging Markets*. Cambridge: Cambridge University Press.

Fischer, Stanley. 2001. "Exchange Rate Regimes: Is the Bipolar View Correct?" *Finance and Development* 38 (2): 18–21.

Gerschenkron, Alexander. 1962. *Economic Backwardness in Historical Perspective*. Cambridge, MA: Harvard University Press.

Johnson, Chalmers. 1982. *MITI and the Japanese Miracle: The Growth of Industrial Policy, 1925–1975*. Stanford, CA: Stanford University Press.

Jomo, K. S., ed. 2003. *Southeast Asia's Paper Tigers: From Miracle to Debacle and Beyond*. London: Routledge.

Jomo, K. S., with Chen Yun Chung, Brian C. Folk, Irfan ul-Haque, Pasuk Phongpaichit, Batara Simatupang, and Mayuri Tateishi. 1997. *Southeast Asia's Misunderstood Miracle: Industrial Policy and Economic Development in Thailand, Malaysia and Indonesia*. Boulder, CO: Westview Press.

Krueger, Anne. 2001. "International Financial Architecture for 2002: A New Approach to Sovereign Debt Restructuring." Address at the National Economists' Club Annual Members' Dinner, American Enterprise Institute, Washington, DC, November 26.

———. 2002. "New Approaches to Sovereign Debt Restructuring: An Update on Our Thinking." Speech presented at the conference on "Sovereign Debt Workouts: Hopes and Hazards," Institute for International Economics, Washington, DC, April 1.

Little, Ian M. D., Tibor de Scitovsky, and Maurice Scott. 1970. *Industry and Trade in Some Developing Countries: A Comparative Study*. London: Oxford University Press.

McKinnon, Ronald. 1973. *Money and Capital in Economic Development*. Washington, DC: The Brookings Institution.

———. 1989. *The Order of Economic Liberalization: Financial Control in the Transition to a Market Economy*. Baltimore: Johns Hopkins University Press.

Ocampo, José Antonio. 2000. "A Broad Agenda for International Financial Reform." In *Financial Globalization and the Emerging Economies*, ed. José Antonio Ocampo, Stefano Zamagni, Ricardo Ffrench-Davis, and Carlo Pietrobelli, 41–62. Santiago, Chile: United Nations Economic Commission for Latin America and the Caribbean.

Pistor, Katarina. 2000. "The Standardization of Law and Its Effect on Developing Economies." Group of 24 Discussion Paper Series 4, United Nations Conference on Trade and Development, Geneva; Center for International Development, Harvard University, Cambridge, MA.

Prebisch, Raúl. 1950. "The Economic Development of Latin America and Its Principal Problems." E/CN.12/89/Rev.1. Economic Commission for Latin America, Department of Economic Affairs, United Nations, New York.

Rodrik, Dani. 1999. "Governing the Global Economy: Does One Architectural Style Fit All?" Paper prepared for the Brookings Institution Trade Policy Forum Conference, "Governing in a Global Economy," Washington, DC, April 14–16.

Shaw, Edward. 1973. *Financial Deepening in Economic Development*. New York: Oxford University Press.

Singer, Hans. 1950. "U.S. Foreign Investment in Underdeveloped Areas: The Distribution of Gains between Investing and Borrowing Countries." *American Economic Review, Papers and Proceedings* 40 (May): 473–85.

Stiglitz, Joseph E. 1994. "The Role of the State in Financial Markets." In *Proceedings of the World Bank Conference on Development Economics 1993*, ed. Michael Bruno and Boris Pleskovic, 19–56. Washington, DC: World Bank.

———. 1996. "Some Lessons from the East Asia Debate." *World Bank Research Observer* 11 (1): 151–77.

———. 1998. "More Instruments and Broader Goals: Moving toward the Post-Washington Consensus." WIDER Annual Lecture 2 (January), United Nations University–World Institute for Development Economics Research, Helsinki.

Stiglitz, Joseph E., and Andrew Weiss. 1981. "Credit Rationing in Markets with Imperfect Information." *American Economic Review* 71 (2): 393–410.

Summers, Lawrence. 1999. "The Right Kind of IMF for a Stable Global Financial System." Speech presented at the London Business School, London, December 14.

Tadokoro, M. 2003. "The Asian Financial Crisis and Japanese Policy Reactions." In *International Financial Governance under Stress: Global Structures versus National Imperatives*, ed. R. Geoffrey, D. Underhill, and Xiaoke Zhang, 223–40. Cambridge: Cambridge University Press.

Wade, Robert. 1990. *Governing the Market*. Princeton, NJ: Princeton University Press.

Weisbrot, Mark, Dean Baker, and David Rosnick. 2005. "The Scorecard on Development: 25 Years of Diminished Progress." Policy paper, September, Center for Economic Policy Research, Washington, DC.

Weisbrot, Mark, Robert Naiman, and Joyce Kim. 2000. "The Emperor Has No Growth: Declining Economic Growth Rates in the Era of Globalization." Policy paper, November, Center for Economic Policy Research, Washington, DC.

White, Gordon, ed. 1988. *Developmental States in East Asia*. Basingstoke, United Kingdom: Macmillan.

World Bank. 1993. *The East Asian Miracle: Economic Growth and Public Policy*. World Bank Policy Research Reports. New York: Oxford University Press.

CHAPTER 7

East Asian Economic Integration
Problems for Late-Entry Countries

CAO SY KIEM

The conditions for growth in East Asia have changed since the 1997–98 crisis. The shifts have exposed many new issues among the less-developed countries in the region.

The significant rise of many East Asian economies during the latter half of the last century was based on the change to a market-driven economy and the adoption of an open-door strategy. The close connection between these two factors has created a unique feature in economic growth in East Asia. The growth has been rapid, long-term, and sustainable and has spread swiftly into many economies in the region.

As conditions for worldwide and regional economic development have altered, these two factors have continued to play a key role in the region's economic prospects. This is clear from the structural adjustment process in many East Asian economies after the 1997–98 economic crisis and the great contribution of the emerging economies, especially China, to the region's current growth performance.

The conditions for growth and development in East Asia have, of course, undergone fundamental shifts since the period prior to the 1997–98 economic crisis. These shifts have exposed many new issues to the less-developed countries in the region. The opportunities and challenges are now quite different in terms of scope, nature, level of difficulty, and implementation. Meanwhile, the less-developed countries have been exerting a negative impact on the prospects for development and economic integration in the whole region. Experience has shown that less-developed countries often have negative impacts during the common integration process, thereby hindering more developed countries from growing more quickly.

To assess East Asia's growth prospects, one must identify the new conditions for growth in the region. It would then be possible to single out the problems faced by late-entry countries, and this could help elucidate the development process in East Asia.

The New Context of Development

The Emergence of East Asia as a Global Economic Hub

Together with the dynamism of China, the rapid recovery of the region's economies since the 1997–98 crisis has turned East Asia into an enormous center of economic activity, especially in the role of the region as the industrial hub of the world. Industrial goods produced in East Asia, especially goods relying on mid-level technology, account for a large and expanding share of global industrial production.

The rapid increase in inflows of foreign direct investment to East Asia and the region's status as an industrial hub of the world have created a strong growth momentum. This has changed the position of East Asia in the global economy, but it has also changed the growth model (the "industrial wave") and the comparative advantages of the region's economies.

Before the 1997–98 crisis, economic development in East Asia followed a pattern called the flying geese formation, which was led by Japan. The participation of China and Vietnam in this formation contributed to maintaining this pattern of development following the crisis. It seems that this kind of orderly participation in development helped East Asia reduce competitive risks, especially for late-entry economies. These latecomers could narrow the gap between themselves and their developed-country predecessors. Nonetheless, although all countries were subject to competition, the gap remained sufficiently wide so that the frontrunner might feel safely ahead.

However, under the impact of the economic crisis and the shifts in the movements of foreign direct investment, the rise of the Chinese economy—giant in terms of the scale and scope of its development—has altered the industrial wave and set East Asia's economic development process on a new course.

First, while the differences in industrial structure among countries in the region have persisted, technological gaps have narrowed. Second, there is a trend toward a division of labor based on a value added chain among countries in the region. This represents a new model for industrial development in East Asia. It is a fresh foundation for closer development links among countries. In principle, all economies that take part in this chain will have many opportunities to benefit from forces for development. Third, because of globalization and knowledge-based economic development, late-entry countries may attempt to catch up to developed countries by skipping over stages in industrial development and moving directly to a higher level of technological sophistication. Shortcuts exist in the development process. The Republic of Korea and Malaysia have demonstrated that such an approach is possible in Asia. China and India have repeated the experiment with considerable success. Of course, to take maximum advantage of this opportunity, there are a number of requirements, such as adequate financing, technology, human resources, markets, a sound strategy, and a degree of economic integration with the region and the world. Such requirements are not readily met by latecomers.

Depending on a country's specific situation and capabilities, the time needed to absorb the structure wave (in the wave model) and to move up the technological ladder (in the value added chain model) varies considerably. In general, the less-developed late-entry countries, notably, the Cambodia–Lao People's Democratic Republic–Myanmar–Vietnam group, have encountered difficulties in participating in the regional system for the division of labor under either industrial model. In the meantime, China, thanks to its economies of scale and its overall strength, has leapfrogged up the technological ladder. It has become a prominent example of the possibility of narrowing economic gaps with developed countries.

The long-term economic prospects of East Asia are bright, and there are many development opportunities for the whole region. The shifts in the development characteristics of countries in the region have already been enormous. The conditions for access and the ability to take advantage of economic opportunities still vary among countries, however. The weaker economies face bigger challenges and difficulties.

Tight integration within the region must be an important goal if the weaker economies are to narrow the gap.

The Rise of China

The rise of China has given East Asia a new appearance. There is a new force for growth, and there have been dramatic changes in modes of operation. There is a new competitive relationship in the region. It has brought new, unprecedented development opportunities and challenges.

China plays the role of a *black hole*[1] in the development process in East Asia. From the perspective of the industrial wave, the emergence of China is having a strong impact in the spread of economic development throughout the region.

First, because of its giant scale and rapid growth, China has altered, on its own, the balance of development in the region. China's significant demand for inputs and its ability to supply outputs to the world's markets have altered the international supply-demand equation dramatically. China is exerting fierce competitive pressure on all countries and markets at various levels. This pressure is multidimensional in that it embraces quality, quantity, durability, and price.

For those countries in the region at a similar or lower level of development, the pressure has been especially furious in the short term and the long term. However, those countries that are at a similar or lower level of development and happen to be China's neighbors will also experience stronger positive effects. From this reasoning, the countries of the Association of Southeast Asian Nations (ASEAN) are certainly being directly and decisively affected by China's emergence as a powerful economic force.

Second, in general, the rise of China has upset the old balance. It has created new development opportunities that are significant for the region and the world. Unfortunately, most East Asian economies, but especially the weaker economies, have seen the situation as containing more challenges than opportunities. This has often precipitated a policy response that aims to protect the economy from the challenges, but fails to take advantage of the opportunities.

The world economy must adapt to the changes caused by China's rapid expansion. This may be achieved in three ways:

- Investing in China to produce goods in China, then selling the goods at a profit in China or on the world market

- Exporting machines, equipment, and modern inputs to China to take part in the production and export process in China, thereby benefiting from the economy's development
- Exporting raw materials and products to China for profit

Depending on its competitive level and strength, each economy will find among these three an appropriate method for adapting to China, taking advantage of the opportunities created by China, or competing with China. The United States and other developed economies have mainly chosen the first way. Middle-level developed economies with mid-level financial resources have followed the second way. The third way has been selected by less-developed economies that have natural resource advantages or that are at a level of competitiveness lower than that of China (Tran Quoc Hung 2004).

Relative to China, the development level of ASEAN countries is generally no higher. Some economies are less developed and in a weaker position financially. This is why ASEAN economies have mainly adapted to China's economic boom in either the second or the third way. The relatively more well developed ASEAN economies (Indonesia, Malaysia, the Philippines, Singapore, and Thailand) have followed the second way. Cambodia, Lao PDR, Myanmar, and Vietnam have chosen the third.

For ASEAN economies, the rapid growth of China has represented a huge opportunity, as well as a sort of challenge ASEAN has never faced before. As a united, integrated economic bloc, ASEAN is a potential rival to China. However, in terms of position and power, trends, and prospects, ASEAN is generally at a disadvantage. ASEAN may become a supplier of raw materials to China in exchange for manufactured goods (the third way) (Thayer 2005). Moreover, ASEAN is involved in the new division of labor in the region, in which China has played a key role.

Vietnam is typical among the less-developed economies in ASEAN and East Asia. For Vietnam, the dangers are greater. Economic cooperation and exchange between Vietnam and China have evolved in the third way. While Vietnam has a surplus in exports with all developed economies (Europe, Japan, the United States), it has an import surplus with China, a developing economy. This seems to be a paradox for Vietnam, where there has been industrialization and modernization and where considerable effort has been taken to narrow the development gap with the rest of the world. For the long-term benefits of development, Vietnam has reason to worry about this paradox.

The reason for Vietnam's long-standing import surplus in its trade with China lies in the division of labor between the two economies:

Vietnam has been specializing in providing raw materials, fuel, and primary agricultural products to China, while China has been exporting low- and medium-technology industrial products to Vietnam. The possibility that the trade and investment relationship between China and Vietnam may evolve toward a North-South model cannot be ignored. Vietnam might become caught in the low-wage trap and remain economically subordinate to China.[2]

There are good reasons for predicting that the economic relationship between the region's less-developed economies and China will also evolve in this way. Such a situation will be adverse for Vietnam and other less-developed countries, but also have a negative effect on the benefits of China's development, the course of East Asian economic integration, and the region's economic development prospects.

Third, because of China's scale, the industrial wave within China may be long-lasting.[3] It may possibly be generally confined within China's borders and not spread to less-developed neighboring economies like Cambodia, Lao PDR, Myanmar, and Vietnam (Tran Van Tho 2005). This is a real possibility given that China is more competitive than the region's less-developed economies. Thus, a normal course of development involving shifts in the structural waves across economies in the region will be blocked. A fact that has a decisive influence on the prospects for latecomer economies in East Asia should be stressed: the structure and inputs of products made in China and exported have been diversified from low-technology, labor-intensive items to high-technology, capital-intensive ones. This is similar to the situation in many economies in the region. This means there is a danger of destabilization in the division of labor in East Asia. Late-entry ASEAN countries (such as Cambodia, Lao PDR, and Vietnam) will encounter difficulties establishing a foothold in this system. Even more developed economies such as Japan, Korea, and Malaysia may have difficulty, though at higher product levels. Weaker economies, if they are unable to compete successfully with China, which is already the case for many products, will be eliminated from the regional labor market. This very real issue renders the economic prospects in East Asia less bright.

New Developments in Regional Economic Integration

Prior to the 1997–98 crisis, even within the flying geese model of development, the performance of East Asia was a simple sum of separate miracle-growth economies. Even ASEAN, the bloc with the most well integrated institutional structure in the region, did not enjoy close, effective economic links.

The 1997–98 crisis revealed the obvious: under normal growth conditions, East Asian economies did not seem to need each other very much (except Japan), and, during the crisis, no one country could save any other country. Malaysia and Thailand are neighbors, and both are also ASEAN members, but, when they were caught up in the crisis, they could not assist each other even though assistance would have been timely and effective.

It can be seen that the three main weaknesses of the economic integration model of ASEAN are as follows:

- The inefficiency of integration the ASEAN way, wherein the key words are voluntary, consensus, and noninterference
- Lack of a powerful institutional body that is able to organize and supervise links among countries in the region so as to overcome national obstacles
- Absence of the driving force of a truly leading nation

Although ASEAN has launched many sound programs aimed at fostering integration and development, the implementation of these programs has often been slow and inefficient. Since the 1997–98 crisis, this state of affairs has been more or less superseded, but the results are still far from meeting expectations.

Recently, with China's participation, followed by Japan and Korea, the process of economic integration in East Asia and within ASEAN has become more dynamic. First, while weaker than many other players, ASEAN is a focal point for regional efforts at integration and is so regarded by ASEAN itself. Australia, China, India, and Japan have undertaken efforts to link with ASEAN and thereby establish long-term relationships with other countries in East Asia. New formulas and models that tend toward a close institutional structure in the region—ASEAN+1 (plus China), ASEAN+3 (plus China, Japan, and Korea), ASEAN+5 (plus China, Hong Kong [China], Japan, Korea, and Taiwan [China]), the Asia-Europe Meeting, and Asia-Pacific Economic Cooperation[4]—are mushrooming in the region. This process has created fresh forces for development in East Asia, increasing development opportunities in the region. The integrating process in East Asia is now fostering the construction and consolidation of economic and financial blocs through coherent institutional structures.

East Asia has also been attempting to build development corridors among ASEAN economies and between ASEAN and China. These programs have good prospects. The speed of implementation has been accelerating, especially in those programs directly related to China. However, it is important to note that, to create better development opportunities and facilitate access to these opportunities by less-developed economies in ASEAN (Cambodia, Lao PDR, Myanmar, and Vietnam) so as to narrow the development gap within the region, these programs must be carried out over a large area under especially difficult geographical, social, and economic conditions (including in southwestern China). In addition, the lack of regular, firm financial guarantees causes problems in implementing the programs rapidly and smoothly.

Bilateral integration processes have also been accelerated. Many countries are cooperating through a series of bilateral investment and trade agreements. Thanks to bilateral agreements, some developed economies (for example, Singapore and Thailand) have preferred to undertake integration and liberalization according to their own capabilities rather than adopt ASEAN's principles of integration. This has helped promote economic development in individual countries. It has also created stronger competition and allowed countries to ignore regional integration principles that are inefficient and obstruct the liberalization process. ASEAN has been investigating and testing these effects, along with new integration formulas such as 10–X (any grouping under the 10 ASEAN members is sufficient for integration programs) and 2+X (only two countries are required).

However, accelerating the bilateral integration process may also have adverse impacts on regional integration efforts. Because they have to implement many bilateral agreements instead of only one multilateral agreement, governments and enterprises may suffer from the "Asian noodle bowl" effect or the "centrifugal" effect, whereby the orientation toward integration is skewed toward bilateral relationships. Increased transaction costs can widen the development gaps among economies.

The presence of outside partners in ASEAN's integration formulas (ASEAN+1, ASEAN+2 [plus Australia and New Zealand], ASEAN+5) and the trend toward an East Asian Economic Community have strengthened the centrifugal effect in ASEAN. ASEAN will become even weaker if it cannot overcome this problem given that it is at an inherent competitive disadvantage relative to China, India, and Japan. Although the ASEAN Economic Community is considered a priority program for dealing with the centrifugal effect and creating a new development power and position for ASEAN, the history of the program and its current status clearly show that implementing it as intended will be extremely difficult (see box 7.1).

Key ASEAN countries are facing political and social instability. Ethnic and religious conflicts and conflicts of interest have been heated in Indonesia, Myanmar, the Philippines, and Thailand. It is unlikely that these situations will be resolved in the near future. Instead of focusing more effort on ASEAN integration operations, these governments are obliged to assign more priority to these domestic issues. The ASEAN Economic Community—the loose institutional structure for ASEAN integration—is thus even more difficult to realize.

These difficulties are augmented by several other factors. These include cultural diversification, the differences in views on and the development of democratic foundations in the region, potential disputes and conflicts between ASEAN members and non-ASEAN countries (for example, the South China Sea conflict), and the lack of a force strong enough to lead the process.

This implies that, to maintain and consolidate their role in the East Asian development process and to increase their competitiveness, which has been lower than that of China, India, and Japan up to now, ASEAN economies need to achieve a breakthrough in their attitude to and steps toward integration. The issue here is no longer the efficiency of

---

BOX 7.1 The ASEAN Integration Gap

ASEAN's level of development as a region is much less than that of the European Union or the North American Free Trade Agreement. Because of the large development gap and low average level of development, ASEAN's impetus toward economic links and integration has been weak, and ASEAN lacks a strong, capable engine for leading the integration process.[5] ASEAN lacks a strong guiding force at its interior. This has imposed huge obstacles on ASEAN integration, but also represents a challenge to ASEAN's will. It is this objective weakness that has generated the trend among ASEAN members to escape from the regional bonds and become involved in establishing bilateral links and integration agreements with powerful partners outside the region, notably China, India, Japan, and the United States. This trend is having a negative impact on ASEAN's prospects because it is eliminating the development advantages that may be fostered by regional integration.

Source: Tran Dinh Thien 2005.

ASEAN integration. Instead, it is the existence of ASEAN as a grouping involved in integration with respect to other partners. Certainly, this is a most critical issue.

Late-Entry Countries and the Prospects for East Asian Economic Integration

ASEAN Issues

ASEAN plays a crucial role in the integration process, as well as in the development process, in East Asia, and it is also attempting to create links with the region's most powerful partners. Without this role, East Asian regionalism would be showing fewer successes. The development of the ASEAN economic integration process is therefore significant for the future of East Asia.

However, our analysis also shows that, first, ASEAN's competitiveness has not been high (McKinsey and Company 2003). It is increasingly difficult for ASEAN to compete with China both in absorbing foreign direct investment and in trading inputs and outputs. The product structure of ASEAN, from developed to developing economies, is generally similar to that of China, but ASEAN does not have the same strong potential of becoming a center for knowledge and of technology development. This suggests that China will surpass ASEAN in competitiveness in the long run. If ASEAN does not aim at becoming a center for the creation and development of knowledge and technologies, it will continue to be left behind.

Second, although the deadline for full implementation of the ASEAN Free Trade Area has matured for some ASEAN members (Indonesia, Malaysia, the Philippines, Singapore, Thailand, and Vietnam) and is approaching for the rest, there is no clear sign of any fundamental institutional reform process or of the establishment of the relevant cooperative and integrative mechanisms in ASEAN. Many serious political and social problems have arisen in ASEAN member countries that cannot be resolved quickly (particularly Indonesia, Myanmar, the Philippines, and Thailand). The governments of these countries have to focus their efforts on dealing with these problems rather than on regional integration and links with other countries. This encourages the centrifugal effect and slows the integration process.

Third, the attitude of Japan and the United States toward ASEAN development and China's strategic response to the region have not been clear. China is set to realize its "going South" strategy. This has also strengthened the centrifugal trend in the region.

At the same time, a strong ASEAN is the best guarantee that ASEAN as a whole and each member country will reap the benefits of cooperating together to compete with the world, but especially with China. In the long term, each ASEAN country will gain the most through cohesion in forming the best division of labor within the region. Besides accelerating the reform process and creating closer bonds, ASEAN should seek to establish a new division of labor in the region based on the principles of the supply chain. Under present conditions, this is the best way to form a movement toward economic integration and improve competitiveness of ASEAN products internationally and regionally. This will enhance ASEAN's bargaining power relative to partners outside the region and create more consensus within the region.

Problems for Late-Entry Countries in East Asia

Cambodia, Lao PDR, Myanmar, and Vietnam are the four late-entry countries that are ASEAN members. In terms of the prospects for integration in East Asia, this group has two characteristics. First, the relative abilities and level of development of these countries are weak. Second, these countries are still dismantling internal economic relationships that are backward. It is extremely difficult, even impossible, for these countries to enter the regional system for the division of labor as promising and equal members. Clearly, these economies face obstacles in improving their status by themselves.[6]

These four countries should accelerate their market reforms (especially Lao PDR and Myanmar) and increase their participation in regional integration. This will require determination in the adoption of strategies and in decisive practical action internally in each country. These countries must also be given strong and steady support and encouragement from outside. All should aim at accelerating market reform and integrating with the regional economy. In East Asia's specific development context, both tasks are important, but cannot be achieved simultaneously. A breakthrough approach is required to position these economies properly for reform and integration. China and Vietnam offer good examples of how to conduct market reforms. The efforts of Cambodia to become a member of the World Trade Organization despite the difficulties show how decisive practical action might be undertaken.

The pressure exerted by the commitment of the late-entry economies to integration will be a powerful motivating force for internal economic reform. Meanwhile, the region's development programs (for example, the implementation of the ASEAN economic corridors) that include the participation of these economies will help create within them the foundations for more rapid growth.

Vietnam

For Vietnam and for several other ASEAN members, a strong ASEAN is extremely important in helping to consolidate the foundations for comprehensive regional integration and integration within the global economy. Vietnam needs to have a specific partnership strategy based on a clear identification of the ideological, economic, political, and social benefits it seeks through ASEAN and elsewhere. Recent progress in improving the country's relationships with the United States and other Western economies needs to be accelerated, because these relationships bring substantial short- and long-term benefits.

Vietnam should assign priority to the process of ASEAN integration. Once strategic partners have been chosen, this process will become a way for Vietnam to increase its international appeal for investment and to enlarge its markets to improve its competitiveness.

Vietnam should take a leading role in restructuring the ASEAN system for the division of labor according to the supply chain principle.

Finally, Cambodia, Lao PDR, Myanmar, and Vietnam individually and ASEAN as an association of countries should assist in formulating an effective economic development strategy for the whole bloc. The successful implementation of a good strategy will assist ASEAN and Vietnam in achieving a significant breakthrough in institutional reform and product competitiveness.

Notes

1. The black hole image is used here to describe China's role as a development center with an especially strong input pull. China represents great opportunities, but it may also come to represent a development vacuum for rivals.

2. This North-South relationship may become more serious if China's growth model changes because of the impact of the appreciation of the yuan.

3. Hu Angang (2003) divides China into four major regions. These "four worlds in one China" show extreme differences in income and development. The per capita income in the highest-income region is similar to that in high-income countries, while

the per capita income in the lowest-income region is between 9 and 12 times less than the corresponding figure in the highest-income region and similar to that in low-income countries.

4. Except for Asia-Pacific Economic Cooperation, the United States has not been represented within East Asian blocs aiming at economic integration. However, the big role that the United States is playing in the development of East Asia suggests that East Asian economic integration will not be successful if the United States takes no part. The United States is a key player in determining the prospects of the process.

5. Only Singapore has reached the income standard of a developed country. Although its development level and gross domestic product per capita are rather high, Singapore's strength and size are small according to most parameters. The biggest ASEAN country is Indonesia, with some 230 million people. Its development level is low, and it has a long history of economic, political, and social instability. Neither country has the capability to lead ASEAN integration and development. Malaysia and Thailand have set themselves the goal of becoming developed countries by 2020.

6. It is interesting to compare the prospects of Cambodia, Lao PDR, Myanmar, and Vietnam with those of the less-developed areas in southwestern China. Even these poorer areas of China are larger and have more people than the four ASEAN members. Moreover, the Chinese government clearly would support the efforts of these areas to establish links with the more well developed areas in eastern China and with other economies. Cambodia, Lao PDR, Myanmar, and Vietnam do not have such advantages.

References

ADB (Asian Development Bank). 2002. "Study on Monetary and Financial Co-operation in East Asia (Summary Report)." Preliminary report, May, Regional Economic Monitoring Unit for the Kobe Research Project Asian Development Bank, Manila. http://www.mof.go.jp/jouhou/kokkin/tyousa/tyou056.pdf.

Hu Angang. 2002. "The Free Trade Agreement Policy for North-East Asia Countries and ASEAN: A View Point from China." Paper presented at the 16th International Symposium, "Co-Design for a New East Asia after the Crisis," Economic Research Center, Graduate School of Economics, and Alumni Foundation of School of Economics, Nogoya University, Nagoya, Japan, February.

———. 2003. *China: The Big Strategies* [in Vietnamese]. Hanoi: Press Publishing House.

McKinsey and Company. 2003. *ASEAN Competitiveness Study, Final Report.* Jakarta: Secretariat, Association of Southeast Asian Nations.

Naisbitt, John, and Patricia Aburdene. 1991. *Megatrends 2000: New Directions for Tomorrow.* New York: Avon Books.

Thayer, Carlyle A. 2005. "The Region's Geopolitical Picture Is Changing: Proposals for Vietnam." Paper presented at the Second High-Level Roundtable Meeting, "Assistance for the 20-Year Review of Doi Moi," Hanoi, June 30–July 1.

Tran Dinh Thien. 2005. *ASEAN Economic Integration: Problems and Prospects* [in Vietnamese]. Hanoi: World Publishing House.

Tran Quoc Hung. 2004. "Coexistence or Competition." *Saigon Economic Times,* November 4.

Tran Van Tho. 2005. "The Pattern of Trade Specialization and Economic Integration in East Asia: Problems of Late Countries." Working paper, March, International Collaboration Projects 2005, Economic and Social Research Institute, Cabinet Office, Government of Japan, Tokyo.

Vo Dai Luoc, Do Hoai Nam, and Nueuyen Xuan Thang, eds. 2004. *Towards East Asian Economic Community.* Hanoi: World Publishing House.

World Bank. 1993. *The East Asian Miracle: Economic Growth and Public Policy.* World Bank Policy Research Reports. New York: Oxford University Press.

———. 1997. *World Development Report 1997: The State in a Changing World.* New York: Oxford University Press.

———. 1998. *East Asia: The Road to Recovery.* Washington, DC: World Bank.

CHAPTER 8

Asia's Challenges

TOMMY KOH

Among the serious obstacles Asia is currently facing are corruption, growing social inequities, and environmental neglect and mismanagement.

I am optimistic about Asia's prospects in this century. I believe that, economically, many countries in Asia will follow Japan's lead and catch up to the West. My ambition for Asia, however, extends beyond economics. My ambition is for Asian countries to achieve comprehensive modernization in this century. My dream is that, one day, Asia will be admired by the rest of the world not only for its prosperity and modern infrastructure, its competitive manufacturing and services industries, but also for its good governance, social equity, cohesive families, cultural achievements, care for the environment, and quality of life. With the exception of Japan, Asia is far from the ideal. In this essay, I wish to discuss three of Asia's challenges: corruption, social equity, and environmental neglect and mismanagement.

Corruption

The most respected annual survey of corruption in the world is carried out by the Berlin-based nongovernmental organization, Transparency International. Transparency International publishes an annual index of countries ranked from the least to the most corrupt. The index is a composite index drawing on 16 surveys from

10 independent institutions that gather the opinions of business people and country analysts. The index defines corruption as the abuse of public office for private gain. The scores range from 10 for the squeaky clean to 0 for the highly corrupt. Transparency International uses the score of 5.0 as the borderline number to distinguish countries that do and those that do not have a serious corruption problem.

The 2005 Corruption Perceptions Index of Transparency International ranks 159 countries (Transparency International 2005).[1] The three least corrupt Asian economies are Singapore, with a score of 9.4 and ranking fifth overall, Hong Kong (China), with a score of 8.3 and ranking 15th, and Japan, with a score of 7.3 and ranking 21st.

Other Asian economies that scored above 5.0 are Taiwan (China), ranking 32nd with a score of 5.9, Malaysia, ranking 39th with a score of 5.1, and the Republic of Korea, ranking 40th with a score of 5.0, which is on the borderline. All the other Asian countries have scores below 5. An Asian country is tied with Chad for the dubious honor of ranking as the most corrupt country in the index. Clearly, corruption is a serious and pervasive problem in Asia.

I hold a dogmatic view of corruption. I think corruption is an evil. Corruption distorts economic decisions. It leads to injustice. Corruption undermines the integrity of public institutions. Asian leaders and thinkers should be united in condemning and combating corruption. They should work with international organizations such as the World Bank and nongovernmental organizations such as Transparency International in increasing transparency, accountability, and integrity and in reducing the evils of corruption, collusion, and cronyism.

I am encouraged by the fact that the president of China, Hu Jintao, the president of Indonesia, Susilo Bambang Yudhoyono, the prime minister of Malaysia, Abdullah Badawi, and the new leadership of Vietnam have all made fighting corruption a major priority of their administrations. It is also encouraging that Asian media and nongovernmental organizations have become more vigilant and vocal in exposing corruption in their respective countries. Efforts should be made to enlist the Asian private sector as a stakeholder in the anticorruption campaign. I am personally very pleased that the president of the World Bank, Paul Wolfowitz, has made fighting corruption an important priority on the Bank's agenda and that the Bank is implementing a new system to minimize the risk of corruption in World Bank–funded projects.

Social Equity

In 1993, the World Bank published a report, *The East Asian Miracle*, that caught the world's attention. The report stated that East Asia had grown more rapidly and for a more sustained period than any other region of the world. The report also concluded that the East Asian economic model seemed to combine growth with equity. East Asia was not only growing more rapidly; it was also more equitable than Africa, Latin America, and the Middle East. Only 13 years after that report, the situation in Asia has changed radically. Asia has become more prosperous, but more unequal. Let us take a look at the facts.

I will use Table 2.8, "Distribution of income or consumption," in *World Development Indicators 2006* (World Bank 2006).[2] The table shows the Gini index. A Gini index of 0 represents perfect income equality, whereas a Gini index of 100 represents perfect income inequality. In real life, there are no countries with a Gini index of either 0 or 100.

The United States is usually regarded as a paradigm of a robust capitalist society with great prosperity, but also a big social divide. What is the Gini index of the United States? It is 40.8. I would like to use Japan as an example of an Asian country that is modern, prosperous, and socially equitable. Japan's index is 24.9. Japan's Gini index is very similar to the index in the Scandinavian countries: Denmark at 24.7, Finland at 26.9, Norway at 25.8, and Sweden at 25.0.

Are there any Asian countries that are as equitable as or more equitable than Japan? There are none. This is a surprising finding given that several Asian countries, such as China, Laos, and Vietnam, are ruled by communist parties and were, at least until recently, poor but relatively equitable.

Are there any Asian countries that are more unequal than the United States? The intuitive answer should be no, but the correct answer is yes. The following Asian economies have a Gini index higher than that of the United States: China at 44.7, Hong Kong (China) at 43.4, Malaysia at 49.2, Papua New Guinea at 50.9, the Philippines at 46.1, Singapore at 42.5, and Thailand at 42.0.

The table also shows income disparities between income quintiles (20 percent shares of the population according to income) in each economy. Let us take a deeper look at the disparity between the top income quintiles (top 20 percent according to income) and the bottom income quintiles (bottom 20 percent) in the various Asian economies. In

Japan, the top quintile accounts for 35.7 percent of gross domestic product. The comparable figure is 50 percent of gross domestic product for China, 50.7 percent for Hong Kong (China), 54.3 percent for Malaysia, 52.3 percent for the Philippines, 49.0 percent for Singapore, and 49.0 percent for Thailand. What about the bottom quintile? In Japan, the bottom quintile accounts for 10.6 percent of gross domestic product. The comparable figure is 4.7 percent of gross domestic product for China, 5.3 percent for Hong Kong (China), 4.4 percent for Malaysia, 5.4 percent for the Philippines, 5.0 percent for Singapore, and 6.3 percent for Thailand.

Asian thinkers and leaders will be surprised to learn that their economies have become more inequitable than the United States. What has brought about this change? What has happened to the East Asian economic model of growth with equity? How might Asia reinvent its economic model so that it will continue to spur high growth and reward achievement, but, at the same time, ensure that prosperity is more equitably distributed?

There are probably many reasons for the trend of the last decade. Asia has become more prosperous, and this has benefited the top income quintile in a disproportionate way. Asian countries have, generally speaking, brought the tax burden down to approximately half the tax burden in Europe, Japan, and the United States. This has also benefited the top quintile. Asians prefer self-reliance and family support rather than a state-funded welfare system, such as those in Europe and the United States. The bottom quintile in Asia has therefore not benefited as much as the bottom quintile in Europe, Japan, or the United States because there is less transfer of wealth from the top to the bottom through the welfare system. Finally, globalization and the competition for talent have raised the wages of the top quintile, whereas the bottom quintile remains stuck in a developing economy. In places like Hong Kong (China) and Singapore, senior executives are paid salaries comparable to the salaries of executives in London and New York, but with half the tax burden. As the same time, consolidation, restructuring, and outsourcing have increased job insecurity and suppressed the wages of the bottom two quintiles in the Asian economies. A globalized world has become, for many people, a more unjust world.

Ironically, the most emotional debate about the growing inequality has taken place in Asia's most equal country, Japan. Income inequality has been rising in Japan since the early 1980s. This is probably due to Japan's rapidly aging population. Nevertheless, Japan's left and right political wings have united in blaming the growing income gap on globalization and on Prime Minister Koizumi's structural reforms and deregulation. In China, a similar debate is taking place. Speaking recently at a discussion on income distribution, President Hu Jintao said that salaries should be market oriented, but that the nation must also focus on fairness. The Labor-Wage Institute, an interdisciplinary research group affiliated with the Chinese Ministry of Labor and Social Security, has suggested capping the salaries of employees in monopoly industries such as electricity, telecommunications, finance, insurance, tobacco, and so on. In Singapore, the issue was highlighted in the 2006 general elections and in a report published recently by the Department of Statistics showing that all households in Singapore, except those in the bottom income quintile, have benefited from the expanding prosperity. The Singapore government has recently introduced a number of measures to help the bottom quintile of the population. In this respect, Singapore serves as an interesting laboratory for the rest of Asia.

It is clear that the issue of growing social inequality should be on the Asian agenda. The challenge is to learn to tweak the economic model so that the social divide will be narrowed and prosperity will be distributed in a more equitable manner without dampening the incentive to work and the motivation to achieve, without raising taxes, and without establishing a welfare system that breeds an entitlement mentality. Can this be done? I do not know, but I hope we will try to reinvent the East Asian economic model of growth with equity.

The Environment

The countries of Asia, with the exception of only a few such as Japan, have done a very poor job in reconciling development and the environment and in managing and using the environment and natural resources. China and India, the two rising giants of Asia, are also two of the most polluted countries in the world. Most of Asia's towns and cities have been ruined by poor planning and mismanagement. Few Asian cities have made it to the list of the world's most livable cities.

What do I consider Asia's worst environmental problems? They are air pollution; contaminated water; lack of modern sanitation; destruction of forests, mangroves, and other natural habitats and the attendant loss of biodiversity; and unlivable cities.

Air pollution is a major problem in Asia. The air quality in most of Asia's major cities is unhealthy. According to a World Bank–Asian

Development Bank study of air pollution in 20 major Asian cities between 2000 and 2003, Delhi is the most polluted city in Asia. Chongqing, Jakarta, Kolkata, and Mumbai are not far behind. Air pollution affects the health of a city's residents. In Delhi, for example, one school child in every ten suffers from asthma. The number of premature deaths due to air pollution in Indian cities is estimated to have increased by 30 percent between 1992 and 1995.

Waste disposal is another major problem in urban areas in Asia. Most Asian cities are unable to cope with the waste they generate. In the Philippines, only 40 percent of solid waste is collected. The rest is dumped in open spaces and waterways. Cities in South Asia are literally drowning in their own waste. In China, only 20 percent of the 168 million tons of solid waste generated each year is properly disposed of. One deleterious consequence of the dumping of waste in waterways, rivers, lakes, and open spaces is that the waste contaminates the sources of drinking water for millions of people.

Water is essential to life. Sadly, only a minority of Asians have access to potable water. The recent spillage of chemicals into the Songhua River in China resulted in the closure of the water system in the city of Harbin for four days. This caused headline news around the world. Countries in Asia should regard the incident as a wake-up call. According to China's State Environment Protection Agency, 70 percent of the water in five of China's seven major river systems was found to be unsuitable for human contact, let alone for consumption. The situation in the other countries in Asia is as bad. We should make it our collective priority in Asia to afford to all our citizens, rich and poor alike, access to safe drinking water as a basic human right.

Asia has, in general, done a very poor job in looking after our forests, mangroves, and other natural habitats. One consequence has been the loss of biodiversity. There are other negative consequences. When parts of Asia were struck by the tsunami on December 24, 2004, we discovered that beaches with mangroves were more well protected from the ferocity of the tsunami than other areas from which mangroves had been cleared for development. Disastrous floods in China and mudslides in Indonesia were probably caused, at least in part, by deforestation. China is, however, making a serious effort to plant trees. In 2005, nearly 560 million people participated in a campaign to plant 2.5 billion trees.

I would like to believe that Asians have awakened to the serious environmental crisis in which we live, but I am not sure. In spite of our economic progress, most Asians still do not have access to safe drinking water, modern sanitation, and clean air. We have polluted our air, contaminated our rivers and seas, and poisoned the land that gives us sustenance. We have not cared for our environment, and we have used our natural resources in an unsustainable manner. We live in towns and cities that have lost their beauty, heritage, and livability. China and India are two of the world's largest emitters of carbon. As Asia becomes a major stakeholder in the world economy, it must also accept its correlative duty to behave as a good global citizen. The future of the human civilization is in peril if we do not succeed in reconciling the human enterprise and the natural world. That future will depend to an increasing extent on Asia's behavior.

Conclusion

I am reasonably confident that, by the middle of this century, Asia will have caught up with the West economically. My dream is that Asia will be admired by the world not only for our prosperity and modernity, but also for our soft power. Three of the obstacles that we have to overcome in order to achieve my dream are corruption, growing social inequity, and environmental neglect. We have to solve these and other shortcomings if we want the West to treat us as equals and if we want the rest of the non-Western world to look to Asia for inspiration.

Notes

1. To access the table, go to http://ww1.transparency.org/cpi/2005/cpi2005.sources.en.html#cpi.

2. To access the table, go to http://devdata.worldbank.org/wdi2006/contents/Tables2.htm. There, at "2.8," click on "Distribution of income or consumption." (The table was accessed in 2006.)

References

Transparency International. 2005. "Table 1: TI 2005 Corruption Perceptions Index." Transparency International, Berlin. http://ww1.transparency.org/cpi/2005/cpi2005.sources.en.html#cpi.
World Bank. 1993. *The East Asian Miracle: Economic Growth and Public Policy*. World Bank Policy Research Reports. New York: Oxford University Press.
———. 2006. *World Development Indicators 2006*. Washington, DC: World Bank. http://devdata.worldbank.org/wdi2006/contents/cover.htm.

CHAPTER 9

Toward an Integrated, Poverty-Free, and Peaceful East Asia

HARUHIKO KURODA

Regional cooperation and integration are key instruments if East Asia is to advance toward realizing the vision of peace, prosperity, and equity.

As one of the world's most rapidly growing regions, East Asia has increasingly become a major force in the world economy. However, the potential of East Asia has not been fully realized. East Asian markets are still fragmented. The need to eliminate systemic poverty remains the single most urgent challenge for many East Asian developing countries. Development gaps are widening across some countries and within some parts of countries. I believe that regional cooperation and integration in East Asia are desirable and necessary to maximize the region's potential and achieve a vision of an integrated, poverty-free, and peaceful East Asia.

This vision has been articulated by the leaders of East Asia on many occasions. In the Joint Statement on East Asia Cooperation, the leaders of the Association of Southeast Asian Nations, plus China, the Republic of Korea, and Japan (ASEAN+3), agreed, at the Manila summit in 1999, to "promote dialogue and to deepen and consolidate collective efforts with a view to advancing ... peace, stability and prosperity in East Asia and the world."[1] The ASEAN+3 Summit, in Phnom Penh, Cambodia, in November 2002, endorsed 26 concrete recommendations of the East Asia Study Group to accelerate regional integration in East Asia, address poverty reduction, narrow development disparities, and maintain peace and stability in East Asia (see Annex 1).[2] The First East Asia Summit, in Kuala Lumpur on December 14, 2005, reaffirmed the desire "of creating a peaceful environment [in East Asia] by further enhancing cooperation and strengthening the existing bonds of friendship among our countries in keeping with the principles of equality, partnership, consultation and consensus."[3] The summit underscored the need for "promoting development, financial stability, energy security, economic integration and growth, eradicating poverty and narrowing the development gap in East Asia through technology transfer and infrastructure development, capacity building, good governance and humanitarian assistance and promoting financial links, trade and investment expansion and liberalization."[4]

Regional cooperation and integration are key instruments in achieving peace, prosperity, and equity in East Asia. They help mobilize concerted efforts across East Asia to sustain economic growth, reduce poverty, and close development gaps, which, collectively, provide an economic basis for regional peace. In the following sections, I will review trends that contribute to the integration of East Asian economies. Subsequently, I will examine challenges associated with the evolution of these trends. I will then try to articulate how regional cooperation and integration may help economies in the region achieve their vision of an integrated, poverty-free, and peaceful East Asia.

East Asian Economic Integration

There are three major trends that contribute to the integration of the East Asian economies: trade, investment, and finance. One of the fundamental economic factors contributing to East Asian integration is deepening regional economic interdependence through trade and investment. Intraregional trade and investment in East Asia have risen rapidly over the last two decades. The continuous domestic trade and investment liberalization efforts undertaken by many economies, the substantial realignment of major exchange rates, particularly the yen-dollar exchange rates in the 1980s, and the remarkable technical progress achieved in information and communications technologies that has reduced communication and logistics costs have been among the most important external factors that have led to rapid increases in intraregional trade and investment flows (Kawai 2005a).

While intraregional trade in Central Asia and South Asia is still at a low level, intraregional trade in East Asia has risen rapidly over the past 25 years. It accounted for 55 percent of East Asia's total trade, including Japan, in 2004, up sharply from the 35 percent in 1980. This share is higher than the 46 percent figure for the North American Free Trade Agreement and only modestly lower than the 62 percent figure for the 15 "old" European Union countries and the 68 percent for all 25 European Union countries (see table 9.1).

TABLE 9.1 Intraregional Trade Share, 1980–2004
percent

Region	1980	1985	1990	1995	2000	2001	2002	2003	2004
East Asia 15[a]	35	37	43	52	52	52	54	55	55
Emerging East Asia 14[b]	22	28	33	39	41	41	43	44	44
ASEAN+3	30	30	29	38	37	37	38	38	39
NIE 4[c]	6	7	12	16	16	15	15	15	14
ASEAN 10[d]	18	20	19	24	25	24	24	24	24
SAARC[e]	4	3	3	4	4	4	5	6	5
Central Asia[f]	—	—	—	—	7	7	6	6	5
NAFTA[g]	34	39	38	43	49	49	48	47	46
Mercosur[h]	11	7	11	19	20	18	14	15	15
Old European Union 15[i]	61	60	66	64	62	62	63	63	62
New European Union 25[j]	61	60	67	67	67	67	68	69	68

Sources: Adapted from Kawai 2005b; based on data from IMF (2006) and the CEIC Asia Database (CEIC Data. http://www.ceicdata.com/economic.htm).
Note: Intraregional trade share is defined as: Xii / {(Xi. + X.i)/2}, where Xii is exports of region i to region i; Xi. is total exports of region i to the world; and X.i is exports of the world to region i.
— = no data are available.
a. East Asia 15 encompasses Emerging East Asia 14, plus Japan.
b. Emerging East Asia 14 encompasses ASEAN 10, plus China, Hong Kong (China), the Republic of Korea, and Taiwan (China).
c. NIE 4 are the newly industrialized economies of Hong Kong (China), the Republic of Korea, Singapore, and Taiwan (China).
d. ASEAN encompasses Brunei Darussalam, Cambodia, Indonesia, Lao People's Democratic Republic, Malaysia, Myanmar, the Philippines, Singapore, Thailand, and Vietnam.
e. SAARC is the South Asian Association for Regional Cooperation (Bangladesh, Bhutan, India, Maldives, Nepal, Pakistan, and Sri Lanka).
f. For purposes of this table, Central Asia encompasses Afghanistan, Azerbaijan, China, Kazakhstan, the Kyrgyz Republic, Mongolia, Tajikistan, and Uzbekistan.
g. NAFTA is the North American Free Trade Agreement (Canada, Mexico, and the United States).
h. Mercosur is the Southern Cone Common Market (Argentina, Brazil, Paraguay, Uruguay, and República Bolivariana de Venezuela).
i. Old European Union 15 encompasses Austria, Belgium, Denmark, Finland, France, Germany, Greece, Ireland, Italy, Luxembourg, the Netherlands, Portugal, Spain, Sweden, and the United Kingdom.
j. New European Union 25 encompasses the old European Union 15, plus Cyprus, the Czech Republic, Estonia, Hungary, Latvia, Lithuania, Malta, Poland, the Slovak Republic, and Slovenia.

The favorable macroeconomic environment and the abundant supply of well-educated low-wage labor also contributed to the expansion of inflows of foreign direct investment (FDI). Since 1980, FDI flows into East Asia have more than quadrupled, reaching 31 percent of world FDI inflows in 2004. Over the same period, East Asia's sustained dynamism fueled an increase in FDI outflows from 5 to 14 percent of world outflows. Notably, much of these flows have been intraregional, from Japan and the newly industrialized economies (NIEs), that is, Hong Kong (China), the Republic of Korea, Singapore, and Taiwan (China), to the countries of ASEAN, plus China, and from the ASEAN countries to one another and to China.

Trade and investment flows have created a virtuous cycle in East Asia. The provision of FDI in the region has been part of the strategy of multinational corporations to relocate their labor-intensive manufacturing production to lower-cost economies and to integrate these offshore production bases into a coherent network of supply chains. Hence, such FDI has generated exports of capital goods and key parts and components from the source economy to recipient economies, exports and imports of intermediate and semifinished products among the FDI-host economies, and imports of finished products to the source economy. Japan took a lead in establishing these sorts of production networks, and it was soon followed by the Asian NIEs and then by some middle-income ASEAN countries, Malaysia and Thailand for instance. Other emerging economies in East Asia—China, Indonesia, the Philippines, and, more recently, Vietnam—also participate in the networks, mainly as FDI recipients because of their different stages of industrial development.

In addition, recent years have also seen a growing number of government-led initiatives to promote free trade areas (FTAs) in East Asia and beyond (see table 9.2). ASEAN accelerated its trade cooperation initiative by advancing the deadline for the implementation of the ASEAN Free Trade Area from 2008 to 2002; the implementation of the ASEAN Free Trade Area was thus begun about six years in advance. ASEAN has established closer economic partnerships with its major trading partners, that is, Australia, China, India, Japan, Korea, and New Zealand, through a series of economic partnership agreements; one of the outcomes of these agreements has been the establishment of various FTAs involving ASEAN and these countries.[5]

ASEAN has also made important progress in regional investment cooperation. Under the ASEAN Framework Agreement on the ASEAN Investment Area, signed in Manila in October 1998, ASEAN countries

TABLE 9.2 **FTAs and Economic Partnership Agreements in East Asia, April 2006**

In effect	Under official negotiation	Under consultation or study
Asia-Pacific Trade Agreement (1976)	Singapore–Mexico (July 2000)	Japan–Australia
Lao PDR–Thailand (1991)[a]	Singapore–Canada (January 2002)	Japan–Chile
ASEAN FTA (1992)	Singapore–Chile	Japan–India
Singapore–New Zealand (January 2001)	Singapore–Pacific-3 (CER, Chile)[b][c]	Japan–Switzerland
Japan–Singapore (November 2002)	Hong Kong (China)–New Zealand (November 2000)	Japan–China–Korea, Rep. of
Singapore–Australia (2003)	Japan–Philippines (agreed in principle November 2004)	China–India
Singapore–EFTA (January 2003)[d]	Japan–Malaysia (signed December 2005)	Korea, Rep. of–Australia
Singapore–United States (January 2004)	Japan–Thailand (agreed in principle August 2005)	Korea, Rep. of–New Zealand
Singapore–Jordan (2004)	Japan–Korea, Rep. of (December 2003)	Korea, Rep. of–India
China–Hong Kong (China) (January 2004)	Japan–ASEAN (November 2005)	Korea, Rep. of–United States
China–Macao SAR (China) (January 2004)[e]	Japan–Indonesia (July 2005)	Korea, Rep. of–Mercosur[f]
Korea, Rep. of–Chile (April 2004)	China–New Zealand (December 2004)	Korea, Rep. of–China
Thailand–India (September 2004)	China–Australia (May 2005)	Singapore–Taiwan (China)
Thailand–Australia (January 2005)	Korea, Rep. of–Canada (July 2005)	ASEAN–European Union
Japan–Mexico (April 2005)	Korea, Rep. of–Mexico (early 2006)	Malaysia–India
China–ASEAN (July 2005)	Korea, Rep. of–United States	Indonesia–India
Singapore–India (August 2005)	Thailand–Bahrain (signed)	n.a.
Thailand–New Zealand (2005)	Thailand–Peru (agreed April 2004)	n.a.

continued

■ TABLE 9.2 **FTAs and Economic Partnership Agreements in East Asia, April 2006**
(continued)

In effect	Under official negotiation	Under consultation or study
Korea, Rep. of–Singapore (2006)	Thailand–United States (June 2004)	n.a.
Korea, Rep. of–EFTA (2006)[d]	Malaysia–Australia (May 2005)	n.a.
China–Chile (2006)	Malaysia–New Zealand	n.a.
Singapore–Panama (2006)	Malaysia–United States	n.a.
Korea, Rep. of–ASEAN (July 2006)	ASEAN–India (January 2004)	n.a.
	ASEAN–CER (February 2005)[c]	n.a.
	ASEAN–Australia–New Zealand	n.a.

Source: Kawai 2005b.
Note: The shaded cells indicate those arrangements within East Asia, that is, ASEAN+3, Hong Kong (China), and Taiwan (China).
n.a. = not applicable.
a. Lao People's Democratic Republic.
b. The Pacific-3 are Chile, New Zealand, and Singapore.
c. CER is the Australia and New Zealand Closer Economic Relations Trade Agreement.
d. EFTA is the European Free Trade Association (Iceland, Liechtenstein, Norway, and Switzerland).
e. Macao Special Administrative Region (China).
f. Mercosur is the Southern Cone Common Market (Argentina, Brazil, Paraguay, Uruguay, and Venezuela).

are committed to opening the manufacturing, agriculture, forestry, fisheries, and mining sectors and to granting national treatment to ASEAN investors by 2010 and to all regional investors by 2020. In Northeast Asia, Japan and Korea signed, in March 2002, the Agreement for the Liberalization, Promotion, and Protection of Investment. Under this agreement, each country extends equal treatment to investors of the other country, except in certain areas (ASEAN 2002).

Financial and macroeconomic interdependence in East Asia has also deepened as a result of market-driven financial integration, including deregulation of the financial system, the opening of financial services to foreign institutions, and the liberalization of the capital account (Kawai 2005b). Macroeconomic interdependence in East Asia has become stronger following the contagious impact of the 1997–98 Asian financial crisis, which prompted East Asian economies to realize the importance of managing financial openness and macroeconomic interdependence at the regional level through closer cooperation. As a result, various initiatives have been launched to institutionalize regional financial and macroeconomic interdependence. For example, ASEAN+3 has undertaken the Chiang Mai Initiative, an economic surveillance and policy dialogue, and initiatives for the development of local-currency bond markets (the Asian Bond Markets Initiative). These initiatives have demonstrated a commitment by the region's leaders to seek cooperative regional solutions to common economic and financial problems.

In summary, all these trends have underscored that East Asian economies have achieved strong economic interdependence, particularly through market-driven integration with global and regional economies. Expansion in trade, in direct investment, and in financial flows has created a naturally integrated economic zone in East Asia. In addition, East Asia has embarked on a series of regional initiatives to institutionalize and manage its economic interdependence (Kawai 2005b).

Challenges for East Asia

In reviewing these trends toward regional economic cooperation and integration, one should remember that East Asia is facing numerous challenges. One of the biggest challenges is the urgent need for poverty reduction and the need for social improvements in developing countries. The impressive growth of East Asia in the past three decades has been accompanied by a dramatic decline in absolute poverty. Despite the abrupt intermission caused by the 1997–98 Asian financial crisis, the share of the population living on less than US$1 a day fell from 34 to 19 percent in Asia as a whole between 1990 and 2003. There were 233 million fewer people living in extreme poverty in Asia in 2002 compared to 1990. East Asia contributed much to this progress. China accounted for 75 percent of the decline. Southeast Asia accounted for around 48 million people in the decline. China, Indonesia, Malaysia, Thailand, and Vietnam may well have already achieved, by 2005, the Millennium Development Goal of halving US$1-a-day poverty incidence by 2015.

Despite major achievements in reducing absolute poverty, systemic poverty across the region remains the single most urgent economic and social challenge. More than 620 million Asians still live on less than US$1 a day, and about 1.9 billion live on US$2 a day. A quick assessment of the incidence rate of US$2-a-day poverty in East Asian developing countries will reveal that the battle to eradicate poverty is evidently far from coming to a close. The large percentages of poor in terms of the US$2-a-day poverty line also highlight the vulnerability of those people who have escaped US$1-a-day poverty. In other words, adverse economic shocks faced by poor people who are rising out of US$1-a-day poverty could easily reverse their economic and social fortunes.[6]

Another challenge for East Asia is the widening development gap among the economies, as well as within each of the economies. East Asia is a diverse region (see table 9.3). The combined population of East Asia is about 1.5 billion people (about 40 percent of Asia's population and a quarter of the world's population), with populations ranging from 2.5 million in Mongolia to 1.3 billion in China. The total gross domestic product (GDP) of East Asia is about US$7 trillion. Three of the 10 largest economies in the world are now in East Asia (China, Japan, and Korea), but so are least developed economies such as Cambodia and the Lao People's Democratic Republic (PDR). While Hong Kong (China), Japan, Singapore, and Taiwan (China) are among the richest economies in the world, with annual per capita income in the US$20,000–US$40,000 range, countries such as Cambodia, Lao PDR, Mongolia, and Myanmar remain among the poorest, with annual per capita income of less than US$500.

Environmental degradation and communicable diseases constitute other challenges for East Asia. The region's rapid economic growth has brought tremendous benefits in terms of poverty reduction. But there are rising concerns over the adverse environmental consequences of rapid economic growth that, in some countries, threaten to undermine the economic gains. Many environmental problems are transboundary in nature, so that addressing them requires coordinated regional actions. The current environmental challenges range from dealing with serious air pollution and global climate change to management of transboundary rivers and protected areas. The region must also learn to deal with the burgeoning volumes of waste products, many of which are hazardous. Several of the most important environmental problems faced by the region, particularly the deteriorating air quality and increasing greenhouse gas emissions, have their origin in the energy sector. Energy use in many developing countries in East Asia is characterized by rapid growth and the dominant use of fossil fuels. The current pattern of energy consumption growth is becoming unsustainable from both

TABLE 9.3 **Selected Indicators for East Asian Economies**

Country	Population (millions)[a] 2004	GDP per capita (US$) 1990	GDP per capita (US$) 2003	GDP growth (%)[b] 2007	Poverty index (head-count ratio, %)[c] US$1 a day 1990	US$1 a day 2003	US$1 a day 2015	US$2 a day 1990	US$2 a day 2003	US$2 a day 2015
China	1,300	364	1,067	8.9	33.0	13.4	0.1	72.2	41.6	7.0
Indonesia	216	612	874	6.5	20.5	6.5	0.4	70.9	50.5	22.6
Philippines	84	921	1,035	5.0	19.7	14.1	0.5	54.9	44.4	26.8
Vietnam	82	226	470	7.5	50.7	9.7	0.1	87.4	54.2	18.5
Thailand	64	1,427	2,227	6.0	10.1	0.7	0.0	43.3	27.8	8.5
Malaysia	26	2,498	4,011	5.8	0.6	0.2	0.0	11.4	9.0	0.2
Cambodia	14	—	314	4.7	46.0	33.8	10.6	84.3	77.3	51.9
Lao PDR	6	227	359	5.8	52.7	28.8	2.4	91.1	74.4	47.4
Mongolia	3	608	424	7.5	28.0	18.9	5.7	70.8	63.9	35.4

Sources: ADB 2005a, 2005b; World Bank 2006.
Note: — = no data are available.
a. Mid-year population.
b. Projections of the Asian Development Bank.
c. For 2015 data, the projections are based on benchmark growth and more equitable distribution.

environmental and energy-security perspectives. By 2020, greenhouse gas emissions in Asia are projected to account for 32 percent of global emissions from the energy sector, much of this coming from East Asia. The threat to the global environment needs to be addressed at both the national and the regional levels. The seriousness of the situation is underlined by the fact that, following on current trends, some large countries in the region seem certain to rely mainly on indigenous coal in the future (see Annex 2).

Greater integration, crossborder mobility, and migration facilitate human contacts and loosen social restrictions, but they thereby play an important role in the spread of communicable diseases. It is estimated that, by 2010, Asia as a whole will overtake Africa in the number of HIV/AIDS cases. Apart from being a great human tragedy for the patients and their families, the continuing spread of HIV/AIDS also entails significant economic losses, particularly for developing economies of East Asia in which labor-intensive industries still have a critical part in economic development. The pandemic threatens to reverse hard-earned gains in poverty reduction in the region. Severe acute respiratory syndrome (SARS), which first appeared in East Asia in 2003, was quickly recognized as a global threat. SARS was barely contained when the first series of H5N1 avian influenza outbreaks were observed in the region. If the influenza virus mutates or combines with existing human influenza viruses, it may acquire the capacity to spread more easily among humans, resulting in a human influenza pandemic. The World Health Organization estimates that 2 million to 7 million people could die in an influenza pandemic worldwide. In November 2005, the Food and Agriculture Organization of the United Nations estimated the total cost of avian influenza outbreaks at US$10 billion. Loss of poultry due to disease and culling has already pushed many rural households into poverty. If a pandemic starts, it would have the potential to halt economic growth in East Asia (see Annex 2).

The Road Ahead

What should East Asia do to respond to these challenges? One of the major challenges to be overcome in combating systemic poverty in the region is the lack of high-quality infrastructure to support economic activity and trade and contribute to job creation. In most developing countries in the region, inadequate and poor-quality power supplies, inefficient transport systems, insufficiently connected or maintained roads, inadequate and aging railroad networks, badly equipped and congested ports and airports, unreliable communications systems, and poor urban infrastructure raise transaction and logistics costs, curtail productivity, and often render investment unviable (ADB 2006a). However, infrastructure investment requires enormous amounts of financial and technical resources. Infrastructure development in East Asia alone will need approximately US$200 billion annually over the next five years, a level of investment far beyond the fiscal capacity of national governments (ADB, JBIC, and World Bank 2005). The private sector has been reluctant to support infrastructure projects because of the large, lumpy investments, long gestation periods, and high risks involved.

To mobilize the necessary resources, countries will have to work together to strengthen regional capital markets in East Asia. It is ironic that East Asia's massive needs for infrastructure investment go unmet, while excess savings find their way to global capital markets. One reason is that East Asian savings are not being efficiently intermediated by the regionwide financial system. It is difficult for intermediaries and savers to find the right investment opportunities in the region. Financial market infrastructure is underdeveloped in many respects, and investor concerns include inefficient pricing and low liquidity. Perceived weaknesses in legal transparency and in regulatory frameworks may also be responsible for discouraging active investment. These issues obviously need to be resolved. By ensuring that more of East Asia's savings remain invested in the region, East Asia might also make a significant contribution to correcting global payment imbalances.

Bilateral or multilateral FTAs often produce desirable outcomes by inducing the participating economies to implement the needed structural reforms. However, there is a risk that the current proliferation of FTAs might sustain market fragmentation in markets in East Asia rather than bringing markets together into a single market. Free trade agreements vary widely in scope, rules, and participation and create an "Asian noodle bowl" effect. The administrative costs associated with managing various types of rules of origin in overlapping FTAs are prohibitively high, particularly for small- and medium-sized trade-oriented firms. If excessively burdensome, rules of this kind can limit rather than promote freer trade and investment. The proliferation of FTAs presents challenges for harmonization and broader integration. Thus, it is important to bring greater coherence to the growing number of overlapping regional trade agreements in East Asia so that they do not become a stumbling block to regional and global trade expansion.

To avoid the noodle bowl effect and maximize the potential benefits of FTAs, East Asia has to draft a clear road map to establish a regionwide FTA (ASEAN 2002). The existing efforts in East Asia such as the ASEAN Free Trade Area and various FTAs between ASEAN and Northeast Asian countries could pave the way for the establishment of an East Asia FTA. Such an FTA should cover not only trade in goods, but also trade in services, investment, and coordination in other regulatory and standards areas. It is important to study the benefits, challenges, and implications of an integrated and comprehensive FTA in East Asia and explore the appropriate architecture.

East Asian economies should also encourage investment among themselves and dismantle barriers to investment. The importance of FDI for the economic development of developing countries is well established. In most cases, investment (including FDI) has a positive impact on direct poverty reduction (Mirza 2002). Developing countries with larger flows of investment generally demonstrate greater success in economic growth and poverty reduction. Economies such as China and Southeast Asian countries that have received most of the FDI over the last two decades accounted for the bulk of the decline in extreme poverty in Asia during 1990–2002. At the ASEAN+3 Summit in November 1999, the ASEAN+3 leaders agreed to strengthen efforts in accelerating investment. The best strategy to increase investment flows is to create an attractive investment climate. This includes establishing sound macroeconomic fundamentals, removing restrictions on investment, providing adequate industrial and social infrastructure, offering tax and other incentives, and putting in place transparent and nondiscriminatory legal frameworks with well-functioning enforcement capabilities.

The high levels of intraregional trade in East Asia, which are comparable to those in the European Union before the 1992 Maastricht Treaty, indicate that even small intraregional exchange rate misalignments may disturb trade and investment flows and build difficulties for regional economies. Indeed, the lack of coordination of exchange rate mechanisms among East Asian economies exacerbated the impact of the 1997–98 Asian financial crisis. East Asian economies are now aware of the critical role of exchange rates for regional financial stability, which is a basis for sustained economic growth, development, and poverty reduction. This underscores the need for intraregional exchange rate policy coordination in the years to come (Kuroda 2006). An important step is to bring greater intraregional exchange rate stability and to help rebalance sources of growth away from the external sector into domestic demand. Given the growing payment imbalances, East Asia needs to see exchange rates that are flexible toward the rest of the world, but relatively stable within the region. There are some encouraging signs thus far. China has started to adjust the renminbi exchange rate and move to greater exchange rate flexibility. This is encouraging given that Korea, Singapore, and Thailand have adopted a de facto or de jure managed floating exchange rate regime with reference to a basket of major currencies (Kawai 2006).

One option for facilitating greater exchange rate policy coordination across countries in the region might be to introduce an Asian currency unit. The unit—a weighted basket of the national currencies of Asia—might facilitate the monitoring of both the collective movement of Asian currencies against major external currencies, such as the U.S. dollar and the euro, and the individual movement of each component currency against the regional average of the unit. The unit might also promote the development of an Asian multicurrency bond market and a deepening of capital markets that would help reduce exposure to external shocks (Kuroda 2006).

Within the ASEAN+3 finance ministers process, there have been recent advances toward doubling the size of the existing swaps under the Chiang Mai Initiative, integrating the initiative with the economic surveillance mechanism, and increasing the percentage of funds that can be disbursed when required. The finance ministers have also agreed on a collective decision-making formula for the mobilization of the Chiang Mai Initiative, the first step toward multilateralization. Additional steps might be taken to expand the initiative to a more solid, multilateral regional financing facility and to make the ASEAN+3 economic surveillance mechanism more effective, for example, by putting it in line with the best practices of the G-7 or the Organisation for Economic Co-operation and Development's Working Party 3 or Economic Policy Committee. It might also be useful for Central Bank governors to join the finance ministers process in fostering effective economic surveillance and policy dialogue.

Significant efforts are needed to address the development gaps in East Asia, which are widening because of the disparities in the level of economic development among regional economies. Intraregional trade and investment might be a propelling force to close these gaps.

The establishment of a generalized system of preferences status and of preferential treatment for the least developed countries would substantially improve the competitiveness of exports from these countries. A good example of such an initiative is the ASEAN Integration System of Preferences, whereby, since January 1, 2002, preferential tariffs of between 0 and 5 percent may be offered to the less developed members (Cambodia, Lao PDR, Myanmar, and Vietnam) by the more developed members on a voluntary and bilateral basis. The scheme is being implemented through products proposed by the less developed members. Indonesia, Malaysia, the Philippines, and Thailand have issued legal enactments to realize the scheme.[7]

Environmental issues are fundamental to East Asia's economic future. Coordinating the crossborder dimensions of environmental issues is a key area as part of efforts to provide regional public goods. Major endeavors include coordinating environmental initiatives among national and subregional organizations; harmonizing standards, regulations, and laws; addressing air pollution, land degradation, and global climate change; and widening the range of financing sources for environmental investments (see Annex 2).

The fight against communicable diseases should be multipronged. Crucial elements include generating awareness, improving coordination among stakeholders, strengthening monitoring capacity, and developing a flexible regional response capacity. There is a growing recognition of the need to strengthen the commitment of stakeholders, build capacity at the national and regional levels, and undertake targeted programs for the benefit of sectors and the poor. With the increasing permeability of international boundaries, the role of regional cooperation in regional public goods to fight the spread of communicable diseases will remain critical (see Annex 2).

Conclusion

The emergence of an integrated East Asia is inevitable and necessary. Strong economic interdependence—particularly through the market-driven expansion of trade, investment, and financial flows—has created a "naturally" integrated economic zone in East Asia. Increasing economic interdependence was one of the main reasons for the contagious impact of the 1997–98 Asian financial crisis. Economic interdependence and the crisis experience have led East Asian economies to intensify their collective efforts to manage this growing economic interdependence. Governments have started to embark on various regional initiatives to promote cooperation in infrastructure, trade and investment, money and finance, and other crossborder issues.

Poverty reduction remains a major developmental challenge for many developing countries in East Asia. Development gaps are also imposing major hurdles to the greater integration of East Asia. Within this context, East Asia should focus on economic cooperation and integration, while ensuring that the region's integration will be economically sustainable, socially inclusive, and environmentally sound. Broadbased support for this process will certainly help realize the vision of an integrated, poverty-free, and peaceful East Asia.

ANNEX 1

Recommendations of the East Asia Study Group
(2002)

Short-Term Measures
(17 concrete measures)

- Form an East Asia business council
- Establish generalized system of preferences status and preferential treatment for the least developed countries
- Foster an attractive investment environment for increased foreign direct investment
- Establish an East Asian investment information network
- Develop resources and infrastructure jointly for growth areas and expand financial resources for development with the active participation of the private sector
- Provide assistance and cooperation in four priority areas: infrastructure, information technology, human resources development, and ASEAN regional economic integration
- Cooperate through technology transfers and joint technology development
- Develop information technology jointly to build telecommunications infrastructure and to provide greater access to the Internet
- Build a network of East Asian think tanks
- Establish an East Asia Forum
- Implement a comprehensive human resources development program for East Asia
- Establish poverty alleviation programs
- Take concerted steps to provide access to primary health care for the people
- Strengthen mechanisms for cooperation on nontraditional security issues

- Work together with cultural and educational institutions to promote a strong sense of identity and an East Asian consciousness
- Promote networking and exchanges of experts in the conservation of the arts, artifacts, and cultural heritage of East Asian countries
- Promote East Asian studies in the region

Medium-Term and Long-Term Measures and Those That Require Further Studies
(9 concrete measures)

- Form an East Asian Free Trade Area
- Promote investment by small and medium enterprises
- Establish an East Asia investment area by expanding the ASEAN investment area
- Establish a regional financing facility
- Pursue a more closely coordinated regional exchange rate mechanism
- Pursue the evolution of the ASEAN+3 Summit into an East Asian Summit
- Promote closer regional marine environmental cooperation for the entire region
- Build a framework for energy policies and strategies and action plans
- Work closely with nongovernmental organizations in policy consultation and coordination to encourage civic participation and state–civil society partnerships in tackling social problems

Source: ASEAN 2002, 4.

ANNEX 2

Selected Regional Public Goods Supported by the Asian Development Bank

The provision of regional public goods is a key element of the approach of the Asian Development Bank (ADB) to regional cooperation and integration. The ADB promotes regional public goods by supporting a variety of actions. The key areas of ADB's focus are the environment, clean energy and energy efficiency, natural disaster responses, communicable disease, governance and anticorruption, and human trafficking. The next few paragraphs describe the challenges faced, the progress made, and the experience gained in promoting regional public goods by the ADB and other development partners in the region.

Environment

1. Asia's rapid economic growth has brought tremendous benefits to the region, but there is rising concern over its adverse environmental consequences, which threaten to undermine the economic gains the region has achieved. Many environmental problems are transboundary in nature, and addressing them effectively requires coordinated regional actions. The current challenges range from dealing with serious air pollution and global climate change to managing transboundary rivers and protected areas. The region must also learn to deal with the burgeoning volumes of waste products, many of which are hazardous.
2. These issues are fundamental to the region's economic future, as well as the health and safety of its people. Along with other donors, the ADB is actively seeking to address these concerns. Coordinating the crossborder dimensions of the environment is a key area of ADB's support for providing regional public goods, as there are few

regional frameworks for managing the environment. Major areas include coordinating environmental initiatives among national and subregional organizations; harmonizing standards, regulations, and laws, sometimes in conjunction with trade integration; addressing air pollution, land degradation, and global climate change; and widening the range of financing sources for environmental investments. Among its initiatives, the ADB has played a leading role in helping the East Asian countries find appropriate measures to address the ongoing problem of dust- and sandstorms that arises primarily from the overuse of fragile drylands in western China and Mongolia. The ADB also played a key role in the ASEAN Agreement on Transboundary Haze Pollution (June 2002), which provides a legal framework to facilitate regional cooperation in addressing the crossborder impacts of haze pollution. In partnership with the United Nations Economic and Social Commission for Asia and the Pacific, the United Nations Environment Programme, and the United Nations Convention to Combat Desertification, the ADB has worked with the governments of China, Japan, Korea, and Mongolia to develop an action plan and design a regional network for the prediction and monitoring of major storm events. As host to the secretariat of the Clean Air Initiative for Asian Cities, the ADB also supports work on a range of other national and regional air pollution concerns.

3. In the Greater Mekong Subregion (GMS),[8] the ADB is working with governments and a number of international and local partners to create a new approach to protecting and managing natural areas. Furthermore, the Biodiversity Corridors Initiative in the GMS is piecing together a network of transboundary protected areas linked with measures to manage adjacent forests, wetlands, and other valuable ecosystems sustainably. Among other benefits, this will preserve the economic value of ecological services provided by these areas, such as the protection of water supplies, while also maintaining the basis for rapidly expanding ecotourism.

4. The ADB is also beginning to work more closely with governments of the region on policies and practices for improved waste management, including issues related to trade in recyclable and reusable products. There is expanding demand for investments to improve municipal solid waste management services, and the ADB will bring to its assistance programs fresh perspectives and knowl-

edge on international best practices on the minimization of waste generation, reuse, and recycling, as well as innovative financing, such as the use of global carbon markets to fund methane gas capture from landfills.
5. With proper attention to both the domestic and the regional environmental concerns arising from Asia's rapid economic growth, the region's development can move forward in an environmentally sustainable manner. This will incur new costs and will not be an easy adjustment, but both the governments and the people of the region increasingly recognize the importance of establishing environmental quality as an integral part of Asia's new prosperity.

Clean Energy and Energy Efficiency

6. A major portion of the environmental problems faced by the region, particularly the deteriorating air quality and increasing greenhouse gas emissions, have their origin in the energy sector. Energy use in Asia is characterized by rapid growth and the dominant use of fossil fuels. The current pattern of energy sector growth is becoming unsustainable from both environmental and security perspectives. By 2020, greenhouse gas emissions in the region are projected to account for 32 percent of global emissions from the energy sector. The threat to the global environment emerging from energy sector growth in the region needs to be addressed at both the national and regional levels. The seriousness of the situation is underlined by the fact that some large countries in the region are likely to rely mainly on indigenous coal in the future.
7. Despite greater recognition of the problems, there are few long-term strategies for adopting cleaner technologies such as energy efficiency, renewable energy, and clean coal technologies. The region's substantial potential for cost-effective renewable energy and energy efficiency improvements remains largely untapped due to market, financial, institutional, structural, and policy barriers. Although many ADB developing member countries have enabled clean energy legislation and set targets, the implementation barriers persist. Much of the knowledge and technology required to address energy and environmental challenges can be generated more efficiently and effectively at the regional level. Furthermore, there are significant opportunities for crossborder energy supply,

which can support a more environment-friendly energy consumption pattern in the region.

8. ADB's energy policy emphasizes renewable energy and energy efficiency in developing member countries. The policy also recommends focusing on regional and global environmental impacts and enhancing regional cooperation and trade in the energy sector. In terms of regional public goods, ADB's contribution in the area of clean energy includes systematically studying the implementation barriers across countries. The ADB has also strongly supported the development of regional energy markets, regional energy trade, regional power transmission and gas pipelines, and related institution-building efforts to promote energy efficiency and energy security. For example, the ADB cofinanced the Nam Theun 2 Hydropower project involving power trades between Lao PDR and Thailand. The ADB also provided technical assistance for developing an efficient and competitive GMS power market.

9. As part of its regional efforts in the area of clean energy, the ADB has brought together donor trust funds[9] under its Renewable Energy, Energy Efficiency, and Climate Change Program to support capacity building, institutional development, and project development activities. In August 2003, the ADB set up a Clean Development Mechanism Facility to provide additional support for projects in the area of renewable energy and energy efficiency, carbon sequestration, and adaptation. In July 2005, the ADB established the Energy Efficiency Initiative to compile and analyze existing knowledge and experience on energy efficiency policies and formulate a clean energy investment strategy with an indicative lending target of US$1 billion per year over the next few years. Another significant step by the ADB is the creation of the Carbon Market Initiative, a proposal to establish a cofinancing facility that aims to provide finance and marketing support to developers and sponsors of projects with a carbon credit content. In 2006, the ADB will be reviewing its energy policy, which will also address clean energy and energy efficiency issues from both country and regional perspectives.

10. There is an increasing sense that the growth of the energy sector in this region will substantially determine future global warming. Given its dynamic track record, the region will certainly face up to this challenge successfully through innovation, adjustments, and collective action. However, the role of developed countries in

terms of funding support and the transfer of technology during the initial period will remain critical.

Natural Disaster Response

11. The recent tsunami in Asia highlighted the crossborder impact of natural disasters and underlined the need to create appropriate regional public goods to address such problems collectively. In the recent past, Asia has been one of the most disaster-prone regions in the world, and the need for policy coordination in disaster response has been increasing in the region. The tsunami experience required a high degree of coordination of donor response. The ADB played a critical role in those regional efforts by organizing a high-level meeting and developing a tracking matrix with the help of other donors. With its own contribution of US$600 million, the ADB also established the Asian Tsunami Fund as a regional facility for others to contribute to this unprecedented human tragedy. Another key regional public good required for facing natural disasters is the establishment of appropriate early warning systems; this is being addressed with the help of donor support. In addition, there is a need to build an effective, well-resourced, and capable regional disaster response system.

12. Besides the above, building knowledge about responses to immediate and potential disasters is a key regional public good. Governments, donors, and other development partners have initiated several individual and collective efforts in this area. For example, to address the risks associated with disaster responses that often bypass routine procedures and safeguards, the ADB organized a regional expert meeting on corruption prevention in tsunami relief jointly with the Organisation for Economic Co-operation and Development and Transparency International to develop knowledge on this vital issue of wide stakeholder concern. Furthermore, experience suggests that international donors need to ensure that the response to one crisis does not adversely affect responses to other crises. To address this challenge, in 2003, key donors agreed to the Principles and Good Practice of Humanitarian Donors, which includes ensuring that funding of humanitarian action in new crises does not adversely affect the needs in ongoing crises. With the experience in dealing with the recent disasters, the region is poised to develop a more comprehensive and effective sys-

tem of disaster response. Support from the donor and international community will be critical for the success of these endeavors.

Communicable Disease Control
HIV/AIDS

13. Mobility and migration play an important role in the spread of HIV/AIDS by facilitating contacts and by loosening social restrictions. The rapid spread of HIV/AIDS in the region strikingly demonstrates the risks associated with greater integration and crossborder mobility. It is estimated that, by 2010, Asia will overtake Africa in the number of HIV/AIDS cases. Apart from being a great human tragedy for the patients and their families, the continuing spread of HIV/AIDS in Asia also entails significant economic losses. It can potentially reverse the hard-earned gains in poverty reduction in the region.

14. The fight against HIV/AIDS needs to be multipronged. Some key elements include advocacy and awareness generation, improving coordination, and strengthening the knowledge base. The ADB has worked closely with national authorities and international agencies to achieve these objectives. In view of their close links, the incorporation of measures to prevent and mitigate the risk of HIV/AIDS in the transport and transportation sectors so as to reduce mobility-linked and crossborder risk factors has been a key area of donor focus, including within the ADB. As more experience is gained, the fight against HIV/AIDS has been evolving in the region. There is growing recognition of the need to strengthen the commitment of regional leaders, build capacity at the country and regional levels, and undertake targeted programs for the poor and the vulnerable. The new strategic framework of the ADB approved in April 2005 addresses these issues. The ADB is also strengthening its collaboration with the Joint United Nations Programme on HIV/AIDS in these efforts. Using the Asian Development Fund grant resources,[10] during 2005, the ADB approved several transport projects with HIV/AIDS components, a regional communicable diseases control project, and an HIV/AIDS prevention and capacity development project in the Pacific. In February 2005, the ADB also established an HIV/AIDS trust fund with an initial contribution from the government of Sweden. The fund will provide support for developing regional knowledge products for program and policy planning.

SARS and Avian Flu

15. During the past few years, new communicable diseases have emerged in the region. The rapid spread of these diseases has reminded the region of the risks associated with greater integration and crossborder mobility. In 2003, SARS, which first occurred in East Asia, was quickly recognized as a global threat. SARS was barely contained when the first series of H5N1 avian influenza outbreaks were observed in the region. If the influenza virus mutates or combines with existing human influenza viruses, it may acquire the capacity to spread more easily among humans, resulting in a human influenza pandemic. The World Health Organization estimates that 2–7 million people could die in an influenza pandemic worldwide. In November 2005, the Food and Agriculture Organization estimated the total cost of the avian influenza outbreaks at US$10 billion. Loss of poultry due to disease and culling has already pushed many rural households into poverty. If a pandemic starts, some economic analyses suggest that it could potentially halt economic growth in East and South Asia in the short run.

16. A problem of this magnitude and wide geographical dimension requires a regional response that includes the provision of a variety of regional public goods, including knowledge, regional frameworks, and coordinated action. During the SARS epidemic, the ADB formulated and initiated an action plan to strengthen emerging disease surveillance and response in the region. Based on its experience in dealing with similar issues in the past, the ADB is responding within a significant regional dimension to the outbreak of avian flu influenza. There is a general agreement that control at the source, when avian influenza still affects only the bird population, is the priority strategy to prevent the pandemic. This implies rapid identification and containment of avian influenza outbreaks. Regionwide coordination and the sharing of information remain critical for the success of such efforts.

17. The fight against avian influenza seems to be long term, requiring collective and sustained effort by all stakeholders. The rapid progress seen in donor collaboration to develop a more flexible regional response to the avian influenza is encouraging. This includes a partnership between the ADB, ASEAN, the Food and Agriculture Organization, and the World Health Organization. Donors are also extending grant assistance to provide some crit-

ically needed regional public goods. For example, apart from US$400 million for lending, the ADB has provided US$68 million in grant assistance for two regional projects. The first project, the Communicable Disease Control Project (US$30 million) in the GMS, is aimed at controlling the outbreak of emerging communicable diseases by improving regional coordination. The second, the Prevention and Control of Avian Influenza in Asia and the Pacific Project (US$38 million), covers all ADB member countries and focuses on both the short-term needs for fighting avian influenza and the longer-term strengthening of the regional capacity to fight emerging diseases.

18. With the increasing permeability of international boundaries, the role of regional cooperation and regional public goods in the fight against the spread of communicable diseases will remain critical in the future. The knowledge and the regional facilities created to fight today's communicable diseases should be developed in a manner to outlive the current diseases, as they are likely to be needed in the future.

Governance and Anticorruption

19. The 1997 East Asian economic crisis demonstrated how financial and governance problems in one country may rapidly affect investor confidence in neighboring countries. It also underscored the need to improve governance and adopt tougher standards to prevent corruption and related destabilizing factors in the region. Transnational corruption is another key governance issue posing a serious threat to market stability and physical security. This requires strong regional mechanisms for communication and coordination. Progress on these governance issues is still at the early stages. The ADB has supported the processes both directly and indirectly. In 1995, the ADB became the first multilateral development bank to adopt a comprehensive governance policy. The policy identified four essential elements of good governance: accountability, predictability, participation, and transparency. Three years later, the ADB adopted its anticorruption policy with the firm view that combating corruption is vital to improving governance and enhancing the impact of investments in developing member countries. This strengthens the regional and global governance architecture.

20. Although much of the work in these areas must take place at the country level, regional initiatives also play a role. A judicious mix of the provision of national and regional public goods can improve the effectiveness of national-level efforts. The donor community is becoming increasingly active in supporting such efforts. For example, the Anti-Corruption Initiative for Asia-Pacific of the ADB and the Organisation for Economic Co-operation and Development provides a regional platform to implement an action plan that will cover transparent systems for public service, anti-bribery actions and integrity in business operations, and public involvement and that will strengthen national-level efforts. The ADB also supports capacity building among developing member country officials in evolving anticorruption strategies, and it disseminates related publications. Following the recent review of the implementation of its governance and anticorruption policies, the ADB is developing a medium-term action plan for governance and anticorruption. This results-based plan will draw on the principle of mutual accountability and include benchmarks for the accountability of international financial institutions in governance and anticorruption work. The ADB will actively encourage developing member countries to strengthen budgetary and financial management systems, and it will contribute toward aligning the priorities for donor support to developing member country strategies for public financial management and procurement.
21. The governance-related challenges facing the region are expected to intensify as the economies of East Asia become more developed, complex, and integrated. There is a need to correspondingly intensify collective efforts to address these issues quickly before the problems become the most potent source of friction for the future growth of the region.

Human Trafficking Prevention

22. Over the past few decades, the centuries-old problem of human trafficking has intensified. Asia has served as the major source and destination of this traffic. In 2003–04, the Asia and Pacific region accounted for about half of the total global trafficking-related prosecutions (United States 2005). The worsening phenomenon of trafficking in women and children can be attributed to push factors such as poverty and unequal development, conflicts, natural disas-

ters, dysfunctional families, and social and gender discrimination, as well as pull factors such as globalization and the global demand for cheap labor, improved communication systems, the attractive image of a better urban life, improved transport and transportation networks, and growing global tourism. While trafficking of men and boys does occur, the majority of trafficked persons are women and girls. Although trafficking is generally associated with sex work, substantial demand for exploitable labor also arises from the wider range of the demand for work, such as bonded labor in industrial and agricultural sectors, domestic work, the entertainment sector, and begging. Over the past decade, various preventive, legal-prosecution, and rescuing-rehabilitation measures have been undertaken by governments and nongovernmental organizations, but the results have been frustrating, partly because of corruption, the lack of commitment, and the complexity of antitrafficking interventions that involve multiple agencies.

23. The key areas for addressing this problem include preventive measures (for example, awareness raising and the empowerment of women and children) and impact monitoring, along with economic development operations, especially crossborder road corridors and other regional economic integration initiatives. Most of these areas need to be addressed at both the country and the regional levels. As the regional development bank, ADB has contributed to these efforts along with other stakeholders. The current approach of the donor community includes regional research, minimizing and mitigating human trafficking vulnerabilities through donor-funded projects, and policy dialogue. Examples of research work that is examining aspects of the human trafficking problem include the ADB technical assistance grant on Preventing Trafficking of Women and Children and Promoting Safe Migration, as well as the ADB project, Reviewing the Poverty Impact of Regional Economic Integration in the GMS. Where trafficking vulnerabilities are identified through donor-funded projects, donors are recommending inclusion of an antitrafficking component in such projects, often in conjunction with an HIV/AIDS prevention component. This is particularly important in crossborder transport corridor and tourism projects. Along with others, the ADB has also facilitated policy dialogue within or between different subregions of Asia, including the GMS countries. Having gained more experience in this area, the ADB needs gradually to move

from a project-by-project, piecemeal approach to a programmatic regional approach that is linked to regional corridor and connectivity planning.

Source: Based on ADB 2006a.

Notes

1. "Joint Statement on East Asia Cooperation." November 28, 1999. http://www.aseansec.org/5301.htm.
2. "Press Statement by the Chairman of the 8th ASEAN Summit, the 6th ASEAN+3 Summit and the ASEAN-China Summit." Phnom Penh, Cambodia, November 4, 2002. http://www.aseansec.org/13188.htm.
3. "Kuala Lumpur Declaration on the East Asia Summit." Kuala Lumpur, Malaysia, December 14, 2005. http://www.aseansec.org/18098.htm.
4. Ibid.
5. To date, ASEAN has signed framework agreements on comprehensive economic partnership with China, India, Japan, and Korea. The negotiations on FTAs with these countries have already been embarked on; they cover trade in goods, services, and investment. The basis for FTA negotiations between ASEAN and Australia and New Zealand is the Joint Declaration of the Leaders at the ASEAN–Australia and New Zealand Commemorative Summit, which was signed on November 30, 2004 (see http://www.aseansec.org/16796.htm). The Agreement on Trade in Goods was signed with China in November 2004 (http://www.aseansec.org/16646.htm), and its implementation commenced in July 2005, while other agreements are under negotiation, with a targeted completion year of 2007.
6. Poverty and Development Indicators Database. Asian Development Bank. http://www.adb.org/Statistics/pov_dev_indicators.asp.
7. For example, see http://www.aseansec.org/16056.htm.
8. The GMS consists of Cambodia, Lao PDR, Myanmar, Thailand, Vietnam, and Yunnan Province and the Guanxi Zhuang Autonomous Region in China.
9. Funds of the governments of Canada, Denmark, Finland, and the Netherlands.
10. Under the ninth replenishment of the Asian Development Fund (ADF IX), 2 percent of the total resources have been earmarked as a grant to support activities targeting HIV/AIDS and other communicable diseases.

References

ADB (Asian Development Bank). 1966. "Agreement Establishing the Asian Development Bank." Asian Development Bank. http://www.adb.org/Documents/Reports/Charter/charter.pdf.
———. 1994. "Bank Support for Regional Cooperation." Asian Development Bank. http://adb.org/Documents/Policies/Support-for-Regional-Cooperation/bank-support-reg.pdf.
———. 2005a. *Key Indicators 2005.* Manila: Asian Development Bank. http://www.adb.org/Documents/Books/Key_Indicators/2005/default.asp.
———. 2005b. *Asian Development Outlook 2005: Promoting Competition for Long-Term Development.* Manila: Asian Development Bank. http://www.adb.org/Documents/Books/ADO/2005/default.asp.

———. 2006a. "Draft Medium-Term Strategy II 2006–2008." Policy Papers (February), Asian Development Bank, Manila.

———. 2006b. "Asia Regional Information Center and Asia Economic Monitor." http://aric.adb.org.

ADB (Asian Development Bank), JBIC (Japan Bank for International Cooperation), and World Bank. 2005. *Connecting East Asia: A New Framework for Infrastructure*, Tokyo launch ed., March 16. Washington, DC: World Bank.

ASEAN (Association of Southeast Asian Nations). 2002. "Final Report of the East Asia Study Group." Report presented to the Sixth ASEAN+3 Summit, Phnom Penh, Cambodia, November 4.

———. 2005. "Overview: Association of Southeast Asian Nations." Association of Southeast Asian Nations. http://www.aseansec.org/64.htm.

IMF (International Monetary Fund). 2006. *Direction of Trade Statistics Database*. CD-ROM. Washington, DC: International Monetary Fund. http://www.esds.ac.uk/international/support/user_guides/imf/dots.asp.

Kawai, Masahiro. 2005a. "Trade and Investment Integration and Cooperation in East Asia: Empirical Evidence and Issues." In ADB, *Asian Economic Cooperation and Integration: Progress, Prospects, and Challenges*. Manila: ADB.

———. 2005b. "East Asian Economic Regionalism: Progress and Challenges." *Journal of Asian Economics* 16 (1): 30–52.

———. 2006. "Toward a Regional Exchange Rate Regime in East Asia." Paper prepared for the Bellagio Conference on "New Monetary and Exchange Rate Arrangements for East Asia," Bellagio, Italy, May 23–26.

Kuroda, Haruhiko. 2006. "Towards Deeper Asian Economic Integration: Progress and Prospects." Keynote speech at the "Asian Business Conference 2006," Harvard Business School, Boston, February 11.

Mirza, Hafiz. 2002. "Regionalization, FDI and Poverty Reduction: Lessons from Other ASEAN Countries." Paper prepared for the Department for International Development (United Kingdom) Workshop on "Globalization and Poverty in Vietnam," Hanoi, September 23–24.

NILIM (National Institute for Land and Infrastructure Management). 2006. "National Institute for Land and Infrastructure Management." Asahi, Japan: National Institute for Land and Infrastructure Management, Ministry of Land, Infrastructure and Transport. http://www.nilim.go.jp/english/eindex.htm.

United States, State Department. 2005. "Maps (with Regional Law Enforcement Statistics)." In *Trafficking in Persons Report*, Chapter IV. Washington, DC: Office to Monitor and Combat Trafficking in Persons, Under Secretary for Democracy and Global Affairs, U.S. State Department.

World Bank. 2006. *World Development Indicators 2006*. Washington, DC: World Bank. http://devdata.worldbank.org/wdi2006/contents/cover.htm.

CHAPTER 10

China's WTO Accession
Implications and Key Lessons Learned

LONG YONGTU

The protracted negotiations leading up to China's accession to the World Trade Organization have had benefits for the country and its relationship with the world.

China's accession to the World Trade Organization (WTO) has taken 15 years of arduous and protracted negotiations. In assessing this process, one finds that it is a worthy undertaking, not only for China, but also for other countries, especially in the context of numerous ongoing trade negotiations at the global and regional levels. Many thought that China, as a major trading country, was to join the WTO as a matter of course. Others thought that, because of the country's sheer size and importance, the WTO had to handle China's accession with the utmost care. Whichever the approach, 15 years of negotiations seem far too long to achieve such a goal, particularly in relation to the average time taken by other countries that have acceded to the WTO.

Oddly enough, as the chief negotiator of China's WTO accession and having had to endure so much difficulty and shoulder so many burdens during this long process, I now believe that it may prove to be a good thing for China to have undergone these difficult years of negotiations. It may seem illogical, but it is true. The key is how one views the accession process. If you look at this process of negotiation only as one in which you have to make endless concessions to your partners and confront endless challenges at home for the sake of obtaining a WTO membership card, then you would find this process very painful and long indeed. If, instead, you look at the process from a strategic point of view, in the framework of China's long-term economic development, as well as its relationships with the rest of the world, you will find that many positive elements have been generated through this historic process.

Building a Consensus

The fact is that many people only perceive the apparent difficulties and pain of the negotiations themselves. They do not know that there is another side to the coin, an even tougher and therefore more significant process, one of consensus building among our own people at home on some major issues that are being confronted not only by China, but also by many other countries, especially the developing ones.

The issues include, although they are not limited to, the following:

- How to address economic globalization
- How to achieve a balance between trade liberalization and economic development
- How to tackle social issues such as unemployment in the restructuring of the economy

It is the process of consensus building around these major issues domestically that turns out to be the more important aspect of China's WTO negotiations.

The fact that China's accession to an international organization would have such a wide impact throughout the world is something we had not expected at all. The important thing is that we in China have successfully and skillfully handled the domestic side of the accession process and have transformed the pressure generated by these negotiations both at home and abroad and turned them into a promoter, a catalyst for China's historic process of economic reform and opening to the outside world, a process started by Deng Xiaoping in 1979.

That is the most significant lesson we can draw from the negotiations: *that we have involved not only dozens of negotiators, but also millions of ordinary Chinese in the process.* To some extent, the process became an unprecedented, massive education program for our people regarding globalization and the restructuring of the economy, with its positive, as well as negative implications for their day-to-day lives. I believe that this striking feature of China's WTO accession—not as a diplomatic exercise in Geneva, but as a range of broadbased activities involving millions of people in a quest for a better life—is a unique experience in the context of contemporary trade negotiations.

The Issues China Had to Confront

To understand this unique feature of China's accession to the WTO, one should examine the major outcomes of the 15 years of negotiations. To acquire the right to WTO membership, China has made numerous commitments, which can be grouped into two broad categories: first, to observe international rules and practices and, second, to gradually open up its markets. By committing itself to international rules and practices, China has addressed some of the fundamental problems it has faced in the economic reform and opening-up process.

First, China is determined to create a market economy based on the rule of law. A sense of rules has certainly been lacking in China. The planned economy the country pursued for several decades was based on the rules of men, and, to make matters more complicated, several thousand years of feudal society had given the "rule of man" deep roots. So, China's economic reform has reached a critical stage, namely, that of making the rule of law an essential element in the country's economic system. It is against this background that China's commitment to international rules and practices arising from the WTO accession negotiations has become an integral feature of China's economic reform process.

As China has committed itself to making its domestic laws and regulations consistent with WTO rules, it started an extensive clean-up of its existing legal system; this "clean-up" includes the massive task of repealing or modifying numerous laws and regulations.

At the same time, China established reasonable legal measures to protect domestic industries and the domestic market in those situations where WTO rules allow them, under the so-called safety-valve mechanism. These measures included, among others, modifying and drafting antidumping regulations, antisubsidy regulations, and special safeguards.

As legal reforms have accelerated hand-in-hand with the accession to the WTO, China's economic reform process has entered a new stage hallmarked by emphasis on the rule of law and the importance of making laws consistent with international practice. This progress in the legal sphere has certainly had a far-reaching impact on China's economic reforms, giving them greater sustainability and international recognition.

Second, after 20 years of reform and market opening and as tremendous progress was being achieved in economic development and the improvement of people's livelihoods, China has also witnessed the emergence of serious market disorders, including smuggling, corruption, bribery, sham goods, tax evasion, counterfeit goods, and pirated software. These have become the tumor in the body of China's economy. The Chinese government launched an extensive campaign against these evils in the marketplace, fully aware of the long-term significance of this action. WTO accession, including the enforcement of international rules, has certainly given the government the full legitimacy to take strong, sweeping measures to deal with these issues.

The government realized that it was dealing not only with an imminent threat to the establishment of a true market economy; it was also addressing fundamental obstacles to creating a society based on values of reliability, honesty, and truthfulness. Therefore, upon completing the accession negotiations, China set up an unprecedented and extensive training program for the whole country on the WTO rules, additionally thought of as a driver to forge the ethical values of honesty and trustworthiness both in business practices and in people's daily lives. This educational program, which was partly a result of the WTO accession, has helped to change the business environment, but, more importantly, the social and ethical environment of the Chinese people in the 21st century as well.

Third, in China's opening-up to the outside world, one of the key achievements is the fact that China has become the premier location for foreign direct investment (FDI) among the developing countries, with a yearly average of US$40 billion in the last decade. FDI today plays an important role in China's economic development. In 2005, enterprises benefiting from foreign investment contributed 57 percent to the overall imports and exports in China and 20 percent of the country's tax revenue and, more importantly, generated more than 20 million jobs. It is of paramount importance to keep up the volume of FDI and improve the quality of these investments.

In spite of all the efforts already made by the government, including an array of measures offering preferential treatment, there is still much room for improvement in China's investment environment. The chief complaint that an increasing number of foreign investors and business people were making to the government before the WTO accession was the lack of a transparent, predictable, and stable legal environment.

In China, there used to be numerous so-called internal regulations governing business practices. These were only known to a few people, a situation that conspired against the desired transparency of law. In many cases, the local regulations were not consistent with national rules, even less with international practices, and they were changing all the time, making predictability almost impossible. As a result, the investment environment has deteriorated in some parts of China, and the government has had to take decisive action to stop random fees and fines, compulsory donations, and unauthorized inspections of foreign capital enterprises. In this connection, China's WTO accession has provided timely recipes for improving the business environment for FDI flows.

In summary, China's WTO commitment to observe international rules has helped China build a market economy based on the rule of law, a market economy characterized by order, and a market economy with a transparent, stable, and predictable legal environment. All these are not only fundamental if China is to move into a truly market-driven economic system, but they are also important if China is to maintain the reputation of its business environment in order to attract more FDI and to avoid unnecessary trade disputes with its fellow WTO members.

The ongoing WTO negotiations have included efforts to introduce more rules, regulations, standards, and so on in such areas as environment and labor. Once these are accepted by WTO members, they will have far-reaching implications for the domestic economic system of the members and the functioning of their governments and companies.

However, it is imperative to avoid as much as possible the practice of a double standard in the implementation of the rules in order to strengthen the rule-based system of the WTO. Paragraph 15 and 16 of the protocol on the accession of China set up different rules for China only in the area of antidumping and product-specific safeguard mechanisms. Even though these provisions were agreed upon under specific circumstances during China's WTO negotiations, they have weakened the position of the Chinese government in its efforts to convince the general public to observe the WTO rules since people have concluded from these provisions that there may be exceptions to the rules and that China is already a victim of these exceptions.

A Two-Way Process

By committing itself to a gradually more open market, China has highlighted some important points to be maintained in its trade policies.

In the first place, China believes that market openness is a two-way process. China, as an increasingly important trading country in the world, cannot simply take advantage of the markets of others; it has to open its own market. This is the principle of mutual benefit and nondiscrimination. It is also of fundamental importance in reducing trade frictions and disputes.

However, China has forcefully held that the opening of domestic markets, especially by developing countries, should be a gradual process. The extent of opening should be in line with the level of development of each individual country. That is why China insisted very firmly on its developing-country status throughout the entire negotiation period.

The opening of markets should serve the growth of markets and be conducive to domestic economic development. Otherwise, it would only lead to a situation, where, as the Chinese proverb goes, "One kills the hen in order to get the egg." It would be a real tragedy for trade negotiators if, after such tough negotiations, they find that the market has been opened, but that, actually, the market has ceased to exist because there is no economic growth and residents have no purchasing power.

Since China and its negotiation partners, especially those from developed countries, have come to a common understanding that only a gradual opening of the Chinese market can produce a win-win outcome for all the parties concerned, some compromises have been reached with regard to opening up markets, including many arrangements during the transition to ensure a gradual process.

These outcomes have taken into account the level of maturity reached in each and every sector under negotiation. Therefore, the arrangements protect the development of these industries from serious risk; on the other hand, the arrangements promote the development of these sectors through healthy and appropriate external competition.

Second, China believes that the main benefit of opening up to trade and investment flows is to catalyze change in Chinese domestic industries, not simply to generate foreign exchange. China is not opening itself up so that foreign products can flood the domestic market; rather, it is opening its markets to enhance the competitiveness of Chinese industries.

Of all the sectors opening up to competition since China's WTO accession, for many constituents, agriculture would be the most vulnerable and therefore the most exposed to massive import competition.

With WTO entry, China's average tariff on agriculture imports fell to 15 percent from 22 percent in trade-weighted terms, affecting mainly wheat, maize, rice, and vegetable oil. It was even predicted that more than 9 million to 20 million farmers would lose their jobs. In terms of first impressions, this may be true. However, it was also believed that China's entry provided a real opportunity to restructure the country's agricultural sector, which has been the least open and lags relatively behind other industries in the reform process.

Compared with advanced countries, China's agriculture does not enjoy a comparative advantage in producing some foodstuffs, including wheat, corn, soybeans, and other vegetable oil crops. China has only 7 percent of the world's arable land, but has to feed 20 percent of the world's population. In addition, many areas of China are short of water. Therefore, as some agricultural experts argue, China should import more grain as this is tantamount to the importation of scarce land and water resources. Given China's size, even if it imports the full tariff-quota volume of grains (about 22 million tons a year), such imports would still amount to less than 5 percent of the country's total production of these crops. This means that food security could be guaranteed even in the very unlikely event of a food embargo. Therefore, China should be resolute in restructuring its agriculture sector so as to move to the more competitive products, such as fruits, vegetables, and meat, because WTO membership will bring greater access to foreign markets.

In any event, WTO entry has certainly exerted a major influence on the government to introduce a more rational and fair policy toward agriculture, strengthening it through better infrastructure and services and by alleviating the financial burden and increasing the incomes of farmers. After China's WTO accession, the Chinese government decided to abandon the agricultural tax, which has been practiced for thousands of years in China and has been considered a negative subsidy in agriculture. Furthermore, China has also increased its domestic support for agriculture within the so-called green box (the WTO category that allows subsidies for agriculture in certain cases). It would be interesting to debate whether this development can be considered positive or negative as a result of China's WTO accession.

The development of the agricultural sector following WTO accession may prove that WTO entry was a turning point for China's agricultural policy and the driving force behind a new phase of seeking to achieve world standards of competitiveness. It has been found that another key benefit of opening up to world trade and investment flows has been the cultivation of new industries to generate massive employment, which is critical for China's sustainable economic development, as well as social stability.

As a result of the WTO market-access negotiations, China has made the most significant offer of opening up the service sector. The service sector is relatively undeveloped in China, accounting for only 35 percent of the country's gross domestic product (GDP) in 2004, which is a lower ratio than that in some developing countries and even more so with respect to that in developed countries, where the service sector accounts for 65–85 percent of GDP. Still more remarkable from the Chinese government's standpoint is that the service sector has a weight in terms of employment in those countries that is similar to its weight in their GDP. As a consequence, the Chinese government is determined to restructure the economy and make special efforts to develop its service industries. Its experience in developing some of its most advanced manufacturing sectors, such as electronic home appliances, has led the government to believe that the Chinese service sector will also follow the same road by opening up to foreign competition.

This is the reason why there has been so much more major market openness in banking, insurance, telecommunications, distribution, tourism, transportation, and professional services. However, in retrospect, for some activities, especially in banking, investment, and securities, more openness might have been arranged under China's WTO agreement, if not for the 1997–98 Asian financial crisis, which hardened the views of Chinese leaders that the opening of the financial sector should be gradual in order not to repeat what had happened in some Southeast Asian countries. In spite of the intention for a more gradual pace in opening up these areas, the service sector in China is, in reality, opening up rapidly and becoming increasingly important in the Chinese economy. We believe that the opening-up of these service sectors will generate massive job opportunities, especially middle- and high-income jobs, which is important to ensure work prospects at home for talented young Chinese rather than compelling them to seek jobs abroad. The paramount consideration of creating more jobs is reflected in opening up not only the service sector, but also some of the major manufacturing sectors.

The automobile industry is a typical case. Long-standing protection of the auto industry has made it inefficient and noncompetitive and has made cars, whether imported or domestically produced, so highly priced that they have been out of reach of most of the population. This has limited the expansion of the domestic market. This is why, for so many years, private car sales increased very slowly in China. Even more worrisome is the fact that many of the service providers fundamental to the auto industry, such as gas stations, auto loan and insurance providers, and distribution and maintenance networks, have not developed; all these services could generate considerable employment.

Gearing Up for Globalization

Fortunately, China has been implementing a policy of opening up to trade and investment flows for the past 26 years, that is, for longer than it took to negotiate China's accession to the WTO, and almost all of its population has benefited from this. As a result of the policy, since 1977, China has doubled its income every 10 years, while, historically, it took Britain 58 years, the United States 47 years, and Japan 35 years to accomplish this. This is why, during the negotiations, it was comparatively easy to convince our people that a gradual process of opening our markets should not be regarded as unilateral concessions. The fact that the negotiations took longer than we expected has to some extent made it easier for us to prepare conceptually and in practical terms for WTO accession.

On the other hand, there has been strong general public support for accession because of the fact that China, during the negotiations, was very firm in protecting its fundamental interests. We need to make sure that the policy of opening up will not lead to mass unemployment, that it will not lead to the destruction of key industries, and that it will not change China's national values, culture, and identity. The opening of the market should be a positive element in China's economic development, not a negative factor.

Another strategic outcome of China's WTO accession is that it helped to get the Chinese people well prepared for economic globalization. It is generally believed in China that, confronted with the historical tide of economic globalization, China, like other countries, must participate actively in the process. We must also participate effectively in order to benefit from this process and not be harmed by it.

It is somewhat ironic that, when China first gained access to the global trading system, there was a rapid development of regional and bilateral trade agreements. We, the trade negotiators, then became quite puzzled about why there had been a need to undertake so much effort to get into the global system if regional and bilateral arrangements could achieve the same purpose. That is why I did not know in the beginning how to handle the negotiations for a free trade agreement with the countries of the Association of Southeast Asian Nations. Gradually, we came to understand that, if the Americans and the Europeans were accelerating their efforts in this regard, Asia's interest might be jeopardized if it did not pursue the opportunities for regional and bilateral agreements. The reality is that intra–East Asia trade is already over 50 percent of the total trade and is approaching the percentage achieved by Europe–North America trade. There should be a mechanism to reflect this trade reality in East Asia and better manage competition within the region, as well as with other regions. Therefore, it is not a question of whether such a trend would be helpful or harmful to the WTO–Doha Development Agenda process. Rather, it is for the WTO, maybe through the Doha process, to develop rules and frameworks to ensure that regional and bilateral arrangements will not weaken the basis of global trade, but, instead, complement the WTO system.

In conclusion, China's 15 years of negotiations have prepared us to participate in economic globalization in general and for a new round of trade negotiations within the framework of the WTO, as well as many regional-level and bilateral-level trade negotiations, in particular. We have discovered that a balanced approach between the opening-up policy and sustaining economic development works for China. Economic development would not take place without a real opening-up policy. That is why we support the Doha round, a new round that will bring greater economic benefits for the world and especially for the developing countries. That is also why we actively participate in the regional-level effort to liberalize trade and investment, which might prove to be the building blocks for global liberalization.

CHAPTER 11

From Confucius to Kennedy
Principles of East Asian Governance

KISHORE MAHBUBANI

East Asia is making great strides in its quest to join the ranks of the developed countries, but there is no consensus on why this is so. This essay examines several possible reasons.

The story of development is a curious one. In the immediate aftermath of World War II, during the height of optimism generated by decolonization, the world held a common assumption that all nations shared a potential to become developed nations. The combination of a benign international economic order, wise free-market economic policies, and a small dose of foreign assistance from the developed world would enable any nation to develop. A half century later, this optimism has been replaced by a general pessimism. In private, many have begun to believe that, perhaps, only Western nations can succeed and develop.

Today, the only region that seems to have the capacity to escape the clutches of this pessimism is East Asia. At the height of the Asian financial crisis around 1997–98, as the East Asian economies began to collapse like dominoes, murmurings were heard that the East Asian miracle had been a mirage. Like the rest of the developing world elsewhere in Asia and in Africa and Latin America, East Asia was also perceived to be heading toward failure in the story of development. Fortunately, nine years after the East Asian financial crisis, East Asia has regained its confidence. The world, too, is becoming convinced that the region is set on a secular path of steady economic growth. Several East Asian nations are now positioned to join Japan as developed nations, achieving within a generation what the West took several generations to accomplish.

A Critical Difference: The East Asian Elites

Despite this new consensus that East Asia is likely to succeed, there is no consensus on *why* East Asian nations are succeeding. The conventional Western narrative on political and economic development does not explain the rise of East Asia. Neither democratic nor authoritarian political systems are critical variables. While participation in free-market economic development is a necessary ingredient, it is not a sufficient one. The role of the state varies greatly in the story of East Asian economic development. All these points suggest that the time has come to start a fresh narrative about East Asian development. This is what this essay means to do.

The critical difference between East Asia and the rest of the developing world is the nature of the elites that have been leading and managing the successful states. Essentially, they have been productive, instead of parasitic elites. While they have achieved and retained power in different ways, they have remained focused on uplifting their nations and societies while in office. With the possible exception of Hong Kong (China) and Singapore, one could not argue that these states have been free of corruption. But, despite the corruption, the elites have continued to focus their energies more on transforming their societies than on preserving their special, privileged status. This is the common element that is found in China and Japan, the Republic of Korea and Taiwan (China), Malaysia and Singapore.

The best way to construct this East Asian narrative is to compare the performance of East Asian elites with the elites of Latin America. Latin America began both the 20th century and the post–World War II era with far greater promise than did East Asia. Argentina was ranked among the 10 richest countries in 1900. The presence of European elites in Latin American societies gave good reason to believe that the elites would learn and transmit the best practices of European societies into Latin America. Yet, by the end of the 20th century, when Singapore had emerged as a symbol of what a small East Asian state could do with no resources, Haiti had emerged as a potent symbol of the other extreme. Even U.S. tutelage could not stop Haiti from dropping toward the status of a practically failed state.

Why did East Asian elites perform better than many of their Latin American counterparts? Any attempt to give a full answer to this question will reveal the complexity of the East Asian story. Culture is certainly part of the explanation. Since the days of Confucius, the ethical fabric of East Asian societies has been laced with the belief that obligation to society is an integral part of being an ethical person. But a similar strain occurs in other societies, including Christian and Muslim societies.

Putting society before self was not the only thought in East Asian minds. Starting with Japan during the Meiji Restoration, East Asian societies gradually began to realize, especially in the 1960s and 1970s, that they had to emulate the best practices of the West if they were to succeed. The one common element found in all the elites of East Asia is that they opened their minds to the study of the West. Thousands went to universities in the United States beginning in the 1950s and 1960s. When they returned home, they brought back the remarkable confidence of post–World War II America that a "great society" could be created by human intervention. The boundless optimism of the Kennedy era infected East Asia, too. Hence, both Confucius and Kennedy explain the rise of East Asia, even though these two personalities seem poles apart in spiritual terms.

This willingness to learn Western best practices and to adapt and apply them may thus be the key distinguishing feature of East Asian elites. In theory, these elites might have been afraid of losing their cultural identity in trying to copy the West. In practice, they retained their deep cultural confidence that they could learn from the West and not lose their souls. Hence, both the capacity to learn and the confidence to accept Western best practices are central elements of the East Asian narrative.

One poorly understood dimension of the East Asian story is the remarkable number of extraordinary leaders who have appeared in the region. Maintaining a developed society requires less effort. Hence, the countries of the Organisation for Economic Co-operation and Development that have experienced mediocre or poor leadership have not suffered too much. On the other hand, no state can be lifted from a poor developing status to a modern developed nation without extraordinary leadership. The Meiji reformers did this for Japan. Deng Xiaoping did it for China. Park Chung Hee did it for Korea. Chiang Ching-kuo did it for Taiwan (China). Equally important, these great leaders surrounded themselves with other remarkable leaders who could pull their nations up.

It is a real pity that no major study has been carried out to compare the impact of leadership on East Asian development. Witness the contrasting stories of Korea and the Philippines. The Philippines began with far greater promise at the end of World War II: higher per capita income, a more well educated elite, better access to the U.S. market, and a remarkably talented population that has thrived in every country outside the Philippines. But the feudal hacienda mentality and poor leadership both under democratic and under dictatorial rule did the Philippines in. Korea had no advantages. Decades of war and occupation had devastated Korea. But it had extraordinary leadership and an elite committed to strengthening their nation, not their own bank accounts. This one comparison makes clear that the performance of elites is a key variable in assessing the fate and fortunes of nations.

Silent Learning

There is another, equally important dimension in the East Asian story that has not been fully understood or described. Even though the societies of East Asia are quite different and their elites seem independent of each other, there has been a lot of silent learning among the elites. Over time, historians will discover the many connections. This is true even though the stories of development appear so different. This essay will try to show some common threads of learning in East Asia.

After its unfortunate detour into a militaristic society in the first half of the 20th century, Japan remained firmly committed to democratic rule in the second half of the century. Today, the story of the Japanese economic miracle is being overshadowed by that of China, which has managed its remarkable economic transformation under communist party rule. Korea began its extraordinary economic growth under a military dictator, Park Chung Hee, while Hong Kong (China) did so under British colonial rule. Given this significant diversity of political systems, what does one find in common in the East Asian story?

To begin to answer this question, it may be useful to show how Japan triggered the first wave of elite learning. Japan was the first East Asian community to wake from centuries of slumber. It took the arrival of the West, especially the naval expedition of Commodore Perry in 1853, to make the Japanese aware of how weak and backward their society had become. The Japanese had also been observing the humiliation of China by the West. They knew that a similar fate awaited

Japan if it did not change course drastically. Hence, a brave group of young reformers overthrew the Tokugawa Shogunate in 1868, restored the Meiji emperor, and firmly embarked on a process of reform. Fukuzawa Yukichi, one of the leading reformers, said, "Our immediate policy, therefore, should be to lose no time in waiting for the enlightenment of our neighbouring countries in order to join them in developing Asia, but rather to depart from their ranks and cast our lot with the civilized countries of the West . . . We should deal with them exactly as the Westerners do."[1] Japan was therefore the first East Asian country to decide that learning from the West was essential for successful development.

What motivated this brave band of Meiji reformers in the late 19th century? Their fundamental concern was for the fate of their nation, not their own fate. They desperately wanted to prevent the humiliation of their country. Hence, they traveled to all corners of the globe to understand what made nations great.

They showed a remarkably pragmatic spirit in applying the lessons they learned. Instead of trying to find one set of formulas or learning only from one society, they were happy to mix and match best practices learned from a variety of sources. Iwakura Tomomi, one of the Meiji reformers, went on a two-year tour of the world with 54 protégés. They were impressed with what they saw and realized the need to change their society completely. For example, they patterned their education system after that of the French centralized system and American curriculum development. They stressed universal primary education followed by expanding secondary education. This end to education according to class allowed for talent-based upward mobility. They also adopted the German system of civil service recruitment through examinations. In the political arena, they conducted an in-depth study of Western systems of jurisprudence and constitutional law. The Meiji reformers also learned Western agricultural techniques to boost the Japanese economy. Goh Keng Swee observed that, "By studying Western techniques, importing Western experts and introducing new strains through experimental stations, Japanese agriculture made great and continuing advances, so much so that today the number of farmers in Japan is smaller than in the early Meiji period, the increases in the country's population having been absorbed in the 'modern' sector" (Goh 1995a, 139).

Goh Keng Swee, one of the founding fathers of modern Singapore, made a significant effort to understand the Meiji reformation. He is widely credited, together with Lee Kuan Yew and S. Rajaratnam, with being responsible for the Singapore success story. He referred to the Meiji reformers in several of his essays. For example, in 1983 when he delivered the fourth Harry G. Johnson Memorial Lecture at the Royal Society, London, on the topic, "Public Administration and Economic Development in LDCs [Least Developed Countries]," he discussed several lessons from Japan's economic development, in particular the Meiji reformers (Goh 1995a).

It is clear that Goh Keng Swee tried to apply the lessons he learned from the Meiji reformers to the development of Singapore. Indeed, his contribution to Singapore's development was not small. Lee Kuan Yew, the then prime minister, said that, whenever he encountered a major challenge in governance, he put Goh Keng Swee in charge of the relevant portfolio. This is how Lee Kuan Yew described Dr. Goh: "Throughout this fight [with the communists] and for the next 21 years until he retired as deputy prime minister in 1984, he was my *alter ego*, always the skeptic, always turning a proposition on its head to reveal its flaws and help me reshape it. He was my resident intellectual *par excellence* and a doughty fighter" (Lee 1998, 510). Thus, Goh occupied several ministerial portfolios, moving from defense to finance, from education to central banking, in the course of his career. Without fail, he overcame major problems each time. He also left behind lasting legacies in each area into which he ventured. Remarkably, he could handle equally well both large and small problems. The Jurong Bird Park, the Singapore Zoo (both the day and night zoos), the Singapore Symphony Orchestra, and the East Asian Institute (which originally began as an institute to study Confucian philosophy) continue to thrive because of the firm foundations he established for them.

I once accompanied Dr. Goh when he paid a call on Paul Volcker, then chairman of the board of governors of the U.S. Federal Reserve System ("the Fed"), in 1985. Before the visit, we discussed the role of the Fed. It became clear to me after a few minutes that Goh had studied both the Fed and the U.S. monetary system in great depth. Indeed, when he ran the central bank equivalent in Singapore, the Monetary Authority of Singapore, he applied Western best practices judiciously. Yet, there was no slavish copying. This was the governing principle of Goh's stewardship: learn the best practices from the rest of the world and adapt them to the unique conditions of Singapore. In so doing, he was behaving exactly like the Meiji reformers had done in Japan almost a hundred years earlier.

If Goh had inherited a "healthy virus" of learning and application from the Meiji reformers, he may also have been inadvertently responsible for passing on some of this "healthy virus" to China. It is little known that China, under the initial guidance of Deng Xiaoping, had made a significant effort to learn from Singapore.

Deng Xiaoping clearly deserves to go down as one of the greatest leaders of all time because of the enormous improvement he brought to the lives of over a billion Chinese people. The 19th-century British moral philosophers of the utilitarian school would have had no hesitation in praising his contributions to Chinese society. It is remarkable how he turned the most populous country of the world on a dime and moved it almost instantly from socialist central planning to free-market economics.

While Deng's enormous contribution is now well recognized, there is little understanding of how his worldview changed along the way. From the age of 20 to the age of 75, when he launched his Four Modernizations Policy, he was a dedicated communist party official. It is true that he witnessed the disastrous Great Leap Forward of 1958–60 and the Cultural Revolution of 1966–76. Twice, he was also purged from the communist party by Mao Zedong and Mao's supporters. Hence, he was acutely aware of the failures of the communist economic system. But what made him decide to opt for free-market economic principles?

The full story may never be known. However, it is worth recalling the challenges he faced when he was rehabilitated and put back in office in July 1977. Apart from dealing with the consequences of the enormous turmoil produced by the Cultural Revolution, he faced a uniquely adverse geopolitical environment. Vietnam was set to invade Cambodia in 1978 after signing a treaty in Moscow on November 3 to secure Soviet protection if China invaded Vietnam in retaliation. Deng went to Washington in January 1979 to explain to President Carter how China would react to the Vietnamese invasion. Zbigniew Brzezinski, President Carter's national security advisor, was present at the meeting, and, in his memoirs, he described Deng's presentation as "the single most impressive demonstration of raw power politics that I encountered in my four years at the White House" (Goh 1995b, 325). Note that it was also during this visit that Deng made the bold decision to expose Chinese society to the remarkable affluence of American society. This was a huge political risk. It proved the falsehood of the long-standing and oft-repeated claims of the Communist Party of China that the American people were poor and oppressed. But Deng's gamble worked. It unleashed the enormous energies of the Chinese population when they learned from American society that better lives awaited them if they opted for free-market economics.

It would have been excusable for any Chinese leader to focus only on geopolitical challenges in such difficult circumstances (as the Soviet leaders appeared to be doing at the time). Yet, remarkably, Deng also focused his energies on the domestic economic reform that China would have to undertake. As part of his response to the Vietnamese invasion of Cambodia in December 1978, he also decided to visit a few states of the Association of Southeast Asian Nations, including Singapore. These visits opened his eyes to the superior economic conditions in Southeast Asia. In a December 2005 interview with *Time Asia*, Lee Kuan Yew described the likely reaction of Deng to his visit to Singapore:

> I'm convinced that his visit to Bangkok, Kuala Lumpur and Singapore, that journey, in November '78, was a shock to him. He expected three Third-World cities; he saw three Second-World cities better than Shanghai or Beijing. As his aircraft door closed, I turned around to my colleagues; I said, "[his aides] are getting a shellacking. They gave him the wrong brief." Within weeks, the *People's Daily* switched lines, [writing] that Singapore is no longer a running dog of the Americans; it's a very nice city, a garden city, good public housing, very clean place. They changed their line. And he changed to the "open door" policy. After a lifetime as a communist, at the age of 74, he persuaded his Long March contemporaries to return to a market economy. (Elegant and Elliot 2005, 6)

After this visit to Singapore, Deng worked even harder to promote economic reform. To get his meaning across to a billion people, Deng had to keep his message clear. He used brilliantly simple and striking aphorisms. The most famous one was his remark, "It does not matter whether a cat is black or white; as long as it catches mice, it's a good cat." Deng wanted to imbue the Chinese people with a spirit of pragmatism to replace the rigid doctrinal approaches of Maoist thought.

He also wanted to provide the Chinese people with a model on which they might rely. He might have used either Japan or the four tigers (Hong Kong [China], Korea, Singapore, and Taiwan [China]). However, Japan and Korea were out as models because they were still political rivals in the Cold War geopolitical setting. Culturally, it would have been difficult for the Chinese population to accept Japan and Korea (hitherto Chinese cultural satellites) as role models. Hong Kong

(China) and Taiwan (China) could not be used because their continued separation from China meant they served as living symbols of one of the most humiliating periods of Chinese history, and China was still recovering from this humiliation. Hence, perhaps by default, perhaps because the Singapore story had its own merits, Deng went around China advocating that China learn a lesson or two from Singapore's development experience. As Lee Kuan Yew recounts in his memoirs, China's attitude toward Singapore changed significantly soon after Deng's visit in 1978. Lee (2000, 668–69) quoted from Deng's speech in October 1979. "I went to Singapore to study how they utilized foreign capital. Singapore benefited from factories set up by foreigners in Singapore: first, foreign enterprises paid 35 percent of their net profits in taxes, which went to the state; second, labor income went to the workers; and third, it [foreign investment] generated the service sectors. All these were income [for the state]," and Lee then added, "What he saw in Singapore in 1978 had become a point of reference as the minimum the Chinese people should achieve."

The Chinese government followed this up by inviting Goh Keng Swee to serve as the economic advisor to the State Council of China on coastal development from 1985 to the mid-1990s. We will never have a full account of all the advice Dr. Goh gave to the Chinese government. Much of it was given in confidence. Still, it is unlikely that Goh would not have mentioned to his Chinese hosts either his study of the Meiji reformers or his own experience in adopting Western best practices. For example, Goh once described Singapore's development experience as follows, "If our experience can be used as a general guide to policy in other developing nations, the lesson is that the free enterprise system, correctly nurtured and adroitly handled, can serve as a powerful and versatile instrument of economic growth" (Goh 1995c) He must have shared this idea with his Chinese hosts as well.

This story of one man who studied Meiji Japan, applied its lessons to Singapore, and then shared with China his experiences in governing Singapore may seem like a very thin thread on which to hang the point that there has been a lot of mutual learning and interconnectedness among the elites of the region as they tried to foster growth and development in their societies. Clearly, there must have been numerous other threads, many of which were certainly much thicker. To unearth all these threads will require more in-depth research.

But some of these threads may remain invisible for a long time. For example, it is well known that the Korean economic success story was based to an extent on lessons learned from Japan. Under normal circumstances, it would have been natural for Koreans openly to acknowledge the lessons learned. However, the recent political history of Japan and Korea has been immensely difficult and complicated. The Japanese occupation of Korea from 1910 to 1945 was painful and brutal. Koreans were not even allowed to speak their language during this occupation. To make matters worse, Japan had, until recently, been reluctant to acknowledge the pain it had caused Korea. Hence, not surprisingly, there is equal reticence on the part of Koreans to acknowledge Japan's positive contributions. The wounds have not healed. It will take time for both sides to agree on the positive dimensions of their relationship.

However, the connections between Japan and Korea are significant. On the surface, one often witnesses popular hostility to Japan in Korea because of the bitter memories of Koreans about the Japanese occupation. Yet, underneath this hostility, there is also a layer of deep cultural respect for Japan and its enormous accomplishments. Many development economists like to point out that, in 1960, per capita gross national income in Korea was lower than that in many developing countries in other regions. Korea's was about US$80, while Ghana's was US$200, and Argentina's was US$2,700. Today, the comparable figures are Korea, US$13,900, Ghana, US$380, and Argentina, US$3,700. Has Japan contributed to Korea's growth in any way?

American historians, who are equally detached from Japanese and Korean sentiments, have made an effort to catalogue the lessons that Korea may have learned from Japan. Dennis L. McNamara, a sociologist at Georgetown University, has traced the beginnings of Korean capitalism and the *chaebols*[2] to the Japanese colonial period (for example, McNamara 1990). Ezra Vogel adds the following:

> After World War II, only the governments of South Korea and Singapore consciously studied the Japanese experience in detail, but the main outlines of the Japanese strategy were well understood by all four of the little dragons. They all knew that Japan began with labor-intensive industries and used the income from exports in this sector to purchase new equipment, while upgrading its training and technology in sectors where productivity gains would allow higher wages. They all saw the crucial role of government in guiding these changes. Having the Japanese model provided both the confidence that they too could succeed and a perspective on how to proceed. (Vogel 1991, 91)

The Deeper Roots of the Contribution of the Elites

As one of the foremost scholars of East Asia, Vogel has tried to understand the deeper roots of the unique characteristics of East Asian elites (although he focuses his study on Japan and the four tigers). In describing these unique characteristics, he highlights four common areas (Vogel 1991, 93–101). They are:

1. *Meritocratic elite.* According to Vogel, the responsibilities of bureaucrats in Confucian societies of the past were broader than those of bureaucrats in the West, and the bureaucrats in Confucian societies enjoyed more authority and respect than did their Western counterparts. They had a sense of responsibility for the overall social order and moral tone of society. In the modern form, the ablest people in society are chosen. They remain dedicated to overall public goals and exercise restraint in their private pursuit of wealth. This concern for overall social order and existing inequities causes them to put more effort into spreading income opportunities.
2. *Entrance exam system.* Examinations are necessary for the selection of new workers as more skills become required. They are also critical in overcoming feudal favoritism. All members of society are thus given the opportunity to access high positions and better opportunities.
3. *The importance of the group.* While East Asian societies do not focus on binding legal codes as greatly as do societies in the West, they have detailed rules about the behavior of an individual in his or her group. Vogel cites the emphasis on loyalty, the responsiveness of people in organizations to group demands, and the predictability of individual behavior in the group setting as characteristics well suited to the needs of industrialization, particularly for those countries trying to catch up.
4. *Self-cultivation.* This is analogous to the Protestant work ethic in its power to strengthen the personal drive for achievement. Self-cultivation was traditionally driven by a desire for more perfect control over one's emotions. It required study and reflection. This can be elevated to an active, purposive form by advancing work-related skills, such as learning new languages, using computers, or understanding foreign markets. This can then be channeled toward improving group performance. It is a restless desire for improvement that looks to the long term and that looks beyond material acquisition.

Vogel selected all four of these characteristics to describe the unique nature of East Asian elites. His emphasis on elite behavior is significant. This may well be the critical variable in the explanation of a society's ability to become a modern developed society. Look at, for example, the qualities Vogel highlights for special mention when he describes the nature of East Asian bureaucracies:

> The bureaucratic system, in its modern form, played a critical role in industrialization . . . The fact that they were selected by meritocratic measures, were reputed to be highly moral, and lived without conspicuous display gave them an unquestioned legitimacy that encouraged public compliance with their decisions and thus helped to provide a stable base of support for their governments . . . Concern for the overall social order led officials to be sensitive to problems of inequality early in the process of industrialization and to make efforts to spread income opportunities to all parts of society. (Vogel 1991, 95)

This list of qualities can be used to administer a simple test for all societies that have so far failed to develop a positive momentum on the road to development: how many of them have implanted these qualities in their elites?

Various development theorists have had great difficulty explaining why countries fail in development. As recently as 2003, the chief economist of the International Monetary Fund, Raghuram Rajan, observed,

> This development dilemma is the single biggest economic challenge the world faces in the longer term. And there isn't an easy solution. It isn't just a case of pouring in more money. We need to better understand how successful development has occurred. Indeed, one of the areas that I find most frustrating is the complete lack of guidance in economics as to how to start a virtuous cycle of development in the poorest parts of the world. (IMF 2003, 363)

The real secret to launching a virtuous circle of development may not lie in getting a country to adopt a certain set of economic prescriptions. These are necessary, but not sufficient. What is far more critical is to transform the nature of the elites running the society. It would be useful, for example, to create an international index of good governance that measures the performance of elites on the basis of, say, the qualities that Vogel has listed above in his description of East Asian bureaucracies. Elite behavior may well be the critical variable in deciding whether countries succeed in development.

The Enabling Environment

This emphasis on elite behavior may be difficult for contemporary Western intellectuals to stomach. The winds of political correctness that have blown through Western academia make it difficult to have a balanced discussion on this subject. It is far more politically correct to praise the virtues of democracy, even if democratic rule is, sadly, unlikely to change the conditions in countries such as Haiti. This is a simple truth. But when such simple truths cannot be stated, real problems emerge in attempting to have rational discourse on these issues.

This problem of political correctness has been aggravated by America's retreat from the golden assumptions of the Kennedy era to the minimalist assumptions of the Reagan era on issues of governance. The Kennedy generation believed that great societies could be created by governments led by good leaders. That generation may have made mistakes, but they believed that leaders and elites could and should transform societies. The Reagan generation, by contrast, believed that good government could only come through least government. Their goal was to shrink government and reduce the role of governing elites on the assumption that the marketplace would make all the right decisions if governments stepped out of the way.

Fortunately, East Asia has been influenced more by the assumptions of the Kennedy generation rather than the Reagan generation. All the East Asian elites believed that both the state and the elites had critical roles to play in leading and changing society. This assumption may have been consistent with their cultural genes. But it helped that the Kennedy era provided a psychological boost to this tendency.

The Kennedy era provided more than a psychological boost. It also provided an enabling environment. If all the East Asian nations had tried to implement the policies of the 1960s in the 1860s, they would have been thwarted by the colonial ambitions of the expansionist European powers in East Asia. The Kennedy generation of the 1960s, by contrast (and for a variety of complex reasons, including Cold War considerations), wanted to see the success of East Asia. The Kennedy generation also retained memories of the ravages of World War II. Hence, they remained firmly committed to maintaining the 1945 multilateral order, including the rules of the forerunner of the World Trade Organization, the General Agreement on Tariffs and Trade, which provided a level playing field for all economies to grow and thrive.

Hence, it would be a mistake to point out only the Confucian dimensions of the East Asian story. These Confucian roots provided enabling cultural conditions. But equally important was the contribution of the American political and economic leadership of the 1960s and the strong encouragement it gave to the elites in East Asia. President John F. Kennedy may have had only a short term in office before he was tragically killed. But, in his short stay, he was able to influence significantly the zeitgeist. This zeitgeist also helped to fuel East Asia's development.

I can write all this with personal conviction. The 1960s were among the most critical, formative years of my life. Growing up in Singapore, we did experience a great deal of political and economic turbulence. Yet, despite all this, we also felt new rays of hope entering our lives. We felt ourselves moving forward toward better times. This optimism proved to be justified. The post–World War II era has been the best that East Asia has ever experienced. America laid the foundations for this era. Hence, in symbolic terms, the story of East Asia has to be portrayed as the journey from Confucius to Kennedy.

The truly good news from East Asia is that this journey has only now begun. Any nation anywhere in the world can join in the journey. The critical variable here is elite performance. With the right elites in place, all nations can progress and succeed.

Notes

1. Cited in Nishikawa (1993), page 8 as reproduced on the Web site of the International Bureau of Education, United Nations Educational, Scientific, and Cultural Organization, Paris, at http://www.ibe.unesco.org/publications/ThinkersPdf/fukuzawe.pdf. The quote is originally found in Fukuzawa (1885). The translation is by Sinh Vinh in *Fukuzawa Yukichi nenkan* [Annals] 11, Mita, Tokyo, Fukuzawa Yukichi kyokai, 1984.

2. *Chaebols* are large enterprise groups in Korea.

References

Elegant, Simon, and Michael Elliot. 2005. "Lee Kuan Yew Reflects." *Time Asia* 166 (24), on the Web on December 5. http://www.time.com/time/asia/covers/501051212/lky_intvu6.html.

Fukuzawa, Yukichi. 1885. "Datsu-A Ron" [Our Departure from Asia]. *Jiji-shimpo,* March 16.

Goh Keng Swee. 1995a. "Public Administration and Economic Development in LDCs." In *Wealth of East Asian Nations: Speeches and Writings by Goh Keng Swee,* ed. Linda Low, 128-45. Singapore: Federal Publications.

———. 1995b. "The Vietnam War: Round 3." In *Wealth of East Asian Nations: Speeches and Writings by Goh Keng Swee,* ed. Linda Low, 313-32. Singapore: Federal Publications.

———. 1995c. *The Economics of Modernization.* Singapore: Federal Publications.

IMF (International Monetary Fund). 2003. "Interview with Raghuram Rajan: Top Economist Calls for Rethink of IMF's Role." *IMF Survey* 32 (22): 361-64. http://www.imf.org/external/pubs/ft/survey/2003/121503.pdf.

Lee Kuan Yew. 1998. *The Singapore Story: Memoirs of Lee Kuan Yew.* Singapore: Times Editions.

———. 2000. *From Third World To First: The Singapore Story, 1965-2000.* Singapore: Times Media Private Ltd.

McNamara, Dennis L. 1990. *Colonial Origins of Korean Enterprise, 1910-1945.* Cambridge: Cambridge University Press.

Nishikawa, Shunsaku. 1993. "Fukuzawa Yukichi." *Prospects: The Quarterly Review of Comparative Education* 23 (3/4): 493-506.

Vogel, Ezra F. 1991. *The Four Little Dragons: The Spread of Industrialization in East Asia.* Cambridge, MA: Harvard University Press.

CHAPTER 12

Economic Integration in East Asia
A Philippine Perspective

FELIPE M. MEDALLA

Regional integration will certainly benefit the more dynamic economies in East Asia. The case of the Philippines is analyzed to show why leaders in other economies may be more skeptical.

This essay starts from two premises: (1) growth in East Asia is beginning to draw more and more from the internal strengths of the more dynamic economies in the region, and (2) the benefits of economic integration will, at least initially, be unequally distributed. Initially, I wanted to look at East Asian economic integration from the point of view of all lagging economies in the region. Such, however, is beyond my competence. So, I decided to focus on what I think is a Philippine perspective.

China and Japan have good reasons for wanting to take the lead in fostering greater East Asian economic integration. The Philippines, on the other hand, has good reasons to be ambivalent about rising economic integration in the region. It gained much less than its more dynamic neighbors after it liberalized trade. It is hard to be optimistic that the Philippines will benefit more than neighboring countries from economic integration.

Yet, it cannot opt out, especially if nearly everyone opts in. It has tried the protectionist approach and failed. The so-called infant industries that the government chose to protect in the 1960s and the 1970s could not be weaned off of protection and the preferential allocation of credit and foreign exchange. There is no reason to repeat the failed import-substitution policies. The Philippines can only hope the rules that govern Asian economic integration will be flexible enough to give it room to handle its sensitive sectors. It can also hope that some integration will occur in Asian labor markets as well.

China and Japan as Leaders in East Asian Economic Integration

Since the late 1990s, governments in East Asia have actively explored the possibility of free trade agreements (in the case of Japan, economic partnership agreements, EPAs). China and Japan have been the prime movers in pushing for agreements that would foster greater economic integration in the region. Japan has successfully negotiated an EPA with Singapore (Japan-Singapore Economic Partnership Agreement) and is almost certain to succeed in doing so with several other countries in the Association of Southeast Asian Nations (ASEAN) as well (for example, the Japan-Philippines Economic Partnership Agreement is expected to be signed before the end of 2006).

China and Japan each certainly have unique motives for wishing to foster greater economic integration in the region. However, they probably also share at least four reasons for this wish. The first is the desire to form a stronger front against possible discriminatory trade practices that may arise as a result of the formation of trading blocs in the West such as the European Union and the North American Free Trade Agreement. Another reason has to do with policy differences with the International Monetary Fund and the United States regarding global macroeconomic management that were highlighted by the Asian financial crisis. The third motive springs from the belief that economic cooperation based on geographical proximity may generate significant political and economic gains. The fourth and possibly the most important reason is the need to reduce dependence on the United States as a market for exports, given the fact that U.S. trade deficits are now large and would eventually have to be reduced by cutting into the growth of imports (by increasing protectionism, limiting economic growth, or depreciating the dollar). In short, these factors will result in changing the region "from a set of countries that rapidly integrated with the world to a region that is aggressively exploiting the sources of dynamism that lie within Asia" (Gill and Kharas 2006, 37).

Japan is working hard to facilitate the formal economic integration of the region by trying to sign EPAs with the Republic of Korea and some ASEAN countries. As pointed out by Baldwin (2002), the pressure on ASEAN countries to enter into trade agreements with Japan will be hard to resist if a Japan-Korea agreement is forged. This is so since Japan is a major market for Malaysian and Thai exports, a significant portion of which may compete with Korean products. By the same reasoning, the pressure on Indonesia and the Philippines to sign an EPA with Japan would be magnified if Malaysia and Thailand sign EPAs with Japan.

Given its complicated relationship with Japan and the United States and its dynamic economy, China should be quite optimistic that it would benefit in political and economic terms from greater regional economic integration. For instance, at the ASEAN+3 (plus China, Japan, and Korea) meeting in 2000, China proposed the creation of an economic expert group that would look at ways to increase ASEAN-China cooperation, including the possibility of a free trade agreement not only with ASEAN, but with Japan as well.

For such a large country that still has an abundance of surplus labor, it is not healthy for China to be too dependent on European and U.S. markets. It is therefore not surprising that China's active pursuit of increased regional economic integration is reflected not only in official Chinese statements (including at the last meeting of the Board of Governors of the Asian Development Bank [ADB] in Hyderabad), but also by China's offer of an "early harvest," whereby cuts in tariffs on ASEAN exports to China would be granted appreciably ahead of the reciprocal grant of the same preferential treatment for Chinese exports by ASEAN member countries.

Ambivalence of Countries Such As the Philippines

Under traditional or standard trade models or theories, all countries stand to gain from free trade. Indeed, under the simplest version of the standard model, there is no obvious reason why peripheral economies should benefit less from freer trade than core or leading economies. In a world where learning by doing, agglomeration and scale economies, and endogenous technological progress determine the direction of trade and investment flows, however, lagging or peripheral countries may gain much less from trade in spite of the fact that the total dynamic gains from trade may be much bigger than the static gains (for example, those arising purely from differences in factor endowments).

So what is the advantage for lagging countries such as the Philippines? Unfortunately, the dynamic forces that drive rapid growth in core or leading countries may also be the same forces that reduce the growth prospects of the lagging countries, at least at the early stages. The free movement of goods and capital allows for greater agglomeration and scale economies, which, in the absence of congestion costs and labor shortages, tend to concentrate growth in a few places.

In contrast to international trade theory, which recognizes that trade tends to concentrate growth in a few countries only after the introduction of the "new economic geography," the literature on urban and regional economics has long held the view that, because of scale and agglomeration economies, trade in goods and the movement of labor and capital within countries tend to concentrate economic activity in a few central places unless congestion costs in the central places put a brake on this geographical concentration of economic activities. Indeed, the primacy of metropolitan centers in terms of their disproportionately large share in total population and gross domestic product (GDP) is testament to the fact that growth tends to be highly concentrated if not only goods, but also factors of production are mobile.

That growth is highly concentrated in the center, however, does not result in political pressure to restrict trade within countries, not only because it is extremely difficult to control the movement of goods within countries, but also because most national tax and expenditure systems are designed to offset at least partially the effects of unbalanced growth. Moreover, people in backward areas may gain from increasing specialization and intracountry trade by migrating to the central places. In the Philippines, for example, the share of the National Capital Region in nonagricultural GDP (and, in all likelihood, in taxes as well) is around 42 percent, but the corresponding share of local governments in the National Capital Region in the block grants from the national treasury to local governments (called the internal revenue allotment) is only 8.1 percent. Moreover, the migration of workers to the richer regions of the country reduces interregional wage differentials and increases remittances to the poorer regions. Regrettably, in the case of international trade, an international tax system does not exist that would, at least partially, redistribute what is expected to be large, but highly unequal gains from trade, and there is not a sufficient movement of labor (because of the high cost of immigration and immigration controls) to reduce wage and income differentials.

It is therefore not surprising that lagging countries in Asia have ambivalent attitudes toward greater regional economic integration. The statement below by the alternate governor from Bangladesh (which is not part of East Asia) at the 39th meeting of the Board of Governors of the ADB perhaps best describes the ambivalence of governments in lagging economies toward greater economic integration in the region:

> The euphoria surrounding globalization seems to be waning as the champions of globalization have in recent times expressed doubts as to its effect on their industries and employment. We still believe in the process of globalization but at our own pace and convenience based on realities on the ground. (Zabihullah 2006, 2)

The above quotation stands in stark contrast with the statement made by China at the same meeting:

> ADB should further regional cooperation, a mission that is enshrined in the ADB Charter. Regional cooperation is full of potential. It is our hope that ADB will continue to play a role as a facilitator and financier. As a facilitator, ADB should give full play to its strengths as a multilateral institution and do more coordinating work, so as to promote deeper regional cooperation. (Jin 2006, 2)

The statement by the Philippine secretary of finance at the annual meetings of the International Monetary Fund and the World Bank Group did not mention Asian economic integration at all and pinned Philippine hopes "on the successful conclusion of the Doha round" (Teves 2005, 4). Unfortunately, the Doha Development Round has thus far failed to reach any agreement and probably never will, a fact that should be well known to the secretary of finance. Moreover, the benign view of the Philippine secretary of finance on the impact of a successful conclusion of the Doha round on the Philippines is not shared by many of his colleagues in the Department of Agriculture. In short, the way things are in the Philippines, there are mixed feelings about the failure of the Doha round. On the one hand, that many international trade issues are unresolved in the Doha round is a good thing from the point of view of government departments, the main constituencies of which are heavily protected by tariffs and trade barriers, to the extent that pressure on the Philippines to liberalize further is reduced. On the other hand, to the extent that the Philippines might have gained from a wider opening-up of developed-country markets and from a significant reduction in agricultural subsidies in the developed countries, the failure of the Doha round is clearly bad for the Philippines. At any rate, those who publicly proclaim that it is a good thing that the Doha round failed far outnumber those who say otherwise. (For example, the title of an opinion piece by a long-time critic of trade liberalization was "Why Monday's Collapse of the Doha Round Negotiations Is the Best Outcome for Developing Countries" [Bello 2006].)

Slow Economic Growth after Trade Liberalization

That the Philippines is not as sanguine as China, Malaysia, or Thailand about the implications of greater economic integration in the region is hardly surprising if one has looked at how the Philippine economy has performed since the second half of the 1980s, when international trade started to be significantly liberalized (beginning with the administration of President Corazon Aquino). As shown in table 12.1, the Philippine economy has lagged behind high-performing Asian economies. With the exception of the last five years, when the Philippines had the third lowest growth rate among the countries shown in the table, per capita GDP growth has been, by far, the low-

■ TABLE 12.1 **Average Annual Per Capita GDP Growth in Selected Asian Countries**
percent

Country	1981–90	1991–2000	2001–04
China	7.7	9.1	8.1
Korea, Rep. of	7.4	5.3	4.1
Indonesia	3.5	2.5	3.3
Malaysia	3.3	4.5	2.1
Philippines	−0.6	0.7	2.2
Singapore	4.8	4.8	1.4
Thailand	6.1	3.5	4.3
Vietnam	—	5.8	5.9

Source: Compiled by the author based on data from the ADB (www.adb.org) and the International Monetary Fund (www.imfstatistics.org).
Note: — = no data are available.

est in the Philippines during the last two or three decades among the Asian countries in the table. Moreover, the Philippine economy actually grew more rapidly during the import-substitution and protectionist decades of the 1960s and the 1970s (not shown in the table) than over the last 20 years.

Weak Influence of the Export Sector on Philippine Trade Policy

In general, a country's trade and industrial policy and the resulting level and structure of trade and nontariff barriers balance the political costs and benefits involved in opening up the economy (as perceived by policy makers). Domestic producers (and their labor unions) who are threatened by cheaper imports lobby for high-tariff protection and trade barriers. On the other hand, consumers are not seen by politicians as an interest group, so exporters may be the only ones who have some interest in lobbying for a more open economy. Exporters, however, will generally not lobby against tariffs or trade barriers that do not directly affect them (although they are indirectly affected to the extent that the trade barriers affect the real exchange rate) and may be placated by exempting their inputs from tariffs and domestic taxes (through bonded customs warehouses or tax and duty drawbacks). Thus, unlike in the case of Chile, tariffs are unlikely to become either uniform or low. Some sectors will receive much higher-than-average protection from foreign competition, and exports will be promoted not by reducing tariffs and trade barriers, but by giving exporters fiscal incentives and waivers of taxes and duties on their imports of raw materials and capital goods.

Since the administration of President Aquino, the Philippine government has unilaterally reduced many tariffs and trade barriers so as to promote consumer interest (partly because they have believed it would result in lower inflation). However, in cases where there has been strong producer, worker, or peasant resistance, the government has often yielded to political pressure and given much higher-than-average protection to certain industries and sensitive agricultural products. For instance, the rates of protection for rice, sugar, motor vehicles, and petrochemicals remain high after two decades of trade and tariff reforms.

In theory, negotiations on free trade areas (FTAs) and EPAs change the political balance in favor of making the economy more open. This is so since negotiations that eventually lead to FTAs or EPAs make it very clear to exporters that they must lobby for the opening up of their country's markets to imports in order to win market access abroad for their exports.

One can argue that FTA and EPA negotiations could give Philippine political leaders greater fortitude to resist lobbying by groups that benefit from the few remaining protected segments (albeit relatively large ones) in the manufacturing and agricultural sectors. Exporters, who normally worry mostly about their input costs and tax incentives, will generally not lobby for opening up domestic markets to foreign competition unless such is the explicit price their government must pay to open up markets abroad for the exporters. The dilemma for Philippine leaders is that there is relatively weak support for free trade agreements because exporters in the manufacturing sector account for a relatively small share of GDP and employment. Moreover, firms that account for a large share of manufactured exports have succeeded, in spite of the existing system of protection, either because they are in duty- and tax-free enclaves and serve niche markets (for example, semiconductors) or are already well served by existing agreements (such as exports of textiles and garments prior to the termination of export quotas under the international Multifiber Agreement or exports of motor vehicle units and parts under the Japan-led ASEAN complementation scheme). On the other hand, the opposition is strong and well organized. (Though small relative to the total population, it is able to coordinate large demonstrations and rallies.) To make matters worse, the academic and intellectual critics of greater economic integration never fail to point out that economic growth has been rather slow since the economy was liberalized. Sadly, export growth rates in the Philippines, although not nominally lower than those in other Asian countries except China, have not contributed significantly to the creation of jobs. Moreover, export growth has decelerated in recent years because of its dependence on growth in the demand for semiconductors (see table 12.2).

In spite of the modest growth in Philippine exports, growth in employment in the country's tradable sectors (manufacturing and agriculture) has been much lower than the growth rate of the labor force. The average growth rate of manufacturing employment during the last 10 years was only 1.6 percent. In the primary sector (agriculture, forest products, fishing, and mining), the growth rate of employment was even lower (0.5 percent). Much of the employment growth has occurred in

TABLE 12.2 **Export Growth Rates in Selected Asian Countries**
percent

Year	Indonesia	Malaysia	Philippines	China	Korea, Rep. of	Singapore	Thailand
2005	19.5	—	—	28.4	12.2	18.8	15.0
2004	17.2	20.5	9.5	35.4	31.0	24.6	21.6
2003	6.8	11.6	2.9	34.7	19.3	15.2	18.2
2002	1.5	6.9	9.5	22.1	8.0	2.8	4.8
2001	−9.3	−10.4	−15.6	7.0	−12.7	−11.6	−7.1
2000	27.7	16.2	8.7	27.9	19.9	20.1	19.5
1999	−0.4	15.3	18.8	6.1	8.6	4.3	7.4
1998	−8.6	−6.9	16.9	0.5	−2.8	−11.9	−6.8
1997	7.3	0.6	22.8	21.0	5.0	−0.1	3.8
1996	9.7	6.0	17.7	1.5	3.7	5.7	−1.9
1995	13.4	25.6	29.4	23.0	30.3	−22.2	24.8
1994	8.8	24.9	18.5	31.9	16.8	30.9	22.2
1993	8.4	15.6	15.8	8.0	7.3	16.6	13.4
1992	16.6	18.7	11.1	—	6.6	7.6	13.8
1991	13.5	16.5	8.0	—	10.5	11.8	—
Average	8.8	11.5	12.4	19.0	10.9	10.5	10.4

Source: Compiled by the author based on data from the ADB Asia Regional Information Center (http://aric.adb.org).
Note: — = no data are available.

the service sector (the great bulk of which is internationally nontradable), wherein employment grew by more than 4 percent. This has resulted in a decline in the employment share not only of the primary sectors, but of the manufacturing sector as well. The primary sector's employment share fell from 43.8 percent in 1995 to 36.4 percent in 2005. On the other hand, the manufacturing sector's employment share fell from an already low 10.2 percent in 1995 to 9.5 percent in 2005, which is a continuation of a long-term declining trend since the share of the manufacturing sector in total employment was more than 12 percent before international trade was liberalized. In short, the employment shares of the tradable sectors declined after the domestic economy became more integrated with the global economy.

That employment growth in manufacturing was very disappointing despite modest export growth may be explained by the fact that much of the export growth is accounted for by only two types of goods: semiconductors and motor vehicle units and parts (including wiring harnesses). As shown in table 12.3, electronic and electrical equipment and parts, and machinery and transport equipment, are the two most rapidly growing exports, accounting for 82.6 percent of the increase in Philippine exports (in U.S. dollars) during the last 20 years. Former mainstays in labor-intensive exports—garments, textiles, and footwear—and primary exports performed poorly. Unfortunately, semiconductors and wiring harnesses have relatively low domestic value added and are less labor intensive than garments, textiles, and footwear. At any rate, trade and employment data will not inspire political leaders to open up the economy. Moreover, because the rise in the exports of electronic and electrical goods occurs largely in enclaves and because the rise in the export of automobile units and parts is not due to free trade, but to managed trade, it is not clear that joining FTAs would be good for employment growth. In short, the claim that freer trade will create a lot more jobs for the Philippines will be met with quite a bit of skepticism. (The Philippines restricted and heavily taxed the imports of completely built vehicles, while taxing the importation of car parts by car assemblers at a much lower rate. This fostered a very inefficient car assembly industry. Exports of cars and car parts rose after the sector was rationalized and became more efficient. This occurred when the government began allowing car companies

TABLE 12.3 Growth in Philippine Exports

Sector	1985 (US$ millions)	2005 (US$ millions)	Increase (US$ millions)	Share in increase (%)	Growth rate (%, compounded)
Primary sectors	2,038	3,441	1,403	4.0	2.6
Electronic and electrical equipment and parts	1,056	28,476	27,420	77.5	16.5
Machinery and transport equipment	30	1,836	1,806	5.1	20.6
Garments, textiles, and footwear	711	2,568	1,857	5.2	6.4
Other manufactured goods	1,007	3,910	2,903	8.2	6.8
Total	4,842	40,231	35,389	100.0	10.6

Source: Compiled by the author based on data from the Bangko Sentral ng Pilipinas (http://www.bsp.gov.ph).

to import completely built vehicles provided such imports are financed by exports of vehicles and vehicle parts. The tariffs are low if the automobile company is a participant in the ASEAN automobile complementation scheme.)

Why There Is Little Support for More Trade Liberalization

Supporters of trade liberalization argue, of course, that economic and employment growth is low *in spite* of trade liberalization. Such arguments, though plausible, may not gain ground with the general public, especially since many of the people who fought in favor of trade liberalization (for example, during the debates regarding Philippine membership in the World Trade Organization) also virtually predicted that it would result in much higher output and employment growth. Regrettably, actual employment and export growth did not come anywhere near the vision that supporters of trade liberalization painted during the debates that eventually led the Philippine senate to ratify the membership of the Philippines in the World Trade Organization.

At any rate, it is very hard to sell to opinion makers and policy makers the argument that people may not be much more well off today compared to the past, but have actually benefited from liberalization because they might have been much less well off if the economy had not been liberalized. In the first place, such an argument requires counterfactual reasoning (comparing what actually happened to the economy to something that did not happen and is therefore hard to visualize). In the second place, it requires that alternative explanations be given for the economy's poor performance (such as external shocks, weak institutions, the absence of population policies, corruption, poor fiscal management, labor market distortions, poor infrastructure, mismanagement of the electricity sector, and so on). However, to the layman or even the typical legislator, the simplistic argument is much easier to follow: the economy did not perform well after liberalization; therefore liberalizing the economy was not a good idea, and it is not a good idea to liberalize further.

There are, of course, obvious gains from liberalization. Consumers certainly get much greater value for their money (in terms of quality and price) because of trade liberalization. The price of air conditioners today, for example, is about the same as it was 10 years ago despite a significant rise in the general price level and the continuous fall of the Philippine peso. Electronic products (for instance, DVD players and computers) have become more affordable, and cheap imported manufactured goods from China have expanded the consumption space of most Filipinos. What best illustrates the gains of consumers is the great number of people going to the shopping centers in Manila's Chinatown that sell virtually nothing except cheap Chinese goods. Unfortunately, policy debates about opening up the economy are never won by pointing out that cheaper, higher-quality imported goods are beneficial for the people. Indeed, to most politicians, cheap imported goods are good only if they do not compete with more expensive domestic products. (Recall the fallacy that, if it is true that exports increase employment, it must also be true that imports reduce employment.) At any rate, closures of uncompetitive factories are a lot more newsworthy than the increased supply of imported products that are cheaper or better. Moreover, among influential religious leaders whose encouragement might have given the politicians some backbone to support greater liberalization, the expansion of the consumption space was, in fact, seen as a bad thing (that is, negatively described as encouraging materialism and commercialism). Of course, the critics of liberalization would have dwindled if liberalization had also created a lot of jobs and not only increased the range and supply of higher-quality, lower-priced products.

However, neither employment statistics nor modern trade theory bears out that this is what happens. Indeed, what happened to the Philippines relative to high-performing Asian economies and Metro-Manila relative to the rest of the Philippines is quite consistent with the new economic geography that predicts some places will tend to grow much more rapidly than others (because of the dynamics of trade and growth, which are triggered by location-specific advantages such as governance, centrality, the size of the domestic market, and so on). Regrettably, Manila and its surrounding regions (Bulacan and Pampanga to the north and Laguna, Batangas, and Cavite to the south) are part of the periphery from the point of view of Asia and the world and are, at the same time, the center from the point of view of the rest of the Philippines. Thus, the Philippines has the worst of both worlds: slow economic growth that is overly concentrated in and around Metro-Manila.

One may, of course, again use the counterfactual argument that the continuation of import-substitution policies and protectionism as practiced until the early part of the 1980s would not have succeeded in making the Philippines a leading economy. This is so since the infant industries that were protected and promoted used a lot of imported inputs and did not become more efficient. They were therefore unable to export even after extended periods of protection. As a result, balance of payments shocks often resulted in increased idle capacity and layoffs. Typically, plants become underutilized when foreign exchange becomes scarce because balance of payments crises usually force central banks to reduce aggregate demand. Since the protected firms survive only because domestic prices are higher than border prices, the protected industries could not eliminate idle capacity by exporting what could not be sold domestically. In short, protectionism worsened the boom-bust cycles. The economy grew rapidly as long as the protected sector had access to cheap foreign exchange (for instance, because of war damage payments by Japan and the United States after World War II and because of foreign borrowing by the government during the administration of President Marcos), but collapsed when foreign exchange became scarce. In turn, balance of payments crises were almost periodic and inevitable because protectionism, which made foreign exchange artificially cheap for protected industries, also discouraged exports.

This was not initially the case in the early stage of import substitution when there were plenty of opportunities for easy import substitution. There were many industries in the 1950s and the 1960s that were otherwise globally competitive, but could not compete with imports because the peso was overvalued. (The official exchange rate was twice the black market rate.) There were two ways to level the playing field for such industries. One was to scrap import controls and devalue the peso. Another was to use foreign exchange, capital rationing, and selectively high tariffs to encourage import substitution. The government chose the latter, with initially encouraging results in terms of output and employment growth. (Some older Philippine economists still look at the early import-substitution period as a sort of golden age for manufacturing.)

However, as opportunities for easy import substitution were exhausted, policy makers chose to allocate resources to industries that were uncompetitive and used a lot of imported inputs. Unfortunately, none or very few of these capital-intensive infant industries became competitive. In short, with the exception perhaps of a few professional economists in government, Philippine policy makers abandoned important substitution and protectionism not because they liked trade liberalization. They did so because the Philippine import-substitution path had reached a dead end. This essay will not attempt to explain why protectionism did not become a springboard for export-led development in the Philippines, unlike the Japanese and Korean experience. (The top four explanations are weak bureaucracy, traditional politics, the rapacity of Philippine elites, and the backwardness of science and engineering, not necessarily in that order.) What is important to note is that Philippine policy makers, on the whole, were quite wary and uncomfortable with opening up domestic markets to foreign competition and opened up the economy only after they had failed in their attempts to achieve high and sustainable economic growth through interventionist trade and industrial policies. In other words, if one scratches the surface of a seemingly market-friendly policy maker hard enough, one is likely to find a protectionist who happens not to trust government. Thus, it is ironic that Philippine tariffs on many manufactured products were raised back to 1997 levels in 2003, after many years of gradual decline, under a president with a doctorate in economics.

In hindsight, the weak commitment to opening up the economy is not surprising. Liberalization did not usher in higher economic growth. It was accompanied by a fall in the share of manufacturing in total employment, and exporter and consumer lobbies were much weaker than the lobbies of the sectors that would be hurt by liberalization. It is therefore quite likely that trade liberalization in the Philippines cannot progress further. What was politically easy to liberalize has already been liberalized. What remains untouched by trade liberalization is the politically most difficult sectors. For instance, there are large potential gains from liberalizing the importation of rice and sugar (given the large difference between border and domestic prices). The sugar lobby is a shadow of its former self, but is still influential when it comes to sugar-importation policy. In the case of rice, on the other hand, the government is torn between having greater economic efficiency and protecting rice farmers (who are, on average, poorer than urban rice consumers, and their plight has historical links with the communist insurgency).

Unfortunately, the government does not have the capability to tax the winners and compensate the losers from trade liberalization. Moreover, weak as the tax system is, it is much stronger and less corruptible than the system of making transfer payments or subsidies. There is plenty of anecdotal evidence that, whenever the government gives money to people who are hurt by policy change or natural calamities, the likelihood that many nonvictims will be toward the front of the queue is quite high. In short, the capacity to supply targeted subsidies may be even weaker than the capacity to administer taxes.

The case of sugar is a different story. A fall in the price of sugar may actually reduce agricultural land prices and make agrarian reform more affordable (since land reform is based on the principle of just compensation). The sugar lobby is not as strong as it used to be. In the past, it was a kingmaker not only in local politics, but in national politics as well. (It was often said that one could not be president of the Philippines without being anointed by the sugar bloc.) However, it remains politically influential in many provinces. Moreover, access to the U.S. markets that is protected by a system of sugar-import quotas actually makes it worthwhile for the Philippines to import sugar for domestic consumption and produce sugar for the U.S. markets, which creates a lot of opportunities for rent seeking.

The Philippines Gains Largely from Consumption and the Export of Labor

It is worth noting that a significant part of the gains from integrating the Philippine economy with the global economy is accounted for by migration (both circular and permanent) by Philippine workers. At constant 1985 prices, Philippine per capita income increased by US$186, from US$631 to US$817. In contrast, remittances per capita increased by US$51 during the same period, which represents more than a quarter (27 percent) of the increase in per capita income from 1995 to 2005.

In current prices, the share of remittances in the increase in per capita income is even greater (see table 12.4). Per capita income increased by US$139, from US$1,085 in 1995 to US$1,224 in 2005. On the other hand, the increase in remittances per capita during the same period was US$69, or one half the increase in per capita income.

Since there was a large real depreciation of the peso after the Asian financial crisis and a large proportion of gross national product (GNP) is nontradable, it is possible that the importance of increases in worker remittances would be overstated if one uses current prices and exchange rates to compare the peso value of domestic production with the dollar value of worker remittances. Moreover, remittances may have negative effects on the international competitiveness of tradable sectors in the Philippines (via the Dutch Disease effect through the exchange rate). However, using 1985 prices to compare 2005 and 1995 values is also

TABLE 12.4 **Share of Worker Remittances and Two Key Exports in Per Capita GNP**

Year	Per capita GNP[a]	Remittances per capita	Valued added in electronic and electrical equipment exports per capita[b]
Constant 1985 prices			
2005 (US$)	817	83	44
1995 (US$)	631	32	12
Increase (US$)	186	51	32
% of total increase	(100)	(27)	(17)
Current prices			
2005 (US$)	1,224	124	66
1995 (US$)	1,085	55	21
Increase (US$)	139	69	45
% of total increase	(100)	(50)	(33)

Source: Compiled by the author based on data from the Bangko Sentral ng Pilipinas (http://www.bsp.gov.ph).
a. GNP = gross national product.
b. Assumed to be equal to 20 percent of total exports of electronic and electrical equipment.

quite problematic. In addition, worker remittances may have large multiplier effects to the extent that many sectors of the economy use imported inputs. For example, transportation and distribution costs and the markups of wholesalers and retailers are counted as value added when imported goods are sold to consumers. (Thus, the value added of the wholesale retail sector in 2005 was 70 percent of the value added of the manufacturing sector, up from 55 percent in 1990.) At any rate, whether increases in remittances account for one-quarter or one-half of the increase in per capita incomes, it is clear that, relative to other countries, Filipinos benefited much more from the integration of global labor and goods markets than from the integration of global production.

Table 12.5 shows the distribution of worker remittances by geographical origin. The United States was by far the largest source, accounting for 60 percent of the remittances in 2005. Europe and the Middle East each accounted for 13 percent, and Asia accounted for 11 percent. Nearly a million overseas workers were reported to have been deployed in 2005. The deployment statistics of the Department of Labor and Employment do not include the bulk of the 1.4 million

TABLE 12.5 **Worker Remittances, by Source**
US$ thousands

Year	Total	United States	Asia	Europe	Middle East	Other
1997	5,741,835	4,109,430	454,791	436,050	25,375	716,189
1998	7,367,989	6,403,215	401,419	329,317	60,682	173,356
1999	6,794,550	4,868,879	645,566	457,671	263,004	559,430
2000	6,050,450	3,944,639	831,779	534,675	594,198	145,159
2001	6,031,271	3,202,230	1,049,551	406,194	711,918	661,378
2002	6,886,156	3,443,547	1,116,336	889,094	1,242,809	194,370
2003	7,578,458	4,299,850	894,310	1,040,562	1,166,376	177,360
2004	8,550,371	4,904,302	918,329	1,286,130	1,232,069	209,541
2005	10,689,005	6,424,848	1,172,373	1,433,904	1,417,491	240,389

Source: Compiled by the author based on data from the Bangko Sentral ng Pilipinas (http://www.bsp.gov.ph).

to 1.6 million Filipinos in the United States who generally do not register with the department when they leave the Philippines. This probably explains why the United States is the biggest source of remittances. Still, it may be that the share of the United States in remittances is overstated since permanent migrants are expected to remit less than circular migrants. One possible reason for the overstatement of the share of the United States in remittances is that remittances from other countries that go through U.S. banks may sometimes be reported as remittances from the United States.

Exports of electronic and electrical equipment accounted for much more than 80 percent of the increase in Philippine exports. If it is assumed that value added is 20 percent of the value of the top export, this value added would account for 17 percent of the increase in per capita GNP between 1995 and 2005 at 1985 prices and 33 percent at current prices (see table 12.4). Combined with the increase in remittances, this sums to 44 percent of the increase in per capita GNP in constant prices over the last 10 years and an incredible 83 percent of the increase in per capita GNP in current prices.

As shown in table 12.6, the rest of the manufacturing sector did not do as well as the production of electronic goods and electrical parts and equipment. The rest of the manufacturing sector's share in GDP declined from slightly less than a quarter in 1991 to 21.1 percent in 2005. Why the production of electronic and electrical equipment and parts showed a totally different trend from the rest of manufacturing is perhaps worth a short digression.

TABLE 12.6 **Share of Traditional Manufacturing in GDP**

Year	GDP (constant 1985 ₱ millions)	Value added in traditional manufacturing[a] Constant 1985 ₱ millions	Share of GDP (%)
1991	717,225	176,829	24.7
1993	712,332	173,787	24.4
1995	766,368	179,723	23.5
1997	849,121	200,746	23.6
1999	888,075	201,867	22.7
2001	958,411	209,593	21.9
2003	1,023,101	218,054	21.3
2005	1,134,907	239,818	21.1

Source: Compiled by the author.
a. Excluding electronic and electrical equipment and parts.

Many parts of Philippine manufacturing were not globally competitive and were therefore unable to prosper when the level of protection from foreign competition was reduced. Electronic and electrical parts and equipment, on the other hand, are produced almost exclusively for export by subcontractors or wholly owned plants of multinational companies. European (for example, Philips), Japanese (such as Fujitsu, Hitachi, NEC, and Toshiba), Korean (for example, LG and Samsung), and U.S. firms (such as Intel and Texas Instruments) probably have very different motives for investing in the Philippines. U.S. electronics firms have been in the Philippines for more than two decades. They operate plants that have direct production links with the mother companies and are not part of an Asian or ASEAN regional production network. (For instance, the payroll of Texas Instruments in Baguio is prepared and electronically transmitted directly at the U.S. headquarters.) Some of the plants that are affiliated with ASEAN firms, on the other hand, are part of a regional production network. Perhaps the best example of the importance of a regional network would be Malaysian- or Singaporean-owned firms in the Philippines that are part of the same regional production network as the Malaysian or Singaporean principals.

Japanese multinational corporations, on the other hand, may have different reasons for being in the Philippines relative to corporations from an ASEAN country. Unlike their European or U.S. counterparts, which are mostly involved in assembly and testing, Japanese electronics firms are producing a wide range of products (semiconductors, hard disk drives [HDDs], automobile wiring harnesses, smart automobile brake systems, and so on) in the Philippines. Their activities have relied on various modes of structure and operation, ranging from wholly Filipino-owned subcontractors to wholly owned subsidiaries in the Philippines. For instance, the HDD industry in the Philippines is dominated by Japanese-owned assemblers and suppliers that belong to the *keiretsu* (industrial groups) of the firms or their Japanese independent contractors. (In contrast, among non-Japanese firms, only Read-Rite, Inc. and Seagate are present in the Philippines, and most U.S. HDD firms established in Malaysia, Singapore, and Thailand have not located in the Philippines.)

The wave of Japanese investments in electronics in the Philippines to a great extent was part of the Japanese expansion into Southeast Asia. With the strengthening of the yen (the high yen, or *endaka*), intense global competition induced Japanese firms to transfer separable production to countries with lower production costs. The case of HDDs, however, was quite unique since most Japanese firms that located assembly operations in the Philippines did not locate similar facilities anywhere else outside Japan. Agglomeration economies probably explain why the assembly of HDDs by Japanese firms was highly concentrated in the Philippines. Still, the firms could have located their operations in another ASEAN country, but a combination of factors, including proximity to Japan (so that Japanese managers may make frequent plant visits) and a good supply of engineers and English-speaking workers (the firms hire only workers with at least two years of college), made the Philippines the preferred (or, in the case of three of the four Japanese HDD firms, the sole) plant location outside Japan. The importance of the ability of workers to speak English to Japanese managers is not surprising since Japanese managers who were working outside Japan generally spoke English and no other foreign language. If a good supply of educated English-speaking workers was important to Japanese firms, it is not far-fetched that it would be at least equally important to European and U.S. firms. (Surprisingly, this is not as well documented, since more studies have been conducted on the motives of Japanese firms for locating in the Philippines.)

Why the Philippines Is Still in the Game

Given that much of the gain of the Philippines in becoming integrated with the global economy has arisen from exports of labor (and the imported goods that this financed) and from exports of electronic and electrical equipment, one could argue that the Philippines could have done equally as well if it had not liberalized trade. This is so since it may well be that exports of labor and electronic and electrical equipment would have increased even if trade had not been liberalized. What promoted exports of electronic and electrical equipment and parts was their exemption from taxes and duties on raw materials and capital equipment. The exemptions were carried out through bonded customs warehouses and duty drawbacks, two incentives that could be offered to exporters independently of the level of protection that is given to domestic industries. In short, very little of the growth in Philippine current account receipts (in the balance of payments) could be attributed to trade liberalization. This fits the pattern for lagging countries in the new economic geography.

Does this mean that there is a high risk that the Philippines would resist free trade agreements or even reverse liberalization? The Philippines did, in fact, raise some tariffs back to 1997 levels in 2003. However, no other, similar reversals have occurred since then. It is, of course, very hard to forecast what politicians will do, but it is probably safe to say that the liberalization will not be reversed. In the first place, protectionism will be driven by the lobbying efforts of uncompetitive sectors of the economy, not by explicit industrial policy.

But the fact that the share of manufacturing in total employment has declined to less than 10 percent (even lower if one does not treat a big part of food processing, such as rice milling, as manufacturing) means that much of what remains in the manufacturing sector is either export oriented or inward looking, but competitive. Moreover, the fact that many people expect smuggling to rise if trade barriers and tariffs are raised means there is only a weak political constituency for raising tariffs. Finally, overseas workers have become a powerful political constituency that would like to get good consumer value for their hard-earned money. For instance, they are allowed to bring home a significant amount of imported goods tax and duty free when they return. (This, in turn, has resulted in the proliferation of duty-free shops that cater not to tourists, but to overseas workers and their families.)

Another factor that militates against a reversal of trade liberalization is widespread skepticism that industrial policies successfully practiced (or perceived to have been practiced successfully) in Japan and Korea will work in the Philippines. In short, Filipinos may not have much faith in globalization and the market, but they distrust the government's ability to pick winners even more.

That the current levels of protection will not be raised is, of course, not the same thing as saying that the Philippines could be easily convinced to join FTAs. The Philippines joined the ASEAN Free Trade Area (AFTA), but there was virtually no visible opposition to AFTA membership, which is a reflection more of the flexibility of AFTA (with regard to the exclusion of sensitive products, for example) than of the willingness of the Philippines to join FTAs. In short, given the low political cost of joining AFTA, being excluded from it was unacceptable. Philippine political and business leaders correctly perceive that the cost to the Philippines of being left out of an FTA would be higher as the number of Asian countries joining FTAs increases.

The Prospects for a Japan-Philippine EPA

Like AFTA, an EPA with Japan is also likely to be perceived as uncontroversial in the Philippines. Given Japan's reluctance to reduce agricultural protection, it is unlikely to ask for free trade in agricultural products. Indeed, the fact that the Philippines is a net importer of rice is probably one of the reasons why Japan chose to have an EPA with the Philippines ahead of all other ASEAN countries except Singapore. That the Japanese are seeking many exceptions for agricultural products does not seem to be a stumbling block from the point of view of Philippine policy makers. In the first place, the Philippines is not a major exporter of agricultural products. In the second place, exports of high-value agricultural goods to Japan would be relaxed during the Japanese off-season. Off-season exports may not be good enough from the point of view of some Philippine producers of high-value agricultural products (such as tropical fruits) who see Japan as a large potential market, but their objections would carry little political weight, especially if Japan offers to expand official development assistance (ODA) loans for infrastructure and agrees to open up its labor markets to nurses and caregivers. Indeed, the biggest concern on the Philippine side in the negotiations with Japan is not the number of products that Japan wants to exclude from the trade agreement, but the number of Philippine nurses and caregivers that Japan is willing to accept. President Arroyo personally communicated this point during her last visit to Japan. The Japanese response, however, was rather cautious (because of strong objections from Japanese health care workers). They offered to allow entry of only 100 nurses. The Philippines would probably accept the Japanese offer in the hope that the entry of 100 nurses might pave the way for a greater deployment of Philippine nurses and caregivers in Japan later.

Finally, the reduction of tariffs on Japanese exports of manufactured goods to the Philippines is not a major concern on the part of the latter. Philippine tariffs on manufactured goods are already quite low. The manufactured goods that will be covered by the Japan-Philippine EPA are also subject to zero or low duties for imports covered by the AFTA. The Philippine automotive industry would probably be most affected by the Japan-Philippine EPA. The Philippine motor vehicle assembly and parts industries, however, are mostly owned by Japanese firms and are not going to object to including motor vehicles in the Japan-Philippine EPA. (Not surprisingly, Ford Philippines was not keen on the idea of including cars in the agreement, but its objections are unlikely to deter the Philippines from signing an EPA with Japan.)

China and the Philippines

A free trade agreement that includes China (through a bilateral agreement or through ASEAN) would probably immediately garner negative reactions from most politicians and businessmen in the Philippines. The image of a juggernaut hollowing out the manufacturing sector in the Philippines comes to mind. Yet, more and more Philippine businessmen are beginning to look at China as a market rather than as a competitor. Indeed, as shown in table 12.7, exports to China are the most rapidly growing area of Philippine exports, surpassing exports to Korea in 2002 and almost matching exports to all ASEAN countries in 2005.

Moreover, Europe and the United States account for a big chunk of Philippine exports, which would be threatened by competition from China whether or not ASEAN or the Philippines has a free trade agreement with China. Thus, competition from China has already resulted in slower growth in the exports of Philippine garments. A similar fate probably awaits Philippine exports of electronic and electrical products to Europe and the United States as electronics products become standardized commodities. In other words, because of 20 years of

TABLE 12.7 **Philippine Exports, by Recipient**
US$ millions

Year	United States	Europe	Japan	China	Korea, Rep. of	ASEAN	Total
1994	5,143	2,428	2,024	164	292	723	13,483
1995	6,160	3,134	2,742	214	444	1,370	17,447
1996	6,966	3,684	3,668	328	371	1,742	20,543
1997	8,815	4,670	4,192	244	474	1,809	25,228
1998	10,098	6,139	4,233	343	510	1,987	29,496
1999	10,445	6,969	4,660	575	1,032	2,512	35,037
2000	11,365	6,991	5,606	663	1,173	2,845	38,078
2001	8,979	6,349	5,054	793	1,044	2,669	32,150
2002	8,683	6,567	5,292	1,356	1,339	3,047	35,208
2003	7,119	6,086	5,756	2,143	1,311	4,003	35,752
2004	7,088	6,895	7,981	2,653	1,113	4,195	39,681
2005	7,402	7,116	7,202	4,077	1,391	4,424	41,221

Source: Compiled by the author based on data from the Bangko Sentral ng Pilipinas (http://www.bsp.gov.ph).

trade liberalization, which has reduced the relative share of the vulnerable part of Philippine manufacturing in total employment, there is not much left in the Philippine manufacturing sector that may be threatened by greater East Asian economic integration.

This is not to say that no segment of Philippine manufacturing will be less well off if tariffs and trade barriers between China and the Philippines are significantly reduced. For instance, the car and motorcycle industries, which enjoy the highest rates of tariff protection among all manufactured goods, will be threatened (but only if the quality of Chinese motor vehicles and motorcycles improves). Yet, the overall impact on manufacturing employment in the Philippines may not be as large as the positive impact in sectors that may expand due to greater access to the Chinese market (such as bananas, pineapples, and mangoes). Finally, given the relatively short distance between the two countries and the large and growing Chinese middle class, the prospects are great for the tourism sector in the Philippines.

Bright as the prospects are, however, there would be substantial psychological barriers to the idea of a free trade agreement that includes China and the Philippines. China's offer of early harvest is a good start, but has probably not tipped public opinion in favor of a free trade agreement with China. Maybe China should change tactics and unilaterally open its markets to the Philippines. Such a move will most likely result in a significant increase in Philippine exports to China, which the latter can ultimately use as a bargaining chip to draw the Philippines into a free trade agreement (for example, by threatening to raise the barriers again).

On ODA and East Asian Economic Integration

There has been quite a bit of talk (such as at the last ADB meeting in Hyderabad) about the need to expand ODA to help lagging economies prepare for economic integration in the region. In particular, infrastructure and human resources are often cited by investors as important factors in the decision on where to locate. On the other hand, despite the fact that economic integration has resulted in a high concentration of economic activities in or around metropolitan areas, there is little resistance to economic integration within countries. This is so because significant fiscal transfers (in both cash and kind) related to integration tend to reduce human resource and infrastructure gaps among regions within countries. Still, many developed countries are nowhere near their commitment to allocate at least 1 percent of GNP to ODA.

However, it is unrealistic to expect ODA to make a major dent in resolving the problem of the lack of international competitiveness in lagging countries such as the Philippines. For example, the government of the Philippines spends much less on infrastructure than do other Asian governments (see table 12.8), and the gap is so wide that infrastructure problems in the Philippines will be properly addressed only if the Philippines undertakes significant fiscal and policy reforms (World Bank 2005).

Nonetheless, ODA can play a strategic role in infrastructure development in the Philippines. Political forces and processes in the Philippines have a tendency to spend too little on infrastructure and spread the already small total investment thinly among the various political districts of the country. In contrast, Philippine exports would probably be more competitive if the Philippines were to give priority to infrastructure investments within a relatively narrow corridor connecting the former U.S. military bases north of Metro-Manila and the Batangas port south of the metropolis.

The reason ODA-funded infrastructure does not have to be spread as thinly as locally funded infrastructure projects is that ODA institu-

TABLE 12.8 Government Capital Expenditures as a Share of GDP
percent

Year	Indonesia	Malaysia	Philippines	China	Korea, Rep. of	Thailand
2004	14.1	6.1	—	—	3.5	—
2003	13.2	9.7	1.6	4.0	4.2	2.8
2002	9.9	9.7	1.7	4.4	4.3	3.7
2001	9.1	10.2	1.6	4.2	4.0	3.7
2000	3.1	7.3	1.8	4.0	3.8	3.9
1999	—	7.1	2.1	3.9	4.6	4.9
1998	—	6.0	1.6	3.2	4.2	6.0

Source: Compiled by the author based on data from the ADB Asia Regional Information Center (http://aric.adb.org).
Note: — = no data available.

tions (such as the ADB, the Japan Bank for International Cooperation, and the World Bank) have quite a bit of leverage if they want to focus infrastructure assistance in a few areas. In short, an alliance between national government agencies and ODA institutions can improve the efficiency of infrastructure investments (to the extent that concentrating infrastructure spending in a few strategic areas is efficient, but not now politically feasible). This presents a dilemma for multilateral and bilateral sources of ODA funds because the emphasis on the Millennium Development Goals tends to result in assigning a higher priority to less developed areas. However, the dilemma can be resolved by deciding that a certain proportion of the ODA should go to the goals and a certain portion should go toward enhancing international competitiveness (the criteria for which may vary from country to country).

Conclusion and Future Prospects

The gains from trade will be both large and unequally distributed if the evolution of trade and foreign investments is driven by learning by doing, endogenous technological change, and scale and agglomeration economies. Thus, advanced countries such as Japan and rapidly growing economies such as China have good motives for taking the lead toward greater economic integration in East Asia. However, economies such as the Philippines that have not performed well for various reasons are also the least likely to be favored by trade and investment flows driven by the forces listed above. Economic integration will result initially in unequal gains from trade. Only much later, after the congestion costs and labor costs have risen in the successful countries, will lagging countries such as the Philippines get a bigger share of the gains from trade.

Yet, the lagging countries cannot opt out. Protectionist development strategies require much better governments than those the lagging countries have (and may, in fact, be the reason they are lagging in the first place). The greater the number of countries joining an FTA, the costlier not being part of the FTA becomes. Moreover, the lagging countries may benefit, too, by exporting labor and by finding niches not requiring agglomeration economies that are as extensive as those in rapidly growing economies.

That trade and investment flows do not benefit all countries equally should not be surprising. Trade and the movement of factors of production within countries have the same effect, creating huge cities even in the least dynamic economies. The difference, of course, is that the fiscal systems of nation states may redistribute gains from the intracountry movement of goods and factors. In the case of the benefits of economic integration, however, little transfer will take place between countries that gain a lot and countries that gain little, and there is not much to be obtained by stepping back from the "trade not aid" to the "aid not trade" debate. The aid will never be sufficient to matter significantly because the countries that benefit most from trade also must address their own strong domestic constituents.

Movements of people may possess the potential to mitigate the problems of the unequal gains from trade. But migrant workers from lagging countries can only hope that successful countries will open their doors and treat them well.

Nevertheless, there is reason to be more optimistic about the prospective benefits going to the Philippines from greater East Asian economic integration, especially with regard to the country's experience with trade liberalization in the 1980s and 1990s. The Philippines did gain from the freer trade in the 1980s and 1990s, but the gains were partially masked by the decline of uncompetitive industries that were exposed to foreign competition by trade liberalization. There were gains from freer trade. It just so happened that there could be no gain without pain since both the production and employment levels of uncompetitive industries would inevitably have to be shrunk as tariffs and nontrade barriers were reduced or eliminated. In a way, the withering away of uncompetitive industries (many of which needed more than twice each dollar equivalent of domestic resources to save a dollar at the prevailing exchange rate) was only a matter of time. And, in a sense, it is better the Philippines made the adjustment at least a decade ago rather than now, when the internal dynamic forces that drive growth in the region are much stronger and the region has become more integrated. In other words, except for agriculture, the social cost to the Philippines of greater East Asian economic integration is going to be much less than the cost the country incurred as a result of trade liberalization in the 1980s and 1990s. Thus, the Philippines has already paid many of its dues, and the remaining dues to be paid are relatively small, especially in comparison with the gains to be derived from becoming integrated with dynamic economies that are much closer to the Philippines than the country's Western trading partners.

Finally, perhaps the best argument for economic integration is that integration will make the fact some countries are ahead and some are behind more obvious. And the peoples of the lagging countries will then start asking their governments the reason why this is so.

References

Abeysinghe, Tilak, and Ding Lu. 2003. "China as an Economic Powerhouse: Implications on Its Neighbors." *China Economic Review* 14 (2): 164–85.

Baldwin, Richard E. 2002. "Asian Regionalism: Promises and Pitfalls." Paper presented at the Korea Institute for International Economic Policy "Conference on Prospects for Economic Cooperation in East Asia," Seoul, September 27.

Bello, Walden. 2006. "Why Monday's Collapse of the Doha Round Negotiations Is the Best Outcome for Developing Nations." *Focus on the Global South*, July 25. http://www.focusweb.org/content/view/984/.

Fujita Masahisa, Paul Krugman, and Anthony J. Venables. 1999. *The Spatial Economy: Cities, Regions and International Trade*. Cambridge, MA: MIT Press.

Gill, Indermit S., and Homi Kharas, eds. 2006. *An East Asian Renaissance: Ideas for Economic Growth*. Washington, DC: World Bank.

Jin Renqing. 2006. "People's Republic of China," trans. the delegation of China. Statement GS-26 delivered at the 39th Annual Meeting of the Board of Governors of the Asian Development Bank, Hyderabad, India, May 4–6.

Krugman, Paul, and Anthony J. Venables. 1995. "Globalization and the Inequality of Nations." *Quarterly Journal of Economics* 110 (4): 857–80.

Lall, Sanjaya, and Manuel Albaladejo. 2004. "China's Competitive Performance: A Threat to East Asian Manufactured Exports?" *World Development* 32 (9): 1441–66.

Lucas, Robert E. B. 2005. "International Migration and Economic Development: Lessons from Low-Income Countries, Executive Summary." Report, Expert Group on Development Issues, Ministry for Foreign Affairs, Stockholm.

Medalla, Erlinda M. 2002. "Trade and Industrial Policy Beyond 2000: An Assessment of the Philippine Economy." In *The Philippines Beyond 2000: An Economic Assessment*, ed. Josef T. Yap, Chapter 3. Makati City, the Philippines: Philippine Institute for Development Studies.

Redding, Stephen. 1999. "Dynamic Comparative Advantage and the Welfare Effects of Trade." *Oxford Economic Papers* 51 (1): 15–39.

Redding, Stephen, and Peter K. Schott. 2003. "Distance, Skill Deepening and Development: Will Peripheral Countries Ever Get Rich?" *Journal of Development Economics* 72 (2): 515–41.

Sheng Lijun. 2003. "China-ASEAN Free Trade Area: Origins, Developments and Strategic Motivations." ISEAS Working Paper, International Politics and Security Issues Series 1, Institute of Southeast Asian Studies, Singapore.

Tecson, Gwendolyn R. 1999. "The Hard Disk Drive Industry in the Philippines." ISIC Report 99-01, Information Storage Industry Center, eScholarship Repository, University of California, San Diego, CA. http://repositories.cldlib.org.

Teves, Margarito B. 2005. "Statement by the Hon. Margarito B. Teves, Governor of the Bank for the Philippines, at the Joint Annual Discussion." Statement delivered at the Boards of Governors 2005 Annual Meetings of the World Bank Group and the International Monetary Fund, Washington, DC, September 24–25.

———. 2006. "Philippines." Statement GS-9 delivered at the 39th Annual Meeting of the Board of Governors of the Asian Development Bank, Hyderabad, India, May 4–6.

World Bank. 2005. *Philippines: Meeting Infrastructure Challenges*. Manila: World Bank Group in the Philippines.

Zabihullah, Md Ismail. 2006. "Bangladesh." Statement GS-38 delivered at the 39th Annual Meeting of the Board of Governors of the Asian Development Bank, Hyderabad, India, May 4–6.

CHAPTER 13

Visions of East Asia
Three Engines for a Way Forward

MARI PANGESTU

Southeast Asia must become a pole of development; political openness must be expanded; and there must be more formal regional agreements.

It is ironic and challenging. Thirteen years after participating in the *East Asian Miracle* study (World Bank 1993), I am now being asked to envision the way forward for East Asia, the major development challenges the region faces, and the region's role in the global economy.

We have come a long way since then. First, there was the miracle, which was not really a miracle, but involved good policy and economic fundamentals such as high savings rates and macroeconomic stability. These still matter. Second, there was the Asian crisis, in which we learned that good policies were not enough and that institutions and governance mattered. Delivering on the types of reforms—policy and institutional—matters even more now as the East Asian economies become open economically and politically. Delivering these reforms while countries are undergoing the transition to democracy and, for some countries, such as Indonesia, a process of decentralization, is a challenging task. Third, there was the rise of China and India, to which all East Asian economies and the rest of the world have had to adjust. The implications of their rise will continue, with consequences for competition, the way countries adjust, and the way the region carries on with the process of regional integration.

This essay is about these three trains of thoughts, the three engines for the way forward, and the three main drivers in each engine so that we may achieve an East Asian region that is prosperous and sustainable and plays an effective role in the world economy.

Engine One: Three Poles Are Better Than Two Poles

The rise of China and India has changed the constellation of the Asian region. China and India, which have abundant supplies of labor and large markets, have become two major poles of growth. Their demand for energy has an impact on energy and commodity prices and has changed the dynamics of trade and investment not merely in the region, but throughout the world, even as the prices of many manufactured products are falling because of these two large economies. Each of these countries is facing the pressures of rapid growth, including unbalanced and, sometimes, widening inequality. A large number of people are still living below the poverty line. The growth of these two countries will continue to pose challenges for the rest of the world, but especially countries that compete with them more directly. The rest of the world, including developed countries, will have to make adjustments. In the interim, there may yet be greater tensions because of more protectionism as countries seek to cope with the fresh competition. China and India will have to consider carefully the impact of their robust growth on the rest of the world.

In the years to come, Southeast Asia must develop into a third pole to rebalance the entire region. This is a challenge for the countries of Southeast Asia. How can this be achieved?

Each of the economies of the Association of Southeast Asian Nations (ASEAN) is at a different level of development. Singapore, on the one extreme, is already at an advanced level of development, but it must also look for new sources of growth by establishing niche sectors. It will continue to grow as a services-based economy. The relatively advanced countries of Malaysia and Thailand have a comparative advantage in export-oriented industries such as electronics, the automotive industry, and, to a lesser extent, textiles and clothing, and, of course, resource-based industries. However, they are also entering newer niche sectors. Indonesia is the largest Southeast Asian country. It has evolved out of crisis and is now in the process of economic recovery. Indonesia is much more richly endowed with natural resources than the other economies and has a comparative advantage in labor-intensive exports. It also will have to enhance value added and maintain its competitiveness. The Philippines has comparative advantages similar to those of other ASEAN countries, but the Philippines is an important exporter of labor services, and remittances are a major contributor to the country's foreign exchange reserves. Vietnam is no longer a transition economy; it has undergone rapid transformation in the last 10 years and is providing stiff competition to countries such as Indonesia. It is expected to become a member of the World Trade Organization in 2006. Cambodia became a member in 2004 and has opened up its economy, but will need more institutional and infrastructure development to attract greater investments. The Lao People's Democratic Republic is still involved in a process of change. Myanmar has internal problems.

In essence, each of the ASEAN countries will have to raise productivity, find niches for specialization, and undertake reform to maintain competitiveness relative to China and also India. It is difficult to compete for large production volumes. Thus, it is best for these countries to undertake specialization, improve quality and design, and enhance the product range.

The ASEAN economies are also at various stages of political and institutional reform. At times, there are hiccups, and more serious problems delay the speed of change. The ASEAN economies must manage this process, with its ups and downs. China's process of political opening-up and institutional change also represents a challenge.

Inequality and the number of people living in poverty are much more severe problems in China and India than in Southeast Asia. Relative to China, Southeast Asia is also by and large ahead in the transition to political openness and democratic institutions.

Collectively, the population of Southeast Asia is close to 600 million. Average per capita incomes are high, and the resource base is rich. There is also a diverse system of production and service delivery. Thus, Southeast Asia could become, sooner rather than later, the third pole in an ASEAN community benefiting from social and economic security. At the moment, the target for achieving this is no later than 2020. The idea of establishing a regional production base and a regional market has been discussed since before the early 1990s when the ASEAN Free Trade Area (AFTA) was introduced. The program to accelerate economic integration through the ASEAN economic community entails addressing tariffs, but also bringing down nontariff barriers, harmonizing or mutually recognizing standards, facilitating trade such as through the creation of an ASEAN single window by 2008, and so on.

If the ASEAN economic community is to be a third pole that acts as a viable counterweight, these efforts must be accelerated. There must be sufficient political will to ensure that national policies are changed so that a single production base, a single market, support services, and infrastructure are developed properly. Southeast Asia views this as a way to compete and be perceived as the alternative pole to the two giant, emerging poles of China and India.

Benefiting from three poles that are developing synergistically, the East Asian region will enjoy relatively high rates of economic growth for years to come. While there will be competition, there are ample differences in terms of resources, sources of comparative advantage, and markets. Each pole will be attractive and distinct in its own right, but there will also be many areas of synergy.

Engine Two: Policy Matters, but Institutions and Governance Matter More

What worked during the East Asian miracle still works today. Stable macroeconomics, good policies, and strong economic fundamentals are still prerequisites.

However, delivering successes in second-generation reform, institutional change, governance, and corruption has become tough in East Asia. The process of expanding political openness and instituting the transition to more stable and mature democracy and the requisite institutions is an even greater challenge. Recent events in Thailand are an indication of the difficulties that Asian countries will continue to face.

However, succeeding on these fronts will become a path-breaking way forward. The question is clear: Might good policies coexist with bad politics?

In January 2004, in a column in the *Jakarta Post*, I wrote the following:

> Economists say "it's politics, stupid," whilst politicians say "it's economics, stupid."
>
> At a recent seminar, a former central banker turned research economist turned top-ranking government official, Andrew Sheng, gave an interesting talk. It had a fancy title, but he indicated that the essence of his talk was the "confessions of a reformer turned bureaucrat." The message was simple enough: both economists and politicians were right. That undertaking

the necessary economic reforms and good governance would always be hit by political constraints, but that good politics at the end of the day had to deliver the goods. So the conclusion is that those in decision-making and leadership positions should set realistic and achievable goals, prioritize two to three (or even one if the constraints are onerous) priorities, and really deliver on them.

After five years of ups and downs in reforms and dramatic political changes, with no clear light at the end of the tunnel, we in Indonesia have also come to the same realization. We have lowered our expectations to achieving all the reforms smoothly in a reasonable period of time. Given institutional, capacity, and political constraints, we know [how] to set our sights at the priorities, set short-term goals that hopefully go toward the more ideal, longer-term framework that will bring the greatest benefit to the most people. So what [do] domestic and foreign investors and the average Indonesian want to see in this important year of change, 2004? What kind of president and what kind of government? We want real change, and, to us, this now means a credible start and an important signal that it is not going to be business as usual anymore. What are the priorities?

Little did I know when I wrote this column that we would have the first president directly elected, with 60 percent of the popular vote, whose vision involves making real change and providing a signal that it is not business as usual. I also had no inkling then that I would be in the category Andrew Sheng calls "reformer turned bureaucrat."

Indonesia has undergone a dramatic transformation in the last eight years. But, I suppose, the basic messages listed above remain unaltered. Prior to the crisis, we went through a process of deregulation and opening of the economy, but there was a lack of political openness. Then the economic crisis and collapse revealed the many weaknesses in the economy and in institutions. It took an economic collapse to bring democracy, showing how a nation can turn a crisis into an opportunity for historic change. And it will take economic development and prosperity to maintain democracy. It will take major transformations on various fronts to advance toward a mature and orderly democratic process, and it will take time. There must be a major change in institutions, including the legal, political, and state apparatus. Most important, the commitment must be made to address corruption and the problems in governance.

The government and those representing the government should lead by example in tackling the issue of good governance and corruption. The proper balance must be struck between the establishment of minute checks to weed out all corruption and more fundamental reforms. It would be difficult to tackle corruption without, for instance, addressing civil service reform. There are no magic bullets, and strengthening governance and combating corruption will take time. Thus, there has to be a long-term commitment. The key will be institutional reforms involving prioritization and sequencing.

Reflecting on the Indonesian experience in introducing change might lead one to propose the existence of three key pillars of activity in the effort to achieve institutional change and good governance and to address corruption.

The First Pillar: Transforming Institutions

Transforming institutions will require strengthening political institutions through the use of a system of reasonable checks and balances. In turn, this will require strengthening the legislative and executive apparatus and instituting methods to enhance accountability in decision making. The ground must be prepared for informed policy decisions and for policy change.

One must collect the proper facts and accurate figures, undertake impact analysis, map out the losers and gainers from any policy change, and come up with a balanced proposal. Meanwhile, one is faced with the pressure exerted by various groups. Navigating among the competing interests is a challenge for the executive, which must make good decisions that will bring the most benefit to the people. Leadership today must produce informed policy decisions. At the top, but especially at the bottom, there must be a feeling of ownership and a willingness to accept many new ideas and policies despite the resistance. The socialization of any new idea or policy takes time, but it must be done. There are consultations. Compromises must be made for many reasons. Even in the case of a policy that is less than ideal, how does one make good compromises so that even this policy is not rendered ineffective? One must manage expectations, picking early winners so as to build a constituency for change, but also making clear that the full impact of some reforms will not be felt immediately.

There should be a sustained effort to strengthen the judiciary, build an effective public service, and manage decentralization. One should undertake civil service reform and create adequate institutional capacity in government ministries. This will be a long-term task. Civil service reform will include the installation of a merit-based system and an appropriate incentive and penalty system. This can occur only in stages. Short of reforming the entire public service, one has to begin by creating islands of excellence, applying methods to reduce the discretionary power of officials, enhancing transparency, and establishing a monitoring system.

Given the length of time administrative reforms will take, a leader must be able to find short-term measures that will signal the seriousness of his or her desire to change and advance the achievement of the longer-term goal.

The government of Indonesia has created islands of best practice within an imperfect system. For instance, a few years ago, the Ministry of Finance created the large taxpayers office. This office manages and administers the tax accounts of large taxpayers. It provides better service, and the officials receive better compensation. Their work is monitored closely. In my ministry, the Ministry of Trade, deregulation and greater transparency are being promoted. We have reviewed 77 regulations of the ministry. We have suppressed those deemed unnecessary, streamlined the requirements for the others and made them transparent, and determined the number of days and the cost of processing individual documents and licenses. All the relevant information is well posted for the benefit of the public. We are also beginning to introduce online systems for obtaining and filing applications so as to make the process more arm's length. Of course, we have only now begun this process, and implementation must be closely monitored to ensure that it is effective. Meanwhile, we are also building up the capacity of other human resources and systems inside the ministry.

Another approach the government is currently developing involves special economic zones. These are areas where islands of excellence and islands of best practice would be created. The proposal is still being worked out, but the aim is to identify rapid, effective ways to establish hubs of economic development that would act as catalysts. These zones will not solicit greenfield investments, but will already include infrastructure and be able to provide access to inputs of production such as labor and supporting industries, clusters of industries, and sufficient area to expand. Most importantly, there will be a single, integrated zonal authority that will provide best practice in terms of services and systems to help investors. This will involve issuing the necessary local and national licenses and permits, supplying a service to assist in resolving problems, and providing efficient administrative support services such as for the customs, import and export procedures, and so on.

The Second Pillar: Providing a Conducive Business Environment

Providing a business-friendly environment has not been the premise of policy in the past. However, the way businesses operate must also change. Businesses that require preferential treatment or concessions to survive are not acceptable in this new era. Private sector leadership must operate within today's different rules of engagement. Leadership and entrepreneurship that foster efficient, effective, and innovative Indonesian businesses must be developed alongside the improvements in public governance. Both private sector and public sector leadership must play a role in creating a proper understanding of conflict of interest and the correct interpretation of public-private partnerships and incorporated enterprises in Indonesia.

The Third Pillar: Leadership at All Levels

It will not be possible to implement all these institutional changes and create best practices unless there is an accelerated program to upgrade human capital. The education, training, and development of a cadre of young people who will carry on the process will be crucial. For all three pillars, leadership is needed in the public sector, the political and legislative arena, the private sector, nonprofit organizations, the press, academia, and so on. Indonesia's demographic structure is that of a relatively young population, and this represents opportunities and challenges. If we invest in the leadership of the next generation, we should not fear the future. A new, revitalized leadership will continue the process and secure Indonesia's transformation and its place in the region.

It is incumbent on all institutions to take responsibility for investing in human resource development and capacity building so as to create the next generation of leadership. The process will take time, and we need continuity and consistency. Otherwise, the longer-term goals will not be achieved. That is why, in the Ministry of Trade, we have spent a lot of time thinking through the appropriate program for identifying, training, and building the capacity of the next generation of leaders in the ministry. There are constraints in the civil service regulations, but the government is also developing a program of administrative reforms that would facilitate breakthroughs in the system. A number of ministries, including the Ministry of Trade, are participating in the program.

Engine Three: Regionalism to Regionalization

In the 1970s and 1980s, the export-oriented strategies of the East Asian economies benefited from an open world trading system. From the mid-1980s onward, during the years of the Uruguay Round (1986–94), the East Asian economies undertook a process of unilateral reforms. This led to "regionalism," or market-driven regional integration. The unilateral opening-up by each country, including a policy of export orientation, whereby exporter-producers could access inputs at world prices, meant that a regional production base emerged. Intra–East Asian trade was a trade in components and parts; the final products were exported to third-country markets. The emergence of value chains reinforced these trends. China remains a center of gravity in regional production.

Is such regionalism sufficient, or must there be greater regionalization? Must there be more formal regional agreements to facilitate an even stronger East Asia. It is important that free trade areas (FTAs) encourage integration rather than fragmentation among markets. After all, FTAs are a means to foster market-driven forces. FTAs that do not facilitate market-driven forces only contribute to higher business costs and greater market fragmentation. For instance, discriminatory or cumbersome rules of origin are obstacles to the regional production base. One should be able to produce components and inputs based on specialization and competitiveness (not merely to satisfy rules of origin). In accomplishing this, one should bear in mind three principles so as to ensure that East Asia regionalization reflects best practice and facilitates rather than hinders market-driven forces.

The First Principle: Open Regionalism

Regionalism in Asia should not be an inward-looking, discriminatory arrangement. When ASEAN formed AFTA, this principle appeared to have been violated. However, ASEAN never meant to create an inward-oriented regional market or an internal ASEAN market.

ASEAN's trade is predominantly with non-ASEAN countries. ASEAN's main objective was to create a competitive regional economy that would attract global investors who would use the region as a production and export platform for global markets.

Nonetheless, the principle of open regionalism is manifest in ASEAN in the reduction of most favored nation tariffs in parallel with and, in some instances, more rapidly than the reduction in the common effective preferential tariffs of AFTA, as ASEAN deepens the economic integration process to achieve ASEAN goals.

The liberalization agenda of Asia-Pacific Economic Cooperation (APEC) is also based on this principle. Liberalization, that is, the removal of trade barriers, is undertaken unilaterally by each APEC member economy, but in a concerted manner. This modality is known as concerted unilateral liberalization.

Some question the efficacy of this modality. However, APEC is a nonbinding process. Therefore, this modality is the only feasible one. If the process has not delivered on expectations, this may well be due to the weak peer process (pressure) that should be driving trade liberalization. Those who are unhappy with the results have demanded radical change in APEC's approach, and they have suggested turning APEC into a free trade area of Asia and the Pacific. This is contrary to the principle of open regionalism. In any case, the political feasibility of the proposal is highly problematic because the region is so diverse. It could well be that, because a regionwide FTA is almost impossible, countries have resorted to subregional and even bilateral arrangements. These have proliferated lately.

The Second Principle: Regional Community Building Is More Than Trade Liberalization

Regional community building is a comprehensive undertaking. It must at least include these pillars of APEC: liberalization, facilitation, and development cooperation. In APEC, these key elements have been translated into the trade and investment liberalization and facilitation agenda and the economic and technical cooperation agenda. In the past few years, two other agenda items have been added, namely, human security and governance.

The focus remains largely on trade liberalization, however. APEC's progress is measured in terms of progress in its trade liberalization agenda. This is so because the goals of APEC community building have been narrowly defined as the achievement of free and open trade and investment in the region by 2010 for the developed economies and 2020 for the developing economies.

In ASEAN, the focus of economic cooperation is on the realization of AFTA, at the latest by 2015 (for some countries in the Cambodia–Lao PDR–Myanmar–Vietnam group and for certain agricultural commodities), while the goal of an ASEAN economic community by 2020 remains ill defined.

FTAs are now seen as the main manifestation of regional community building. They are being broadened to include investment, competition policy, and a number of behind-border issues. These more comprehensive agreements are called new age agreements, economic partnership agreements, or comprehensive economic cooperation agreements. In principle, they enshrine the three pillars of APEC, some more explicitly than others. For instance, the Japanese economic partnership agreement explicitly includes economic and technical cooperation.

The problem is that these agreements involve hard-nosed negotiations among participating economies about exchanging concessions. Confidence and community building are reduced to a bargaining game. Other aspects of cooperation have been overshadowed by this exercise in bargaining. This is not Asian community building through sharing, solidarity, and mutual support.

East Asia community building, which was proclaimed as an alternative to APEC community building because it does not involve countries such as the United States, is in danger of falling into the same trap as other regional initiatives. It is unable to get beyond forming an FTA to develop an institutional identity.

The Third Principle: ASEAN Should Be at the Center of Regionalization in East Asia

ASEAN should be a central part of the process of regionalization in East Asia. There is much discussion at the moment on who should be included in East Asia. In the ASEAN and dialogue-partner process, it has been taken to mean ASEAN, plus China, Japan, and the Republic of Korea (ASEAN+3). In last year's seminal East Asia Summit at the leaders level, it was taken also to include Australia, India, and New Zealand.

How should East Asia regionalization then evolve? One path that might be examined is the consolidation of various trade agreements in East Asia into a single FTA, which would then be linked with other parts of the world.

ASEAN has played a significant role in this. ASEAN leaders realize that strengthening intra-ASEAN cooperation and linking it to other parts of the world would maximize the potential for creating greater trade and investment opportunities.

Asia's economic integration is designed to be more thorough than a conventional FTA arrangement. ASEAN+3, for instance, is already committed to moving forward to greater monetary and financial cooperation. Regional monetary and financial cooperation would contribute to global financial stability. Greater monetary and exchange rate policy coordination would be especially beneficial to the highly export-oriented and deeply interdependent economies of East Asia.

In theory, ASEAN could play a significant role in maintaining coherence and consistency in all these initiatives because it is at center stage whether we are talking about ASEAN+3 or ASEAN+1 (ASEAN, plus China), which has already progressed to liberalization in goods; agreements have been signed with China and Korea. It seems that, even with greater East Asian economic integration, ASEAN will play the central role. It would be difficult to solve the leadership issue within a wider effort at economic integration in East Asia.

This is the main challenge for ASEAN, as well as for the region as a whole. The ASEAN economic community must be strengthened in reality, not merely in form. The acceleration in 11 priority sectors must be realized beyond the liberalization of trade in goods. This will require serious effort at removing nontariff barriers and accelerating trade facilitation. In trade facilitation, some progress has been achieved through mutual recognition agreements in two sectors, electronics and professional services.

For the customs, there is agreement on implementing an ASEAN single window by 2008. This requires each ASEAN country to build up a national single window. All documentation for the clearance of goods, including export and import documents and customs clearance documents, must be automated and linked to banking and shipping documents. The processes and documentation will be synchronized within all of ASEAN by 2008. The advantages are, of course, speed, greater accuracy, less discretion, less potential for underinvoicing and smuggling, and access to a more precise regional database on trade.

One could ask: Is this enough? Probably not, and ASEAN will thus still need to accelerate the process of broadening integration and to strengthen its efforts to create an ASEAN economic community, perhaps before the target date (2010 for the 11 sectors and 2020 for all sectors).

In the ASEAN+1 processes that are ongoing, we can see glimpses of potential ASEAN leadership. The main principles of the approach might be a good basis for general principles and for leading by example. These principles are as follows:

- Start with a comprehensive framework that includes goods, services, investment, nonborder issues, and economic and technical cooperation
- Sequentially, start with tariffs on goods and work on the remainder
- Liberalize tariffs on goods by (1) ensuring substantial coverage, that is, 90 percent in the normal track and 10 percent in the sensitive track; (2) realizing that elimination is the target, that is, zero tariff is the final target; and (3) establishing liberal and simple rules of origin (40 percent cumulative value added, AFTA rules of origin, with some changes in tariff headings or for some products)

This framework has been adopted in the case of the ASEAN-China and ASEAN-Korea FTA framework and in the FTA in goods components. It has also been used as the basis for negotiations with India, Japan, and Australia and New Zealand, where progress has been slow.

Of course, we still face the challenge of instituting best practices for the remaining components of the FTAs. If ASEAN is to pay a leadership role in this area, it must review the basic principles and ensure that it can also lead by example in these other areas.

References

World Bank. 1993. *The East Asian Miracle: Economic Growth and Public Policy.* World Bank Policy Research Reports. New York: Oxford University Press.

CHAPTER 14

Political Foundations for Sustainable Growth in Asia

MINXIN PEI

Asia must not allow strong economic fundamentals to obscure the political risks inherent in rapid modernization. Any economic progress must be based on solid political foundations.

In the annals of economic development, many countries in Asia have achieved consistently superior economic performance in the last half century. Their record in poverty reduction, sound economic management, and export growth has surpassed that of most other developing countries. From the 1960s to the 1990s, Asia was home to some of the world's most dynamic and successful dragon economies, such as Hong Kong (China), the Republic of Korea, Singapore, and Taiwan (China).[1] Today, the two Asian giants, China and India, are reshaping the global economic order through rapid growth. At the current rates of growth, Asian economies will remain the world's most dynamic for the foreseeable future.

A major source of growth for Asia will continue to be the region's integration with the global economy. Indeed, few would dispute that Asia has been a primary beneficiary of the globalization of trade and investment. The region has gained shares in global output, trade, and investment. The domestic economic momentum that has powered Asia's growth, such as the high savings rate and the migration of rural surplus labor into urban areas, remains healthy. Regional economic integration is also proceeding at a rapid pace, driven primarily by private sector activities in trade and investment and secondarily by emerging institutional arrangements such as regional free trade agreements (Krumm and Kharas 2004). The robustness of Asia's economic health is all the more remarkable considering the devastating effects of the East Asian financial crisis of the late 1990s. Indeed, few expected the region to rebound from the catastrophe so quickly and well (World Bank 2000).

Still, it would be naive to take Asia's growth for granted. Behind the region's increasing prosperity and impressive dynamism lurk dangers and risks that, if ignored and mismanaged, could slow Asia's ascendance (Stiglitz and Yusuf 2001). On the geopolitical front, Asia is home to three potential flash points: Kashmir, the Korean Peninsula, and the Taiwan Strait. Any miscalculation or crisis mismanagement could ignite a dangerous military confrontation with unimaginable consequences. But the most likely and most potent source of disruption is rising discontent with political leadership, lack of government integrity, and misguided public policies in most of Asia. In Thailand, public anger over Prime Minister Thaksin Shinawatra's questionable business deals fueled mass rallies that ultimately drove the Thai politician, a man with a reputation for strong leadership, from office in disgrace in 2006. Thaksin's Philippine counterparts have fared little better. Alleged corruption forced President Joseph Estrada from office in 2001. Recent allegations of corruption have politically crippled Gloria Macaraeg Macapagal-Arroyo, Estrada's successor. In Korea, Prime Minister Lee Hae Chan resigned under a cloud in March 2006 after it was discovered he had played golf with an indicted businessman and had engaged in gambling. Lee's boss, President Roh Moo-hyun, narrowly survived impeachment in 2004 after his repeated political missteps cut into his public support and allowed the opposition to exploit his ineffective leadership.[2] In Taiwan (China), the pro-independence president, Chen Shui-bian, has accomplished nothing during his six years in office except for constantly playing the divide between mainlanders and native-born Taiwanese and provoking Beijing with moves that might lead to formal independence for the island and to an all but certain military conflict with China. With the economy stagnating and public disappointment running high, President Chen narrowly won reelection in March 2004 under controversial circumstances. (He survived an attempted assassination on the eve of the election, but the government later claimed that the chief suspect had committed suicide.) Hong Kong (China), East Asia's financial and services hub, which returned to Chinese rule in July 1997, has had its share of economic and political turmoil. Shaken by a succession of financial shocks and public health crises, the residents of the former British colony have grown dissatisfied with the performance of their postcolonial government. In July 2004, more than 1 million Hong Kong (China) citizens took to the streets to demonstrate against a proposed security law that might have threatened their civil liberties. Responding to mass discontent, the central government of China was eventually forced to ask Hong Kong (China)'s chief executive, C. H. Tung, to retire two years ahead of schedule.

Unquestionably Asia's star economic performer since the late 1970s, China is also encountering rising skepticism about the sustainability and correctness of its leadership's pro-growth strategy. Including rising income inequality, rampant official corruption, deteriorating social services, and large-scale environmental degradation, the social costs of China's economic rise have become more visible and more politically unsustainable (Pei 2006a).

The biggest political surprise in Asia occurred in India in May 2004. By all accounts, the coalition government led by the Bharatiya Janata Party had delivered robust economic performance and had implemented effective market-oriented reforms. Yet, a slight majority of the Indian electorate appeared to believe that the fruits of these reforms had been unevenly distributed. Exercising their democratic right, India's voters replaced the Bharatiya Janata Party with the Congress Party, which had promised to give more attention to those left behind by India's impressive economic progress.

Why is a region that is doing well by many conventional economic indicators experiencing rising public discontent about government? Will the discontent precipitate instability and slow economic progress in the region? How should Asia's governments respond to a public that is increasingly assertive and often unforgiving?

I argue that governments in Asia must not allow strong economic fundamentals to obscure the political risks inherent in experiencing rapid economic modernization. Indeed, any sustained economic progress must be based on solid political foundations that are constantly rebuilt and strengthened. In the 1960s and 1970s, national experiences unique to the region helped build the political coalitions and institutions that were later credited with making superior economic performance possible (Rowen 1998). These political coalitions have frayed in recent years. Political institutions that were once so suitable for mobilizing resources for rapid growth are adapting poorly to an era in which government integrity and social equity are assuming political importance. China's enormous success in the past three decades and the daunting challenges ahead illustrate this argument. The Chinese example encapsulates the Asian experience of balancing many critical developmental objectives in the course of rapid modernization. Whether and how China maintains its forward momentum and manages these challenges are not only important to the welfare of its 1.3 billion people, but also critical to the peace and prosperity of the entire Asian region.

Why Sustained Economic Growth Requires Solid Political Foundations

Although the idea that any society aspiring to achieve superior and sustained economic growth needs solid political foundations may sound self-evident, only a small number of countries have managed to build and maintain such foundations. Although definitions of what constitute sound political foundations may differ, the experience of the most successful East Asian economies suggests that political systems with the following characteristics and capabilities are more likely to achieve sustained rapid economic growth and maintain social peace:

- A broadbased societal consensus on the desirability of market-oriented reforms
- An encompassing political coalition that rallies support from various segments of society behind reform-minded leaders
- Strong technocratic capabilities for macroeconomic management, the means for resource mobilization, and effective institutional mechanisms to control corruption
- Public policies designed to mitigate the undesirable effects of rapid economic growth, especially income inequality
- A system for the rule of law that protects property rights, enforces contracts, and enhances the predictability of the policy environment

It is worth noting that not every successful East Asian society has enjoyed all of the pro-growth political conditions in equal measure. The political foundations have been stronger in some countries than in others. And, within individual countries, some constituent parts of the foundations have been sturdier than others. Although no systematic research has been undertaken to demonstrate the link between the strength of these political foundations in a society and the sustained economic performance of that same society, political economic theory would suggest that this link not only exists, but is most likely positive.

That there is a relationship between strong political foundations and sustained, superior economic performance is intuitive. But less well understood is how such foundations were first built and whether, once built, they can be maintained. Based on the experience of the first-generation tiger economies, as well as nearly all other high-performing Asian economies, two commonalities stand out: crisis and leadership. Political and economic crises have precipitated radical policy changes in most Asian countries for several reasons. Typically, severe political and economic shocks discredit and delegitimize preexisting policies because these policies are believed to have caused political and economic catastrophes. At the ideological level, crisis paves the way so that new ideas and values may gain dominance and influence development policies. Crises frequently lead to the exit from power of the old ruling elites responsible for the failings of the government. These old elites are replaced by new elites eager to reestablish political legitimacy by delivering better performance. Crises also provide the new elites with a fresh political mandate, which, in turn, creates more room for undertaking high-risk, but potentially high-return reforms that would be politically impossible under the old regime.

Yet, profound political and economic crises alone do not always create the political openings for radical policy shifts. Only countries blessed with the appropriate political leadership can seize the opportunities generated by such crises to break decisively with the past. Table 14.1, which briefly summarizes the turning points in Asia's most successful economies, shows that the combination of crisis, leadership, and policy response has paved the way for the initial economic takeoff in the region over the past half century. Furthermore, the direct result of the policy response to the crises in these countries was revived economic growth, but also a significant strengthening of the political foundations for economic development. In nearly all the countries that made a decisive break with their failed pasts, leaders were able to articulate a clear vision for a different future. An encompassing societal consensus on market-driven growth was achieved, largely thanks to the proven failures of the old economic strategies and policies. To varying degrees, radical leftist or statist ideologies were abandoned. A broad-based governing coalition, including political elites, technocrats, the military, the intelligentsia, and private entrepreneurs, has minimized conflicts among key interest groups and has focused energies on top developmental priorities. In many countries, the ruling elites wisely adopted public policies, such as the expansion of access to

TABLE 14.1 The Leadership Response to Crisis in Selected Asian Countries

Economy	Crisis	Leadership	Postcrisis response
Taiwan, China	defeat in war; popular revolt on Taiwan (China) (1947–49)	Chiang Kai-shek and Chiang Ching-kuo	land reform, privatization, local elections, equitable growth policies, export-led development strategy (1950s and 1960s)
Korea, Rep. of	political gridlock, loss of public confidence, illegitimate election, rampant corruption (1950s)	Park Chung Hee	restoration of macroeconomic stability, land reform, investment in education, government-directed credit to key industries, capable civil service (1960s and 1970s)
Singapore	breakup with Malaya (1965)	Lee Kuan Yew	institution of the rule of law, investment in education, competent civil service, clean government
Malaysia	ethnic riots (1968)	United Malays National Organization, coalition	policies favoring Malays, encouragement for foreign direct investment and export-led growth
Indonesia	failed coup and collapse of the old regime (1965)	Suharto	restoration of macroeconomic stability, use of technocrats and international expertise, encouragement for foreign direct investment
China	Cultural Revolution (1966–76)	Deng Xiaoping	decollectivization of agriculture, economic liberalization, opening to the West, and ending of mass political terror
Vietnam	economic stagnation and invasion of Cambodia (1979–86)	Communist Party of Vietnam, collective	agricultural reform, withdrawal from Cambodia, opening to the West, encouragement for foreign direct investment
India	balance of payments crisis (1991)	Prime Minister Narasimha Rao and Finance Minister Manmohan Singh of the Congress Party	radical economic liberalization, deregulation, integration with the global economy

Source: Compiled by the author.

education and health care, that contributed to poverty reduction and social equity, thus strengthening the political legitimacy of pro-growth strategies.

However, the political foundations that were carefully constructed following these reform-initiating crises must be reinforced constantly.

In particular, the two institutional pillars for maintaining growth momentum and broad political support—the rule of law and political mechanisms for government accountability and integrity—must be continuously strengthened to constrain the state, already relatively strong in most Asian countries, from dominating market forces or becoming predatory. In retrospect, building the rule of law and maintaining government accountability and integrity were the two tasks that even the most successful East Asian societies failed to perform entirely. Rapid economic growth quickly lifted standards of living, but, except in Hong Kong (China) and Singapore, failed to produce legal, regulatory, and political institutions effectively to protect property rights, limit state power, and curb political corruption. In the 1990s, unconstrained by such institutions, most societies in East Asia fell victim to crony-capitalism (incestuous ties between the political elites and the economic elites), with disastrous economic, social, and political consequences. The 1997–98 East Asian financial crisis was, in large part, caused by the region's weak institutional capacity in financial market regulation, corporate governance, and public sector governance. In this regard, the lesson of Indonesia is the most tragic and the most instructive. For three decades, Indonesia achieved world-beating developmental success, albeit under authoritarian rule. But the pace of institution-building, especially in vital areas such as the rule of law, political accountability, and democracy, lagged far behind economic growth. As a result, the authoritarian regime, centered on President Suharto's family and its network of crony-capitalists, grew increasingly venal and neglected the public's need for equity and social justice. At the same time, the Indonesian state's capacity to regulate its financial system remained woefully inadequate, allowing insider dealing and related party lending to go out of control. Politically, the public grew disenchanted with an authoritarian regime that was seen as incurably rapacious and corrupt, despite the three decades of unmatched economic prosperity. Thus, when the East Asian financial crisis hit in 1997–98, Indonesia had neither the financial strength nor the political foundations to weather the storm. The authoritarian regime, along with the country's rickety banking system, collapsed in spectacular fashion. Practically overnight, an erstwhile success story became a poignant negative lesson.

Regrettably, unlike the political and nationalist upheavals in the 1960s and 1970s that later ushered in system-transforming reforms, the East Asian financial crisis did not produce similar long-lasting changes (except in Korea and Singapore).[3] One reason might be the relatively short duration of the crisis and the mildness of the suffering (except in Indonesia). Another and more important explanation is that, except in Korea and Singapore, political leaders failed to seize the opportunities created by the crisis to initiate reforms and strengthen the political foundations for sustained growth. A few badly needed technical reforms were undertaken, such as enhancing the supervision of the banking sector, instituting minor corporate governance reforms, and maintaining significant foreign currency reserves to prevent another financial crisis. However, countries generally did not attempt to introduce policies that would make governments more accountable or make the process of growth more inclusive and socially equitable.

Weak political foundations do not necessarily affect short-term economic performance. Indeed, the strong recovery in Asia following the crisis both masked the weakness of these foundations and reduced the pressures for reform. Fragile political foundations reduce the political support available to sustain rapid growth, and this allows social and economic dislocations. When large segments of the population perceive that the benefits of rapid growth are being unjustly distributed, they question the legitimacy of the government's pro-growth policies and may take political action to contest them. Policy responses to rising public discontent against perceived social injustice and government insensitivity should include short- and long-term strategies. A long-term strategy must be centered on building the institutions that will make the political process more inclusive, the government's commitments to good governance more enforceable, and the fruits of economic growth more equitably distributed. The short-term strategy should use the tools of public policy, such as taxation, health care, and education, to provide relief to social groups that have benefited (relatively) much less from rapid growth. If implemented well, these policy responses will bolster the political support for sustained reform and development.

Rebuilding Political Foundations for Growth: The Case of China

Few major economies have achieved as stellar a record of rapid growth as China in the past three decades. Since the onset of economic reform in 1979, China has maintained an annual growth rate of 9.2 percent and lifted more than 200 million people out of abject poverty. Its per capita income rose from roughly US$150 in 1978 to about US$1,700 in 2005. China has also become deeply and extensively integrated with the global economy. Its foreign trade skyrocketed from US$20 billion in 1978 to more than US$1 trillion in 2005, elevating China to the world's third largest trading nation. In the same period, investor-friendly policies and China's comparative advantage as a low-cost manufacturing site attracted over US$600 billion in foreign direct investment and turned the Chinese economy into a pivotal link in the global supply chain. Economic success has transformed Chinese society and greatly improved the quality of life of the average person. Today, roughly 45 percent of the population lives and works in urban areas, compared with about 20 percent in the late 1970s. Physical mobility and access to information have grown equally rapidly. Economic liberalization has enabled millions of Chinese entrepreneurs to establish their own businesses and acquire private wealth undreamed of under orthodox communist rule. The result is an extremely dynamic society.

Yet, China's economic success has incurred real and significant social costs, which are weakening public support for market-oriented reforms. Ironically, while the West was becoming increasingly alarmed at the impact of China's rapid growth, China itself was beginning to worry about the direction and sustainability of this path. This paradox is most evident in the recent, contentious policy debate among China's political elites over the causes of many socioeconomic problems, especially rising income inequality, the lack of affordable education, the poor access to health care, and runaway corruption.

The facts appear to back up the arguments of many critics of China's single-minded pro-growth strategy of the last three decades. There was the impressive achievement of poverty reduction, the rising standards of living, the social modernization, and the integration with the world economy, but there, alongside, were also significant and worsening social deficits.

Rising Income Inequality

Admittedly, China was an unusually, if not excessively, egalitarian society under the radical rule of Mao Zedong. But the level of income inequality has risen significantly during the reform era, particularly since the 1990s. Various estimates put the range of the Gini coefficient in China today at between 0.42 and 0.48, implying a 50 percent increase in the level of income inequality since the beginning of economic reform.[4] Of course, the most important factor in the increase in income inequality is expanding rural-urban income disparity. The disparity was narrowing in the 1980s thanks to agricultural reform, but has since risen to the highest level in the history of the country.[5] It is widely recognized that the causes of rising income inequality are numerous and complex. This is also a global phenomenon (although the rate of increase varies from country to country). What appears to make rising income inequality politically sensitive and potentially polarizing is the combination of two issues: corruption and the declining provision of public goods.

Corruption

The abuse of power by government officials for personal gain exacts real economic costs, but also directly worsens socioeconomic inequality. Corruption allows politically powerful or connected individuals to gain unfair economic advantage. In a transition economy, such an advantage may easily be turned into enormous private wealth. State-owned properties, such as land and industrial assets, are being sold off to private investors, usually through an opaque process and at prices far below fair market value. Additionally, the decentralization of power, necessary so as to provide local officials with greater incentives and more autonomy to improve their economic performance, also creates opportunities for corruption. Despite a lack of good data on the extent of corruption in China since the late 1970s, several indicators suggest that the scourge of corruption is serious and spreading. The number of legal and judicial cases involving large sums of money has risen significantly since the 1980s, as has the number of senior government officials implicated in corruption scandals. Published official data indicate that the enforcement of anticorruption measures has fallen off in recent years.[6] Corruption has assumed more insidious characteristics as well. It is now being perpetrated by collusive local officials. The practice of accepting bribes in exchange for giving bribers powerful positions in the government has become widespread. Most worrisome, corruption has hit some of China's most crucial industries, such as financial services, transportation, and construction. Corruption has emerged as one of the principal causes of public discontent.

The Declining Provision of Public Goods

To be fair, China's performance in providing health care and education to its people compares favorably with the performance of countries at similar levels of economic development, as shown by China's relatively high scores on the Human Development Index (UNDP 2005). However, the Chinese government has significantly reduced its contribution to health care and education expenditures in the last two decades. According to Chinese official data, government spending on education fell about 20 percent as a share of total education expenditures in the 1990s. The central government contributes only 1 percent to the entire rural education system. Public spending on health care fell even more steeply. In the 1980s, public spending accounted for 36 percent of all health care costs; in 2000, the share fell to less than 15 percent.[7] As a result, individual citizens have begun to bear greater financial risks and responsibilities for their access to health care and education. Many have been priced out of the market. Government data show that about two-thirds of Chinese citizens lack any form of health insurance, and more than half forgo medical care when they get sick. Besides health care costs, educational outlays, including school fees for primary education and college tuition, have become unaffordable relative to incomes. Declining access to health care and educational opportunities increases inequality directly because it particularly hurts the poor and underprivileged and creates a vicious cycle of poverty and shortages of human capital.

Fortunately, the Chinese government, especially under the new leadership, has become aware of the rising social deficits and begun to respond to public pressure to reorient China's development. President Hu Jintao and Premier Wen Jiabao have publicly pledged to pursue a people-based development strategy and place less emphasis on growth rates. Reacting to rising incidents of social unrest, the new leadership has called for a more responsive government and for social harmony and has launched a series of initiatives to address the social deficits accumulated during the 1990s. The government has abolished a regressive agricultural tax and raised spending on health care and education in rural areas. By and large, these policy responses have constituted the initial steps toward building fresh political foundations for sustained growth. They are guided by a new vision (people-based development and social harmony) and backed up by specific policies aimed at spreading the fruits of China's rapid growth to underdeveloped rural areas. China's new leaders face daunting challenges in balancing the imperatives of high growth and the pressures of social frustration and public disenchantment with socioeconomic inequality and injustice. They also have enormous assets at their disposal, such as three decades of experience in managing a transition economy, growing fiscal resources, achieving strong performance in exports and the balance of payments, boosting entrepreneurial private firms, and welding deep and extensive links with the global economy. To increase the odds of success, Beijing needs to take additional, more aggressive steps to mitigate socioeconomic inequality and reduce the stockpile of social deficits. Chinese leaders need to understand that credible public policy commitments must be backed up by political and institutional arrangements that function as enforcement mechanisms. Policy initiatives aimed at benefiting the poor and the disadvantaged would be more credible if the beneficiaries were incorporated into the political process or their representatives influenced policy. Similarly, pledges to improve governance and combat corruption will gain credibility if they are accompanied by specific measures to strengthen judicial independence and empower civil society.

Conclusion

The experience of Asia's successful economic development in general and China's in particular confirms that the political support for economic reform and growth must, like the social contract, be renewed constantly. No government can expect to derive permanent legitimacy from economic performance that occurred in the past, however impressive that may have been. In the six decades since the end of World War II, visionary leaders in many Asian countries have been able to turn crises into opportunities and build the political coalitions needed to take their economic development in new directions. Their legacies have created favorable economic conditions for their successors to continue the journey to peace and prosperity. But the generation of visionary leaders, themselves a product of unique historical circumstances (war and revolutions), is gone, and Asia's new leaders must find fresh visions to inspire their societies and reenergize their peoples. They may have a better chance of success if their new social contract is based on three broad principles:

- Socioeconomic equity: Public policies, especially those on health care and education, must be designed to mitigate the negative effects of rapid growth. Without such policies, no societal consensus will be sustainable.
- Compensation for losers: In today's environment of the hypercompetitive global marketplace, rapid technological change, and

short-lived comparative advantage, governments must develop political mechanisms to compensate losers. Specifically, socially disadvantaged groups must have opportunities to organize and gain access to political power. Only political arrangements that empower such groups will credibly defend the interests of the disadvantaged. On balance, the benefits of compensating the losers, most likely reflected in greater social stability, will outweigh the costs (higher social spending).

- Good governance: Increasing governing capabilities and maintaining the integrity of the government will confer enormous competitive advantages, but also help strengthen societal cohesion and political legitimacy. Policies and political mechanisms designed to fight official corruption are therefore of paramount importance because no governments can expect to maintain public support if their officials engage in corrupt activities with impunity.

To be sure, these principles are well known and self-evident. But it is remarkable that so few governments and leaders in developing countries have been able to articulate these principles in coherent policy platforms or incorporate them into effective public policies. In the age of information revolution and globalization, leaders in Asia today have no choice but to try to prove the cynics and pessimists wrong. The alternative vision—social disharmony, economic stagnation, and political strife—is not the one any self-respecting leader in Asia should entertain.

Notes

1. The most influential work is World Bank (1993).
2. The impeachment was overturned by the country's Supreme Court.
3. One may also argue that China took advantage of the crisis to force mass layoffs and bankruptcies among state-owned enterprises.
4. The Gini coefficient at the end of the 1970s has been estimated at about 0.28.
5. The urban-rural income ratio is 3 to 1 today, although, if various hidden urban subsidies are included, the real ratio becomes much higher.
6. As measured by the percentage of officials prosecuted in the courts. See Sun (2004).
7. The figures are cited in Pei (2006b).

References

Krumm, Kathie, and Homi Kharas, eds. 2004. *East Asia Integrates: A Trade Policy Agenda for Shared Growth.* Washington, DC: World Bank.
Pei, Minxin. 2006a. *China's Trapped Transition: The Limits of Developmental Autocracy.* Cambridge, MA: Harvard University Press.

———. 2006b. "The Dark Side of China's Rise." *Foreign Policy* (March/April).
Rowen, Henry S., ed. 1998. *Behind East Asian Growth: The Political and Social Foundations of Prosperity*. London: Routledge.
Stiglitz, Joseph E., and Shahid Yusuf, eds. 2001. *Rethinking the East Asian Miracle*. Washington, DC: World Bank; New York: Oxford University Press.
Sun, Yan. 2004. *Corruption and Market in Contemporary China*. Ithaca, NY: Cornell University Press.
UNDP (United Nations Development Programme). 2005. *Human Development Report 2005, International Cooperation at a Crossroads: Aid, Trade and Security in an Unequal World*. New York: Oxford University Press.
World Bank. 1993. *The East Asian Miracle: Economic Growth and Public Policy*. World Bank Policy Research Reports. New York: Oxford University Press.
———. 2000. *East Asia: Recovery and Beyond*. Washington, DC: World Bank.

CHAPTER 15

The Asian Network Economy in the 21st Century

ANDREW SHENG

The Asian bureaucracy must make the key transition from a paternalistic top-down governance structure to a pluralistic market economy structure.

When asked about the impact of the French Revolution on China, the late Premier Zhou Enlai is reputed to have remarked that it was too early to tell.

The French Revolution occurred at the rise of the industrial revolution, when Asia accounted for nearly 40 percent of world gross domestic product (GDP) (Maddison 2003).

This essay is an attempt by a Western-trained Asian to reflect on how recent concepts of modern markets apply to the emergence of the Asian economy and how ready Asia is to take its rightful place in the 21st century.

The question of why Asia declined even as the West emerged in the 18th century is one that has vexed Asian and Western historians. Asian intellectuals who attribute the recent rise of Asia to Confucian values tend to forget two important points. First, large parts of Asia, notably India, do not have a Confucian tradition, and, second, many Chinese reformers argued in the late 19th and early 20th centuries that it was precisely the conservative Confucian values and incentive systems that were blocking attempts to advance technologically and institutionally to meet the Western challenge. Harking back to the best of Brahmin, Confucian, or Bushido spirits could not deter the encroachment of a Western canon in the 19th century. Nor do they account for the recent emergence of the Asian economies.

Some Western historians attribute the decline of Asia to institutional and governance frameworks that were not friendly to markets and technological progress. They are perhaps closer to the mark. It is one of the great puzzles of Asian intellectual history: why had the concept of the market as an efficient system of social governance never evolved in Asia? This was despite the flourishing bazaars, the commerce, and the trade between Asia and the West over the Silk Road since the classical age of Greece. I have yet to find a Chinese historical text that enunciates the concept of the market, although there are numerous descriptions of how various trades were conducted in ancient times. The concept of the market as a social mechanism that is more efficient than other forms of social governance is decidedly a Western invention.

A clue in understanding why, historically, the market was not conceptualized or cultivated actively to achieve development in Asia lies in the preeminence of the Asian bureaucracy. Despite all its ups and downs working under enlightened or despotic leaders, including colonial conquerors, the Asian bureaucracy, notably in China and India, remained the bastion of intellectual culture, civilization, and tradition. But it was also the inward-looking, self-satisfied complacency of Asian bureaucracy, combined with the corruption and profligacy of the ruling elites, that grossly underestimated the technological ascendancy of the West. The Asian ruling class, dominated by the bureaucracy, lost touch with the fact that technological change came from market-competitive forces. The top-down controls of the Asian paternalistic mindset meant that markets served only as a source of revenue for the state. In both China and India, traders were much lower than bureaucrats on the social scale. Historically, merchants could only influence state policy through corruption or by ensuring that their children or relatives would become bureaucrats through the competitive examination system.

More than anything else, it was the humiliation caused by colonization and war that drove home the realization that Asian institutions had to change everything, even down to the core values. As the Asian elites became more and more exposed to Western trade, technology, and education, they slowly altered the bureaucracy. Once political leaders had convinced them of the need to change, bureaucracies helped propel the Asian economies toward economic and social rejuvenation. This movement toward change led the way in the revival of Asian economies after World War II.

The reemergence of Asia has not been smooth, despite the momentum. The Asian crisis of 1997–98 was a rude awakening, even in advanced economies such as the Republic of Korea. Organisation for Economic Co-operation and Development status does not guarantee protection against the ferocious animal spirits of global markets. Becoming an advanced economy requires a deep institutional ability to manage national and global risks, level the playing field, promote transparency in economic and social behavior, and be a partner in global growth that is shared with equity and stability.

More than anything else, the Asian crisis was a test of the quality of private and public governance in Asia.

The East Asian Miracle

There are several explanations for East Asia's rapid rise. There is the school that focuses on conventional Asian values. Other observers attribute the rise to the monsoon rice-growing economy. Rice planting generates a social cooperative spirit. Farmers need to work together to irrigate and till the soil, as well as to harvest. During the seasons when farmers are not tilling or harvesting the land, the women learn dexterity in weaving and handicrafts. These characteristics account for the high quality of the Asian labor force in learning and adapting to manufacturing skills, as well as the importance of social infrastructure.

The Asian miracle may also be a demographic phenomenon. Japan grew quickly in the 1960s and 1970s because of the rise of a young, skilled workforce and access to markets in Europe and the United States. Today, China is growing rapidly because of its large young labor force. The workforce accounts for around 70 percent of the country's population (see figure 15.1), one of the highest shares in the world. When Japan's workforce reached that population share in the second half of the 1960s, the Japanese economy was also growing at double-digit rates. India, which does not have a one-child policy (unlike China), is about 10–15 years behind in terms of this workforce share of the population.

It is also no accident of history that the path of modernization in Asia has been heavily influenced by Western thought: Marxism in China, the Democratic People's Republic of Korea, and Vietnam, and Fabian social development in India and many parts of the former British Empire. Both influences led to fairly closed models of development until the end of the Cold War. On the other hand, export-led technocratic nationalism was the leitmotif that propelled Japan and

FIGURE 15.1 **Workforce Share of the Population in China, India, and Japan, 1950–2050**

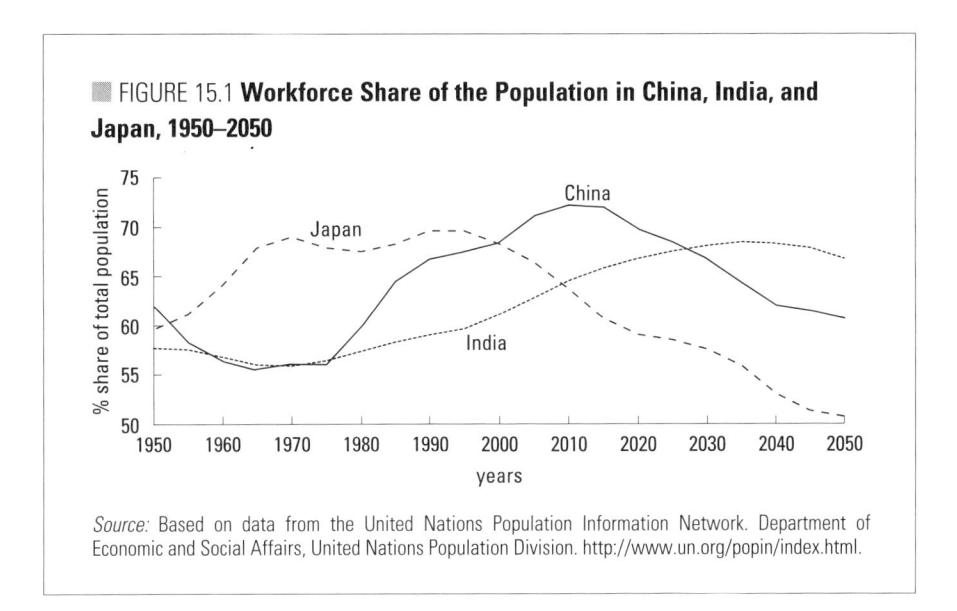

Source: Based on data from the United Nations Population Information Network. Department of Economic and Social Affairs, United Nations Population Division. http://www.un.org/popin/index.html.

the Asian dragons into industrialization. Japan's willingness during the Meiji era to adopt Western technology and even bureaucratic forms enabled it to take the lead on the path to industrialization.

Asians like myself have been fortunate to grow up in a period since World War II of unprecedented peace and stability characterized by functioning global institutions. The United Nations coordinates efforts to resolve world conflicts and improve world health, and world trade and finance have prospered in a context of lower tariff barriers under World Trade Organization conditions. In the financial arena, the Bretton Woods institutions have contributed to development and aid through the World Bank, while the International Monetary Fund has overseen the rising integration of global financial markets.

Asia accounts for 55 percent of the world's population, one-quarter of the world's exports, and slightly more than one-fifth of world nominal GDP, compared with the United States, which accounts for less than 5 percent of the world's population, 14 percent of exports, and one-third of world GDP. Europe is more comparable to the United States: 6 percent of the world's population, 36 percent of exports, and 20 percent of world GDP.

In trade terms, the world is now practically tripolar. Asia is the smallest pole, but the most rapidly growing. The North American Free Trade Agreement (Canada, Mexico, and the United States) encompasses a population of 430 million, but a US$13 trillion economy.

The European Union has a slightly larger population, at 460 million, but a smaller GDP, at US$12 trillion. Asia (essentially East and South Asia) has a population of over 3 billion, but only US$8 trillion in GDP. However, in capital market terms, the United States alone accounts for 55 percent of global market capitalization using the weighting in the Global Capital Markets Index of Morgan Stanley Capital International; the European Union accounts for an additional 17 percent, and the whole of Asia accounts for 13 percent.

The rise of China and India added over 2.5 billion workers and consumers to the market economy (Prestowitz 2005). Within the next 40 years, the four population giants, Brazil, China, India, and Russia, are expected to grow more quickly and become larger than the G-7 (Canada, France, Germany, Italy, Japan, the United Kingdom, and the United States) did over the last 40 years. Estimates of Goldman Sachs suggest that China will overtake Japan as the second largest economy by 2016, while India's economy will be larger than Japan's by 2032 (Wilson and Purushothaman 2003). The Goldman Sachs estimates assume that China will grow in real terms by an average 7.2 percent per year to 2010, while India will grow at 6.1 percent. Recent regional forecasts of the Asian Development Bank suggest that East Asia, excluding Japan, would grow in real terms by 6.7 percent a year to 2010, Southeast Asia by 6.9 percent, and South Asia by 7 percent (Roland-Holst, Verbiest, and Zhai 2005).

Japan and the Asian Economy

No proper analysis of the rise of Asia is possible without an understanding of the key role Japan has played as the first Asian economy to reach industrial-country status. Japan was able to do this because the nation adopted a growth model led by the manufacture of exports, supported by a technology- and export-friendly bureaucracy, and financed through mild repression in the banking system. The mercantilist approach of backing winners, which was led by the Ministry of International Trade and Industry and supported through the main banking system (Vittas and Wang 1991), proved so effective that the Republic of Korea, Taiwan (China), and other East Asian countries tried to imitate the system, with varying degrees of success.

Japan's model was essentially a dual economy structure. The externally oriented manufacturing sector was extremely efficient, but the protected services sector, such as property, distributive trades, and finance, lagged behind global efficiency. A McKinsey study (Kondo et al. 2000) on the Japanese economy revealed that the best Japanese industries—autos, steel, machine tools, and consumer electronics—account for only 10 percent of GDP, but show productivity levels that are 20 percent above the global competitors. However, 90 percent of GDP is accounted for by nonexport sectors, such as domestic production and services, that show productivity levels 63 percent below levels in the United States.

Japan was able to industrialize because its government coached companies and groups of companies interlinked via communal or clan ties into becoming world-class manufacturers and exporters. The competition among these groups to meet significant consumer requirements enabled them to make sophisticated products by copying, at first, but later on through innovations in production, design, and marketing (Ohmae 1982). For example, the Toyota Way illustrated the extent to which Japanese corporate philosophy, engineering technology, and process could be combined to achieve standards of quality control, marketing, and global reach that made Japanese products the standard setters in many areas (Liker 2004).

Companies like Toyota evolved a process to manage manufacturing so that end products of the highest quality could be sold at reasonable cost. They were able to do this because the corporate philosophy was identical to the philosophy of a corporate citizen. Each worker had ownership through this philosophy. Each worker believed that the value he added helped to make a better product for the consumer, for the company, for the nation, and for himself. Every worker was a quality controller and a process manager. The corporate philosophy, the process, the people, and the problem-solving capacity formed a value chain that extended beyond single companies.

Japanese companies clustered together to achieve critical mass and then extended the production and distribution chains vertically and horizontally to destination markets such as Europe and the United States, but also to the rest of Asia. This Japanese advance in the theory and practice of production, the value chain along geographical and product space, was a major innovation and contributed greatly to the development of Asia.

Yet, the rise of Asia is complex. One cannot describe it properly purely through the single discipline of economics. The realization that markets are social institutions and function like networks that are path dependent has introduced into the mix other disciplines, including sociology, politics, demography, management, corporate governance, information technology, and engineering, as well as the lens of history and the history of economic thought (Fligstein 2001).

The Network Economy

How do we weave together all the confusing, profound changes in Asia? In 1996, Professor Manuel Castells aptly named the convergence of globalization, information, and communication technology and the consequent changes in society and culture "the rise of the network society." With the Internet, the global economy has become a market "with the capacity to work as a unit in real time on a planetary scale." In his view, "the global economy emerging from informational-based production and competition is characterized by its *interdependence*, its *asymmetry*, its *regionalization*, the *increasing diversification within each region*, its *selective inclusiveness*, its *exclusionary segmentation*, and, as a result of all these features, an extraordinarily *variable geometry* that tends to dissolve historical economic geography" (Castells 1996, 106).

It is perhaps no coincidence that the rise of globalization and the rise of financial innovation occurred at the same time as the rise of free-market fundamentalism (Stiglitz 2002). With amazement and puzzlement, we have all lived through the Asian crisis, the irrational exuberance during the technological bubble of 2000, and the challenges to corporate governance and to free-market capitalism. More recently, advances in behavioral and institutional economics, such as those achieved by Oliver Williamson and Nobel Laureate Douglass North, help us to understand the behavior of firms and their role in the marketplace (Williamson 2005). At the same time, work on the natural laws of networks by physicists such as Professor Albert-Laszlo Barabasi (2003) suggest that an understanding of network behavior might be applied to market behavior.

Indeed, network theory helps us understand how markets behave, but also how Asia has evolved its production and finance chains.

First, a network is a set of interconnected nodes. It may be a network of individuals, firms, or institutions (market participants) connected in order to exchange information, products, and services. Such exchanges are possible because the participants share common values, rules, processes, codes, or standards. Standards facilitate interconnectivity and interoperability. Common standards enable more efficient communication and lower transaction or friction costs. The more widely used a common standard, the larger the network.

Second, nodes do not connect with each other at random. Metcalf's law applies; it states that the value of a network goes up as the square of the number of users (Shapiro and Varian 1999). To increase their own value, nodes seek to connect to other nodes or a hub through what Barabasi calls "preferential attachment." In order to attract more nodes to link, the hub would have to offer more "free goods" through the "the more you give, the more you receive" principle, or what I call the "network altruism" principle. This explains the "loss leader" sales attraction in supermarkets and Google offering free Web addresses and superior search services to gather more enthusiasts.

Third, hubs and clusters are efficient because the shortest route between two distant nodes may be through a hub. The more the efficient hubs cluster together and share and exchange information, the greater the network externality because each node benefits from higher efficiency in accessing information and knowledge and can cooperate in producing greater output (Economides 1993). Economies of scale increase with clusters and critical mass mostly because production and distribution processes (including exchanges of information and decision making) occur at a more rapid pace, as just-in-time processes illustrate.

Fourth, preferential attachment and network externalities, taken together, explain why there is a winner-take-all situation common to networks. The hubs compete with each other until one leading hub emerges. We have already seen how winning standards and distribution networks such as VHS, Wal-Mart, Coca-Cola, and Microsoft achieve market leadership in a short time. The rich-get-richer aspect of networks may be seen in the way markets have become more and more concentrated among an ever smaller number of big players. A large number of small players feel marginalized. For example, there were over 100 stock exchanges in the United States during the 19th century, but, with the arrival of the telegraph and now Internet, the market is dominated by NYSE and NASDAQ. Physicists have discovered that networks behave according to power laws. The most common power law is Pareto's Law, which says that 20 percent by number accounts for 80 percent by effect. Physicists have also noted that the presence of power laws often signals a transition from disorder to order (Barabasi 2003, 72).

Fifth, networks are scale free and not static, because each hub continually seeks to increase its links through its own competition or cooperation strategy. If one hub becomes dominant, the smaller hubs may cooperate or ally with other hubs to compete with the dominant hub. At the local level, some networks may become dominant through law or state control, but, because there is no universal law, there is no single architect for the global network of markets. The world is always evolving through continuous competition between different hubs arising from innovation, technology, and random events. As there are competing standards, so there are competing values and competing networks. Networks are therefore path dependent because they emerge from different social, historical, and political environments.

Finally, since markets are competitive by nature, they adapt and evolve around their environments. Hong Kong Monetary Authority Chief Executive Joseph Yam once observed that "free markets simply move around any (legal or regulatory) obstacles put in front of them." Markets operate through four key arbitrages: information arbitrage, taxation arbitrage, regulatory arbitrage, and governance arbitrage. In local markets, if there are obstacles to growth, the market simply moves offshore, which is why we have witnessed the rapid growth of offshore financial centers relative to onshore financial markets. In the language of London Business School Professor John Kay (2004), markets are, by their very competitive nature, pluralistic and disciplined, adaptive, and with good feedback mechanisms, and, consequently, much more resilient and stable than we realize.

Once we begin to look at markets as networks in an engineering or sociological sense, we move outside classical economics into the realm of political and institutional economics. The architecture of markets is already common terminology. There are, in fact, three basic network topologies or structures: the star or centralized network, the decentralized network, and the distributed network. The star system is the most vulnerable in the event of a failure of the central hub. The star system exists where there is a single dominant hub. Sometimes, decentralized networks with several large competing hubs appear as markets become concentrated among larger and larger players (or hubs). The Web, on the other hand, is so widely distributed that it is much more resilient to viruses and hacker attacks because it does not have a single hub. The self-organizing behavior of the Web ensures survival.

The market is a network. Property rights are delineated, traded, and exchanged across it. A local market is a local area network, and the global market is a network of local networks. If market networks follow power laws, this explains the inherent procyclicality of financial markets (Borio 2005).

The Asian Supply Chain Network

Our quick survey of network theory gives us a clue how the global supply network evolved. Ford's production line revolutionized manufacturing by standardizing the products, components, and processes. The efficiencies of production through lower transaction costs, including staff training and learning costs, created value. Now, information technology, automation, innovation, and competition have converged to the point that manufacturing has become more flexible. It has higher quality standards and is more responsive to consumer needs. More than anything else, information technology has driven globalization, so that the world is increasingly operating as one global network where ideas, capital, and products flow with less and less concern for geographical borders. Through the World Wide Web, manufacturers are able to source production and restructure operations and delivery systems to serve global customers. Production need not be carried out at the point of distribution, but may be outsourced to a place where it is more efficient to produce.

We can trace the rise of the global supply chain to the earlier rise of multinational companies. Trade among the affiliates, subsidiaries, and related companies of multinational companies probably account for about 45 percent of global trade.

In Asia, a World Bank study identified four waves of trade and change (Yusuf, Altaf, and Nabeshima 2004). The waves of global chain decomposition are reminiscent of the Japanese flying geese formation, where industrialization moved from the lead goose, Japan, through newly industrialized economies to the Association of Southeast Asian Nations and then China (Ozawa 2005).

At the domestic level, the idea that enterprises operate together as networks is not new. Japanese enterprises grouped together initially as clan-based industrial groups or *zaibatsus*. When these were broken up after World War II, the components were still knit together in groups called *keiretsus*. The Korean variety is well known as *chaebols*, of which Samsung has emerged as a world-beater in electronics. In the 1960s, there was already awareness that multinational enterprises were using horizontal and vertical integration of production across national borders. The American firms led the way by setting up production companies in Europe and Japan.

By the 1970s, as costs rose in Japan, production began to be outsourced to the newly industrializing economies, such as Hong Kong (China), Korea, Singapore, and Taiwan (China). At about the same time, a large number of Indian and Taiwanese graduates and workers in Silicon Valley decided to set up plants in Bangalore and Taiwan (China) where they could produce goods and services cheaper than in the United States and where local governments were eager to offer assistance because they welcomed the foreign direct investment (FDI). This was the beginning of the spread of the global supply chain back into Asia.

In the second wave of export-led growth in the 1980s, Indonesia, Malaysia, the Philippines, and Thailand began to receive FDI in special development zones. Malaysia was one of the first to benefit from FDI from both Japan and the United States. Footwear, textiles, and consumer electronics were followed by machinery, electronics, chemicals, and transport equipment.

There were two lines of FDI, each with its own networks. The U.S. investments in electronics in Penang, Malaysia, were the first signs that American firms were taking advantage of the cheaper labor, good infrastructure, and tax benefits to move production overseas (Ernst 2004). All the output was exported because Malaysia had little internal demand for electronic chips and components.

Much of the Japanese outward FDI went toward consumer durables and automotive manufacturing, where advantage was also taken of local tax and customs incentives. Initially, these factories served local markets, but, as the Japanese realized that the quality of production in Malaysian and Thai factories was comparable to that in Japan, these factories became part of the supply chain that fed components into the main plants in Japan and other parts of the world.

Japanese manufacturers worked in clusters, and Japanese investments in an auto plant in Thailand, for example, would bring along Japanese component manufacturers, whose networks expanded to include the local component manufacturers, once the quality and timeliness of supply had risen to Japanese requirements. The non-Japanese suppliers and distributors in Asia prospered with the supply chain.

By the mid-1980s, it had become clear that there were five types of networks: supplier networks, producer networks, customer networks, the standards coalition network, and technology cooperation networks

(Ernst 1994). Global supply chains combined rapid geographical dispersion and two types of clusters (Ernst 2005). The first cluster consisted of centers of excellence in research and development, typically close to good universities and defense research centers, and the second cluster revolved around precision mechanical engineering or cost- and time-reduction centers that could drive down production costs.

At the same time, companies such as Li and Fung in Hong Kong (China) used information technology and their network of suppliers in Asia to provide a global distribution and sourcing supply chain (DeMeyer et al. 2005). This was also a major innovation in the supply chain for distribution. Much of the regional distribution chain relied on the Chinese diaspora of entrepreneurs scattered throughout Asia, but located particularly in Hong Kong (China), Singapore, and Taiwan (China). European, Japanese, and U.S. multinational companies used the network of firms of the Chinese diaspora to help in production and distribution. Wal-Mart, Ahold, Carrefour, and Tesco are some of the names of the large retail chains outside Asia that relied on Asia for their supplies, but also expanded their own retail networks in Asia to distribute their goods globally. The distribution networks depended also on specialist skills, such as quality control and outsourcing.

In addition, the Indian diaspora, particularly those people with high technical skills working in Silicon Valley, backward-integrated to India to build up the software business and information technology outsourcing. The Indian model of an invisible, services-oriented production network deserves far more study to appreciate the management and processing innovations involved and to highlight the great significance of this model at the forefront in development.

By the 1990s, the high cost of production in the newly industrialized economies had driven investments toward China. China's position in the global supply chain was consolidated during the Asian crisis, when production began moving to areas where cheap labor was available in an environment with good technological capability and good infrastructure. Those Asian countries that had suffered through huge problems in domestic banking during the Asian crisis found that they had lost production to China, which offered stable financial facilities and a large domestic market that provided a means to reduce the risk. Smaller production centers, such as Singapore, that did not have large domestic markets had to move up the value chain in order to compete.

In a short 10 years, China has emerged as the world's fourth largest trading nation and second largest producer of information technology hardware, with close to 14 percent of the world market (Yusuf, Altaf, and Nabeshima 2004, 6). Today, 75 percent of the world's toys, 36 percent of its television sets, and 31 percent of its crude steel are produced in China. China alone was taking in more than US$50 billion in FDI annually, even exceeding the United States as the leading destination of global FDI flows.

Global supply networks have had a tremendous impact on regional trade. Intra–East Asia trade grew from about one-quarter of all trade in the region in 1971 to more than half in 2004 (Damuri, Atje, and Gaduh 2006). Trade integration has moved beyond the Association of Southeast Asian Nations. China has also emerged as the aggregator of Asian trade and production for reexport to the West. In 2005, it ran a net trade surplus of US$114.2 billion with the United States, but it ran net trade deficits with Taiwan (China) (US$58.1 billion), Korea (US$41.8 billion), Japan (US$16.4 billion), Southeast Asia (US$15.6 billion), and Australia (US$5.1 billion).

As David Roland-Holst (2006) so insightfully pointed out, what we see in today's global economy is a process of supply chain decomposition, whereby FDI is leading to the distribution of production tasks across an international matrix of intermediate producers. In East Asia, this process has advanced rapidly and pervasively, facilitated by both Western FDI and a regional cascade effect, as more advanced Asian economies reallocate production to less advanced ones. He calls this "bamboo capitalism": firms and markets sprout from the nodes in the root system that supports global intermediate supply.

Despite Asian trade integration, the essential point is that the ultimate trade destination remains primarily the United States and then Europe. The U.S. demand for goods and services spawned the global supply chain. Essentially, the opportunity to supply the U.S. economy with cheaper, better goods resulted in the spread of the global supply chain throughout Asia.

The Asian Financial Network

From the balance sheet point of view, assets have to be financed by liabilities of either equity or debt. The global production supply chain had huge implications for the transformation of Asia, but financing was crucial to the network economy.

First, since the main buyer was the largest economy with the best credit standing, its demand for high-quality goods at value prices created the supply and distribution network to support that demand. This meant that credit financing for the Asian supply chain, with subcontractors or original equipment manufacturers and component suppliers lower down the chain, was never a serious problem. Markets cannot grow if the end buyer is a major credit risk.

Second, a distinctive feature is that the financial network relied primarily on the domestic banking channel, while capital market developments were driven largely by the non-Asian supply of FDI and foreign portfolio investments. The result was an imbalanced growth strategy. The strategy was vulnerable to the sort of sudden withdrawals of capital flows that culminated in the Asian crisis. In the absence of a strong regional lender of last resort, the Asian economies built up large foreign exchange reserves and current account surpluses, so that Asia became the primary funder of the global imbalances.

The funding for U.S. direct investments in host countries was never a problem. These investments were funded out of equity or through direct borrowings from local credit markets in local or foreign currency. Asian banks had no credit concerns about providing trade financing nor about supplying bridging finance for FDI projects in Asia. For Japanese FDI in non-Japan Asia, the availability of trade credit for work in progress was rarely in doubt because leading Japanese producers were cash rich and were able to provide both investment and trade credit for non-Japanese component suppliers lower down the production chain. Japanese banks had no credit worries over financing Japanese FDI or financing distributors of Japanese products.

Third, Asia remains a bank-dominated financial system for well-known reasons. In the classic flying geese formation, the other Asian economies mimicked the Japanese bank-financed manufacturing export model and never moved up the value chain in the financial sector by deepening capital and derivative market skills. Many were happy financing the booming domestic mortgage market, domestic property developers, or government-led enterprises. This shortsighted strategy meant that higher-value financial intermediary skills were dependent on markets in London and New York.

The result was overreliance on short-term funding to finance trade credit and long-term investment. The Japanese supply chain model depended on funding from Japanese banks for the keiretsu investments overseas, as well as the trade credit that these leading manufacturers offered their component suppliers and distributors. The ultimate income source was in dollars, but, to avoid the impact of currency fluctuations, Japanese trading houses tended to buy in dollars from Asia and lend in Japanese yen. To keep the yen relatively competitive, there was also considerable outflow in yen official credits.

The Japanese supply chain was therefore the first to undertake the carry trade by borrowing cheaply in yen and lending and investing in higher-return FDI in non-yen countries. Unfortunately, Asian recipients of these yen credits and FDI did not fully understand the risk management implications of the supply chain model and the financial network. They used the capital inflows in foreign currency to invest in local currency assets, particularly stocks and real estate, creating the conditions for the onset of the Asian crisis.

It is thus no coincidence that Thailand, the largest recipient of Japanese FDI in the 1990s, was vulnerable to supply chain pressures. Between 1995 and 1997, Thai companies (especially suppliers to Japanese manufacturers) depended heavily on trade credit from Japanese companies to fund their activities. A number were drawing down heavily on bank borrowing to fund their real estate and non-manufacturing activities. Japanese banks are especially important in Thailand, accounting for over half of all international bank lending. The combination of yen weakening and the decline in the Nikkei index in 1997 caused Japanese banks (under capital rules) to cut back on their credit to Japanese firms, as well as their foreign exchange loans to Thailand. The combination of the cut in bank credit and the sharp reduction in trade credit exacerbated the credit deflation. Since there were insufficient foreign exchange reserves to meet capital outflows, the Thai baht devaluation sent a tsunami shock wave across the Asian financial network (Love, Preve, and Sarria-Allende 2005).

There is now agreement that the Asian crisis was a case of a surge in capital inflows into a dollar-based zone. This led to a rise in the real effective exchange rate, which led to growing current account deficits in the crisis economies. Much of the surge in capital inflows was caused by the Japanese FDI coming into the region between 1990 and 1996, including Japanese bank lending to support the spread of the Japanese supply chain. The spread of the supply chain was necessary to maintain Japanese competitiveness in exporting to the world by using cheap labor, but it also involved the development of an Asian backyard market. The European banks and the fund managers joined the herd of inflows into the region.

After the sharp appreciation of the yen in 1995 to nearly 85 to the dollar, the yen began to depreciate, and Japanese banks began to face mounting losses on domestic loans. The pressure to boost capital ratios reduced their appetite for international lending. By 1996/97, the appearance of a significant premium on their international interbank funding, plus the impact of a weaker yen on their capital adequacy, had forced them to reduce their dollar exposure. Almost 80 percent of their international loans were booked to Asian borrowers, so Japanese banks had their largest international exposure toward Asia (Jeanneau and Micu 2002).

In the five years to 1997, roughly US$200 billion flowed into Asia. In 1997 and 1998, roughly US$160 billion flowed out, of which Japanese bank lending withdrawals accounted for roughly US$65 billion. Indeed, between the end of 1996 and the end of 2000, the Japanese banking system had a net international lending exposure reduction worldwide of ¥20.8 trillion or US$170 billion, the largest retrenchment in recent banking history.[1] As Japan went into deflation, short-term interest rates were brought to zero, and hedge funds and smart investors engaged in a feast with the carry trade by borrowing cheap yen and buying Asian assets that yielded a higher spread in dollars. Once the baht devalued, much of the carry trade had to be unwound in a hurry. Asia experienced a bank run, but domestic central banks did not have enough foreign exchange reserves to meet the run on foreign currency. The Asian global supply chain was without a lender of last resort.

We might conceive of the global market as a network among local networks that operate according to local standards. Broadly, there are three or four dominant international currencies, namely, the dollar, the euro, the yen, and pounds sterling, which make the local networks interoperable. The exchange rate is not only an asset price, but also a network standard. In the postwar Bretton Woods model, the global financial system used essentially the dollar standard fixed against gold, while all other local currencies were effectively pegged against the dollar, so that, de facto, there was one leading standard across the global financial system.

Since World War II, when the U.S. dollar replaced sterling as the premier international currency, it attained a dominant power law status. We might argue that the United States is today the superhub of global financial markets. The U.S. economy accounts for 4 percent of the world population, 30 percent of global GDP, and half of world market capitalization, and the U.S. dollar is used in roughly 60 percent of all trade and financial transactions. Global foreign exchange reserves are roughly 60 percent in dollars, 20 percent in euros, and the rest in yen, sterling, and other currencies. The dollar has contributed significantly to the stable growth of global trade.

The history of the emergence of the United States as the dominant economy in the world is well documented, but it is useful to remember that, after World War II, the U.S. economy accounted for 46 percent of world GDP. One reason there is preferential attachment to the U.S. dollar as a standard is that the U.S. financial market still provides superior infrastructure and transparent protection of property rights through common law and that, until very recently, the track record of the United States in macroeconomic terms has been superior. Specifically, through appropriate monetary and fiscal policies, the U.S. dollar has been a benchmark currency that has not suffered from severe inflation or political shocks.

Since the United States is the final customer, a dollar standard would be the most efficient for all the suppliers to the United States. A dollar standard imposes fiscal and monetary discipline on the economy. Hong Kong (China) relies on this discipline to make sure the economy adjusts to the dollar standard, not the other way around. A fixed exchange rate standard demands a huge amount of discipline in the domestic economy, since one cannot use flexibility to achieve competitive advantage. It also ensures that both the private sector and the public sector must maintain financial discipline, but also match the productivity levels of the dominant standard.

The Asian financial network has two main contending standards, the dollar and the yen. The yen's role has been declining as a share of global foreign exchange trading since 1989, when it had a 13.5 percent share of daily trading; now, the share is 10.4 percent, whereas the dollar's share has been maintained at roughly 44–45 percent (BIS 2004). This is so despite the fact that Japan is the third largest economy after the United States and the European Union. Japan's GDP of US$3.75 trillion is nearly half the total Asian GDP, and Japan has financial assets worth nearly double the assets of the rest of Asia put together.

The underutilization of the yen has several possible causes. One has to do with the fact that Japanese companies export in dollars and import in yen. Another is that the short-term capital market is relatively underdeveloped in Japan, so that transaction costs in yen tend to be higher than transaction costs in dollars (Dominquez 1999). Of course, the volatility in the yen-dollar exchange rate, which moved from 85 yen in 1995 to 137 in 1997, was a factor causing borrowers and investors to worry about borrowing or holding yen.

The Japanese economy is so large in Asia that one cannot divorce Asian economic and financial development from consideration of the interactions between Japan and non-Japan Asia. The Asian crisis was not merely a crisis of four countries outside Japan. It was a crisis that included Japan, which had been suffering through a deflation and an adjustment for 15 years after the Japanese bubble of 1989–90. For example, International Monetary Fund staff estimates suggest that "the downturn in Japanese domestic demand and the depreciation of the yen against the dollar could lower GDP in the Asia-5 countries by almost 1 percent in 1998. On the other hand, the Asia crisis is estimated to lower Japan's GDP by 1–1.25 percent in 1998" (Shimizu 2000).[2] If the yen had depreciated beyond 146 in August 1998, and the Chinese yuan had followed, the ensuing disaster would have been tremendous.

When the yen became strong, non-Japan Asia benefited from Japanese FDI and the shift in production and exports to non-Japan Asia. When the yen became weak, the reverse happened, and production shifted back to Japan. Hence, the dual-standard Asian supply network was subjected to unnecessary volatility and stress, especially because people in non-Japan Asia expected the inflows of capital to be permanent. Prior to the Asian crisis, non-Japan Asia was essentially on a dollar standard, as Professor McKinnon (2005) rightly points out.

The real design flaw in operating a de facto dollar standard is that either you must maintain very high dollar reserves, as Hong Kong (China) did, with minimal external liabilities, or you must have access to a dollar lender of last resort. Prior to the crisis, everyone thought the International Monetary Fund was, subject to appropriate conditionality, the lender of last resort. Asian central bankers did not keep sufficient reserves because they did not have proper international balance sheets that might have helped them understand their true net international position. Indeed, from Indonesia to Korea, people discovered that greater foreign exchange liabilities had been committed offshore than anyone had realized. The second mistake was to underestimate global market volatility in exchange rates and in exchange flows. The contagion that spread from Asia to Russia and Brazil caused market volatility to move by as much as 15 standard deviations.

The Asian global supply chain was therefore a single supply chain with two financial channels and two standards. On the one hand, the

United States was the leading consumer, the provider of the global dollar standard, and the leading banker for Asia's external savings. On the other hand, Japan, as the main hub of the supply chain, had a bank-dominated system based on yen funding. The rest of Asia traded mostly in dollars and had assets in domestic currency and net liabilities in foreign currency, creating a vulnerability to currency and maturity mismatches. The architecture was vulnerable to currency and liquidity shocks.

The hard facts can now be gathered through the Lane and Milesi-Ferretti (2006) data set on global net international assets from 1970 to 2004. As a result of persistent current account surpluses and despite rising exchange rates versus the dollar, Japan's net foreign asset position rose from US$12.2 billion (6.0 percent of GDP) in 1970 to US$293.3 billion (9.9 percent of GDP) in 1989. Over this period, similarly, the net foreign asset position of the United States deteriorated from US$65.5 billion (6.3 percent of GDP) in 1970 to negative US$152.2 billion or (−2.8 percent of GDP) in 1989. By then, Japan was clearly a net creditor to the rest of the world.

Why were Asians willing to put their hard-earned savings with the United States at the risk of exposing themselves to depreciation there? The answer is that we are in Bretton Woods II, in which Asia is satisfied with export sales and with low returns on a dollar exposure. In exchange, Asia obtains open markets in the United States and American skills in venture capital and in reinvestment in Asia (Dooley, Folkerts-Landau, and Garber 2005; Spencer 2006). The imbalance is actually a total equity return swap that is mutually beneficial and could be sustainable. Holders of dollars are willing to pay seigniorage and more to ensure that the world's leading banker remains both the banker and the consumer.

As the issuer of the dominant currency standard, the United States was, at the end of World War II, the banker to the world, with a strong current account surplus and a net creditor position equivalent to 10 percent of U.S. GDP in 1952. By the end of 2004, after running persistent current account deficits, the net external debt of the United States (with FDI at market value) was US$2.5 trillion, or 22 percent of U.S. GDP. The United States had foreign assets of US$10 trillion (85 percent of GDP) and liabilities of US$12.5 trillion (107 percent of GDP). However, 70 percent of U.S. foreign assets were in foreign currency, and the United States was unique in that almost all its liabilities were in U.S. dollars. Gourinchas and Rey (2005) estimate that a 10 percent U.S. dollar depreciation would lead to the transfer of 5.9 percent of U.S. GDP from the foreign holders of its liabilities to the United States.

Before the Asian crisis, the Asian authorities assumed that, since the United States was the banker to the world, either the U.S. Federal Reserve or the International Monetary Fund would be the dollar lender of last resort. This expectation appeared to be confirmed because the United States had stepped in during the Mexican crisis of 1994. But it was not to be. Moreover, it is now abundantly clear that the International Monetary Fund was never designed to be a lender of last resort. It might provide some liquidity. However, with only US$300 billion in assets, it has less than 0.5 percent of the total international assets in the global financial network (over US$85 trillion); meanwhile, 70 percent of its loans are concentrated in only three countries.

Implications of the Global Network Economy for Growth in Asia

We have one global network, but we also have different standards. What are the implications? By switching standards, one would generate different gain and loss allocations in terms of flows and balance sheets across the world. If the law of one price applies, then, ideally, we should have a single global currency and a global lender of last resort. We have seen that, since Bretton Woods I, this is not feasible politically. The dominant standard may therefore decide whether to maintain or enhance its dominant status or allow other standards to take up some of the burden.

Two possibilities are discernible. As Asia grows in gravitas in terms of wealth, the rest of the world would like Asia to rely more on domestic engines of consumption in Asia, rather than such significant dependence on American consumers. By and large, there is reasonable consensus even within Asia that this is the correct course of action. A point of disagreement is whether Asian savings patterns are able to change rapidly given the demographic profile and the fact that much of the social security infrastructure is not yet in place, and domestic financial systems are not yet ready to recycle domestic savings.

The second possibility revolves around whether Asians should change the one supply chain and two standards into a more robust regime. The recent moves by the Association of Southeast Asian Nations, plus China, Japan, and the Republic of Korea, at Chiang Mai, Thailand,

(China) and Singapore, with their highly global, integrated public and corporate governance, could absorb the shocks with resilience. China and India, as well as other transitional economies that are not yet entirely following global standards and price levels, were protected by their relatively closed systems, including exchange controls. But, as they open up, they will also have to deal with the adjustment process.

The Asian bureaucracy must make the important transition from a paternalistic top-down governance structure to a pluralistic market economy structure. However able and determined, a top-down model dominated by a small elite can no longer manage large complex market economies open to wide public choice and rapid technological change. As markets become more open and as network friction costs are reduced, consumers, savers, and skilled labor will have the choice of moving across borders with ease. The law of one price is beginning to become a reality.

I am optimistic that private- and even government-led corporations in Asia would, through global competition, make the transition with relative ease. However, it is in the arena of government bureaucracies where the real battle of market change will have to take place. Asian bureaucracies, in the first years of independence, were the vanguards of change, flush with the idealism of freedom, united by the vision of a new society, and eager to prove to the world that Asians could stand on their own. But, as Asian economies reach the middle age of prosperity, the old bureaucratic traits of conservatism, complacency, and nationalism may combine with the venality of regulatory capture, corruption, and incompetence. The record of privatization throughout Asia has been patchy precisely because bureaucrats are loath to give up their interests as proxy owners and managers. Reforms demanded by the market are slow in coming because many bureaucracies are large and have vested interests in the status quo.

To be fair, many bureaucrats, even in the West, have not understood the important differences between the roles of the state as owner, regulator, and facilitator of business in terms of achieving market efficiency. As society becomes more complex, the bureaucracy is the only agency available to address market and social failures such as inequality, pollution, energy wastages, and terrorism.

The principal-agent problem is everywhere evident in markets. Society demands that the agent (the bureaucracy) must be able to deliver what the market and society want in terms of long-term value-creation and greater social equality and stability. The Asian bureaucracy must be able to manage the process of transition to the market economy without wasting the fruits of development and demographic endowment through lack of focus, incompetence, or corruption.

Asians have evolved managerial innovations such as the Toyota Way, the Li and Fung Global Distribution System, and the Indian software outsourcing model. Asian production and distribution systems can evolve and innovate to global standards and beyond. They have already been able to make important leaps. They have created value and wealth and generated resources so the state might address what the state is good at addressing: education, health, security, regulation, and social infrastructure.

But as Asian bureaucracies have become large and unwieldy, they have lost focus. Many social commentators think that changing politicians through the electoral system can solve this problem. Elected politicians find that the greatest challenge is not simply the right policies, but the capacity of the bureaucracy to identify the policies, offer the right options, and implement them effectively. A defensive bureaucracy that digs in against the demands of the market and the public demand for greater efficiency, transparency, and accountability only delays and impedes the inevitable adjustment to globalization. But the politicians are ultimately accountable to the public. They should set the goals and requirements of the bureaucracy.

Political, business, and civil society leaders must bear much of the responsibility for the readiness of the economy to meet globalization because they are responsible for the bureaucracy. The success of the market economy stands or falls on the professionalism, competence, and integrity of the bureaucracy, from the smallest village official to the cabinet office secretariat. It is time for the bureaucracy to stand up and be counted.

In the modern network economy, among the irreplaceable roles and responsibilities of the state is the creation and enforcement of standards, codes, and rules of the game, as well as establishing the property rights infrastructure of a market economy that is fair, transparent, robust, flexible, and efficient.

Markets are the most important deliverers of the efficiency necessary to achieve social equity and sustainability, but issues of fairness and public goods still require the intervention of the state. The state should be a partner, not a private sector adversary. Asian bureaucracies will have to rise to this important challenge.

The old order of success is no guarantee of the future success of the new order. If crisis is an event, reform is a process. For reform to be successful, it must be managed as a process. The real challenge for Asia in the 21st century is to manage the process of transition to Asia's rightful place in the global economy. Altering the management of this process so as to meet the goal will be a big challenge in years to come.

Notes

1. Web site of the Ministry of Finance, Japan, on the net international asset position of Japan.
2. The Asia-5 are Brunei Darussalam, Hong Kong (China), Japan, Singapore, and Taiwan (China).

References

Barabasi, Albert-Laszlo. 2003. *Linked: How Everything Is Connected to Everything Else and What It Means to Business, Science and Everyday Life*. New York: Plume Books.
BIS (Bank for International Settlements). 2004. "Triennial Central Bank Survey of Foreign Exchange and Derivatives Market Activity in June 2004." Regular publication, December 6, Bank for International Settlements, Basel, Switzerland.
Borio, Claudio. 2005. "The Search for the Elusive Twin Goals of Monetary and Financial Stability." Paper prepared for the conference organized by the IMF Institute and the Monetary and Financial Systems Department, "Financial Stability: Central Banking and Supervisory Challenges," International Monetary Fund, Washington, DC, September 6–7.
Castells, Manuel. 1996. *The Rise of the Network Society*. Vol. I of *The Information Age: Economy, Society and Culture*. Cambridge, MA: Blackwell Publishers.
Damuri, Yose Rizal, Raymond Atje, and Arya B. Gaduh. 2006. "Integration and Trade Specialization in East Asia." CSIS Economics Working Paper WPE 094, East Asia Bureau of Economic Research and Center for Strategic and International Studies, Jakarta. http://www.csis.or.id/working_paper_file/66/wpe094.pdf.
DeMeyer, Arnoud, Peter Williamson, Frank-Jürgen Richter, and Pamela C. M. Mar. 2005. *Global Future: The Next Challenge for Asian Business*. Singapore: John Wiley & Sons (Asia) Pte. Ltd.
Dobbs-Higginson, Michael S. 1993. *Asia Pacific: Its Role in the New World Disorder*. London: Heinemann.
Dominquez, Kathryn M. 1999. "The Role of the Yen." In *International Capital Flows*. National Bureau of Economic Research Conference Report, ed. Martin Feldstein, chap. 3.2. Chicago: University of Chicago Press.
Dooley, Michael, David Folkerts-Landau, and Peter Garber. 2005. "International Financial Stability: Asia, Interest Rates and the Dollar." Global Markets Research paper, October 27, Deutsche Bank Global Research, Deutsche Bank, New York.
Economides, Nicholas. 1993. "Network Economics with Application to Finance." *Financial Markets, Institutions and Instruments* 2 (5): 89–97.
Ernst, Dieter. 1994. "Inter-Firm Networks and Market Structure: Driving Forces, Barriers, and Patterns of Control." BRIE Research Paper, University of California, Berkeley, CA.
———. 2004. "Global Production Networks in East Asia's Electronic Industry and Upgrading Prospects in Malaysia." In *Global Production Networking and Technological*

Change in East Asia, ed. Shahid Yusuf, M. Anjum Altaf, and Kaoru Nabeshima, 89–158. Washington, DC: World Bank.

———. 2005, "The New Mobility of Knowledge: Digital Information Systems and Global Flagship Networks." In *Digital Formations: IT and New Architectures in the Global Realm,* ed. Robert Latham and Saskia Sassen, 89–114. Princeton, NJ: Princeton University Press.

Fligstein, Neil. 2001. *The Architecture of Markets: An Economic Sociology of Twenty-First-Century Capitalist Societies.* Princeton, NJ: Princeton University Press.

Gourinchas, Pierre-Olivier, and Hélène Rey. 2005. "From World Banker to World Venture Capitalist: U.S. External Adjustment and the Exorbitant Privilege." CEPR Discussion Paper 5220 (September), Center for Economic Policy Research, London.

Ho, Corrine, Guonan Ma, and Robert N. McCauley. 2005. "Trading Asian Currencies." BIS Quarterly Review, March, Bank for International Settlements, Basel, Switzerland.

Jeanneau, Serge, and Marian Micu. 2002. "Determinants of International Bank Lending to Emerging Market Countries." BIS Working Paper 112 (June), Bank for International Settlements, Basel, Switzerland. http://www.bis.org/publ/work112.htm.

Kay, John. 2004. *The Truth About Markets: Why Some Countries Are Rich but Most Remain Poor.* London: Penguin.

Kojima, Kiyoshi. 2000. "The 'Flying Geese' Model of Asian Economic Development: Origin, Theoretical Extensions, and Regional Policy Implications." *Journal of Asian Economics* 11 (4): 375–401.

Kondo, M. J., W. Lewis, V. Palmade, and Y. Yokohama. 2000. "Reviving Japan's Economy." McKinsey Quarterly 4, McKinsey Global Institute, Washington, DC.

Lane, Philip R., and Gian Maria Milesi-Ferretti. 2006. "The External Wealth of Nations Mark II: Revised and Extended Estimates of Foreign Assets and Liabilities, 1970–2004." IMF Working Paper 06/69, Research Department, International Monetary Fund, Washington, DC.

Liker, Jeffrey. 2004. *The Toyota Way: 14 Management Principles from the World's Greatest Manufacturer.* New York: McGraw-Hill.

Love, Inessa, Lorenzo A. Preve, and Virginia Sarria-Allende. 2005. "Trade Credit and Bank Credit: Evidence from Recent Financial Crises." Policy Research Working Paper 3716, World Bank, Washington, DC.

Maddison, Angus. 2003. *The World Economy: Historical Statistics.* Paris: Organisation for Economic Co-operation and Development.

McKinnon, Ronald I. 2005. *Exchange Rates under the East Asian Dollar Standard: Living with Conflicted Virtue.* Cambridge, MA: MIT Press.

Ohmae, Kenichi. 1982. *The Mind of the Strategist: The Art of Japanese Business.* New York: McGraw-Hill.

Ozawa, Terutomo. 2005. "Asia's Labor-Driven Economic Development, Flying-Geese Style: An Unprecedented Opportunity for the Poor to Rise?" APEC Study Centre Discussion Paper 40 (July), Asia-Pacific Economic Cooperation Study Center, Columbia University, New York.

Pan, Lynn. 1990. *Sons of the Yellow Emperor: A History of the Chinese Diaspora.* Boston: Little, Brown and Company.

Prestowitz, Clyde. 2005. "Three Billion New Capitalists: The Great Shift of Wealth and Power to the East." New York: Basic Books.

Rohwer, Jim. 1995. *Asia Rising: Why America Will Prosper as Asia's Economies Boom.* Singapore: Butterworth-Heinemann Asia.

Roland-Holst, David. 2006. "Global Supply Networks and Multilateral Trade Linkages: A Structural Analysis of East Asia." Working paper, March 31, University of California, Berkeley, CA.

Roland-Holst, David, Jean-Pierre Verbiest, and Fan Zhai. 2005. "Growth and Trade Horizons for Asia: Long-Term Forecasts for Regional Integration." ERD Working Paper 74 (November), Economics and Research Department, Asian Development Bank, Manila.

Shapiro, Carl, and Hal R. Varian. 1999. *Information Rules: A Strategic Guide to the Network Economy.* Boston: Harvard Business School Press.

Shimizu, Yoshinori. 2000. "Convoy Regulation, Bank Management, and the Financial Crisis in Japan." In *Japan's Financial Crisis and Its Parallels to U.S. Experience.* Special Report 13 (September), ed. Riyoichi Mikitani and Adam S. Posen, 57–99. Washington, DC: Institute for International Economics.

Spencer, Michael. 2006. "A Guide through Bretton Woods II." Global Markets Research paper, April 10, Deutsche Bank Global Research, Deutsche Bank, New York.

Stiglitz, Joseph E. 2002. *Globalization and Its Discontents.* New York: WW Norton.

Vittas, Dimitri, and Bo Wang. 1991. "Credit Policies in Japan and Korea: A Review of the Literature." Policy Research Working Paper 747, World Bank, Washington, DC.

Williamson, Oliver E. 2005. "The Economics of Governance." *American Economic Review* 95 (2): 1–18.

Wilson, Dominic, and Roopa Purushothaman. 2003. "Dreaming with BRICs: The Path to 2050." Global Economics Paper 99 (October 1), Goldman Sachs, New York. http://www.goldman-sachs.com/insight/research/reports/99.pdf.

Yusuf, Shahid, M. Anjum Altaf, and Kaoru Nabeshima, eds. 2004. *Global Production Networking and Technological Change in East Asia.* Washington, DC: World Bank.

CHAPTER 16

Does China Need to Change Its Industrialization Path?

WU JINGLIAN

The path to industrialization and the growth strategy being followed in China have become unsustainable. A new reform agenda should be pursued.

In recent years, the industrialization path that should be followed and the growth strategy that should be preferred have become major issues attracting attention across China. The Chinese government put forward the slogan "following a new industrialization path" in 2002 and the requirement of following a resource-economizing development approach with Chinese characteristics in 2004. However, another characterization and practice have actually been in play, that is, it has been contended that the Chinese economy has, as a totality, moved into a development phase of industrialization through heavy industry and opened up a broad space for investment growth. Many local governments have pooled physical and financial resources for the launch of large-scale projects in such sectors as automobiles, steel and iron, and aluminum electrodes in an attempt to drive economic growth by way of the high-level development of heavy industry and chemical industries. During the process of the drafting of the 11th Five-Year Plan (FYP), 2006–10, this author criticized such a line of thinking and practice and ignited a profoundly influential debate between and among economists and policy makers. Now, the Chinese government has formulated the 11th FYP in accordance with the principle of "following a new industrialization path"; however, for the plan to be implemented effectively, efforts should be made to push ahead with reforms in the growth strategy and other critical fields.

This essay will first offer an overview of the industrialization path followed and the growth strategy adopted over the past half century, while the second part will analyze the institutional impediments facing efforts to transform the growth strategy. The third part will turn to an explanation as to why such a path and model have already become unsustainable, and the fourth part will put forward the reform agenda that should be pursued. The last part will respond to critiques about the viewpoints raised by this author during the two-year debate.

The Zigzagging Road of China's Industrialization Drive

With the beginning of the 1st FYP (1953–57) in 1953, China comprehensively adopted the Soviet industrialization strategy, which was characterized by the top priority granted to heavy industry as the guiding principle in economic development. During the 1st FYP, China concentrated its human, physical, and financial resources and, with the assistance of the Soviet Union, created and upgraded 156 major engineering investment projects, among which the vast majority were heavy-industry projects: investments in heavy industry accounted for 85 percent of the aggregate industrial investment during those five years. It was predicted that, by adopting such a guideline, China would be able to speed up the industrialization process appreciably, achieving industrialization throughout the country in approximately 15 years (1953–67), and basically build China into a great industrialized socialist country (Propaganda Department, Central Committee of the Communist Party of China, 1953).

In the first few years, implementation of the 1st FYP did not make satisfactory progress. Despite the fact that, driven by heavy industry, the Chinese economy achieved rapid development, given the abnormal development of heavy industry and the seriously worsening economic structure, the national economy was in very unstable condition. Against such a background, in 1956, Mao Zedong put forward his requirement of speeding up the development of light industry and agriculture, while top priority was granted to the development of heavy industry (Mao 1956).

Nevertheless, China did not make any substantive change in its growth strategy and continued to attempt to sustain a high growth rate in output by means of inputs of capital and other resources. As a result, the year 1958 saw the launch of the Great Leap Forward campaign, which imposed high growth targets on output in such heavy industries as steel and coal. Although the Great Leap Forward campaign resulted in a seriously worsened economic situation and huge losses in wealth and even human lives, this growth strategy, featuring high targets, a high level of inputs, a high rate of growth, and low efficiency, was not changed at all until the end of the Great Cultural Revolution in 1976.

In the wake of the Great Cultural Revolution, a reflection occurred both within and outside the government on the development path that had been followed in the preceding years, and it was realized that China could not possibly achieve industrialization and modernization smoothly if the country were to continue to follow this path of extensive (factor-driven) development. In 1980, the Central Committee of the Communist Party of China and the State Council formally put forward the guideline of "embarking upon a new path with a relatively realistic speed, relatively good economic returns, and more real benefits for the people."[1] In 1996, based on the experience of the early period of the reform and the drive toward openness ("opening-up"), the National People's Congress passed the 9th FYP (1996–2000) and the "Vision Targets" for national economic and social development by 2010, which set out the "realization of the transformation of the economic growth strategy from an extensive (factor-driven) one to an intensive (productivity-driven) one" as a basic task for the 9th FYP. The 10th FYP (2001–05) regarded economic restructuring and upgrading as the main thread of economic development during those five years.

In the course of the two decades of reform and opening-up, efforts to eradicate the influence of the Stalinist socialist industrialization path targeted the outcomes or results; no thorough revamping was undertaken of the root causes of these outcomes, in particular, the mindset and institutional arrangements underpinning the traditional industrialization path. Because the institutional and policy legacy compatible with the traditional industrialization path is still in existence on a massive scale and continues to play a role, practices that rely on substantial investments and high consumption to sustain high growth rates tend to be readopted easily.

Institutional Foundation of the Traditional Industrialization Path and Growth Strategy

The reason China's economic growth strategy has failed to achieve a transformation toward intensive growth in line with the requirements of modern economic growth is, fundamentally speaking, related to institutional factors. In other words, a series of institutional arrangements tends to support and encourage the traditional industrialization path and growth strategy.

First and foremost, the government retains control over important resources. The market economic system that China has managed to establish initially is still government dominated; the market's basic role in allocating resources is far from sufficient, and the government maintains the power to allocate many resources. For example, enterprises either wholly owned or absolutely controlled by the state retain their monopoly positions in important sectors. Given the fact that reform of the banking system is not yet completed, the allocation of credit and capital resources is still considerably influenced by administrative authorities at various levels. In particular, over the past five years, as a result of the urbanization process, land has become ever more important. However, the land that has been expropriated from farmers has not been allocated by the market mechanism; instead, this has been done by governments at various levels.

Second, political achievements are measured by the growth rate in gross domestic product (GDP) at the center stage. Starting in 1995, China's national economic accounting system was changed from the material product balance sheet system, which only accounts for material production activities, to the system of national accounts, which accounts for production, distribution, and consumption as an integral totality. However, the tradition of regarding high GDP growth rates and the emulation of advanced countries in the material production field as national objectives that should be achieved at all costs still plays the dominant role and is the major yardstick against which the political achievements of party and government leaders at each level are measured. This yardstick of political achievements is employed in both superior and subordinate levels and in the horizontal comparison of different localities by the official media. Consequently, government officials at different levels of the hierarchy have a motivation to use their power to allocate resources for the sake of achieving high output growth rates.

Third, a production-oriented value added tax regime is in place. At present, the Chinese government collects half of its tax revenues through the value added tax. The level of value added tax revenues is directly linked to the level of the value of local aggregate output. This has also been an incentive on the part of various levels of governments to take advantage of the power in their hands to encourage and support investments in the construction of processing industries and big heavy- and chemical-industry projects that generate significant output and hefty tax revenues.

Fourth, the prices of resources are distorted. Under the traditional growth strategy, to ensure that resource- and capital-intensive industries are profitable and to achieve the target of rapidly developing industry, particularly heavy and chemical industries, the state usually forced factor prices to go down to a very low level (Lin, Fang, and Zhou 1999, 28–66). Nowadays, this sort of situation whereby the prices of factors, such as land, energy, freshwater, capital, labor, and foreign exchange, are seriously distorted still exists.[2] World Bank studies demonstrate that, because energy prices cannot reflect the true cost and the scarcity of energy, China's energy consumption has increased by at least 9 percent (see table 16.1).

Negative Consequences of an Aberrant Industrialization Path and Growth Strategy

At the turn of the 21st century, China witnessed a massive wave of investments in heavy and chemical industries. A series of negative effects of this growth strategy was quickly exposed, and these effects led to serious macroeconomic imbalances.

In the first place, the national economy could not allocate resources according to the principle of taking advantage of strengths, while avoiding weaknesses and bringing advantages into play, and its overall efficiency dropped.

The basic characteristics of China's resource endowments are abundant human resources, scarce natural resources, capital resources in short supply, and vulnerable ecological resources. Among these, the most salient feature is that the per capita ownership of natural resources is considerably below the world average (see table 16.2).

Given these resource endowments, if there were a sound resource allocation mechanism, China's industrial structures would obviously be oriented toward industries low in energy consumption and resource inputs and capable of capitalizing on China's advantage in its abundant supply of human resources that are adept and skilled. Only under such circumstances can minimum resources generate maximum value. However, by following the old industrialization path, China may easily tumble into the pitfall of taking advantage of weaknesses, while avoiding strengths, whereby certain sectors or localities may achieve some

TABLE 16.1 **Impact on Efficiency and Energy Consumption of Unsubsidized Energy Prices**

Country	Average subsidies (as % of the reference price)	Cost of subsidies (US$ billions)	Increase in economic efficiency (as % of GDP)[a]	Decrease in energy consumption (%)	Decrease in CO_2 emissions (%)
Iran	80.4	3.6	2.2	48	49
Venezuela	57.6	1.1	1.2	25	26
Russian Federation	32.5	6.7[b]	1.5	18	17
Indonesia	27.5	0.5[b]	0.2	7	11
Kazakhstan	18.2	0.3	1.0	19	23
India	14.2	1.5	0.3	7	14
China	10.9	3.6	0.4	9	13
South Africa	6.4	0.08	0.1	6	8
Total or average	21.2	17.2	0.7	13	16

Sources: Data of the International Energy Agency; Myers and Kent 2001.
a. Subsidies may increase total consumer and producer surpluses. The consumer surplus is defined as the difference between the price consumers are willing to pay and the price actually paid, while the producer surplus is defined as the difference between the amount actually received for each unit of commodities sold by the producer and the price that the producer is willing to pay. If the total of the consumer and producer surpluses is smaller than the amount of transfer payments (subsidies), the subsidy policy has created a net loss in social welfare. As a result, the elimination of the subsidies will increase economic efficiency.
b. Calculated on the basis of prices and exchange rates prior to the 1997 financial crisis.

TABLE 16.2 **Per Capita Ownership of Resources in China Relative to the World Average**

Resource	Per capita ownership in China	Percent of the world average
Farmland	0.1 hectares	42
Freshwater	2,257 cubic meters	27
Forests	0.12 hectares	20
Potential total mineral reserves	US$9,300	58
Coal (proven and extractable reserves)	98.9 tons	53
Petroleum (surplus reserves)	2.7 tons	11
Natural gas (proven and extractable reserves)	769 cubic meters	3
Iron ore	36 tons	71

Source: Data drawn from "China Energy Development Strategy Study," 2004, Scientific Information Center for Resources and Environment, Chinese Academy of Sciences.

growth and gains at the expense of serious welfare losses on the part of society as a whole.

For example, China boasts the world's largest labor force, which is relatively high quality. Whether this huge potential can be unleashed will have a direct impact upon whether China's overall efficiency can be increased in a sustainable fashion and whether the people's livelihoods can be improved generally. It follows, therefore, that job creation is a serious task directly affecting sustained economic development and affecting social stability. However, theoretical analysis and practical experience both show that the services industry and small enterprises are the major creators of new jobs and that resource-intensive and capital-intensive heavy and chemical industries have a weak capability in creating new jobs and offer limited job opportunities. If massive resources were to be allocated to the development of high-output, low-employment industries, the employment situation would, as a consequence, inevitably worsen.

Beginning in the second half of the 1990s, along with the heavy-industry orientation and capital intensiveness in industrial structures, while investments grew by a significant margin, the elasticity coefficient of job creation relative to GDP growth was declining, from 0.453 in the 1980s to 0.11 in the 1990s and further down to 0.098 in the first four years of the 21st century (Wu 2006). According to the National

Bureau of Statistics, China's registered urban unemployment rate had risen to 4.3 percent by 2003, up from less than 3 percent before 2000, pointing to a problematic unemployment situation (see figure 16.1). At present, the 150-million-strong surplus labor in China's rural areas needs to migrate to nonagricultural jobs in cities and townships, while the cities and townships must absorb their own local labor force, which is increasing by 15 million on an annual basis. In recent years, urban and industrial development has spread into farmlands on a massive scale, with tens of thousands of farmers losing their lands each year. It has been reported that the number of landless farmers throughout the country has now reached 20 million.[3] As these landless farmers cannot find jobs in nonagricultural sectors in cities and townships, serious social problems have occurred.

Also, for example, in recent years, some localities in China have produced high-energy-consuming and high-pollution products in massive quantities and exported them in return for foreign exchange revenues. Take aluminum electrodes for instance. In recent years, demand for aluminum ingots on the domestic and international markets has increased. Coupled with the fact that the production of aluminum electrodes may benefit from preferential electricity tariffs, various localities have, as a result, increased the production of aluminum ingots. In 2003, China exported 1.25 million tons of aluminum ingots, a dramatic rise

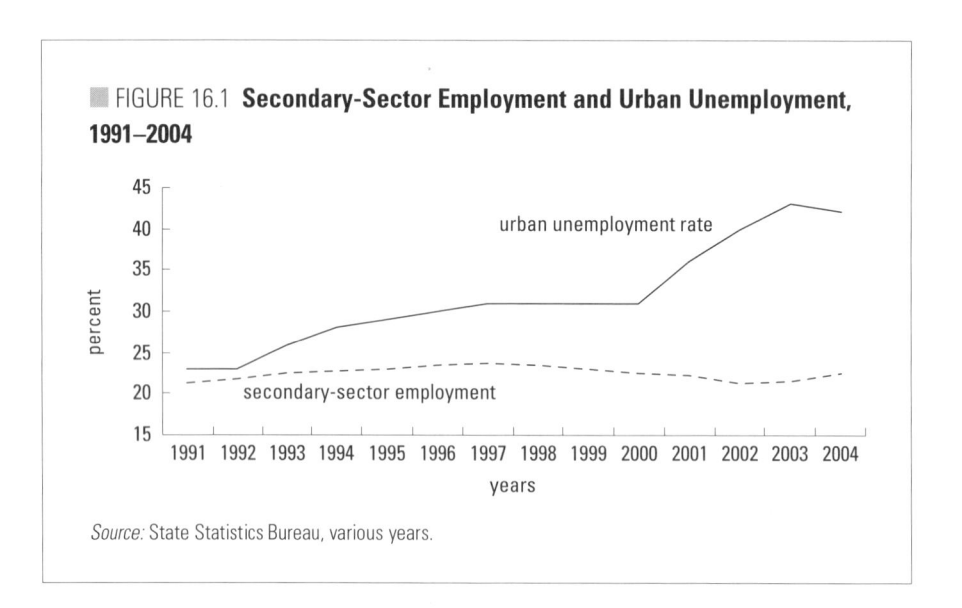

■ FIGURE 16.1 **Secondary-Sector Employment and Urban Unemployment, 1991–2004**

Source: State Statistics Bureau, various years.

of 0.5 million tons over 2002. Given China's short supply of aluminum oxide, in order to export aluminum electrodes, massive amounts of aluminum oxide needed to be imported, which, after the electrolytic process, were then exported. Each ton of aluminum electrode exported was equivalent to the exportation of 15,200 kilowatt hours. As a consequence, in 2003, an additional 7.5 billion kilowatts of electricity were consumed, and, because of the massive imports by Chinese enterprises, the price and international freight costs of aluminum oxide rose, respectively, by 130 and 140 percent. After adjusting for cost increases, the profits on the accounting books of exporters edged up by only US$90 million. If deductions are made for (1) the opportunity costs (approximately US$1.1 billion) resulting from the additional use of electricity, (2) the cost underestimates caused by distorted factor prices, (3) the massive consumption of nonrenewable resources, and (4) environmental costs, this gives a net loss amounting to US$1 billion in national wealth.[4] Because of the incentives for high profits on accounting records, various localities have put massive funds into the construction of aluminum electrode plants. Since 2004, the country's annual aluminum electrode capacity has reached 8 million tons, and another 5 million tons in capacity are planned or under construction. However, this unreal prosperity is unsustainable. In 2005, the aluminum sector already found itself faced with the dilemma of sectorwide losses.

Second, efforts in connection with technological innovation and product upgrading have been relaxed. China has abundant human resources, but these are, on average, characterized by a low level of educational attainment and a generally low cultural and technical level. This, however, does not suggest that China can make both ends meet only by relying on quantitative increases in extensively processed products and by selling physical labor to others. On the one hand, through development over the course of many years, China has gradually established a scientific and technological infrastructure that is complete in sectoral coverage and that also represents a material and technological basis for widely employing and developing technologies of the late 20th century. On the other hand, unlike other developing countries, China has a labor force that is better educated, more disciplined, and innovative, and, even in absolute quantitative terms, Chinese scientists and technologists capable of shouldering the task of technological innovation are not limited in number.[5] In relation to the development of high-tech industries, China cannot expect to succeed overnight and technologically upgrade the national economy as a whole. Yet, in some localities where conditions are ripe, China should endeavor to and may perfectly expect to achieve technical and product upgrading, as exemplified by efforts in the manufacturing sector to reach upstream and downstream into high-value-added activities such as independent research and development and brand-name marketing.

Nevertheless, in the institutional and policy environments as described elsewhere above, many localities and enterprises have, in pursuit of short-term interests, preferred to depend upon massive inputs of inexpensive labor, capital, and natural resources in the production of products with low technological content and have tried to excel through quantitative expansion. They have been unwilling or unable to make progress in human capital accumulation and independent technology development. For instance, Beijing is one of the cities with the highest concentration of technical resources in the world; if the potential of its intellectual resources could be unleashed, Beijing would have unlimited prospects of economic development. However, after several years of efforts to implement its guiding principle of establishing the Zhongguancun high- and new-tech development zone into a high-tech base for innovation and a high-tech product manufacturing base, the city has been forced to admit that it is difficult to achieve high GDP and fiscal revenue growth in the short term by means of the development of high-tech industries. As a result, in the face of pressures in the form of the need to boost GDP growth targets and fiscal revenues, it has no choice but to turn to general processing industries that are low in technological content but high in output value as a priority in economic development.

Third, severe shortages have now appeared in relation to land, freshwater, coal, electricity, petroleum, transportation, and other scarce resources. Adoption of a growth strategy that massively consumes resources has resulted in the very uneconomical consumption of China's scarce resources and the rapid emergence of severe bottlenecks in resources such as land and freshwater already not in abundant supply. As remarked by Ma Kai (2004), minister of China's National Development and Reform Commission, in 2003, China's GDP accounted for approximately 4 percent of the world total, while its resource consumption accounted for a percentage far higher than that of GDP (see table 16.3).[6]

Wang (2005) points out that the coefficient of elasticity of electricity consumption of various countries around the world during the process of industrialization has been around 0.8 percent, that Japan's coefficient

TABLE 16.3 China's Resource Consumption as a Percentage of the World Total

Crude oil	Crude coal	Iron ore	Steel products	Aluminum oxide	Cement
7.4	31	30	21	25	40

Source: Ma 2004.

of elasticity of energy consumption during the accelerated industrialization phase in the 1960s and 1970s was merely 1.21, and that, although in the range of 0.8 and 1 over the past 40 years, the corresponding figure for China during the past few years has jumped to 1.6 at a time when the majority of provinces have resorted to measures imposing limits on the usage of power supplies. This obviously has a direct link with the fact that China's industrial structure is characterized by significant irregularities and that the development of high-energy-consuming heavy and chemical industries has been too rapid.

China does not have rich petroleum reserves, and its primary energy resource is mainly raw coal. In 2000, China produced 998 million tons of raw coal. In the first three years of the 10th FYP, although the output of raw coal grew at 15 percent on average, the demand was still not being met. This has, in turn, provided incentives for some coal mines to go ahead with predatory mining beyond their capacity. At the same time, some coal mines where the safety devices did not meet regulatory requirements continued operations, as a result of which disasters frequently occurred. China's death rate per ton of coal ranks first in the world. Meanwhile, some visionary individuals have, for many years, been calling for measures to curtail the production and consumption of high-emission automobiles; however, to support the development of the automobile sector, such measures have not yet been unveiled. China has now become the world's second biggest oil consumer, next only to the United States. In 2004, China imported 123 million tons of crude oil, accounting for 4 percent of the total volume of domestic consumption.[7] The continuously increasing degree of reliance upon petroleum, which is a strategic resource, will seriously affect China's economic security.

At the same time, many localities have made great efforts to develop high-energy-consuming industries as an important step in rejuvenating the local economy. According to the Xinhua News Agency, in recent years, some provinces in western China have exerted big efforts to establish "high-energy-carrier industrial parks" and plan to turn their jurisdictions into a "world-class" high-energy-consuming product base. The outcome is that some localities previously free from the problem have started to face power and coal shortages.[8] China's huge demand for energy from across the world has led to dramatic rises in energy prices. As statistics of the People's Bank of China show, on the international market, the prices of coal and crude oil rose by 41.7 percent and 30.2 percent, respectively, in 2004 relative to the same period of the previous year.[9] Xu Kuangdi (2004), fellow of the Chinese Academy of Engineering, points out that, if China were to follow the beaten track of the traditional industrialization approach, its energy consumption would be more than China and the world at large could bear.

Resources such as land and freshwater are nontradable goods that are difficult to obtain through international trade. Under the current growth strategy, resource bottlenecks have given rise to hard constraints on the economic development of some localities. For example, China's per capita possession of land is far lower than the world average. Furthermore, the population is unevenly distributed on the land, with 94 percent of the population living off 46 percent of the country's territory, hence the need to cherish land as if it were gold. However, in high profile projects and political achievement projects that have been undertaken over the past few years, the phenomenon of the serious wastage of land resources can be found everywhere. One may readily come across huge buildings, huge squares, and massive development zones where a production unit easily occupies up to one thousand *mu* of land for flower planting. (A mu is approximately 666.7 square meters.) As indicated by a report of the Ministry of Land and Resources in 2004, in recent years, governments at various levels have established 6,866 development zones of different sorts, which have occupied 38,600 square kilometers (579,000 mu) of land, most of which is farmland.[10] Coupled with land allocated for other uses, in 2003 alone, the area of China's farmland dropped by 38.1 million mu. The acreage of arable land in the city of Shenzhen is similar to that of Hong Kong (China). Hong Kong (China) has been under development for over a century, but, by the year 2003, it had developed only 22 percent of its arable land.[11] With its GDP accounting for only one-sixth that of Hong Kong (China), Shenzhen has, in recent years, found itself experiencing land shortages, without large patches of land for development or even survival. Some people have put forward requests for transfers of land from neighboring districts.[12]

Fourth, China's ecological environment has worsened at an accelerated pace. China's extensive urban construction and industrial development, in particular the development of heavy and chemical industries, which involve substantial energy consumption, high water consumption, significant pollution, and large-scale occupation of land, has given rise to environmental degradation that has not been brought under effective control. Some localities have found that their basic manufacturing and living environments are being destroyed.

In the course of industrialization, China's environmental degradation has been getting worse by the day.[13] The amount of solid industrial waste increased from 580 million tons in 1990 to 816 million tons in 2000. At present, the daily volume of sewage discharge is around 130 million tons, and nearly half the river courses of seven major river systems are seriously contaminated. Many cities have serious air pollution. The coverage of acid rain accounts for one-third of the nation's area. Countrywide, the area affected by diminishing surface water and serious soil erosion has reached 360 million hectares, or 38 percent of the territory. The spread of desertification has reached 170 million hectares, or 18.2 percent of the country's territory (Han 2004). According to World Bank statistics in 1997, losses caused by air and water pollution were equal to 3 to 8 percent of China's GDP (UNDP 1999, 74).

The North China Plains produce half of China's wheat and one-third of its corn and, at the same time, is an area with serious shortages of water. Nevertheless, in recent years, Beijing, Hebei, Shanxi, and Tianjin have been making great efforts to develop coal, steel, and automobile industries that are highly water consuming. In Hebei Province alone, there is a nearly 60-million-ton steel and iron smelter capacity, a considerable portion of which is based upon high-consumption, high-cost, and high-pollution smelters.[14] Even among larger-scale and more technologically sophisticated steelmakers, to produce 1 ton of steel requires the consumption of 16 tons of water. When there is no supply of surface water, underground water is tapped to make up for the shortage. According to a report by the Sandra National Laboratory in the United States, 55 billion tons of water were obtained from the Hai River in the year 2000, 21 billion tons more than the river's sustainable supply volume of 34 billion tons. Such a gap is closed by tapping underground water. An underground water measurement report released by the Chinese Institute of Geological and Environmental Monitoring in August 2001 shows that the water table in the North China Plains was dropping more rapidly than previously reported. Overtapping has greatly depleted the shallow water storage layer; as a result, well-diggers have to turn to the deep water storage layer. The report says that the average water table of the deep water storage layer in Hebei Province dropped by 2.9 meters in the year 2000 alone, with the water table in some cities of the province dropping by as much as 6 meters. In light of the fact that the deep water storage layer cannot be replenished, the depletion of the deep water storage layer in the North China Plains is causing this region to lose the last bit of its water reserves (Brown 2003, 24).

Fifth, the development of the services industry, which has an important bearing upon the increase in the overall efficiency of the national economy, has been inhibited. The traditional version of socialist political economy defines services as nonproductive labor, and the command economy focuses its attention on the growth of material product. Under the influence of such theories and policies, the output of China's services industry has consistently and seriously been on the low side. Because of structural adjustment, which has taken place over the course of many years since the start of the reform and opening-up drive, the output value of the tertiary sector accounted for around 33 percent of China's GDP at the turn of the millennium, lower than both the average level in the rest of the world (60 percent) and the average level in low-income countries (45 percent)[15] (see figures 16.2 and 16.3).

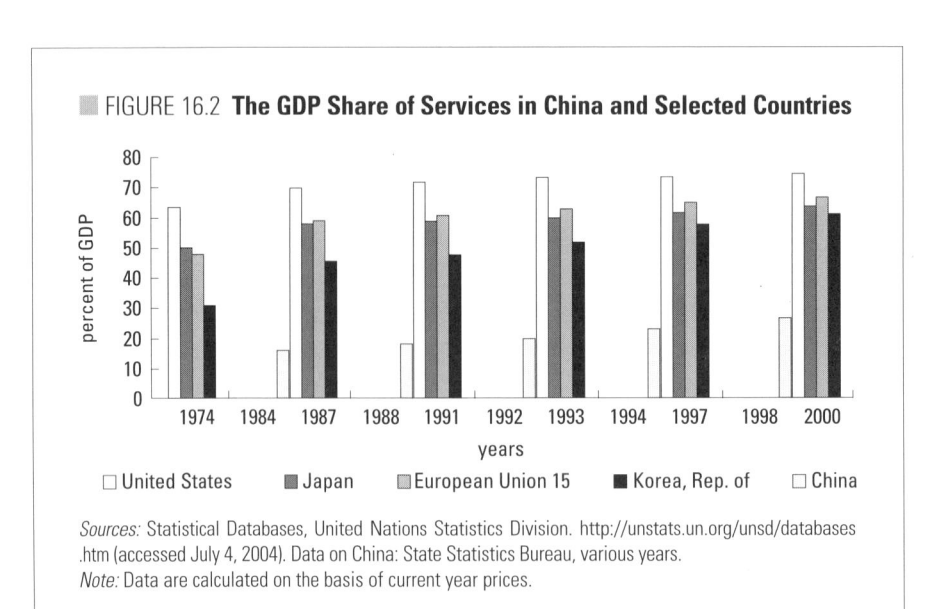

FIGURE 16.2 The GDP Share of Services in China and Selected Countries

Sources: Statistical Databases, United Nations Statistics Division. http://unstats.un.org/unsd/databases.htm (accessed July 4, 2004). Data on China: State Statistics Bureau, various years.
Note: Data are calculated on the basis of current year prices.

In the wave of efforts to strengthen the heavy-industry component in industrial structures on the part of some localities in the past few years, China's services industry, as a percentage share of GDP, decreased instead of increasing as the distortions in industrial structures became more salient (see table 16.4).

A major trend in the development of the services industry in the 20th century was that the productive services sector was evolving more rapidly than the consumptive services sector. The productive services sector has witnessed development in a number of aspects. One is so-called integrated logistics management or supply-chain management that regards logistic services as a critical link in the supply chain. In a supply chain, the marketing and distribution phase usually captures the vast majority of value added and profits. Even within the manufacturing sector, there has been vertical consolidation of such activities as research and development, design, supply-chain management, brand marketing, after-sales services, and financial services. As a result,

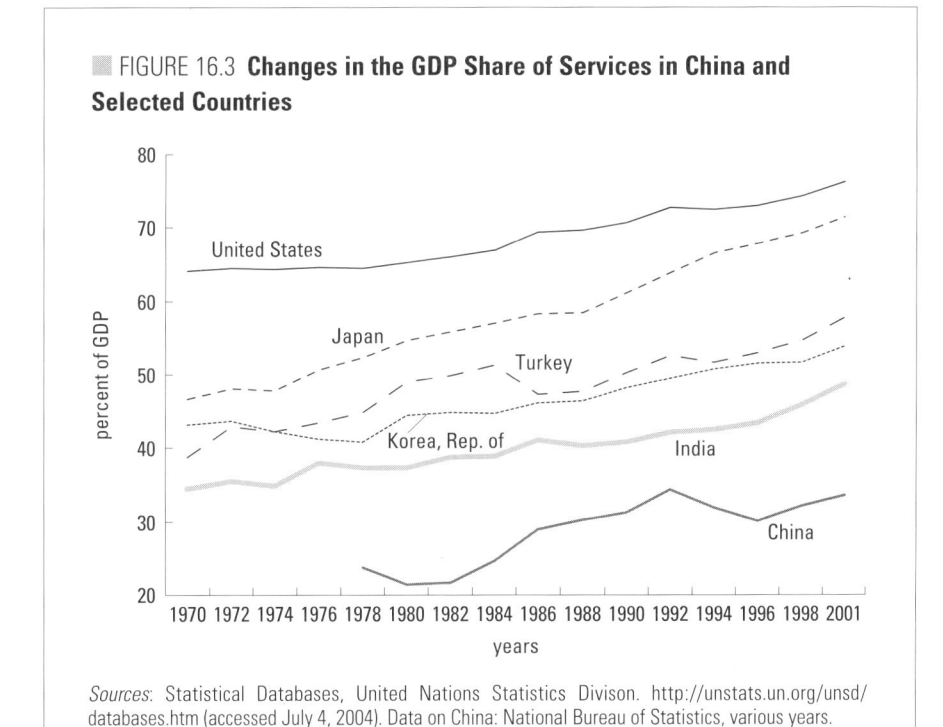

■ FIGURE 16.3 **Changes in the GDP Share of Services in China and Selected Countries**

Sources: Statistical Databases, United Nations Statistics Division. http://unstats.un.org/unsd/databases.htm (accessed July 4, 2004). Data on China: National Bureau of Statistics, various years.

TABLE 16.4 GDP Share of the Output Value of the Tertiary Sector, 1980–2004
percent

1980	1984	1990	1994	2000	2001	2002	2003	2004
21.4	24.7	31.3	31.9	33.4	33.6	33.5	33.1	31.9

Source: National Bureau of Statistics, various years.

modern manufacturing is integrated with the services industry and, thus, becomes the services-manufacturing industry. As they are laggards in terms of service operations, Chinese enterprises are usually reduced to the status of selling their physical labor and engaging in economic activities low in the value chain in terms of value added and profit margins, such as simple processing and assembly; they turn over the hefty profits arising from research and development, design, brand marketing, and financial services to others. The selling price of a product that a Chinese enterprise (original equipment manufacturer) manufactures for a foreign enterprise is very low and usually one-fourth or even one-tenth of that of the vendor. The original equipment manufacturer only obtains a meager processing income.

In a commentary carried in January 2004, the *Wall Street Journal* cited Logitech International as an example of the role China plays in the global division of labor. This company, headquartered in California, has a factory in Suzhou, which exports 20 million units of the Wanda wireless mouse to the United States. The mouse sells for US$40 per unit in the United States. According to a breakdown of that price, Logitech gets US$8 (20 percent); distributors and retailers capture US$15 (37.5 percent); Motorola, Inc. and Agilent Technologies, Inc., Logitech's spare parts suppliers, snatch US$14 (35 percent); and China obtains the remaining US$3 (7.5 percent). This amount of US$3 needs to cover the wages of 4,000 employees in Suzhou and the energy, transportation, and other administrative costs. The total income of Logitech's 450-person marketing team in California is far higher than the total income of the 4,000 Chinese employees in the Suzhou plant. As remarked in the commentary in the *Wall Street Journal*, Logitech's Suzhou warehouse might be called the current global economy in miniature.[16]

Because the value added and profit margins of their export products are too low, many Chinese exporters can only win through volume, and they sustain their business operations by increasing their export volumes. These exports will, in turn, inevitably lead to trade frictions, increase antidumping investigations, and add to the difficulties of export operations. Some commentators have characterized the situation caused by the traditional growth strategy by saying that we have consumed a large quantity of nonrenewable resources, suffer from environmental pollution, and shoulder a bad name for dumping, while the lion's share of profits is not in our hands.

Sixth, for a developing country such as China, capital is a very valuable, scarce resource that needs to be highly cherished and effectively employed. However, with the rise of the heavy-industry trend in many localities in the 1990s, as demonstrated by economist Robert Solow in his analysis of early growth models, growth driven by investment has resulted in a decline in the return on investment and an increase in investment's share of GDP (Easterly 2002, 26–50). The share of investment in China's GDP rose from about 25 percent at the beginning of the reform and opening-up drive to over 40 percent starting in 2003 (see figure 16.4).[17] At the same time, the efficiency of investment displayed a downward trend, with the incremental capital-output rate, a measure of investment efficiency, rising from 2–3 percent before 1997 to 5–7 percent thereafter (see figure 16.5).[18]

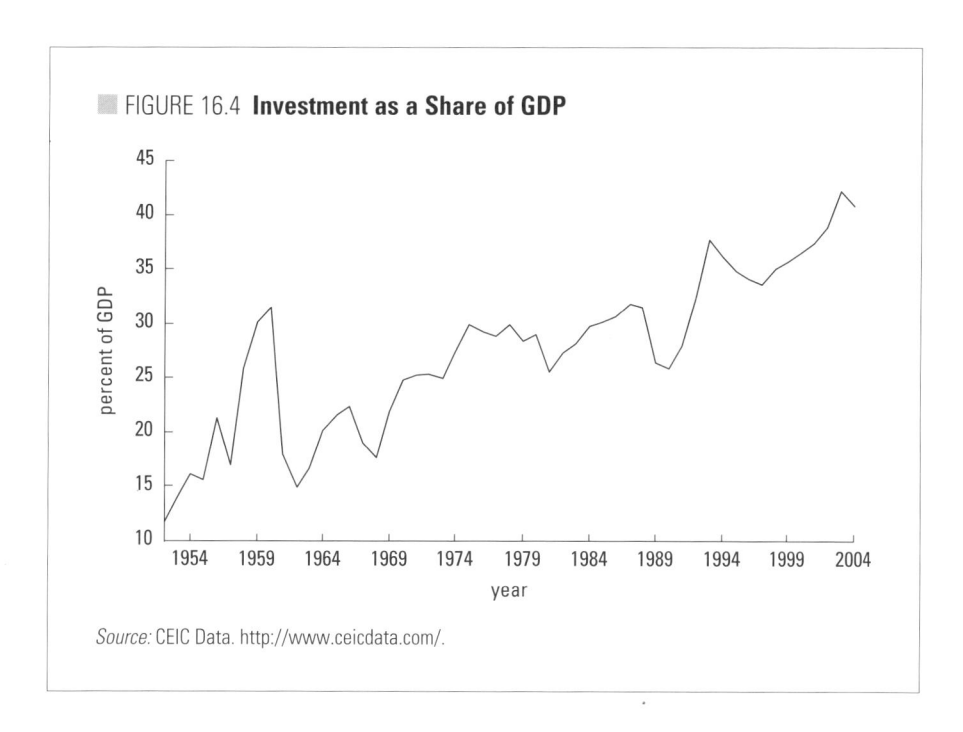

FIGURE 16.4 **Investment as a Share of GDP**

Source: CEIC Data. http://www.ceicdata.com/.

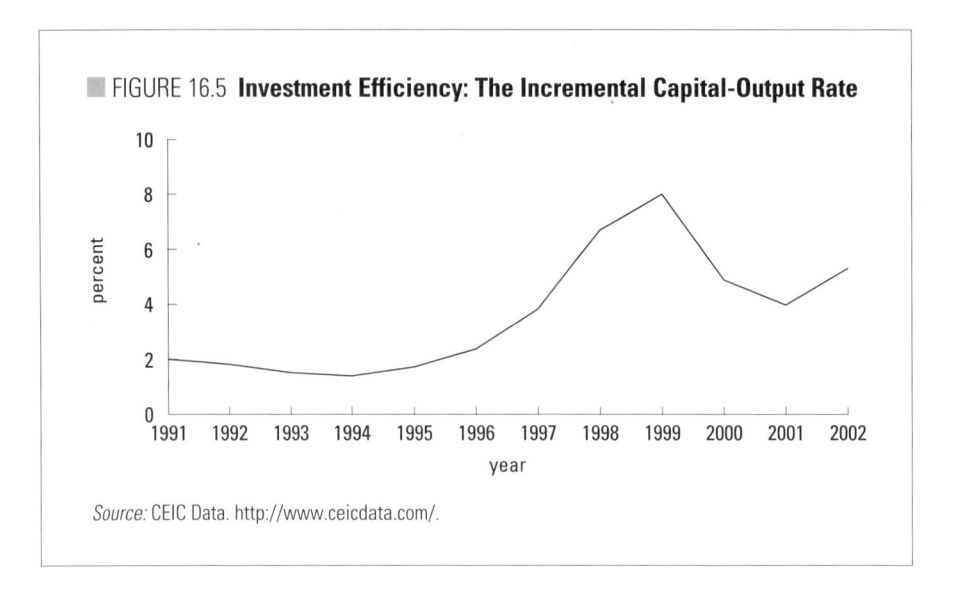

FIGURE 16.5 **Investment Efficiency: The Incremental Capital-Output Rate**

Source: CEIC Data. http://www.ceicdata.com/.

After careful analysis of the growth path of the Chinese economy over the past 20 years, Professor Zhang Jun confirms this consequence of overinvestment (Zhang 2003, 228–339).

The short-term consequences of the constant rise in the investment rate and the distortion of the structure of investment and consumption are that (1) capacity expands too rapidly, while demand is ultimately insufficient; (2) incomes among low-income groups rise only slowly, resulting in increasing income inequality between the rich and the poor; and (3) the external trade surplus and the country's foreign exchange reserves increase on a massive scale, reducing the room to maneuver in connection with the use of macroeconomic policy.

The long-term consequences are the accumulation of financial risks. Given that, in recent years, the overinvestment wave has basically been supported by loans extended by commercial banks, the consequences will inevitably be reflected in China's financial system and lead to a hidden financial problem in the form of mounting nonperforming loans within the banking system. Since the growth supported by bank loans is a kind of borrowed prosperity,[19] at a time when the investment rate is not high, the risk of bad loans will be accumulated quietly during the upswing period of the business cycle. When the business cycle is in its downswing period or when there are external shocks, the systemic risk across the financial system will become overt. Currently, in China, the incremental capital-output ratio remains high and has reached a level similar to that in some East Asian countries before the 1997 financial crisis, namely, to increase GDP by Y1, it is necessary to invest Y5. As Professor Krugman (1999) points out, the fact that some countries had adopted an investment-driven growth strategy was one of the reasons the East Asian financial crisis occurred. We have to learn from the lessons that history has to offer, take preemptive measures, and avert such a crisis in China.

The Crux Lies with Unswerving Efforts to Stick with Reform

China should thoroughly transform its economic growth strategy, embark on a new industrialization path, and regard the development of an energy-saving and environment-friendly economy as the basic guiding principle for the 11th FYP and an even longer time frame. Only by chartering such a path can China, in the years to come, achieve sustained and relatively rapid growth and smoothly realize the target of making the nation wealthy and the people rich. Based on the historical experience of advanced countries, China, as a developing country in the mid-to-late phase of industrialization, needs to exert efforts in the following areas so as to change its growth strategy and improve the quality of its growth: (1) encourage indigenous innovation and product upgrading and promote the use of science-based technologies in various areas of the national economy; (2) undertake great efforts to develop the services industry, in particular the productive services sector; (3) make use of modern information and communications technologies to increase the efficiency of various industries in the national economy; and (4) work hard to raise job opportunities so that a larger share of the workforce can shift from low-efficiency agriculture to higher-efficiency urban nonagricultural jobs.

To achieve the target of transforming the growth strategy, it is imperative to deepen economic and political reform, eliminate the institutional impediments to the transformation of the growth strategy, and improve the market economic system. With regard to the structural reform of the economy, of most current importance is (1) to continue with adjustment in the profile of the state-owned economy according to the policy of making advances in some sectors, while exiting from others in an effort to break down sectoral monopolies by state-owned enterprises and push ahead with reform in the nontradable share of state-owned enterprises; (2) to speed up the market-oriented reform of the financial system; and (3) to reduce the government's administrative interference in prices and correct the distortions in factor prices and so on. It should be noted that the crux of the effort to improve the market economic system lies with the government.

China's situation at present, as remarked by Premier Wen Jiabao, is that "governments at various levels are still taking care of many things that they should not be doing and cannot do well in, while they are not doing a good job in relation to the things that governments should be doing."[20] To ensure the development and effective functioning of the socialist system, it is necessary to build a limited, but effective government. A limited government means that, unless and until the market fails, the government should refrain from interfering in market transactions and the micro-decision-making behavior of enterprises and that different localities, sectors, and enterprises should allocate resources according to their own preferences. An effective government requires that the government perform its various responsibilities at low cost. Among such responsibilities, the most important are, in the first place, to provide an environment of the rule of law for the normal functioning of the market economy and to administer justice fairly and impartially; second, to rely on aggregate tools to ensure macroeconomic stability; third, to provide free and compulsory education and build up a good educational system; and fourth, to provide minimum security for the well-being of the population as a whole and build up a safety net that covers the whole society.

Efforts to push ahead with government reform need to be integrated with efforts to improve the market economic system. In the majority of situations, excessive interference in the allocation of resources by the government is concomitant with the imperfections of the market system. The imperfections of the market system provide an excuse for the government's excessive interference, while the government's interference makes it difficult for the market system to improve and can make it yet more imperfect. At present, this situation is the worst in factor markets, in particular the market for land for urban development, the credit market, and the capital market. It therefore follows that, to achieve greater progress in government reform, it is essential to push ahead in nurturing factor markets and the reform of the financial sector, while speeding up the development of the norms and institutions necessary for the market mechanism to play its proper role, particularly in the allocation of land, credit, and capital, and facilitating the government's withdrawal. One of the core tasks is to streamline the pricing regime of various factors of production. Today, because of insufficient nurturing of factor markets and excessive interference by the government, the prices of labor, capital, land, and natural resources are distorted to differing degrees; some are severely distorted. The crux of reform is to bring into play the market mechanism's price-setting role and eliminate distortions so that prices can fully reflect the scarcity of resources and the opportunity costs, and provide a scientific basis for the decision-making process of microeconomic entities.

An important policy move designed to facilitate government reform is the reform of the monitoring and evaluation mechanism of government performance. There used to be an idea that the current evaluation method, whereby officials are assessed only in a top-down manner and there is no bottom-to-top election or monitoring, should not change; the emphasis was placed, instead, on improving evaluation criteria. As a matter of fact, it is extremely difficult to come up with a set of scientific evaluation criteria. What is important is to increase the transparency of the government performance evaluation process and the effective use of the general public's democratic rights, so that various stakeholders and the general public may actively participate in the monitoring and evaluation of the government and its leading officials.

Government reform, in essence, is the process of having the government reform itself; given that this exercise will involve the powers and interests of a multitude of officials, it is inevitable that all kinds of difficulties and barriers will exist. As a result, efforts to push ahead with government reform will, first and foremost, require government leaders to have the political determination to overcome difficulties and stumbling blocks. At the same time, this cannot occur without the monitoring and empowerment of various quarters of society. In 2004, the Chinese government formulated the "Outline of Efforts Comprehensively to Push Ahead with Administration according to Law," which is a road map for the next 10 years in government reform, with the establishment of a government based on the rule of law as the target. The current major task in efforts to advance government reform is to show firm political determination, overcome all sorts of impediments and resistances, and implement this outline.

Notes

1. "The Guideline of Economic Construction in the Years to Come," *People's Daily*, December 2, 1981.

2. It is only for the sake of supporting the export-oriented policy that the foreign exchange rate of the home currency is undervalued instead of being overvalued as in the import-substitution scenario.

3. "Urban Development Cannot 'Kick Away' Landless Farmers," Xinhua News Agency, Beijing, March 8, 2003.

4. In 2004, in Zhejiang Province alone, there was a power shortage of over 75 billion kilowatt hours, and over half of all private enterprises, on average, suffered from power stoppages for 11.3 days on a monthly basis. The direct economic losses caused by power shortages reached Y100 billion, equivalent to Y1.33 in opportunity costs for each kilowatt of electricity (compare to the Y8.36 in Shanghai). See "Country-wide Power Shortages Have Caused Severe Losses and the Massive Power Shortages Are Attributable to Natural (30%) and Man-Made (70%) Disasters," *China Business Times*, December 22, 2004. If one takes only this factor into consideration, the Y800 million accounting profits in the aluminum electrode sector have generated over Y10 billion in losses in national wealth.

5. In 2001, the number of students enrolled in Chinese institutions of higher learning reached 15.1 million, ranking first in the world. (See UNESCO 2004, 7.) Chen Zhiwu (2004) also points out that, although from the perspective of the quality of the population as a whole the Chinese population is low in educational attainment, "in terms of the absolute figure, the number of people in China that have received higher education is in the vicinity of 50 million (representing 5.7% of the total adult population), or nearly half of the U.S. labor force, bigger than the labor force either in the U.K., France, Italy, or Germany, and bigger than the total population of Spain."

6. Of course, considering that China is currently at the initial stage of modernization, its massive buildup in infrastructure needs to consume a larger share of raw materials such as steel products and cement for each unit of GDP output. In addition, due to factors such as exchange rates, China's GDP as a percentage of the world total may have been underestimated, and thus the amount of physical inputs into each unit of China's GDP may have been overestimated. Even if such factors are taken into consideration, the problem of high input levels and low output in the Chinese economy is still a serious one. For example, in the past few years, India has achieved economic growth rates ranging from 6 to 8 percent with an investment rate of less than 20 percent of GDP, while China has only realized 7–9 percent GDP growth with an investment of nearly 50 percent of GDP.

7. "Speech of Mr. Fu Ziying at the Meeting for the Establishment of the Iron Ore Branch of the CCCMC," March 10, 2005. http://fuziying2.mofcom.gov.cn/aarticle/speech/200508/20050800327172.html.

8. Chu Guoqiang, Liu Jun, and Xiong Congming, "Beware that China Becomes a Center for the Transfer of the World's High-Energy-Consuming Industries," Xinhuanet, Beijing, December 8, 2004.

9. "Analysis and Prediction of the Industrial Situation in 2004–05: The Energy Bottlenecks Will Continue in 2005," *Shanghai Securities Daily*, January 20, 2005.

10. "China's Farmland Saw a Net Loss of Nearly 40 Million Mu in 2003," Xinhua News Agency, February 24, 2004.

11. Hong Kong Special Administrative Region of the People's Republic of China. "Table 31: Land Usage (as at 31 December 2003)." *Hong Kong 2003*. http://www.yearbook.gov.hk/2003/english/append/app6_31.html.

12. Data are taken from Shenzhen Government, "Statistics Bulletin 2003 on National Economic and Social Development." (A page of relevant statistics is available in Chinese at Shenzhen Government Online, http://www.shenzhen.gov.cn/jingji/tongji/2003yxqk/200404190207.htm.) Also, see "Surplus Land Only Enough for 10 Years of Development," *Nanfangdoushibao*, March 8, 2004.

13. A considerable portion of the foreign direct investment that China has absorbed is in the high-energy-consuming and high-polluting industries that advanced countries shift out of their own territories. The products of these industries are ultimately exported in large quantities to advanced countries so that these countries have completed the shift of their own pollution elsewhere. See Diamond (2005), in particular page 370, in rela-

tion to the amount of foreign direct investment involved in shifting pollution-intensive industries to China.

14. In regard to other negative consequences of the strategy adopted by Hebei Province of centering around steel in the development of heavy and chemical industries, also see Hu (2004).

15. The relatively low percentage share of the services industry in China's GDP is partly due to the technical reason that the output value of services in the manufacturing sector is not included. However, even if this factor is eliminated, it still remains that China's services industry accounts for a relatively low percentage share.

16. Andrew Higgins, "As China Surges, It Also Proves a Buttress to American Strength," *Wall Street Journal*, January 30, 2004 (A1 edition).

17. This figure is far higher than the highest level posted by Japan, a country with a propensity for overinvestment, during its high-speed growth period. Based on data provided by Weijian Shan, even during the high-speed industrialization phase at the turn of the 20th century and during the postwar recovery period, the United States did not have an investment rate over 20 percent. In Japan, the highest level of the investment rate was 32 percent in the 1960s and 1970s. See Weijian Shan, "China's Yuan is Overvalued," *Asian Wall Street Journal*, June 23, 2005.

18. As pointed out by China's National Development and Reform Commission Minister Ma Kai, 10–20 percent of GDP in France, Germany, India, and the United States is used for investment purposes, while the figure for China is 40–45 percent. In the former countries, to increase GDP by an additional Y100 million, Y100 million to Y200 million of investment is required, while to achieve the same result in China in the past few years, the requirement has been an investment of Y500 million (Ma 2004).

19. Weijian Shan, "The Great Paradox in the Growth of the Chinese Economy," *Caijing Magazine*, 2003.

20. Wen Jiabao, "Explanations about the Proposal with Regard to the Formulation of the 11th Five-Year Plan," October 19, 2005. http://news.sina.com.cn/c/2005-10-20/10187217226s.shtml (in Mandarin).

References

Brown, L. 2003. *Plan B: Rescuing a Planet under Stress and a Civilization in Trouble*. Beijing: Dongfang Publishing House.
Chen Guangyan. 2004. "The Sustainable Development Strategy: Shenzhen and China." Speech presented at the Shenzhen Development Forum, Shenzhen, China, October 22.
Chen Zhiwu. 2004. "Why Is It 'Hard Labor' that the Chinese Sell?" *New Fortune* magazine, September.
Diamond, Jared. 2005. *Collapse: How Societies Choose to Fail or Survive*. London: Penguin.
Easterly, William. 2002. *The Elusive Quest for Growth: Economists' Adventures and Misadventures in the Tropics*. Beijing: CITIC Publishing House, 2004.
Han Baojiang. 2004. "Reflections on the Worries and Concerns about China's Development." *Outlook Weekly*, February 16.
Hu Angang. 2004. "From Black to Green: Views on the Transformation of the Economic Growth Model in Hebei Province." Transcript from a conference held in Hebei Province, July 25.
Krugman, P. 1999. *The Return of Depression Economics*. Beijing: China Renmin University Publishing House.
Lin Justin Yifu, Fang Cai, and Zhou Li. 1999. *The China Miracle: Development Strategy and Economic Reform*, revised edition. Shanghai: Shanghai People's Publishing House and Sanlian Publishing House.

Ma Kai. 2004. "Develop and Implement the Concept of Scientific Development and Push Ahead with the Fundamental Transformation of the Economic Growth Strategy." Speech presented at the China High-Level Forum Annual Conference, March 21. http://www.people.com.cn/GB/jingji/8215/32688/32689/2403665.html.

Mao Zedong. 1956. "On the Ten Major Relationships." *Selected Works of Mao Tsetung*, Vol. 5. Beijing: People's Publishing House, 1977.

Myers, Norman, and Jennifer Kent. 2001. *Perverse Subsidies: How Tax Dollars Can Undercut the Environment and Economy*. Washington, DC: Island Press. Quoted in Chen Guangyan 2004.

National Bureau of Statistics. Various years. *China Statistics Almanac*. Beijing: China Statistics Publishing House.

Propaganda Department, Central Committee of the Communist Party of China. 1953. "Fight to Mobilize All Available Resources and Build China into a Great Socialist Country: Outlines for Learning and Disseminating the Party's Overall Line in the Transitional Period." *Compilation of Documents for Reading for Socialist Educational Courses*, Vol. 1: 341–74. Beijing: People's Publishing House, 1957.

UNDP (United Nations Development Programme). 1999. *China Human Development Report 1999: Transition and the State*. Beijing: China Financial and Economic Press.

UNESCO (United Nations Educational, Scientific, and Cultural Organization). 2004. "Synthesis Report on Trends and Developments in Higher Education since the World Conference on Higher Education (1998–2003)." UNESCO. http://portal.unesco.org/education/en/file_download.php/73780badda28a3f7839bbea447c5e4edSynthesisE.pdf.

Wang Shucheng. 2005. "Model C: Self-Disciplined Development." Speech presented at the China Water Conservancy Magazine and Building a Water-Saving Society High-Level Forum, June 3.

Wu Jinglian. 2004. "To Comprehensively Increase the Economy's Overall Competitiveness Is the Inevitable Course for Zhejiang's Economic Development." *Investigation and Research Reports* 93 (July 21), Beijing, Development Research Center of the State Council.

———. 2005. "Earnestly Solve the Problem of the Industrialization Path and the Growth Strategy: Speech at the 3rd Plenary Session of the 10th National Congress of the Chinese People's Political Consultative Conference on March 7, 2005." *Wenhui Daily*, March 9.

———. 2006. *Choices of China's Economic Growth Strategy*. Shanghai: Shanghai Far East Publishing House.

Xu Kuangdi. 2004. "China Must Follow a New Industrialization Path: Speech at China International Steel and Iron Conference on March 23, 2004." News dispatch, Xinhua News Agency, Shanghai, June 6.

Zhang Jun. 2003. *China's Industrial Reform and Economic Growth: Problems and Explanations*. Shanghai: Sanlian Bookstore and Shanghai People's Publishing House.

CHAPTER 17

Reflections on Financial and Monetary Developments in Asia

JOSEPH YAM

Three challenges facing central banks in Asia are the development and integration of financial markets, monetary cooperation, and the management of international reserves.

The economies of Asia are again a focus of the attention of international economic organizations, multinational enterprises, investment banks, and hedge funds. After having been thought of as a dynamic growth pole in the early and mid-1990s, the region was somewhat forgotten, at least as a place to invest one's capital, in the immediate aftermath of the financial crisis of 1997–98. Now, as China has grown to become the fourth largest economy in the world and continues to grow at breakneck speed, as Japan appears to be coming out of a decade-long economic slump, and as other economies in the region are showing signs of healthy growth, the region is back on the radar screen of international investors and commentators.

With the rise of China as a major manufacturing hub, the region has seen a remarkable increase in economic integration as measured by trade in goods. For example, since the late 1990s, intraregional trade has accounted for over half the growth in the exports of the emerging economies in the region (Zebregs 2004). While the integration of financial markets is lagging, important initiatives are being proposed, and concrete actions have been taken to deepen this integration. Further developments are likely to lead to significant changes in financial relationships among the economies in the region in the years to come. Although full monetary integration is still only a distant possibility, the deepening of financial links has important implications for how the transition to closer monetary cooperation among central banks in the region should proceed.

This essay will focus on three aspects of financial developments and relations in East Asia: the process of financial integration and its implications for financial stability, the consequences of greater financial integration for the process of monetary integration, and the growth of official international reserves and what this may mean for reserve management.

As will become clear in the course of the discussion, these topics are closely related to each other and to the integration of the region with financial markets in the rest of the world. What I propose in this essay is not a detailed blueprint for efforts to promote and manage the integration process, but a vignette of the developments I see shaping progress and debates in the region in the coming years.

The Case for Financial Integration in East Asia

Concrete steps are being taken to further financial integration in Asia because financial integration is felt to contribute to a more efficient allocation of resources in the region, thereby supporting continued economic growth. Moreover, integration also contributes to greater financial stability.

The fundamental characteristic of financial integration is that net savers in an economy may have access to any investment vehicle regardless of the geographical location of the saver or the issuer of the investment product. Similarly, entrepreneurs seeking funds to finance capital expenditure plans may, in a financially integrated area, have access to sources of credit irrespective of geographic location.

Financial integration permits the efficient transfer of funds between economic units that have savings in excess of their investment plans to economic units for which the opposite is true. As a result, net savers will receive the highest return on their funds, and investors will obtain credit on the lowest available terms. In addition, financial integration enhances competition in each locality since savers and investors are not constrained to deal only with local suppliers of financial services, but may search for the most efficient supplier in the entire integrated area.

It is uncontroversial to suggest that financial integration within a given jurisdiction will be beneficial for the economy as a whole. Few would question that financial integration within the United States, for example, has made a positive contribution to that country's economy. Similarly, expanding financial links across provinces in China would make the mobilization of the high savings and the allocation of capital there more efficient, leading to sustained economic dynamism. But the benefits of financial integration need not occur only within a single jurisdiction. Observing from afar the process of economic integration in Europe, it is clear that financial integration across national borders will make a positive contribution to the region's economic development.

Financial integration across economies here in Asia has not proceeded as far as it has in Europe and North America, even though the degree of economic (particularly trade) integration within the region has been rising sharply. In the financial sphere, Asian economies are less integrated with each other than they are with economies in the rest of the world. I believe that economic integration brought about by market forces and reflecting comparative advantages in production within the region can best be served by a level of financial integration that is similar.

It is difficult to provide empirical evidence to support the hypothesis that the optimal degree of financial integration is the same as or close to the degree of economic integration within a region. There are theoretical difficulties in identifying measures of optimality. There is no established measure of the actual degree of financial integration, let alone the degree of economic integration.

Lack of empirical evidence notwithstanding, it seems unproblematic to suppose that the synergy driving economic integration can best be harnessed financially by the stakeholders themselves, who know better what they are doing and take a longer-term view, rather than by people who are motivated largely by relatively short-term financial rates of return and who are acting in accordance with credit assessments conducted many miles from where the action is.

Regrettably, for a variety of reasons, financial integration in Asia lags considerably behind economic integration. Currently, a sizable portion of gross savings in Asia finds its way into the debt instruments of governmental and quasi-governmental issuers in industrialized economies, while investment in Asia is financed, to a significant extent, through capital from those same countries. This state of affairs seems incongruous and is a reflection of the relative lack of integration between financial markets in Asian economies. It seems to me quite likely that the cost of capital for enterprises in Asia would be lower if there were a deep and well-functioning corporate bond market in the region to tap the considerable pool of savings, much of which now flows instead to industrial countries.

The dependence of regional investment on funds from external sources is not only incongruous; it also exposes the region to the sudden stop phenomenon, whereby the flows of capital dry up abruptly, wreaking havoc among real economic activities. This well-documented feature of international capital flows, which is especially costly to emerging market economies, has led to greater policy conservatism toward financial openness, at least in this region. This has limited and slowed the pace of financial integration. I argue that it is for precisely this reason that financial integration in Asia should be pursued more vigorously.

A large and financially integrated regional market is an effective defense against volatile global financial flows. There is, I believe, a nonlinear relationship between vulnerability to financial instability and the size of financial markets. The small financial markets are not attractive to international capital because of their lack of liquidity; so, there is little volatility generated by the inflow and outflow of international capital. At the other extreme, where financial markets are very large relative to international capital, sudden movements of the latter will only lead to ripples that are not big enough to cause any concern about financial stability. The most vulnerable financial markets are the medium-sized ones. They have adequate liquidity to attract international capital, but they are small enough so that short-term trends are dictated by larger operators who are looking for short-term gains.[1] There is also the temptation, for some, to engage in manipulative behavior, amplifying volatility and vulnerability to financial instability.

Of course, merely increasing the effective size of a financial market cannot substitute for sound macroeconomic policies as a guard against volatile capital flows. Indeed, I believe that the authorities in the region are committed to prudent monetary, exchange rate, and fiscal policies. But I am also convinced that expanding the effective size of Asian financial markets through greater integration across jurisdictions may increase the ability of our economies to absorb the volatility of international capital as effectively as the U.S. and European markets. It is therefore heartening to observe that several official initiatives toward greater financial links in the region are bearing fruit, notably the Chiang Mai Initiative and the Asian Bond Funds Initiative. The former was created partly with the objective of allowing central banks to hold back on the accumulation of international reserves, a topic I will discuss elsewhere in this essay. The Asian Bond Fund has been created specifically to encourage the development of bond markets in Asian economies and ultimately to establish an integrated regional market. The process leading up to the agreements related to Asian Bond Funds 1 and 2 has shown that cooperation between central banks in the region can successfully deal with technical and conceptual issues. This bodes well for the development of the initiatives.

Articulating the economic case is necessary, but not sufficient to convince participants that increased financial integration is a worthwhile objective. Other, practical steps must also be taken. First, links must be established between jurisdictions across the whole infrastructure—the trading, payment, clearing, settlement, and custodian systems—for money and for financial instruments. This would facilitate the movement of savings between jurisdictions and make crossborder transactions more efficient. These links are not difficult or costly to establish. The technology—electronic messaging platforms of acceptable security—is already available and in international use.

The second element involves the relaxation of nonsupervisory restrictions on the access by foreign financial intermediaries to domestic financial markets. The size of financial intermediaries as measured, for example, in terms of capital, is often a barrier to market access, but, as we know, size is not necessarily a good indicator of quality. Measures of capital adequacy that are assessed objectively according to risk provide a better safeguard. Greater competition, no matter from where it comes, enhances efficiency, although, in the interest of financial stability, allowance should be made to enable weaker domestic institutions to cope.

The third element is the harmonization of standards in the financial system. Harmonization, at least the adoption of minimum acceptable international standards, is essential for improving investor confidence and enriching the flow of capital within the region. It would also be conducive to the stability and integrity of the financial system. I would emphasize the word international in terms of the standards. There is no reason to develop regional standards that are different from the standards that have already been developed by international financial institutions, professional bodies, and supervisory agencies.

The fourth element concerns the strengthening of cooperative efforts in financial system development. In Asia, we have been making good progress in our efforts to develop the domestic and regional debt markets through various regional forums and involving international financial institutions. In the context of developing Asian Bond Fund 2, for example, we have achieved a few firsts, including introducing the first exchange-traded bond index fund in Asia, arranging matters so that two Asian markets now allow exchange-traded funds, and opening up the yuan interbank bond market to foreign investors.

The final step toward creating an integrated Asian financial market requires the relaxation of statutory restrictions on crossborder capital flows. This is likely to be the most difficult step, in part because it depends on the ability of the financial system in individual jurisdictions to cope with the risks.

This raises the issue of the need for a strong and efficient regulatory framework. Greater financial integration across jurisdictions creates two new sources of risk for domestic financial institutions. The first and most obvious is the risk of currency mismatches when crossborder transactions involve different currencies, as they are likely to do in Asia. Although monetary integration is a topic often mentioned in the region, realizing monetary integration, if this occurs, is almost certainly going to take considerably more time than it will take for financial markets to become more closely linked. Meanwhile, financial systems will have to be robust with respect to fluctuations in exchange rates that may impact the assets and liabilities of financial institutions differentially. Of course, the financial turbulence in 1997 and 1998 has already alerted regulators and the private sector to these risks, but, if financial integration leads to increased crossborder financial commitments for domestic financial institutions, the size of the risks may become larger.

If integration has the desired effect of increasing cross-jurisdictional intermediation between savers and investors or if it leads to the establishment of cross-jurisdictional subsidiaries and branches, the nature of the credit risks faced by financial institutions may also change. Exposures to different business cycles will increase, as will exposures to different sources of idiosyncratic risk. Supervisory agencies need to make sure that appropriate risk control measures are implemented in individual institutions and that the available institutional capital adequately reflects the market, credit, and operational risks faced by institutions as they become exposed to foreign markets.

In Hong Kong (China), we are well on our way to implementing the latest international standards in this respect, that is, the Basel II standards. As the bank supervisor, the Hong Kong Monetary Authority has been working with banks and legislators to ensure that we are able to implement the new standards by January 1, 2007. We have also been working with other regulators in the region through the Working Group on Banking Supervision of the Executives' Meeting of East Asia–Pacific Central Banks to share our experiences on the implementation process. As financial flows increase within the region and as financial institutions increasingly operate in several jurisdictions, it is essential that this process proceed across the region.

The Implications of Financial Integration for Regional Monetary Arrangements

The successful introduction of the euro and the success of the European Central Bank in delivering monetary stability have naturally raised the question whether it would be appropriate for East Asia to contemplate monetary union. Studies have been undertaken with the goal of determining whether such a development would be desirable based on optimum currency area considerations. Not surprisingly, there is no clear-cut answer, but a number of authors suggest that East Asian economies are no less an optimum currency area than Europe when Europe started the process toward union.[2]

But, in discussing monetary union, one must bear in mind that a monetary union among a set of economies implies a single common currency, which, in turn, requires a single, common central bank. The decision to establish a monetary union therefore becomes intensely political because it involves ceding sovereignty over an institution that is a symbol of economic independence. In Europe, monetary integration was a political process, as well as an economic one. Indeed, without strong support by the political leadership in France and Germany, monetary integration might not have come about at all.

While I do not want to offer predictions about the political relationships among candidates for monetary union in East Asia, it seems safe to assume that any such union is many years away. After all, the process in Europe took more than 20 years between the first proposals and the launch of the euro. The implication is that East Asia is likely to find itself with substantially liberalized and integrated financial markets, together with different currencies in each jurisdiction, for a considerable time. This raises an important question. What is the nature of the monetary and exchange rate arrangements in a region characterized by highly integrated financial markets side by side with numerous independent currencies and central banks? It is well known that free capital mobility, independence in monetary policy, and a fixed exchange rate are not compatible. An economy must choose only two of the three as a basis for its monetary system. For example, Japan has opted for monetary independence and a floating exchange rate, whereas Hong Kong (China) has chosen a strict, nondiscretionary version of a fixed exchange rate, thus forgoing monetary autonomy. In both economies, international capital mobility is complete. Currently, some economies maintain significant controls on capital movements and are therefore able to conduct an independent monetary policy, while pursuing a policy of exchange rate stability. China is a particularly revealing example. To varying degrees, other countries in the region, such as the Republic of Korea, Malaysia, and Thailand, are also relying on restrictions on international capital movements in order to maintain a degree of control over domestic monetary conditions and exchange rate movements.

As financial integration in the region proceeds along the lines suggested in the previous section, policy makers will increasingly have to choose between monetary independence and exchange rate stability. The Hong Kong Monetary Authority has already made this choice by opting to forgo monetary independence altogether. This has been a highly successful strategy. It has delivered substantial benefits. The financial system is fully integrated with world capital markets, but there is a degree of monetary and financial stability that arguably would not have been achievable under other likely monetary strategies.

It has been suggested that economies in the region should tie their currencies together by pegging them to a common currency basket as a transition arrangement similar to the European Exchange Rate Mechanism. I would caution against such an approach; it may well increase the risk of a recurrence of currency crisis in the region. As Issing (2006) points out, the speculative attacks in the European Monetary System during the 1992 crisis arose in part because central banks were setting interest rates that were not consistent with the goal of maintaining fixed exchange rate parities. It would be a sad irony if the desire for monetary integration and exchange rate stability in East Asia led to agreements on a common exchange rate policy that would precipitate another currency crisis in the region.

To avoid such an outcome, it may be necessary to pursue coordination among monetary policies without relying on a common exchange rate policy.[3] One possibility would be for like-minded central banks to coordinate the setting of goals for independent domestic monetary policies, which would lead to similar levels of policy interest rates when the economies are at similar cyclical positions. If policy makers so desired, such coordination might naturally evolve into closer monetary cooperation through the creation of a common institutional framework for monetary policy decisions. By avoiding explicit exchange rate commitments, central banks would not set themselves up for the kind of foreign exchange speculation that featured in the financial crisis of 1997–98. At the same time, they could start building the institutional infrastructure necessary for the establishment of closer monetary cooperation.

I see at least three advantages to such an arrangement. First, the risk of exchange rate crisis in the region will be minimized because central banks that pursue independent monetary policies are not committed to defend any particular exchange rate levels. Second, the cooperation between central banks in the definition of policy objectives and the building of institutions will bring benefits whether or not the final outcome is full monetary union. Third, the arrangement is flexible in that central banks can take part in particular aspects of the arrangement without committing to full monetary integration.

Growth and Investment of Official Reserves

The rapid growth of official reserves in East Asia since the financial crisis is now well known. For the region as a whole, the U.S. dollar value of reserves increased from US$660 billion at the end of 1998 to US$2.3 trillion at the end of 2005.[4] Japan alone held US$831 billion at the end of 2005, while China had US$819 billion. Hong Kong (China) had a more modest US$117 billion, but, as we shall see, this may still be quite large relative to some measures of reserve adequacy. The rapid growth and the large size of these reserves suggest three interrelated questions. What are the motives and reasons for the accumulation, and will the accumulation continue? What constitutes an adequate level of international reserves? In what financial instruments should reserves be invested?

In coming years, we are likely to find answers to these questions by observing the actions of central banks. These actions will undoubtedly differ because institutions face different circumstances and constraints. Nevertheless, there will be trends.

There is, of course, no single motive or reason for the persistence in accumulating reserves. Supply and demand factors are at work. The supply factors leading to reserve accumulation are the capital flows that have entered the region, as well as current account surpluses. In the absence of official interventions, these factors tend to appreciate local currencies, and authorities have judged it prudent to resist at least part of this appreciation by intervening in the foreign exchange market and accumulating reserves. The major demand factor during the past six to eight years is, without doubt, the desire on the part of regional central banks to build up a stock of reserves as a buffer against possible swings in capital flows in the future. There is a view in the region that holding a substantial stock of international reserve assets may prove advantageous if international borrowing possibilities dry up suddenly or if capital flows precipitously change direction. There is a sentiment that, in such circumstances, one is better served by one's own guaranteed resources rather than by the uncertain prospects of credits from multilateral institutions, even if there is an opportunity cost associated with holding accumulated reserves.

The supply and demand factors are bound to have finite duration because countries with current account imbalances will eventually find that corrective action is in their interest and because central banks that are accumulating reserves will, at some stage, realize that the insurance value of an additional dollar in foreign exchange reserves is not worth the opportunity cost entailed. A major reason for the postcrisis current account surpluses in East Asia (except China) was the fall in investment rates. As economic growth resumes, investment will follow sooner or later, thus narrowing or eliminating the savings-investment gap. In China, the high savings rate is likely to fall as the economic policy strategy of the authorities begins to emphasize domestic consumption and as improvements in the social security system reduce the precautionary savings of households.

I would like to offer some thoughts on how to measure reserve adequacy and what might be done with "excess" reserves.

If we view international reserves as a kind of insurance against unforeseen events, what events are we insuring against? The traditional answer is that we need to keep international reserves equal to some multiple of monthly import payments in the event that export receipts suddenly dry up. In today's world of large and volatile capital flows, the traditional answer is, of course, not adequate. As central bankers, we need to pay attention to the possibility of sudden stops or reversals in capital flows. The so-called Guidotti rule for assessing reserve adequacy is one response to such concerns. This rule suggests that central banks should hold reserves that are no smaller than the scheduled interest payments and amortization of foreign debt in the coming 12 months. While this is a useful point of departure for thoughts about reserve adequacy, it does not fully address the vulnerability of an economy to potential capital flows. For example, in circumstances such as those facing Hong Kong (China), the rule is not particularly helpful because we do not have any external debt, at least as regards the official sector.

More generally, therefore, it must be recognized that owners of domestic liquid assets may, on some occasions, collectively decide to convert some portion of these assets into foreign exchange, potentially leading to strains on the domestic financial system and pressures on the exchange rate. The monetary authority, which is required to maintain financial stability, must then be able to supply a corresponding amount of foreign exchange to the market. Hence, one element that enters the assessment of reserve adequacy will be the size of short-term liquid assets in the domestic financial system. But what proportion of liquid assets may be said to be "at risk"? This depends in part on the volatility of the demand for these assets, a quantity that may be estimated based on past behavior.

According to this line of reasoning, the authority responsible for determining the appropriate amount of international reserves needed for self-insurance will have to determine what types of domestic assets risk being withdrawn from the financial system and converted into foreign currencies. The authority will then have to assess the volatility in the private sector's demand for these assets. Using these data, together with an estimate of the opportunity costs of holding highly liquid international reserves, the authority might obtain a rough estimate of reserve adequacy. I believe that authorities are already reasoning along these lines and will do so even more in the years to come. My guess is that, as time passes, many will come to the conclusion that the reserves already accumulated have surpassed the needs of self-insurance.

Insurance principles also suggest that the pooling of resources will reduce the amount of resources required by each of the members of the pool. This idea lies behind the Chiang Mai Initiative. If, one day, this becomes a blueprint for a multilateral agreement, as I hope and believe it will, then the need for international reserves from each of the participants will be reduced. It is therefore useful to start contemplating the mandate that should be given to reserve managers with respect to dealing with any excess of actual holdings relative to the amounts considered required.

There are essentially two approaches to this problem—one is for the authorities to divest themselves of the excess reserves, and the other is to manage the excess according to objectives that are different from those applied to the reserves required for insurance purposes. Because international reserves, by definition, are denominated in foreign currencies, divesting may not be a feasible option if it would lead to undesirable pressures on the exchange rate.[5] Converting foreign exchange proceeds from the sale of external assets into domestic currency would tend to appreciate the domestic currency, which may be contrary to the objectives of the central bank. The only case in which such pressure would not materialize is if the domestic private sector is willing to add to their foreign assets as the central bank reduces its holdings. Prasad and Rajan (2005), of the International Monetary Fund, have proposed an interesting method of divesting official international reserves under conditions where the domestic private sector has a latent demand for foreign currency–denominated assets. They believe such a situation exists in China at the moment due to restrictions on holdings of external assets by the private sector. The essence of their proposal is that the domestic authorities should authorize the creation of mutual funds that would sell shares denominated in domestic currency to the public. The proceeds would be used to obtain foreign exchange from the central bank for the acquisition of external assets. While their proposal might be a solution for some jurisdictions that have strict controls on the purchase of the foreign assets of the private sector, it is not applicable to countries without such controls, a fact explicitly recognized by the authors.

Excess reserves could also be used to buy back external government debt. Of course, this assumes that there is some official external debt to buy back, which, as already noted, is not necessarily the case for all jurisdictions. In any event, such a buyback should be evaluated in the context of an optimal portfolio allocation strategy. Such a strategy would involve consideration of a number of assets beyond the traditional, highly liquid securities of a small number of sovereign issuers, and it would include agency bonds, highly rated corporate bonds, equities of top-rated corporations, commodities, and maybe private equity. As with the liquid reserves used for self-insurance, the management of the portfolio could be carried out by the central bank according to a specific mandate specifying the risk-return trade that it should be aiming for. Alternatively, a special government agency could be established for this purpose, like the Korean Investment Corporation, the Government Petroleum Fund in Norway, or the Government of Singapore Investment Corporation. I believe that, in the coming years, an increasing number of central banks will take steps to distinguish explicitly between different portions of their international reserve holdings and determine investment strategies involving specific risk-return profiles for each portfolio. This will lead to reserve management strategies that emphasize liquidity for the traditional insurance portion of international reserves and national wealth management for the excess reserve portion. The principles that should determine the optimal size and composition of an official national wealth management portfolio will have to be elaborated, and the conflicting interests of current and future generations of citizens will have to be addressed.

Concluding Remarks

This essay has focused on three challenges that I believe will frame discussions among central banks in Asia in the coming years: the development and integration of financial markets, the evolution and nature of monetary cooperation, and the management of international reserves. Properly managed, the challenges can lead to the emergence of a stronger, more resilient, and more efficient financial and monetary system in the region. I hope that the ideas spelled out in this essay will aid the discussions in regional forums such as the Executives' Meeting of East Asia–Pacific Central Banks and various working groups in the context of the Association of Southeast Asian Nations or of Asia-Pacific Economic Cooperation, as well as in international financial organizations more generally.

Notes

1. Empirical evidence consistent with this line of reasoning can be found in Kaminsky, Lyons, and Schmukler (2000).

2. Ito and Park (2004) review the empirical literature.

3. I rule out the possibility of adopting Hong Kong–style currency board arrangements in other jurisdictions on the grounds that central banks have shown a preference for monetary policy autonomy.

4. These figures are based on data from *International Financial Statistics* (International Monetary Fund) and refer to the reserves of the countries in the Association of Southeast

Asian Nations (except Brunei Darussalam because of data unavailability), plus China, the Republic of Korea, and Japan.

5. In the case of Hong Kong (China), divesting is not even an option given our linked exchange rate system.

References

Issing, Otmar. 2006. "Europe's Hard Fix: The Euro Area." Draft working paper, Oesterreichische Nationalbank, Vienna.
Ito, Takatoshi, and Yung Chul Park. 2004. "Exchange Rate Regimes in East Asia." In *Monetary and Financial Integration in East Asia: The Way Ahead*, Vol. 1, ed. Asian Development Bank, 143–88. Basingstoke, United Kingdom: Palgrave Macmillan.
Kaminsky, Graciela, Richard Lyons, and Sergio Schmukler. 2000. "Economic Fragility, Liquidity, and Risk: The Behavior of Mutual Funds during Crises." Draft research paper, World Bank, Washington, DC.
Prasad, Eswar, and Raghuram Rajan. 2005. "Controlled Capital Account Liberalization: A Proposal." IMF Policy Discussion Paper 05/7, International Monetary Fund, Washington, DC.
Zebregs, Harm H. 2004. "Intraregional Trade in Emerging Asia." IMF Policy Discussion Paper 04/1, Asia and Pacific Department, International Monetary Fund, Washington, DC.

CHAPTER 18

The Internal and External Environments of China's Development over the Next Five Years

ZHENG BIJIAN

The coming years will witness a marked improvement in the Chinese economy. They offer a window of opportunity, but there will also be significant difficulties.

One of the easiest ways to observe recent developments in China is to read the Guidelines of the Plan for National Economic and Social Development for 2006–10 (the Guidelines of the 11th Five-Year Plan), which was deliberated upon and approved by the Fourth Plenary Session of the 10th National People's Congress, held in March 2006. The reason: this document is a program of action that aims at laying a solid foundation for the country's rapid and sound development in the first two decades of the 21st century.

One Part of the Equation: The Domestic Situation

China's major decisions during the new era have been closely associated with a correct understanding of the internal and external environments facing the country. The first 20 years of the 21st century represent an important window of opportunity for efforts to build a moderately prosperous society.[1] This has been the assessment of the Chinese government on the basis of its analysis of the situation. China's 11th Five-Year Plan (FYP) has been formulated as a result of an in-depth examination of the internal and external environments the country will face.

Let us start with the internal development environment and the features of the different stages of China's growth. As I see it, the 11th FYP period will be China's golden age of development, but also a period of major challenges.[2]

China's growth demonstrates that the 10th FYP period (2001–05) witnessed the first steps in China's comprehensive efforts to build a moderately prosperous society. It was a seminal period and a period of extraordinary achievements. Under the guidance of Deng Xiaoping's theory and the important concept of "Three Represents,"[3] we have put forward and are implementing a scientific outlook on development and a strategy for constructing a harmonious socialist society. Economic development is our top priority in the pursuit of national rejuvenation. We are concentrating our efforts to achieve this goal through reform and greater openness ("opening-up"). As a result, China's economy has grown, and the country's overall national strength and international status have been significantly enhanced.

China's level of urbanization had risen to 43 percent by the end of the 10th FYP period, up from 36 percent toward the end of the last century, and the population in cities and towns had increased from 459.1 million to 562.1 million by the end of the year 2000. Clusters of cities connected by transportation, energy, and information networks are gradually taking shape. Several major city clusters are full of vitality and dynamism. Urban development is advancing by the day, and cities are running more smoothly.

As a sign of its economic strength, by the end of the 10th FYP period, China's gross domestic product (GDP) had risen to Y 18.2 trillion, up from Y 10.1 trillion, an increase of 80 percent relative to the end of the 1990s, while budgetary revenues more than doubled, from Y 1.3 trillion to Y 3.2 trillion. Living standards have improved. This is evident in the increase in the retail sales of consumer goods nationwide to Y 6.7 trillion, up by 97.7 percent compared to the end of the 1990s. Per capita disposable income among urban residents rose from Y 6,280 to Y 10,490, while per capita net income in rural areas reached Y 3,255, up from Y 2,253.

As regards the progress in industrialization, infrastructure, and information technology systems, industrial structures have been enhanced in terms of overall competitiveness. Basic industries such as transportation and energy have grown rapidly. A relatively modern, integrated transportation network, encompassing air, rail, waterways, and expressways, is emerging. The penetration rates of fixed and mobile phones top

57 percent and 30 percent, respectively, and the number of Internet users is expected to exceed 100 million.

Our national economy is now more well positioned to cope with risks and disasters. Over the past five years, we have managed to address the impact on the economy and public order of the outbreak of severe acute respiratory syndrome (SARS) and major natural disasters. Automobile manufacturing and agriculture, which were projected to experience serious difficulties following China's accession to the World Trade Organization, have witnessed stable and healthy development and enjoy good prospects. Reform in the banking sector is accelerating, and reform of the exchange rate mechanism is being pushed through. Other financial sectors are being steadily liberalized in accordance with our commitments to the World Trade Organization. The financial system has greatly boosted its ability to weather risks.

Meanwhile, social services have made progress. The achievements in socialist democracy, the promotion of "spiritual civilization,"[4] and the building of a harmonious socialist society have been remarkable.

In short, our work during the 10th FYP period advanced our country to a higher level and laid a solid foundation for greater development during the 11th FYP period.

During the 11th FYP period, the Chinese economy will enter a new phase of long-term, rapid, and sustained development. In the absence of such development, it will be difficult to resolve conflicts of interest. We need to grow steadily; otherwise, these conflicts of interest will become acute as we move ahead.

Experts estimate that, during 2006–15, cities and towns throughout the country will see 5.5 million local residents enter the workforce each year. Moreover, if the annual urbanization rate is 1 percent, cities will need to absorb 10 million more surplus laborers from rural areas each year. As reform reaches more deeply into state- and collective-owned enterprises, 4.5 million workers will lose their jobs each year. If one takes into account the cumulative unemployed population, cities and towns will need to offer a total of 24 million new jobs each year. The pressures on job creation are therefore great. Between 2006 and 2015 and possibly even all the way to 2020, if only to meet the needs of job creation, China's annual GDP growth rate should not be lower than 7 percent. It follows that slow economic growth will render it impossible to meet these requirements.

On the other hand, there is a need to strive for steady development. If one follows the traditional model of economic growth driven by investment, investment often becomes overheated, and it is hard for consumption to play a leading role. Prices tend to rise, and, more often than not, job creation lags. Such a model can easily lead to huge fluctuations in the economy that are characterized by drastic falloffs in growth once macroeconomic controls and regulations are exercised or by drastic upswings once macroeconomic controls and regulations are relaxed. Thus, rapid, stable, and healthy economic development depends on the implementation of a scientific approach, which means transforming patterns of growth, adjusting economic structures, stimulating and expanding domestic demand, and fine tuning macroeconomic controls.

Beyond doubt, the 11th FYP period will be a golden age of development and will witness a marked improvement in the Chinese economy because of the following favorable conditions.

First, the mix in household consumption is gradually changing. Industrialization has entered a phase of accelerated restructuring, and urbanization is accelerating. The experience of other countries indicates that, when a country's per capita GDP is growing from US$1,000 toward US$3,000, household consumption shows a shift from the subsistence level to a higher level of comfort, that is, a shift from seeking enough food to eat and enough clothing to wear, from gaining access to durable consumer goods, and from acquiring permanent shelter to seeking access to more nutritious, higher-quality food and better clothing, improved living conditions, better durable consumer goods, and expanded services. This shift will lead to rapid growth in heavy and chemical industries and, especially, the automotive, construction, and building materials industries. Industrial structures will be improved and technologies upgraded.

Second, China abounds in labor resources, and human capital will increase rapidly. By the year 2010, the labor supply will total 800 million people, 25 million of whom will possess fresh degrees at the undergraduate and postgraduate levels. This large pool of lower-cost labor will constitute a strong comparative advantage in favor of China's economic growth.

Third, in terms of access to capital, China has a relatively high domestic savings rate, and this represents a source of investment for industrial development.

Fourth, along with urbanization and the modernization in transportation and in information technologies, particularly digital communications, the infrastructure, expressways, railways, ports, airports, and information networks in Chinese cities will witness steady improvement. During the 11th FYP period, the modernization in China's industrial sector and various areas of infrastructure will advance to a new stage.

Fifth, the socialist market economic system will gradually improve, and social harmony and political stability will be consolidated and enhanced.

All these areas represent favorable conditions for socioeconomic development during the 11th FYP period.

In the meantime, we are soberly aware that this "golden age of development" will also be a period of significant difficulties. Specifically, during the 11th FYP period, China will continue to be confronted by three major challenges.

First and foremost is the challenge of resources, especially energy. China ranks third in the world in terms of aggregate natural resources. It is a major energy producer. Its total reserves in primary energy resources are estimated at 4 trillion tons of coal equivalent. However, it lags far behind the world average in terms of per capita ownership of energy resources and consumption. In 2005, China's per capita exploitable oil reserves stood at less than 3 tons (accounting for 11.1 percent of the world average), while its per capita extractable natural gas reserves were about 1,000 cubic meters (4.3 percent), and its per capita extractable coal reserves were about 90 tons (55.4 percent).

Although oil does not occupy a dominant position in the structure of China's energy consumption, it should be noted that, since China became a net oil importer in 1996, crude oil imports have generally displayed a rapidly rising trend. In 2005, the country imported 126.8 million tons of crude oil, which represented a degree of import dependence of 42.9 percent. It is projected that, by the year 2020, China's demand for oil will amount to 500 million tons, which is a degree of import dependence of nearly 60 percent. Oil security will become an increasingly pressing problem.

China's ownership of freshwater resources is one-fourth the world average. Of the 666 cities, 440 are in short supply of water. It is estimated that, by the year 2030, China will be included on the list of countries with a serious shortage of water.

Because China's manufacturing sector is developing rapidly (albeit at a generally low level of scientific, technological, and engineering sophistication), its unit and aggregate consumption of resources, including energy, is among the highest in the world. Coupled with this is the massive shift of manufacturing to China, which has brought about a considerable increase in energy and water consumption. Consequently, resource shortages, particularly in energy, are becoming a major problem during China's "peaceful rise."

The second challenge is the environment. In the course of its rapid industrialization and modernization, China has encountered serious environmental pollution, ecological degradation, huge consumption and wastage of resources, and environmental damage resulting from low recycling rates. These problems have evolved into a bottleneck in the sustainable development of the Chinese economy. This is an important reason why the Chinese leadership has put forward the scientific approach to development.

The first major problem in China's ecological environment is soil erosion. According to calculations based on the results of a satellite remote-sensing survey conducted in 1992, the area affected by soil erosion represented 1.8 million square kilometers, or 18.7 percent of the territory of China.

Another problem is rapid desertification. China is the one of the countries in the world undergoing the most severe desertification. In the northern part of the country, the area covered by deserts and water-poor drylands exceeds 1.5 million square kilometers, approximately 15.5 percent of China's territory. Since the 1980s, desert land has been spreading at an annual rate of 2,100 square kilometers. In the course of 25 years, 39,000 square kilometers of land have given way to desert.

The third problem is the reduction and slow recovery of forest resources. China's forest coverage is only 61.5 percent of the world average per country (world rank: 130). Per capita forest coverage is 0.13 hectares, less than one-fourth the world average (world rank: 134).

The fourth problem is worsening water pollution. According to a city monitoring survey conducted in 1987, 42 percent of the sources of drinking water for cities were seriously contaminated, and 63 percent of the water in cities was polluted to varying degrees. Of the 532 rivers surveyed, 82 percent were contaminated to some extent.

The fifth problem is serious air pollution.

The third major challenge is the series of dilemmas encountered in the course of coordinating economic and social development. Among the most difficult and risky problems during the 11th FYP period is, first, the high economic growth rate relative to the slow rise in the level of employment. China's economic growth is currently driven largely by investments and exports, less by domestic consumption. The reason is that the investments are mainly focused on infrastructure and the related industries, which do not create many jobs. Along with the progress in technology and the increase in organic capital formation, investment by state-owned enterprises and foreign direct investment are able to provide only limited employment. This is the fundamental reason why, despite the rapid growth in China's economy, job creation has been sluggish in taking up the surplus labor from rural areas and the expanding labor force in cities and towns.

Another difficulty is represented by the widening income disparities between cities and rural areas, urban and rural residents, and various regions. In general, income is increasing across the board, but at different rates. In 2005, according to data provided by the National Bureau of Statistics, the net per capita income of farmers reached Y 3,255, while the per capita disposable income of urban residents crossed the Y 10,000 threshold and reached Y 10,493. The disparity between urban and rural residents in terms of per capita income was thus 3.2 to 1, and there have been signs that it may expand. In terms of growth momentum, the net income of farmers was increasing from a small base and at a low rate; the most optimistic forecast is that the annual growth in this income sector will probably be around 6 percent during the 11th FYP. In comparison, the disposable income of urban residents has a larger base than the net income of farmers, and it is expected to register a minimum growth rate of around 8 percent during the 11th FYP. As a result, it is probable that the income gap between urban and rural residents will continue to widen.

In terms of regional development, 65 percent of the increase in GDP is being generated in the eastern part of the country. About 80 percent of foreign direct investment benefits the east; so do 60–80 percent of bank lending, job opportunities for university graduates, and exports. As a consequence, much still needs to be done if the development disparity between the eastern and western parts of the country is to be appropriately controlled during the 11th FYP.

The two sets of problems outlined above lead to dilemmas in China's economic and social development. Thus, there is a need to sustain the rapid growth of GDP, while quickening the pace of social development; to preserve the momentum of robust growth in the east, while promoting the development of the central and western parts of the country; to push ahead with urbanization, while providing support to rural areas; to emphasize equity and to reduce social and economic gaps, while maintaining the vitality of the country and increasing efficiency; to absorb more foreign direct investment, while optimizing investment structures; to open up markets and encourage technology imports, while strengthening the capacity for independent scientific and technological innovation; to deepen reform in all areas, while upholding social stability; and to encourage competition, while caring for the disadvantaged. The list goes on well beyond the scope of this essay. All these issues have to be addressed at the same time. *To address these issues, one should not emphasize only one side of each dilemma, while neglecting the other side. Rather, one should look at both sides and adopt balanced and coordinated measures in order to achieve rapid, but sound development.*

The "three major challenges" described above are caused mainly by the gap between the expanding material and cultural needs of the people on the one hand and the less than advanced level of productivity and the relatively short supply of resources on the other. They are the reflection of the fact that China is still at the elementary stage of socialism and will remain there for a long time to come.

Precisely under these circumstances, the structural problems in the economy of China—in industries, in urban and rural areas, and in regions—are becoming more pronounced. Precisely under these circumstances, there is an urgent need to promote urbanization; to address the complex problems among farmers, in agriculture, and in rural areas; to undertake structural adjustment; and to expand domestic demand, while transforming the pattern of growth, boosting the capacity for independent innovation, and fostering skills and talents. Precisely under these circumstances, the host of problems that affect the real interests of the people at large, including employment, social security benefits, poverty reduction, school enrollment, health care, environmental protection, occupational safety, and income distribution, has developed into pressing issues calling for greater attention. Also, precisely under these circumstances, it has become an unshakeable guideline that more profound reform in economic structures and more wide-ranging structural reform must continue to be regarded as the fundamental driving force during the 11th FYP period and over the longer term. The 11th FYP reflects a major decision formulated on the basis of a full consideration of the characteristics of the stage of development of China and in response to the above challenges.

Overall, we must draw up our plan for the 11th FYP period taking account of opportunities and of challenges. We must consider the needs of different sectors, regions, and groups of people and try our best to achieve coordinated development that is relatively rapid and truly steady.

The Other Part of the Equation: The International Environment

Let us now focus our attention on the international environment facing China and the characteristics of the country's external economic relations at this stage.

In my view, the 11th FYP period will continue to witness deepened interdependency and frequent frictions between China and the rest of the world.

Since the start of the 21st century, the international environment as a whole has been stable. Global economic development and even the economic and social development of a particular country or region require a peaceful environment. In turn, maintaining peace, which includes counterterrorism and nuclear nonproliferation efforts, requires international cooperation in a wide array of areas. The alignment of global political forces favors the maintenance of a stable international environment.

At the same time, the trend toward economic globalization is advancing and deepening. Scientific and technological progress is leading to changes by the day, and the mobility of factors of production and geographic shifts of industries are gaining in speed. As countries strengthen their cooperation in trade, investment, technologies, and labor services and bring into play their comparative advantages, the economic interdependence between China and the rest of the world will become more profound.

The external environment as a whole is favorable for China's development.

First, relationships between major powers will continue to undergo change. In regard to China's path of peaceful development and its international environment during the 11th FYP period, it is crucial to handle relations with major powers properly. In the wake of the Iraq war, the relations between the United States and other major powers are in a phase of repair, and the trend toward multipolarization is growing. The competition in overall national strength among major powers will be intensified, with each trying to gain strategic advantage. China's peaceful rise will present more economic opportunities to various major powers. China's position in the relations among major powers will steadily advance.

Second, cooperation among developing countries will be enhanced. For China's peaceful rise and the country's endeavor to gain a favorable international environment during the 11th FYP period, good relations with other developing countries are essential. Solidarity and cooperation with these countries in the international economic sphere will help establish a new international economic order and speed up industrialization in the developing world. In addition, China's exchanges with other developing countries in the economic, political, cultural, and diplomatic fields will be expanded and deepened as the Chinese market grows.

Third, China faces both opportunities and challenges in its relations with surrounding countries, but, in general, the opportunities outweigh the challenges. Our geographic position makes it important to develop good relations with our neighbors. In accordance with the guidelines of "creating an harmonious, amicable, and prosperous neighborhood" and the principle of "putting aside disputes," we have maintained sound relations of cooperation with neighboring countries and gradually solved boundary issues. We are in consultation with relevant countries with the aim of rationally exploiting the oil and gas resources in the East China Sea and the South China Sea without prejudice to our national sovereignty.

Fourth, as international relations evolve and regional cooperation is strengthened, China will have an even larger scope for development. Because China is a developing country, multilateral diplomacy has become an important arena for exchanges and cooperation with other countries.

At the same time, the international environment is complex and shifting. Factors of destabilization that are harmful to world peace are on the rise. Developed countries will maintain their superiority in the economic, scientific, and technological fields for a long time to come. The imbalances in global economic development are intensifying. The competition for resources, markets, technologies, and skills and talents is becoming fiercer, and trade protectionism is increasing. These issues pose a new challenge for China's socioeconomic development and security.

Talks about a "China threat" have been heard here and there. This is not conducive to China's growth. The theory that China represents a military threat has not yet faded, while the assertion that China represents an economic threat has sprung up, and trade disputes and other economic frictions are becoming more noticeable and more numerous. Since China's accession to the World Trade Organization and following the elimination of restrictions such as quotas, there have been strong surges in Chinese exports in areas such as textiles. Some people in Europe, Japan, and the United States contend that China's economic growth and Chinese exports are causing energy shortages, affecting local production and jobs, and leading to global shifts of industries.

We must study the reasons behind these contentions and make a proper response. We should not allow them to mislead us in our judgment of overall trends in the international environment. We should continue to follow the path of peaceful development with determination and act as a responsible country. In this process, in answer to the concerns and worries of the international community, we should demonstrate by our actions that, along with rapid economic growth, China is making efforts to diversify its energy supplies, address its energy problems mainly by relying on its own efforts, transform its pattern of growth and mode of consumption, and build itself into a resource-conserving society. All this will hopefully help the world understand more accurately China's strategy and policies for "peaceful development" or "peaceful rise."

It should be noted that, with China's rapid development, we have left behind the old model of regulating development on our own and entered a new stage of accelerated growth by making use of international and domestic markets and resources. This change has caused China to be more interdependent with the world economy. The huge domestic demand for investment and consumption is the main driving force behind China's economic growth. In terms of retail sales within the country, over 99 percent are balanced in supply and demand; some even show a little surplus. In 2005, China's market for capital goods was valued at Y 8.9 trillion; the consumption of retail goods reached nearly Y 6.7 trillion; and the market for services was worth between Y 3 trillion and Y 4 trillion. Concerning China's relationship with international markets, the country's imports and exports represented US$1.4 trillion in 2005, and, calculated at the current exchange rate, its foreign trade dependence ratio had risen to 62.4 percent. In 2005, China exported US$762 billion and imported US$660.1 billion in goods, including some resources in short supply within China. China has increasingly become a huge market for the world economy and a classic example of international interdependence; the message is that no country can develop in isolation.

In a process associated with, rather than isolated from economic globalization, especially in the years since China's accession to the World Trade Organization, frictions in foreign trade and investment have increased day by day. Because developed countries are plagued by weak domestic demand and industrial structures that are incompatible with the needs of economic globalization, trade disputes arose between China and the European Union and the United States over such products as textiles, footwear, and furniture in 2004 and 2005. Chinese enterprises have frequently been subjected to antidumping and safeguards investigations and intellectual property disputes involving trade and manufacturing. More and more technical, ecological, and environmental barriers and product safety barriers against Chinese products have also been erected.

In short, China must maximize benefits and minimize risks and seek mutually beneficial and win-win results in this international economic environment in which greater interdependence and more frequent frictions between China and other countries coexist. This will, in turn, make it necessary for us to enhance our ability to make accurate scientific assessments of the situation, see clearly our direction of development amid changes in the international and domestic situation, seize the opportunities, create good conditions for development, and hold the reins of general development.

The Next Five Years and Beyond

Looking at the international and domestic environment during the 11th FYP period and beyond and the complex and changing situation, we may conclude that the next five years will be an important period linking the past to the future in China's comprehensive efforts to build a moderately prosperous society. We must firmly grasp opportunities, respond to various challenges, resolve major problems that have existed for a long time, overcome development bottlenecks and institutional obstacles, gear our efforts toward scientific development, strengthen our capacity for independent innovation, deepen reform and opening-up, and promote harmony throughout the country. Then, we will surely be able to turn the five years of the 11th FYP period into a critical phase for the transformation of the current model of economic growth and for economic restructuring and institutional reform, all this with a view to making progress in socialist economic, political, cultural, and social development and laying a solid foundation for smooth development over the next 10 years.

Taking a more profound and long-term view, we can also see that the 11th FYP formulated by the Chinese government is a more vivid reflection of three inevitable trends in China during the first half of the 21st century.

The first is that the Chinese people will continue to make every effort to develop their country. The 1.3 billion Chinese people are both eager and capable of doing this. In itself, this is a strong propeller for the country's socioeconomic growth. When over 1 billion people become rich, they will represent not only a unique pool of human resources, but also a huge reserve of purchasing power and a domestic market with the biggest potential in the world. During the 11th FYP period, if China's annual per capita GDP continues to grow at an average rate of 8 percent, its per capita GDP will have reached US$2,483 by the year 2010, and aggregate GDP will, in constant prices, have risen to approximately Y 26.8 trillion. Meanwhile, the domestic demand for investment and consumption will have reached Y 9.4 trillion and Y 17.4 trillion, respectively. These figures can be expected to continue to expand.

Such a level of domestic demand is quite sizable in world economic and historical terms. This will, in turn, require that we make persistent efforts to raise the level of productivity. In a certain sense, we might even say that, from the leadership to the man on the street, all the efforts being undertaken in China at present and in the years to come are aimed at responding to the huge domestic demand generated by the 1.5 billion population peak that is expected to be reached in the 2030s or 2040s. This also means that, for a very long period of time, the Chinese people will be focusing their energies on addressing their own economic and social development issues.

As Deng Xiaoping used to emphasize again and again, we should concentrate on our own work and work for the entire Chinese people ourselves. We do not seek world hegemony, but, rather, want to ensure a better life and higher level of development for over 1 billion Chinese people. Attainment of this goal in itself will be a huge contribution to world development and human progress. No big latecomer power in modern history ever acted as China is acting during its rise.

The second trend is that the Chinese people will continue to participate in economic globalization on the basis of independence and self-reliance (even in terms of energy, the focus is on self-reliance). We will rely on both domestic and international markets and resources and embrace greater interdependence and win-win cooperation with other countries. Given the fact that countries vary in their resources, geographic location, demographics, and stage of industrial development, regionalization and specialization in the division of labor are intensifying. This dictates that countries must bring into play their own comparative advantages and conduct exchanges and undertake collaboration with one another in a bid to learn from one another's strong points and achieve win-win outcomes. This is why, during the 11th FYP period, China will make more conscientious efforts to link itself with economic globalization rather than shying away, by building Chinese-style socialism through hard work, by relying on its own comparative advantages in economic development, and by sharing the benefits accruing from development.

We should soberly assess the changes in the supply of and demand for resources on the global scale and the increasingly fierce competition for resources. However, resource shortages and price increases will drive technological progress, promote resource- and energy-conserving models of growth and modes of consumption, and facilitate the search for and discovery of new alternative resources and sources of energy so as to change the general public's lifestyles and patterns of production. For this reason, intensified efforts to increase the capacity for independent innovation in knowledge and technology represent a requirement for China within the context of economic globalization, as well as the most dynamic driving force behind China's economic development.

At the same time, we should also assign top priority to international economic and technological exchanges and cooperation. The first 20 years of the 21st century will be a period in which regional economic cooperation evolves at an accelerated pace; in terms of preferential trade arrangements, customs unions, common markets, economic unions, and economic integration, there will be more profound changes. These developments are conducive to a lowering of trade frictions and the costs of exchanges, thus bringing huge economic benefits to all participants. New development opportunities will undoubtedly come our way if we firmly align ourselves with this trend, proactively participate in regional economic cooperation initiatives like ASEAN+3 (the Association of Southeast Asian Nations, plus China, Japan, and the Republic of Korea) and other regional economic cooperation mechanisms in Asia and the Pacific, and facilitate the development of regional economic cooperation organizations. China will persist in opening up and taking part in economic globalization—no other big latecomer country has ever done this during its rise.

The last trend is what we have defined as the great renaissance of the Chinese nation in the middle of the 21st century and China's peaceful rise as the harmonious development of "material civilization," "political civilization," "spiritual civilization," "social civilization," and "ecological civilization," as the rise of the population's ethical standards and the development of harmonious relations internally and externally, and as the construction of a harmonious socialist society. This means that there is a great renaissance of Chinese civilization on the basis of socialism, which, in turn, signals a great change in Chinese society and a great transformation of the Chinese nation in the first half of the 21st century. Such a definition has become a fundamental guideline, and it is a peaceful, civilized, and open pathway. As Chairman Mao Zedong, founder of the New China, remarked in the 1950s, China would become a big, powerful, yet amicable country. This is certainly a great objective. We are pursuing it earnestly and will persist in doing so. Again, no big latecomer country has ever done this during its rise.

In conclusion, during the 11th FYP period and beyond, China is bound to face major challenges, as well as opportunities in various areas. Under the strong leadership of the Central Committee of the Communist Party of China, with Comrade Hu Jintao as general secretary, we have clearly analyzed the international and domestic situation and bear in mind the risks and the uncertainties, yet remain confident. We shall continue to emancipate our minds, be ready to blaze new trails, persist in reform, promote innovation, and work hard in a down-to-earth manner. I am sure we will be able to make new achievements and add new glory to our country's history.

Notes

1. The concept of a "moderately prosperous society" was put forward during the 10th five-year plan period (2001–05). The concept recognizes that, with the considerable progress achieved through economic growth, the major challenge is now not only to increase per capita incomes, but also to adopt broader objectives to enhance social welfare.

2. Experience in some market economies indicates that, when a country's per capita gross domestic product is between US$1,000 and US$3,000, society often undergoes dramatic social and economic transformations. With per capita GDP now exceeding US$1,000, China is at precisely this stage of dynamic change, and, indeed, it is being confronted with both challenges and opportunities.

3. "Three represents" is the notion that the Communist Party of China must represent the requirements of the development of China's advanced productive forces, the development of China's advanced culture, and the fundamental interests of the vast majority of the people in China. The theory was initiated by then President Jiang Zemin in 2000 and later written into the Party Constitution in 2002 and eventually the State Constitution in 2004.

4. "Spiritual civilization" is a term used to denote general intellectual activities, including initiatives in ethics and morality, science, and culture.

About the Authors

Aun Porn Moniroth is chairman of the Supreme National Economic Council, the Cambodian government's interdisciplinary research organization for all socioeconomic matters; chief economic adviser to the prime minister; and secretary of state for economy and finance. He plays a leading role in establishing the government's policy platform in economics, trade, investment, and related areas. In addition, he is a member of the Board of Governors of the National Bank of Cambodia and serves as an alternate governor for Cambodia on the Boards of Governors of the World Bank Group and the Asian Development Bank. Dr. Aun Porn Moniroth has served as an eminent person of Cambodia on two Eminent Persons Groups for the preparation of reports and recommendations to the heads of state and government and other leaders of the Association of Southeast Asian Nations. He is the author of various publications on democracy and the economic development of Cambodia, as well as on globalization and economic integration in the region. He received a PhD in political science from Moscow State University and a diploma in international business from the Moscow School of Business.

Roberto F. de Ocampo is president of the Asian Institute of Management. As secretary of finance (1994–98) during the presidency of Fidel V. Ramos, he was widely recognized as the principal architect of a resurgence in the Philippine economy. At that time, he was also a member of the Boards of Governors of the World Bank and the Asian Development Bank and an alternate governor of the International Monetary Fund. He has served as chairman and chief executive officer of the Development Bank of the Philippines and as chairman of the Asia-Pacific Economic Cooperation Finance Ministers. In 1995, he was named Finance Minister of the Year by *Euromoney* magazine. He was named Asian Finance Minister of the Year by *Euromoney* magazine (in 1996) and *Asiamoney* magazine (in 1997). In September 2001, Dr. de Ocampo was named by the French Republic to the Ordre National de la Legion d'Honneur with the rank of Chevalier. He received a master's degree from the University of Michigan and a postgraduate diploma from the London School of Economics.

Toyoo Gyohten is president of the Institute for International Monetary Affairs, a foundation within the Bank of Tokyo–Mitsubishi UFJ, where Professor Gyohten is senior adviser. He also serves as special adviser to the prime minister. He graduated from the University of Tokyo in 1955 and joined the Tax Bureau at the Ministry of Finance the same year. He then received a Fulbright Scholarship and undertook graduate studies at Princeton University. His long career at the ministry included five years of overseas experience at the International Monetary Fund and the Asian Development Bank, where he was one of the founding members and served as special assistant to the president. After returning to Tokyo, he held various positions in the Finance Bureau, the Banking Bureau, and the International Finance Bureau, where he was director general. He was subsequently vice minister of finance for international affairs, chairman of Working Party III of the Organisation for Economic Co-operation and Development, and visiting professor at Harvard University, Princeton University, and the University of St. Gallen, in Switzerland. In 1991, he joined the Bank of Tokyo (now the Bank of Tokyo–Mitsubishi UFJ) and was elected chairman in June 1992. He is author (with Paul Volcker) of *Changing Fortunes*.

Yujiro Hayami is professor at the National Graduate Institute for Policy Studies, Tokyo, and adviser at the Joint Graduate Program of the National Graduate Institute for Policy Studies and the Foundation for Advanced Studies in International Development. He graduated from the University of Tokyo and received a PhD from the Department of Economics and Sociology at Iowa State University. From 1956 to 1966, he was a research associate at the National Research Institute of Agricultural Economics in the Japanese Ministry of Agriculture, Forestry, and Fisheries. Since then, Dr. Hayami has been actively teaching at universities in Japan and the United States, including Aoyama Gakuin University, Cornell University, Tokyo Metropolitan University, the University of Minnesota, and Yale University. He has received significant recognition in Japan for his contributions as an economist and is deservedly renowned worldwide for a dozen major books on agricultural development, agricultural policy, and development economics.

Jomo K. S. has been assistant secretary general for economic development at the United Nations Department of Economic and Social Affairs since January 2005. He was professor in the Applied Economics Department, Faculty of Economics and Administration, University of Malaya, until November 2004 and was on the board of the United Nations Research Institute for Social Development from 2002 to 2004. He was a founding member and the first chairperson of International Development Economics Associates, a worldwide network of economists engaged in research, teaching, and the dissemination of critical analyses of economic policy and development issues. He received graduate degrees from Yale and Harvard and has taught at Cornell, Harvard, the National University of Malaysia, the Science University of Malaysia, the University of Malaya, and Yale. He has also been a visiting fellow at Cambridge University and a visiting senior research fellow at the Asia Research Institute, National University of Singapore. Dr. Jomo has authored, edited, or translated dozens of monographs and books and is on the editorial boards of several learned journals.

Cao Sy Kiem is vice chairman of the Central Party's Economic Committee, the Vietnam National Board of Finance and Monetary Policies Consultancy, and the Vietnam Learning Promotion Association, and he is chairman of the Vietnam Association of Small and Medium Enterprises. He received a PhD in economics from the National Economics University of Vietnam. Dr. Kiem has been director of the State Bank of Thai Binh Province and governor of the State Bank of Vietnam.

Tommy Koh is ambassador-at-large at the Ministry of Foreign Affairs of Singapore and chairman of the Institute of Policy Studies, the National Heritage Board, and the Chinese Heritage Centre. Professor Koh was dean of the Faculty of Law at the University of Singapore in 1971–74. He was Singapore's permanent representative to the United Nations in 1968–71 and 1974–84. He has also been ambassador to the United States, president of the Third United Nations Conference on the Law of the Sea, and chairman of the Preparatory Committee and the Main Committee of the United Nations Conference on Environment and Development. He has served as the founding executive director of the Asia-Europe Foundation and was Singapore's chief negotiator for the United States–Singapore Free Trade Agreement. Professor Koh was a visiting professor at the Institute for International Studies, Stanford University, in 1994–95 and is a visiting professor at Zhejiang University (China). He received a degree in law from the National University of Singapore, a master's degree in law from Harvard University, and a postgraduate diploma in criminology from Cambridge University.

Haruhiko Kuroda is president of the Asian Development Bank and chairperson of the bank's Board of Directors. He has been professor at the Graduate School of Economics at Hitotsubashi University, Tokyo, and special adviser on international monetary issues to the Cabinet of Prime Minister Junichiro Koizumi. He joined the Ministry of Finance in 1967. While deputy director-general of the International Finance Bureau, he was responsible for official development assistance and relations with multilateral development financial institutions. He served as president of the ministry's research arm, the Institute of Fiscal and Monetary Policy, for one year. During terms as director-general of the International Finance Bureau and vice minister of finance for international affairs between 1997 and 2003, Mr. Kuroda helped design and implement the Miyazawa Initiative, Japan's response to the 1997–98 Asian financial crisis. Under his leadership, Japan helped establish the Chiang Mai Initiative, a network of currency swap agreements designed to avert another crisis. Mr. Kuroda holds a degree in law from the University of Tokyo and a master's degree in economics from the University of Oxford.

Long Yongtu has been secretary-general of the Boao Forum for Asia (China) since 1997. The Boao Forum strives to promote the development goals of Asian countries through greater regional economic integration. Mr. Long is dean of the School of International Relations and Public Affairs, Fudan University. He received an undergraduate degree from Guizhou University and studied economics at the London School of Economics. He joined the Ministry of Foreign Trade and Economic Cooperation in 1965 and served at the Permanent Mission of China to the United Nations from 1978 to 1980. From 1980 to 1986, he worked for the United Nations Development Programme. Subsequently, Mr. Long was deputy director-general at the China International Center for Economic and Technical Exchanges. In 1997, he was appointed vice minister at the Ministry of Foreign Trade and Economic Cooperation and chief representative for trade negotiations. He became chief negotiator during China's prolonged and successful efforts to join the global trading system, first for the General Agreement on Tariffs and Trade and then at the World Trade Organization.

Kishore Mahbubani is dean of the Lee Kuan Yew School of Public Policy, National University of Singapore. With the Singapore Foreign Service from 1971 to 2004, he had postings in Cambodia, Malaysia, and Washington. He was permanent secretary at the Foreign Ministry from 1993 to 1998 and served two stints as Singapore's ambassador to the United Nations. He was president of the United Nations Security Council in January 2001 and May 2002. Mr. Mahbubani is the author of *Can Asians Think?* and *Beyond the Age of Innocence: Rebuilding Trust between America and the World*. He was an undergraduate at the University of Singapore and received a master's degree from Dalhousie University, Halifax, Nova Scotia. He served as a fellow at the Center for International Affairs at Harvard University from 1991 to 1992.

Felipe Medalla is professor, School of Economics, University of the Philippines. He received a PhD in economics from Northwestern University. From 1998 to 2001, he was the secretary of socioeconomic planning in the Cabinet of President Estrada. He has been director-general of the National Economic and Development Authority and chairman of the Population Commission Board, the Philippine Institute for Development Studies, and the Foundation for Economic Freedom, a nongovernmental organization advocating for freer trade and more open markets. He has been dean of the School of Economics, University of the Philippines; visiting research scholar at the Center for Southeast Asian Studies, Kyoto University; vice president for planning and finance at the University of the Philippines; president of the Philippine Economic Society; and executive director of the Philippine Center for Economic Development.

Mari Pangestu is minister of trade, Republic of Indonesia. She obtained undergraduate and master's degrees from the Australian

National University, Canberra, and a PhD in economics from the University of California, Davis. Dr. Pangestu has been a member of the Governing Board of the Centre for Strategic and International Studies, Jakarta. From 2002 to 2004, she was the co-coordinator of the Task Force on Poverty and Development for the United Nations Millennium Project. She has also been program coordinator at the Trade Forum of the Pacific Economic Cooperation Council, a private networking organization comprising two dozen member economies in the Asia Pacific region. She was an external lecturer in international economics at the University of Indonesia, Jakarta, as well as an adjunct professor at the Australia Japan Research Centre, the Australian National University. Dr. Pangestu serves on the Board of External Editors of the *Asian Journal of Business* (University of Michigan) and the *Bulletin of Indonesian Economic Studies* (the Australian National University).

Minxin Pei is senior associate and director of the China Program at the Carnegie Endowment for International Peace, a prestigious interdisciplinary research organization on foreign policy. He was born in Shanghai and received an undergraduate degree from the Shanghai Foreign Language Institute, where he also taught for three years. He obtained a master's degree from the University of Pittsburgh and a PhD in political science from Harvard University. His doctoral dissertation was awarded the university's Edward Chase prize for the best essay in the field of political science. He was a MacArthur visiting assistant professor of political science at Davidson College in 1991–92. From 1992 to 1998, he was on the faculty at Princeton University. He has also been a recipient of the Edward Taylor National Fellowship at the Hoover Institution of Stanford University, the Robert McNamara Fellowship of the World Bank, and the Olin Faculty Fellowship of the John M. Olin Foundation. Professor Pei is the author of well-respected books on Chinese economic and political affairs, and he is a frequent guest on radio news programs.

Andrew Sheng, a chartered accountant by training, has a background in Asian financial development and reform. He has served as chief economist and assistant governor at Malaysia's central bank, senior manager at the World Bank, and deputy chief executive at the Hong Kong Monetary Authority. He was chairman of the Securities and Futures Commission of Hong Kong from 1998 to 2005. Chief adviser to

China's Banking Regulatory Commission, Mr. Sheng continues to write and lecture extensively on financial sector issues in Asia. He chairs the annual Capital Markets Roundtable of the Organisation for Economic Co-operation and Development, in Tokyo. He is also adjunct professor at the Graduate School of Economics and Management, Tsinghua University, Beijing, and the Tun Ismail Ali Professor of Monetary and Financial Economics at the University of Malaya.

Wu Jinglian is a senior research fellow at the Development Research Center of the State Council, China. He was one of the chief economic advisers to former Chinese Premier Zhu Rongji. Professor Wu graduated from the Department of Economics, Fudan University, Shanghai. He served as professor at the Institute of Economics, Chinese Academy of Social Sciences. He was also deputy director of the Programming Office for Economic Reform, the State Council. He is currently professor of economics, Graduate School of the Chinese Academy of Social Sciences; professor and member of the Academic Council, China Europe International Business School, Shanghai; and editor in chief, *Gaige (Journal of Reform)*. Professor Wu's areas of research interest include theoretical economics, comparative institutional analysis, and policy issues in China's economic reform. Professor Wu has published many books and research papers. Among these is the influential *Jianshe Shichangjingji De Zongtigouxiang Yu Fangansheji* (The Road to a Market Economy: Comprehensive Framework and Working Proposals).

Joseph Yam is chief executive of the Hong Kong Monetary Authority. He initiated his civil service career in Hong Kong (China) as a statistician and then as an economist in the Hong Kong Government Secretariat. His involvement in monetary affairs started when he was appointed principal assistant secretary for monetary affairs in 1982. He helped put together Hong Kong's linked exchange rate system. He was subsequently appointed deputy secretary for monetary affairs in 1985 and director of the Office of the Exchange Fund in 1991. Mr. Yam was responsible for many of the reform measures introduced, beginning in the mid-1980s, to strengthen Hong Kong's monetary system and to develop financial markets. These measures contributed to monetary stability and to Hong Kong's development as an international financial center. Mr. Yam was instrumental in the establishment of the Hong Kong Monetary Authority in 1993. He has been recognized over the years for his work on domestic and regional monetary and financial development and for piloting Hong Kong (China) through the Asian financial turmoil.

Zheng Bijian is chairman of the China Reform Forum, an academic organization that provides analysis on domestic and international issues related to China. He has drafted key reports for five National Congresses of the Communist Party of China. Mr. Zheng received a degree in political economy from the Graduate School of Renmin University. He has served as a member of the Research Center of the Secretariat of the Central Committee of the Communist Party of China; political assistant to Hu Yaobang, then general secretary of the Central Committee; vice director general of the Research Center of International Studies of the State Council; vice president of the Chinese Academy of Social Sciences; director of the Marxism-Leninism Research Institute; vice minister of the Propaganda Department of the Central Committee; executive vice president of the Central Party School of the Central Committee; and member of the 14th and 15th Central Committees. A member of the Standing Committee of the 10th Chinese People's Political Consultative Conference National Committee, he is also senior adviser at the China Institute of International Strategic Studies.

About the Editors

Indermit S. Gill is a sector manager in the Poverty Reduction and Economic Management unit in the World Bank's East Asia and Pacific Regional Office, where he is also economic adviser to the chief economist. Before his current assignment, he was the economic adviser to the vice president of the Poverty Reduction and Economic Management unit, as well as head of the network. During 1997–99, he worked as a senior country economist in the Brazil Country Management unit. Upon his return to Washington and between 2000 and 2002, he served as lead economist for human development in the Latin America and the Caribbean Regional Office. He has a PhD in economics from the University of Chicago.

Yukon Huang was the World Bank director for Russia and the Central Asian Republics from 1992 to 1996 and country director for China from 1997 to 2004. He joined the World Bank in 1976 and, for most of his career, has worked as an economist and operations division chief covering countries in South and East Asia. Prior to his work with the Bank, he taught at various universities in Malaysia, Tanzania, and the United States and also worked at the United States Department of the Treasury. Yukon Huang has a bachelor's degree in economics from Yale University and a PhD from Princeton University.

Homi Kharas is the chief economist of the East Asia and Pacific Region of the World Bank and director of the region's Poverty Reduction and Economic Management unit. Dr. Kharas joined the World Bank in 1980 and has worked in the Research Department (1981–86), the Latin America and Caribbean Region (1993–97), and the Economic Policy

Department (1997–99). He worked in the East Asia and Pacific Region in 1986–90 and 1992–93 and has been working there since 1999. Dr. Kharas completed his undergraduate studies at the University of Cambridge and his PhD in economics at Harvard University.

Index

A
accountability, Cambodia, 48–49
AFTA. *See* ASEAN Free Trade Area
agricultural sector, 84–85
   Cambodia, 43, 47–48
   China, 183–185, 297–298
   economies of scale, 86–87
   Java, 94–101
   vegetable marketing operations, 97
air pollution, 146–147, 167, 328
aluminum electrode plants, China, 292–293
ambivalence, 205–208
ASEAN, 20, 55, 61, 70–71, 74, 120
   Cambodia, 30
   competitiveness, 137
   development, 132
   economic community, 234
   economic integration, 134
   economies, 232–233
   Free Trade Area (AFTA), 137, 223, 233
   integration, 134, 135–137
   integration gap, 136
   issues, 137–138
   regionalization and, 241–243
ASEAN+3, 60, 61, 120, 122–123, 124
   Cambodia, 37–38
   summit, 149–150
ASEAN 10, 60
Asia-5
Asian Bond Funds, 313
   Initiative, 38, 278

Asian Development Bank (ADB), public goods, 166–176
Asia-Pacific Economic Cooperation, 120
assets, domestic liquid, 319
Association of Southeast Asian Nations. *See* ASEAN
Aun Porn Moniroth, vii, 3, 21, 338
authors, vii–xi, 3–4, 338–340
avian flu, 172–173

B
bamboo capitalism, 270
Bangladesh, economic integration, 207
banks and banking, 271
   central banks, 62–63, 74–75
   crisis, 112–113
   Japan, 273
   system, 73, 273
bilateral relationships, three, 78–81
biodiversity, 147
bond market, 61–63, 67, 75, 123, 313
   Asian Bond Funds, 38, 278, 313
   currencies, Cambodia, 38
bureaucracy, 259, 280–281
   system, 199
business environment, 238

C
Cambodia, 138, 348
   economic growth, 39
   economic integration, 24–52
   globalization, 39–47

349

Cambodia (*Continued*)
  rural population, 40
  trade, 39-40
capital
  China, 301
  flow, 58, 59, 114
  markets, 61, 62, 75, 159, 326
  restrictions, 314
central banks. *See* banks and banking
chaebols, 197, 267
challenges, 142-148, 155-158
change agents, 19-20
Chiang Mai Initiative, 38, 61, 161
China, 129-130, 138, 232, 244, 246, 247
  black hole role, 131
  Cambodia, 35
  competition with, 9-11
  economic integration, 207
  environment, domestic and international, 323-337, 350
  financial crisis, 121-122
  future, 334-337
  growth, 66, 71
  history, 286-287
  income inequality, 146
  industrialization, 285-308, 350
  information technology, 270
  institutions, 287-289
  issues, 180-182
  labor surplus economy, 116
  leadership in economic integration, 204-205
  negotiation, 179-180, 183
  per capita income, 251-252
  Philippines and, 224-226
  process, two-way, 182-186
  rebuilding political foundations for growth, 251-255
  reform efforts, 303-305
  renaissance, 336-337
  reserves, 317
  resource endowments, 289, 291
  rise of, 131-133
  strategy, aberrant, 289-303
  technology, 130
  "threat," 332-333
  trade, 270
  U.S. and, 79
  workforce, 260, 262, 291-292, 294
  WTO and, 178-187, 349
civil service reform, 237
closed-door solutions, 278
clusters, 265, 269
coal, China, 295
colonialism, 259
  globalization and, 86
  legacy, 84-85
commodities
  industrial, 87
  manufactured goods vs, 110
  production, 88
communicable diseases, 156, 162, 171
  avian flu, 172-173
  HIV/AIDS, 171
communication infrastructure, 101-102
community-based trade network, rural industrialization and, 87-91
community building, regional, 240-241
competition
  with China, 9-11
  with the West, 7-9
competitiveness, markets and, 266
Confucian tradition, 190, 201, 258-259
congestion costs, 228
consensus building, China, 179-180
consumers, trade liberalization and, 213-214
consumption
  China, 326
  future, 277
  Philippines, 217-221
contract farming, 94, 102
contracts
  credit, 100-101
  enforcement, 88-91, 101
cooperation, China and, 332
corporations
  governance, 121
  government-led, 280
  philosophy, Japan, 263
corruption, 88, 142-143, 148, 173-174, 245, 349
  Cambodia, 46-47

China, 181, 253
  perceptions, 65–66, 143
  Perceptions Index of Transparency International, 143
credit
  costs, 99–100
  Java, 99–100
  policy, 111
  processes, 58
crisis, 248, 250
  leadership and, 249
  prevention and mitigation, 117
currency, 320
  bonds, 38
  Cambodia, 36–37, 38
  common, 36–37, 64–65, 67, 75, 316
  devaluation, 111–112, 273
  dominant, 273–275
  EU model, 65
  foreign currency assets, 117
  framework, 279
  movements, 118
  rate stability, 63
  standards, 278
  U.S. dollar and, 114
currency-basket system, 64
currency-swap network, 123, 124

D

debt
  foreign, 114–115
  servicing cost, 77
decentralization, Cambodia, 49
demand, domestic, China, 335
demographics, growth and, 260
Deng Xiaoping, 71, 194–196, 335
de Ocampo, Roberto F., vii–viii, 3, 21, 338–339
deregulation, domestic, 87–88
desertification, China, 328
destabilization, factors, 332
devaluation. *See* currency, devaluation
development, 188, 349
  China, 333, 335
  corridors, 135
  dictatorship, 72–73
  failure, 199

gaps, 149, 156, 161–162
  regulating, 333
diversity, 2
dollar standard, 272–273, 274–277
domestic disintegration, 4
  avoiding, 16–19
domestic trade network, 87, 88
donor trust funds, 169
dragon economies, 244
dual economy model, 262–263, 279–280

E

East Asia
  reasons for success, 189
  renaissance, 2
East Asian miracle, 260–262
  regional differences, 107–109
East Asia–Pacific Central Banks (EMEAP), Executives' Meeting, 62
East Asia Study Group recommendations
  further study, 165
  long-term, 165
  medium-term, 165
  short-term, 164–165
ecology. *See* environment
economic cooperation, 74, 76, 336
economic corridors, Cambodia, 33
economic development, 348, 349
  late-entry countries, 138–139, 349
  regional cooperation and, 107–127
economic globalization, 331
  China and, 335–336
economic growth
  sustainability, Cambodia, 33
  trade liberalization and, 208–209
economic hub, 129–131
economic indicators, 157
economic integration, 128–141, 150–155, 162–163, 226–227, 244–245, 349
  Cambodia, 30–35, 47–50, 348
  key perspectives, 26–30
  management of, 47–50
  new developments, 133–137
  regional, 134
economic partnership agreements (EPAs), 153–154, 204, 209–210
economic vulnerability, 115

economic zones, 237–238
economy, advanced, 260
education
   Cambodia, 43, 45
   China, 254
electricity, China, 294–295
electronic and electrical equipment, Philippines, 219, 220, 221
elites, 189–191
   behavior, 199–200
   contributions, 198–200
   enabling environment, 200–201
   learning, 191–197
   meritocratic, 198
emergency financing, 117
employment, 211–212, 214, 216
   China, 328–329
   Philippines, 222
   trade liberalization and, 215
   see also jobs; workforce
energy and energy efficiency, 168–170
   China, 295, 327
   consumption and prices, 290
enterprises, networks, 267
entrepreneurship, 101, 108–109
environment, 146–148, 156, 158, 162, 166–168, 349
   China, 296–297, 328
equity, 144–146
   China, 329–330
ethics, 190
euro, 279
exams, entrance exam system, 198
exchange rates, 63, 161, 272–273, 320
   monetary independence and, 316–317
   risk, 77
exports and export sector, 219, 222
   Cambodia, 41, 42
   China, 300–301
   GDP and, 57
   growth rates, 210–213
   Philippines, 209–213
   sales, 276
export/import profiles, Cambodia, 31
export-oriented manufacturing model of development, 279

F
factory system, 89
family-based rural enterprises, 88–89
farm producers, mobilizing, 91–101
farming, contract, 94
FDI. *See* foreign direct investment
finance and financing, 150, 152, 154–155
   long-term, 59
financial architecture, 115
financial cooperation, 63, 67, 74–76, 313–314, 348
   regional, 119–124
financial crisis (1997–98), 55–67, 73, 188–189, 250–251
   Cambodia, 29
   economic recovery, 116
   international responses, 120
   Japan, 275
   lessons from, 66–67, 116–119
   management, mechanisms and institutions, 117
   policy responses, 115
   prevention mechanisms, 116–117
financial development, 309–322
financial governance, Cambodia, 33–35
financial integration, 310–315
   benefits, 36–37
   Cambodia, 35–38
   current development, 37–38
financial interests, policy and, 113
financial intermediation, Cambodia, 36
financial liberalization, 111–116
   Cambodia, 36–37
financial markets
   deregulation, Cambodia, 36
   infrastructure, 159
   integrated, 314
financial networks, 11–12, 270–277, 278
   regional, 13–15
financial reform, agenda, 117
fiscal profligacy, 120–121
flying geese formation, 129
foreign currency assets, 117
foreign direct investment (FDI), 53–54, 57–58, 84, 116, 129, 152, 268, 271, 272
   Cambodia, 32, 42
   China, 181, 252, 329, 330

foreign exchange, 215
forests, 147, 328
four tigers, 70–71
free trade, 84
   agreements, 74, 222
   ASEAN, 137
free trade areas (FTAs), 152, 153, 159–160, 209–210, 239
French Revolution, China and, 258
funds and funding, 114
   financial liberalization and, 113
   short-term, 271–272
   transfer of, 310
future, 69–81, 158–182, 348

G

Gill, Indermit S., xv, 346
Gini index, 144
global imbalance, 77
globalization, basis, 72–73
   Cambodia, 39–47
   China, 186–187
   globalization.
   megalopolis-centered system, 84–85
   rural-based development and, 82–106
   second wave, 86–87
   see also economic integration
global output, 6–7
Goh Keng Swee, 192–194, 196
governance, 65, 173–174, 234, 236, 280, 349, 350
   Cambodia, 27, 43
   good, 256
   principles, 188–202
government
   accountability and integrity, 250
   administrative interference, 303–305
   administrative resources, Cambodia, 28–29
   capital expenditures, GDP and, 227
   evaluation and monitoring, 305
   intervention, East Asian miracle, 109–111
   resources and, 288
Great Cultural Revolution, 287
Great Leap Forward campaign, 287
Greater Mekong Subregion (GMS), 167
   Cambodia, 33

greenhouse gases, 168
gross domestic product (GDP), 261
   China, 288, 291, 301, 324, 324, 329–330, 335
   exports and, 57
   growth, 53, 54, 208
   investment and, 301
   pre- and post-crisis, 55
   services, 298
   tertiary sector, 300
   world, 6
group, importance of, 198
growth, 4, 6–11, 108
   Cambodia, 27
   China, 328–329
   criteria for success, 247
   political foundation and, 247–251
Guidotti rule, 319
Gyohten, Toyoo, viii, 3, 21, 339

H

harmonization, financial system standards, 313
Hayami, Yujiro, viii–ix, 3, 21, 339–340
health and health care
   China, 254
   communicable disease, 156, 158, 162, 171
   see also communicable diseases
HIV/AIDS, 171
Hong Kong (China), 245–246
   reserves, 319
   standards, 314–315
Huang, Yukon, xv–xvi, 346–347
hubs, 265–266
human trafficking, prevention, 174–176

I

image, Cambodia, 40
imports, 213–214
import substitution, 85–86, 214–216
income, 2
   China, 251–252
   Philippines, 217
income disparities, 65, 144–146
   Cambodia, 27–28, 45
   China, 252–253, 329

India, 232, 244, 246
  diaspora, 269
  workforce, 262, 269
Indonesia, 235, 237, 250
industry and industrialization
  China , 133, 292-293, 295-296, 297, 299, 324-325, 350
  clusters, 102
  dualism, 109
  industrial wave, 129, 133
  Japan, 263
  Philippines, 222-223
  production, 129
  strategy, 85-86, 289-303
  uncompetitive, 229
inequality, 330, 233, 349
  Cambodia, 44-45
information
  asymmetric, Cambodia, 46
  -based production and competition, 264
information and communications technologies, 303
  China, 270, 326-327
infrastructure, 101-102, 158-159
  Cambodia, 33, 42
  Philippines, 226-227
innovation, 303
  managerial, 281
  technological, China, 293-294
institutions, 65, 234-235
  -building, 250
  Cambodia, 43
  China, 287-289, 294
  policy, 62
  reform, 118
  transforming, 236
insurance principles, 319-320
integration, 80-81
  benefits, 40-44
  bilateral, 135
  Cambodia, 40-47
  negative impacts, 44-47
interest rates
  agriculture, 99
  risk, 77
International Monetary Fund
  financial crisis, 115
  role, 118, 122
international relations, China and, 331

Internet, 264
investment, 150, 152, 154, 310
  China, 186, 301-302
  flows, benefits, 228
  functional vs strategic state, 110
  overinvestment, 302-303
  regional, 63, 76, 160, 162, 312
  see also foreign direct investment
issues, 69-70

J
Japan, 103
  ASEAN and, 137-138
  Asian economy and, 262-264
  development assistance, 109
  economy, 275
  elite learning, 191-192
  financial crisis, 121-122
  globalization, 72-73
  income inequality, 145-146
  investment, 76
  leadership in economic integration, 204-205
  outsourcing, 89-91
  Philippines and, 220-221, 223-224
  recovery, 70
  reserves, 317
  supply chain, 271-272
  U.S. and, 78-79
  workforce, 260
  yen standard, 274-275, 276
Java
  operations, 97
  vegetable marketing, 94-101
jobs, 303
  Cambodia, 28, 33
  China, 185-186, 291, 292, 325-326
  unemployment, 33
  see also employment; workforce
Joint Statement on East Asia Cooperation, 149
Jomo Kwame Sundaram, ix, 3, 21, 340
jusridictions, intermediation, 314

K
kanban, 91
keiretsu investments, 271-272
Kharas, Homi, xv, 346
Kiem, Cao Sy, ix, 3, 22, 340